JOURNAL FOR THE STUDY OF THE OLD TESTAMENT
SUPPLEMENT SERIES
410

Psalms and Liturgy

edited by
Dirk J. Human and Cas J. A. Vos

T&T CLARK INTERNATIONAL
A Continuum imprint
LONDON • NEW YORK

Typeset by Tradespools, Frome, Somerset
Printed on acid-free paper in Great Britain by MPG Books Ltd, Bodmin, Cornwall

CONTENTS

PREFACE

On the 21st and 22nd of August 2003, a symposium took place at the University of Pretoria's Faculty of Theology to discuss the theme of 'Psalms and Liturgy'. We were delighted that various highly-regarded researchers and experts in the fields of Psalms and Liturgy, participated in this symposium. This book is a result of the symposium.

This book has been woven together by many different threads. There are the threads which represent various theological and religious traditions and which lend the book a particular colour and texture. At the same time, another tapestry has been created with the inclusion of a variety of theological analyses, which ultimately enrich the content.

This book examines the manner in which the psalm texts are woven together. This fine network is approached with curiosity, then delicately unravelled. Attention is given to how the colours of the various environments and worlds are imprinted upon the psalm texts. Also examined with curiosity, is how the threads weave different psalms together. The Christian 'voice' of the religious and theological tradition is listened to intently, while the richness of the psalms is unveiled.

The influence and the power of psalms in the religious tradition has recently been re-discovered. It is being acknowledged that religious traditions originate from the saturated roots of Israel. Hence, the liturgical fervour with which attempts are being made to bring psalms alive again and help them become relevant in the church.

In this book, particular attention is also given to the liturgical impact of the psalms. The question of how the psalms fit in and how they can be experienced in a post-modern, religious congregation, is both raised and answered in this book. Finally, the book seeks to affirm that the 'voice' of the psalms once again rings clear in the context of worship.

Should the reader wish to harvest the rich fields of the psalms, he or she will return jubilant and with an abundance of sheaves to take home.

We want to extend our gratitude to Yolande Steenkamp, Linda Piegl and Jaco Gericke for their work on the manuscript. In various ways they have contributed to the ortographical setting of this book.

Cas J. A. Vos   Dirk J. Human

ABBREVIATIONS

AB	*Anchor Bible*
ABD	*Anchor Bible Dictionary*
ACW	*Ancient Christian Writers*
ALw	*Archiv für Liturgiewissenschaft*
ATD	*Das Alte Testament Deutsch*
BBB	*Bonner Biblische Beiträge*
BEThL	*Bibliotheca Emphemeridum theologicarum Lovaniensium*
BI	*Bibliography Index*
BKAT	*Biblische Kommentar zum Alten Testament*
BN	*Biblische Notizen*
BZ	*Biblische Zeitschrift*
BZAW	*Beihefte zur Zeitschrift für die alttestamentliche Wissenschaft*
CBQ	*Catholic Biblical Quarterly*
COT	*Commentaar op het Oude Testament*
CThM	*Calver theologische Monographien*
DBW	*Dietrich Bonhoeffer: Werke*
FAT	*Forschungen zum Alten Testament*
FOTL	*The Forms of the Old Testament Literature*
FzB	*Forschung zur Bibel*
HBS	*Herders biblische Studien*
HKAT	*Handkommentar zum Alten Testament*
HThKAT	*Herders theologischer Kommentar zum Alten Testament*
HTS	*Hervormde Teologiese Studies*
HUCA	*Hebrew Union College Annual*
JBL	*Journal of Biblical Literature*
JS	*Journal for Semitics*
JSOT	*Journal for the Study of the Old Testament*
JSOTSup	*Journal for the Study of the Old Testament Supplement Series*
JSS	*Journal of the Semitic Studies*
LD	*Landschaftsdenkmale der Musik*
NCBC	*The New Century Bible Commentary*
NEB	*Die Neue Echter Bibel*
NEB	*New English Bible*
NRSV	*New Revised Standard Version*

OBO	Orbis Biblicus et Orientalis
ÖBS	Österreichische biblische Studien
OTE	Old Testament Essays
OTL	Old Testament Library
OTS	Oudtestamentische Studien
POT	De Prediking op het Oude Testament
QD	Quaestiones Disputatae
RHR	Revue de l'histoire des religions
SBAB	Stuttgarter biblische Aufsatzbände
SBB	Stuttgarter biblische Beiträge
SBL	Society of Biblical Literature
SBS	Stuttgarter Bibelstudien
SK	Skrif en Kerk
TB	Theologische Bücherei
THAT	Theologisches Handwörterbuch zum Alten Testament
ThPh	Theologie und Philosopie
TRE	Theologische Realenzyklopädie
TThSt	Trierer theologische Studien
TThZ	Trierer theologische Zeitschrift
VE	Verbum et Ecclesia
VT	Vetus Testamentum
VTS	Vetum Testamentum Supplements
WBC	Word Biblical Commentary
WMANT	Wissenschaftliche Monographien zum Alten und Neuen Testament
WUNT	Wissenschaftliche Untersuchungen zum Neuen Testament
ZAW	Zeitschrift für die alttestamentliche Wissenschaft
ZThK	Zeitschrift für Theologie und Kirche

Contributors

Marcel Barnard is professor in Liturgics and lecturer in Homeletics, Evangelical-Lutheran Seminary, Faculty of Theology, University of Utrecht, Utrecht, the Netherlands.

Georg P. Braulik, Benedictine, is professor in Old Testament Studies, Catholic Faculty of Theology, University of Vienna, Vienna, Austria.

Brian Doyle is associate professor in Old Testament Studies, Catholic University of Leuven, Leuven, Belgium.

Alphonso Groenewald is research fellow, Department of Old Testament Studies, University of Pretoria, Pretoria, South Africa.

Dirk J. Human is professor in Old Testament Studies, Department of Old Testament Studies, Faculty of Theology, University of Pretoria, Pretoria, South Africa.

Jörg Jeremias is professor in Old Testament Studies, Faculty for Protestant Theology, Philipps University, Marburg, Germany.

Louis C. Jonker is senior lecturer in Old Testament Studies, Department of Old and New Testament, University of Stellenbosch, Stellenbosch, South Africa.

Jurie H. le Roux is professor in Old Testament Studies and Head of Telematic Education, Department of Old Testament Studies, Faculty of Theology, University of Pretoria, Pretoria, South Africa.

Eckart Otto is professor in Old Testament Studies, Protestant Faculty of Theology, Ludwig Maximillian University, Munich, Germany.

Niek A. Schuman is professor in Liturgics (formerly in the Department of Old Testament Studies), Faculty of Theology, Free University of Amsterdam, Amsterdam, the Netherlands.

Stephanus D. Snyman is professor in Old Testament Studies, Department of Old Testament Studies, University of the Free State, Bloemfontein, South Africa.

Hans Ulrich Steymans, Dominican, is associate professor in Old Testament Studies, École Biblique et Archaéologique Française, Jerusalem.

Pieter M. Venter is professor in Old Testament Studies, Department of Old Testament Studies, University of Pretoria, South Africa.

Cas J. A. Vos is professor in Practical Theology (Homiletics and Liturgy) and Dean of the Faculty of Theology, University of Pretoria, Pretoria, South Africa.

Marcel Barnard

Utrecht, the Netherlands

1. *Introduction*

In 1988, the South-African painter Marlene Dumas (she lives in the Netherlands) painted an intriguing canvas. In oil, a naked body is visible, laying backward with slightly spread out legs across a table or a box covered with a white cloth. In fact the strokes of oil paint only evoke the suggestion of a body. Whether it belongs to a man or a woman cannot be determined. The face is rather a conjecture of a face than an articulated visage. The title of the canvas is *Waiting (for meaning)*[1]. It didn't have to wait long for that. The body has been interpreted to be female, even as the waiting Danaë from Greek mythology, locked in chastely in a room, but nevertheless visited by Zeus in the form of a golden rain and made pregnant. In a book about the artist and her work an art historian writes:

> 'Those who search for meanings in Dumas' work are opening Pandora's box. Her paintings and drawings suggest a wealth of possibilities, but — none of them offers a definite answer. They have unleashed many interpretations, so many in fact that the artist has gradually come to call herself "Miss Interpreted". Generally, the attribution of meaning is based on the depiction and the title, which are both understood to be the representations, i.c. the articulation, of intentions. This is not consistent with the way in which Dumas' paintings have come about. Just as her work does not arise from a single idea or motivation, its meaning cannot be defined in one-dimensional terms' (Van den Boogerd 1999a: 54f.).

In response to Dumas' painting, the poet Antjie Krog, countrywoman of Dumas, wrote a poem with the same title *Waiting for meaning* (Krog 2000: 56). I cite the beginning and the end of that poem:

> 'n vreemde lover laat jou anders vashou...
> ... ons veroorsaak mekaar:
> jy daar, ek hier –
> voos gekneus en

---

1. Marlene Dumas, *Waiting (for Meaning)*, oil on canvas, 50×70 cm., Kunsthalle Kiel (Germany); reproduction in Van den Boogerd (1999b: 52).

behoorlik strotomgedraai
(Krog 2000: 56)[2]

Krog interprets Dumas, and I, in turn, allow myself a free interpretation of this poem. Lovers cause each other. But – and that is what the poem is actually about – a long relationship also can become useless, meaningless. The lovers do not exist with each other any more ('jy daar, ek hier') but apart from each other. The secret of the relationship, of the meaning given to one another, has disappeared. A different lover makes a riddle out of the beloved again. They become who they were not before, new people. They owe their new existence to one another and give meaning to each other. Yet it cannot be ignored that the lover may prove to be an all-devouring fire, the beloved a *femme fatale*. The bounds of passion are the fall.

The painting of Marlene Dumas and the poem of Antjie Krog, in my opinion, succinctly describe the interaction between psalm texts and the people singing them. The psalm is a body, a lingual body, to be loved, *waiting for meaning*. The songs are waiting to get meaning, and these meanings are given to the psalms by the mouth singing them, like the lover tastes his beloved and gives meaning to her life. Every lover, every singer will look for new secrets, will give new meanings to every psalm.

The song may alienate the singer from himself forever, though. Alternatively, the other way around, the interpreter may bring the psalm beyond the borders of his own lingual body. In this process of interpretation, naturally the lover will bring in his or her cultural baggage. It is obvious that a Dutchman gives other meanings to 'desert' in his country, rich in water, than an African in the dry steppe of this continent. In this way, meanings are evoked through a double contextualization: an anthropological and a cultural one, the singer and his environment.

2. *A reading exercise with pastors: Psalms in Lent*

Interesting experiences with this meaning giving process occurred during continuing education courses with pastors, in which the services of Lent were prepared together. In this preparation, not only Bible and service book mattered, not only the exegesis and the prescribed liturgy, but particularly the tapping and application of creativity and the *liturgia condenda*: the liturgy originating from the creative hermeneutical process. That process must be initiated; the texts must start 'streaming'. One of the methods we employ is noting first reactions on the psalms, readings and prayers given in the *lectionarium*. For this we take the Dutch translation of

---

2.   'a different lover holds you differently/.../... we cause each other/: you there, me here – punch drunk and seriously strangled' (my own translation).

the text as a starting point. These first associations are thematically assessed and then integrated into the subsequent homiletic and liturgical process.

I shall give an example that is relevant to the subject of this article. In 2001, a study week of this kind expressly focused on the entrance psalms of the *quadragesima*.[3] Allow me to share with you some of the associations the participants had with the psalms.

First, a few notes on Psalm 91, the entrance of *Invocabit*:

'He who lives in the shelter of the Most High
who lodges under the shadow of the Almighty,
says of the Lord, 'He is my refuge and fortress,
my God in whom I put my trust.'[4]

One of the participants listening to this Psalm imagined the Provence, like Van Gogh painted it. A second one rather saw a convent in which she felt safe behind the thick walls, where 'the arrow that flies by day' could not hit her. Opposed to these pleasant images was the association of a participant saying: with this psalm I feel like a small child in front of a parent, in front of majesty, and it makes me feel anxious. Simply, the fact that colleagues can interpret a single psalm so differently is instructive already: ''n vreemde lover laat jou anders vashou.'

Less tangible, but not less interesting, is asking participants to name images from psalms with colours, or even to supply paint and brushes and let them paint. This exercise concerns qualities other than the rational and is based on the assumption that sentimental values are of great importance in liturgy as well. They do not always play an important role, yet even these can be thematically expressed. We are used to saying that, at least during Lent, the entrance psalm colours the whole Sunday. But then, which colour is that? The spiritual blue, that pulls the spirit on its waves towards infinity, the sunny yellow, in which everything brightens up, the green of the summer vegetation, or the deep and mysterious indigo or purple? To Psalm 25, the psalm of the way and the entrance for *Reminiscere* and for *Oculi*, a pastor said: 'I see bright, sharp colours; a bright, blue way and the purple of a broad longing for God. For God himself I see orange.' Somebody else spoke of a blue longing and of a green oasis with God. Yet another one coloured that intense longing yellow and named it a 'light of great intensity'.

Naturally, this exercise is subjective, even though colour principles seem to obey certain laws, at least in the northern Atlantic world, and many

---

3. Course 'Psalmen in de veertigdagentijd', 22–26 Januari 2001, at *Theologisch Seminarium Hydepark*, Doorn (Netherlands) under guidance of dr. Anne Marijke Spijkerboer and the author of this article. Seven pastors participated in the course.
4. Translations of the Psalms from the *Revised English Bible*.

colours seem to have more or less fixed meanings referring to certain feelings (Itten 1970). My point is that it makes a difference whether a pastor prepares the service from an awareness that the tone is set by a bright yellow, by a mysterious purple or by a hopeful green.

In response to Psalm 43, the entrance of *Judica* ('How deep I am sunk in my misery, groaning in distress!'), somebody said: 'I collapsed on the floor with a big bang and suddenly realized that a human being in distress is so lonely, that even the closest neighbour becomes a stranger. Nevertheless, such a person is longing for removal of the loneliness.' This is an insight that, in homilies and prayers, may result in a powerfully experienced presence of the pastor in the congregation.[5]

Another example[6] is Psalm 24, the entrance psalm of *Palm Sunday*:

'Lift up your heads, you gates,
lift yourselves up, you everlasting doors,
that the king of glory may come in.'

One of the participants imagined a festival gate with balloons, flags, horses and trumpets. 'I am that gate myself', another one said, 'with open arms I am waiting there for the messiah'. 'We, the congregation, are the gate', a third one said, 'we are excitedly and eagerly looking forward, it is carnival with drums and tooters, and magnificent weather'. 'Enter the liturgy like at a feast' and 'the congregation as the gate expecting the Lord with open arms' – these are magnificent images to be thematically appropriated and to be elaborated on and used in sermons directed at the youth, as well as part of general homilies and prayers. Images like these cannot be expected directly from exegetical work alone.

3. *Presuppositions of the reading exercises with pastors*

In the following paragraph, I shall reflect on the method of working sketched above. This procedure challenges listeners or readers to attribute meanings to texts (psalms in this case) or to see the psalms as textual bodies *waiting for meaning*. The method is itself based on a number of presuppositions I must make explicit.

First, the method takes the *liturgical* context in which the psalms are sung absolutely seriously, in the sense that the listener really is evaluated as a listener, the singer as a singer, and not as a theologian, an exegete, a Hebraist (or Graecist). Frequently, the process of giving meaning gets into

5. This was a different course: 'Vieren in 't voren', 27–31 Januari 1997, at *Theologisch Seminarium Hydepark*, Doorn (Netherlands) as well, under guidance of the author of this article.
6. From the course 'Psalms in Lent'.

its stride in response to texts heard, spoken or sung *in popular language*. This often occurs wholly unconsciously.

The churchgoer is a believer and not a theologian. The reaction of the churchgoer is evoked by both the text and the context of the listener. We will use this liturgical fact as a starting point of the hermeneutical process the pastor goes through even before the service commences. I suppose, as I said before, that the 'first brain wave' makes the text 'stream'. In other words, the first brain wave initiates the hermeneutical process. This process involves a continuing discussion between the text on the one side and the listener and his or her situation on the other. This does not mean, however, that every first brain wave will turn out to be useful in the end. Every idea is adapted and corrected by the presented text.

In other words, the exegesis is not lacking in our method; yet it is not the first step in the process of preparing a sermon. In the particular methodology, the primary process of giving meaning is made conscious and is thematically expressed. The hermeneutical process, meanings evoked by the text and the context during the first hearing will join the meanings the text releases at a later stage, after a careful exegesis of the texts. The exegesis in turn, however, is also strongly influenced by the meanings evoked initially, for the exegete asks the text specifically those questions he or she is interested in.

Maybe a text does not even exist apart from its interpretation and so separated from context. (I am referring to the post-modern adage: 'il n'y a pas de hors-[con]texte' [Derrida]), but I cannot pursue that matter in the space of this article. For the psalms, the fact that we read them in a Christian context or, more precisely, in the context of a Christian service, should always be taken into account. Within every new context, a text gets new meanings. In my view, though, this does not cancel out a certain independence of the text in relation to its interpretation.

Secondly, we make the assumption that the church expects a number of activities to take place during the service: singing psalms, engaging in readings and prayers, etc. In short, therefore, the subjects from the *lectionarium*. These subjects more or less constitute a unity. I do not need emphasize the fact that during certain periods (for instance, Lent, in our example above) this unity is more evident than at other times (for instance, during the Sundays after Pentecost).

So I am supposing that the scriptures are read in an ordered manner on Sunday, and not following the more or less arbitrary ideas of the pastor. In this we should constantly realise that the delineation and combination of the pericopes and the psalms are, in itself, already an artificial intervention in the scriptural structures and relations. The combination of the chosen texts constitutes as it were one new text, to be shaped further by the congregation in the active process of giving meaning. On this assumption, a *lectionarium* is an important part of the objective content of the liturgy.

The objective and more or less coherent offering of the *lectionarium* meets the subjective interpretation of the listener in our example of the pastors preparing a service.

Thirdly, the method assumes the unity of liturgy and sermon. More precisely stated: the sermon is considered to be an inextricable part of the liturgy. The homily is an interpretation of the scriptures, yet 'scripture' is more than (one of) the scripture readings. *Adiutorium*, entrance psalm and *graduale* are 'scripture' as well. The Word (with a capital W) is read, sung, heard, interpreted and answered in the liturgy. *My basic theological assumption is that this hearing, interpreting and answering belongs to the Word (with a capital W again!).*

In the texts of Scripture, praise and complaint, judgment and blessing, prayer and thanksgiving, singing and sighing, etc. have all been handed down together as the Bible which is, in the ecclesiastical sense, the Word of God. Already in the Scriptures itself, the Word is not the 'naked Word', but the Word heard and answered. In the Reformed sense, the liturgy is in service of God's Word. Therefore, though it does not coincide with that Word, in its prayerful bondage to the Word, the congregation trusts that the human words get a part in the Word of God. The congregation looking for the force field of the Spirit can trust that its liturgy will be incorporated in the dynamic of the Word. In the service we assume two subjects, God and man, both of whom are interested in each other correlatively, although, in my opinion, God remains the primary subject of the liturgy. He bears the assembly of the congregation. In this sense we can say that the word in the service is the celebrated and remembered word, which begins streaming (which 'happens', as the Scripture says) during the dual act of listening (reading, interpreting and preaching) and answering (praying, calling, praising, singing, moving and acting). *In other words, in the liturgy, a fabric of texts is forming, which is both the happening Word of God and the human answer in response to it.* In this way, the liturgy is much like a subject known in Dutch creative education as 'textile art'.

4. *Reading psalms in secularized culture*

Pastors preparing for services and reading the psalms in that frame are also part of a certain culture. In the given example of the Western European, this is a strongly secularized culture. Remarkably enough, the interest in psalms is growing there, and from this interest the relationship between the western North-Atlantic world, the Scriptures, and the God of the Scriptures can be ascertained. Once more I shall give an example. Some years ago, a booklet with the title *Nieuwe Psalmen* (Beerens 1995) was published in the Netherlands. Flemish and Dutch poets drew inspiration from the psalms and made new poems, mostly inspired by a specific psalm.

Sometimes their new verse got the general title 'Psalm' or 'A Psalm' or 'Apocryphal Psalm'; 'Psalm 151' or even 'Psalm 10501'. Together, we read psalms from this booklet during the study week mentioned before, because we assumed that Dutch churchgoers are secularized to a high degree too. Pastors preparing their services cannot be adequately aware enough of meanings generated outside (but what's outside?) of the church.

Hans Kloos, in his collection 'Een Psalm – A Psalm' (Beerens 1995: 89f.) addresses someone in the second person who eventually turns out to be 'God'. I will single out a few fragments from that poem (and thus do it shamefully wrong – a practice which, by the way, is accepted as normal in the Christian service, as we saw before ... !):

> 'Much they told me
> about you
> ...
> And that's how I
> came to believe in you.
> ...
> And that's how you
> grew big, bigger than me,
> God...
> And that's how I
> became small in you.
>
> ... And that's how I
> merged into the silence of the fearful child,
> stone tablets and the crowing of a coq,
> in the light that was
> when you said I should be silent.
> That's how I became small.
> And then I
> resurrected from you.
> It hurted.
> And then I began
> to see me, being alone,
> flesh...
> ...
> And I often
> told that you weren't there,
> alone. And much
> I still have left; ...
> ...
> That's how you became my story.'

The poet tells in his psalm how faith arose in him and grew, how God made him small and forced him to be silent, and, finally, how he liberated himself from that God, 'resurrecting from him'. He uses biblical images and metaphors describing his own development and secularization. Finally the words and stories – and the psalms – *remain*, but God disappeared from them. They became his own words and his own stories, even when they were handed down from old times.

In other words, initially the language evokes a truth, 'God', but this evoked reality frightens the interpreter and even silences him, after which the interpreter recovers his strength and liberates himself from the evoked truth. In this song, the 'you' as a reality is undone. Or, to put it differently once again, the story and the song of the metaphorical language remained, but 'God' as a stable point of reference within or beyond language disappeared. The meanings became floating, related to the interpreter only.

In his collection, the well-known Dutch poet Leo Vroman goes a step further still, when in his 'Psalm' (Beerens 1995: 91) he addresses a 'System', which even though he 'speaks' to it and it 'speaks' to him, does not have any personal features. In several songs inspired by the psalms, in the end no track of God can be found in these modern verses. Nevertheless, the psalms are still seen as fascinating, as documents in which the deepest and highest, the fiercest and most tender human feelings and experiences have been expressed. As universal human documents, the psalms have lasting meaning as well.

5. *The draft of liturgical science as an integrated and cultural-anthropological study*

After an introduction, this article described the primary way in which the pastor gave meaning to a number of psalms during a study week in which the services of Lent were prepared together. Subsequently, we reflected on the theological presuppositions of that method of preparation of the service. Then we listened to the way psalms are read and rewritten in modern Dutch culture. In the present section we will reflect on this new phenomenon of the universal, cultural understanding of the psalms in connection with their ecclesiastical understanding as discussed before. This will be *a draft of an integrated theological and cultural-anthropological approach of liturgical science*. Finally we will describe a fortunate example of such an integrated approach.

Psalms, and other parts of the Scripture as well, get new meanings in different theological, anthropological and cultural contexts. Of course (even though I didn't mention them yet) I am referring to the three classical Christian and ecclesiastical reading codes of the psalms: *vox Christi ad Patrem, vox Ecclesiae ad Patrem de Christo* and *vox Ecclesiae ad*

Christum.[7] It goes without saying here that these were a rereading and a reinterpretation of the originally Jewish songs. They are new meanings given to the old songs in a new context, opening only for a new audience.[8] Naturally, reflecting on shifting meanings, I also thought of the roots the psalms themselves had in the *Umwelt* they originated in and the influences they underwent as a result of this. This is another aspect I will not discuss here.

In this article my attention is focused on contemporary psalm interpretations, not only in cult, in liturgy, but also in culture. This approach originated in a research programme focused on the dynamic of cults and culture (Barnard 2000; 2001a; 2001b). In this programme, liturgy is defined broadly as a science of Christian rites and symbols. The theological perspective is included in the adjective 'Christian', the cultural-anthropological one in the nouns 'rites and symbols'.

The primary focus of this approach is cultural-anthropological, but the theological perspective is not neglected. In brackets, I note that within the anthropologically oriented study of liturgy the choice for a cultural-anthropological perspective implies a restriction already. By this I mean that there are still other possible anthropological approaches available. These include the psychological perspective, the sociological perspective, or the perspective of the theory of social action.

It is obvious that cult and culture etymologically have a root in common. Both words can, as is probably known, be traced back to the Latin word *colere*: to cultivate the land, to care, to cherish, to worship. People move between the laws of nature and the endeavour to influence them, to have them their own way between natural bounds and sensible meanings.

The American cultural-anthropologist Roy Rappaport in his last book *Ritual and religion in the making of humanity*, published posthumously, analyzes religion, language and culture as coherent human phenomena.

> 'Humanity... is caught between natural laws that it never fully comprehends and *meanings* that it must fabricate in the absence of much to prevent it from constructing self-destructive or even world-destroying follies' (Rappaport 1999: 406).

We move, he says, between '*humus* and *humanitas*' (Rappaport 1999: 406. Italics mine – MB), and use strategies which give sense and meaning to our

---

7. Literature about psalms and their use in liturgy is available in abundance. For a short overview about psalms in liturgy, see e.g. Fischer and Hucke (1987).

8. See for example Van der Leeuw (1946: 169): 'The gospel is latent in the Old Testament. It must become patent. That is what the old church sensed when it added a Gloria after every psalm, the praise of the Trinity. This places the fullness of Christian confession in a short, lapidary form as a summary behind every psalm prayer'.

existence because they influence the laws of nature and protect man against himself as well. This process is the cultural process.

Significant for us is the notion that culture is about meanings given to life and everything connected with it, about values assigned to the different dimensions and domains of life. The cult, the service, the liturgy, assigns *religious* values to phenomena. A Christian cult assigns *Christian* values to phenomena. In Christian liturgy, meanings are generated through a biblical and ecclesiastical perspective, without primary and general cultural meanings disappearing. It rather concerns a new layer, which is laid over the old one, making the old layer more or less invisible.

'Desert', using that example once more, is not only what it is in geography, but in a more general sense has the meaning of a barren and uninhabitable land, an area without variation and pleasure (Van Dale 1976). From a biblical perspective, a 'desert', for example, is also associated with a time of ordeal and a domain of self-reflection, for exodus/liberation, etc.

A second, more complicated example has obvious parallels with the modern revision of the psalms we heard a fragment from. In a Christian perspective, many meanings can be imagined for the notion of 'God', ranging from the Creator and Liberator of Israel, the Father of Jesus and the Sender of the Spirit, to Christ and the Spirit themselves. Nevertheless, in Western culture and for the majority of believers, secular meanings play a role as well. These are meanings in which 'God' is not an obvious and stable point of reference of religious language any more. Many have 'liberated' themselves from him.

So both cult and culture relate to meanings, without neglecting the natural bounds. This last specification explains the importance of, for instance, geography on culture, and also on liturgy. It is not a coincidence that, in the North-Atlantic world, Christmas is considered the main feast of the year, whereas in these regions Pentecost has great meaning only in ecclesiastical social life.

When a cultural-anthropological perspective is chosen in liturgical science, the dynamics of cult and culture are in the picture. The psalms are lingual bodies *waiting for meaning*. The meanings assigned to these bodies need not necessarily be based on Christian (or Jewish) inspiration. From a Western, secularized perspective, this is essential: none of the ministers participating in the reading exercise had *Christian* first reactions on the Psalms! Hans Kloos's psalm, from which I cited before, shows the opposite: how the God of the psalms begins living an own life in the first-person narrator and frightens him, and how he finally liberates himself from that God without entirely growing apart from Him. Here we have an interpretation of the psalms that is characteristic for West-European secularized culture. Moreover, we cannot assume that a person singing a psalm in church, has not been influenced deeply by these meanings as well.

Our experience with pastors, during the course in which they prepared a number of services together, taught us that, even from a Christian perspective, many meanings are possible. The choice the pastor makes will itself subsequently evoke many alternative other meanings. It is a complex and multi-layered meaning system, and once more it becomes clear how differentiated and complicated the hermeneutical process bearing the liturgy actually is.

This article is written from a Western, European, secularized perspective. In different cultures and contexts, Psalms are interpreted differently. I refer to a fascinating book, *The Bible in Africa*, edited by Gerald West and Musa Dube (West & Dube 2001). The volume does not only contain general sketches of the interpretation of the Bible in Africa (West 2001). More specifically, it also includes examples of African readings of the texts. Adamo's article 'The use of psalms in the Igbo Christianity of Nigeria' (Adamo 2001) shows a completely different reading of the poems compared with what we are used to in Western societies. He speaks of 'vernacular hermeneutics' (Adamo 2001: 336). In the Bible, and especially in the psalms, Nigerian Christians found substitutes for means and powers that were labelled as 'pagan' by missionaries. '...the African Indigenous Churches of Nigeria have appropriated the Psalms by classifying them according to their own cultural hermeneutical categories as: protective, curative or therapeutic, and success Psalms' (Adamo 2001: 337). Psalms and verses of Psalms are used in combination with or as substitution for traditional medicine, powerful words, amulets, protective devices and success words. Adamo concludes: 'African Indigenous Christians are not passive receivers of Christianity' (Adamo 2001: 348).

6. *Willem Breuker's Psalm 122*

We considered the meanings pastors assign to psalms and modern Dutch authors give to the old songs of Israel. We let these meanings play an important role in the process of the preparation of services. We reflected on the presuppositions this starting point is based on, and we gave a short draft of our concept of the liturgy in which we chose an integrated theological and cultural-anthropological perspective.

Finally, we would like to present a project which aims for an integration of these examples. It was initiated and organized by the *Prof. Dr. G. Van der Leeuw Foundation, Meeting Centre of Church and Art*. The foundation was named after the first post-war minister of Education, Arts and Sciences in the Netherlands. As an internationally famous professor in phenomenology of religion and in liturgical science, he was the founder of modern Dutch liturgical science seeking for the integration of theological and cultural-anthropological perspectives.

The goal of the Van der Leeuw Foundation is to award commissions in several branches of the arts. In 1996, on the 50th anniversary of its existence, the Foundation commissioned the Jazz musician and composer Willem Breuker to compose *Psalm 122*. Breuker, not having any bond with a church and preferably presenting himself as an atheist, accepted the commission. Theologically he was counselled mainly by Prof. Dr. Karel Deurloo, at the time professor for Old Testament at the University of Amsterdam. The work had its premiere in 1997 and was performed by the Willem Breuker Kollektief, the Trytten Strings, the Choir for New Music (conducted by Huub Kerstens), the narrator and synagogue chazan Peter Halpern and the Two Musketeers' Barrel Organ from Middelburg (province of Zeeland). Of a later performance, a CD was made.[9] I must remark, though, that this composition expressly is a concert composition, and is not meant for liturgy. As a result, this example has its limitations.

The Psalm, in fact a modern *oratorium*, has two introductions placing the song in a modern context:

'Jerusalem! Here I stand with my travel weary feet at your gate. With a poem I want to greet you.' (CD Booklet, cited in translation)

Then, the narrator tells how he thought of Jerusalem, living in exile, and how he sung the song of the city. How he tried to live in peace with his haters. And how glad he was when, with his mates, he went up to the city, depicted as follows:

'Jerusalem, you are a people's city. You are built of peoples, a round dozen. We are twelve, twelve names which together are Israel. As we follow together the paths that lead up to your gates, we build you as our city, with our living bodies. We ourselves are the proof that you live, Jerusalem.' (CD Booklet, cited in translation)

'We? Who are we? The people who hear! Across the confusion of the world, we have heard a voice: "It is I who lead you out of slavery. It is I who occur in your liberation. I shall be there with you. This is my name, which you cannot speak."

The gods paled at that voice. Before our eyes, the earth became a pure human domain. Jerusalem became the navel of the earth, because that unutterable name from there pervaded the whole world. Since then we bow down no more for god or superpower; but if we go up to Jerusalem, it is to give thanks to that name, the name of the liberator, the voice who says: I shall be there.' (CD Booklet, cited in translation)

---

9. CD 9803, to be ordered at: BV Haast, Prinseneiland 99, 1013 LN Amsterdam, tel. +31.(0)20.6239799, fax +31.(0)20.6243534

Jerusalem is everywhere on earth. It is today's Jerusalem, but in those days, when this piece of music was composed, it was also Sarajevo, today it is Kabul or many a city in Africa. Perhaps it even is Baghdad? The people are the Jewish people, but not only that one: it is the men and women who, shoulder to shoulder and all over the world form a new Jerusalem:

> 'A city like a woman. Built with living stones. A city for people, a city where walls and buildings stand shoulder to shoulder, a community. As you are constructed, so would I have my poem. With sounds and words my verses reach out their hands to one another.' (CD Booklet, cited in translation)

Right from the beginning the author of this version, Karel Deurloo, integrates modern culture and exegesis in the introductions, being the undeniable context in which the psalm is read. But a theological and a cultural perspective have not been integrated only in the text. They have been integrated in the composition as well. The musical idiom is highly surprising for a psalm: a mixture of jazz and a Hebraizing recital, performed by a jazz collective, strings, barrel organ and choir. In the *oratorium*, the psalm sounds in Dutch, Hebrew and English, and in this way literally makes audible that the longing for *this* Jerusalem surpasses every national longing (an actual notion!)

7. *Conclusion*

It is clear that a description of this project cannot equal listening to its CD recording. Nevertheless, in this article I chose to give a description of this project in order to show how a psalm, *waiting for meaning*, may get meaning from a modern cultural perspective and from a theological-exegetical perspective at the same time. As far as I am concerned, this psalm, composed and performed in this way, makes audible what modern liturgical science means when it argues for an integrated liturgical practice, and when it analyses the current practice theologically and cultural-anthropologically. When, in this analysis, (too) big gaps appear between the two perspectives, it still leaves suggestions for improvement.

Bibliography

Adamo, D.T. 2001 'The use of Psalms in the Igbo Christianity of Nigeria', in G. West & M.W. Dube (eds.), *The Bible in Africa: Transactions, Trajectories and Trends* (Boston/Leiden: Brill Academic Publishers): 336–349.

Barnard, M. 2000 *Liturgiek als wetenschap van christelijke riten en symbolen* (inaugural lecture, University of Amsterdam, Amsterdam: Amsterdam University Press).

—2001a 'Prinses Diana als postmoderne heilige en een kerkdienst in een museum: Tendensen in de dynamiek van cultus en cultuur vanuit een West-Europees perspectief', *Verbum et Ecclesia*, 22/2: 209–230.

—2001b 'Dynamiek van cultus en cultuur', in M. Barnard & P. Post (eds.), *Ritueel bestek. Antropologische kernwoorden van de liturgie* (Zoetermeer: Meinema): 47–62.

Beerens, M., Joosten, J., Rouwenhorst, H. and Thewissen, M. (eds.) 1995 *Nieuwe Psalmen* (= *Parmentier* 6/4) (Nijmegen: SUN).

Fischer, B. and Hucke, H. 1987 'Poetische Formen', in H.B. Meyer and Hj. Auf der Maur, B. Fischer et alii (eds.), *Gestalt des Gottesdienstes* (Gottesdienst der Kirche. Handbuch der Liturgiewissenschaft, 3; Regensburg: Verlag Friedrich Pustet): 180–188.

Itten, J. 1961 *Kunst der Farbe* (Ravensburg: Otto Maier Verlag).

Krog, A. 2000 *Kleur kom nooit alleen nie* (Cape Town: Kwela Boeke).

Rappaport, R. 1999 *Ritual and Religion in the making of humanity* (Cambridge Studies in Social and Cultural Anthropology, 110; Cambridge: Cambridge University Press).

Van Dale 1976 *Groot woordenboek der Nederlandse taal* (Utrecht/Antwerpen: Van Dale Lexicografie, 10th edn.).

Van den Boogerd, D. 1999a 'Hang-ups and Hangovers in the Work of Marlene Dumas', in D. Van den Boogerd, B. Bloom, and M. Casadio, (eds.), *Marlene Dumas* (London: Phaidon Press Limited): 30–85.

Van den Boogerd, D., Bloom, B. and Casadio, M. (eds.) 1999b *Marlene Dumas* (London: Phaidon Press Limited).

Van der Leeuw, G. 1946 [1940] *Liturgiek* (Nijkerk: Callenbach).

West, G. 2001 'Mapping African Biblical Interpretation: A Tentative Sketch', in G. West & M.W. Dube (eds.), *The Bible in Africa: Transactions, Trajectories and Trends* (Boston/Leiden: Brill Academic Publishers): 29–53.

West, G. and Dube, M.W. (eds.) 2001 *The Bible in Africa: Transactions, Trajectories and Trends* (Boston/Leiden: Brill Academic Publishers).

PSALTER AND MESSIAH. TOWARDS A CHRISTOLOGICAL
UNDERSTANDING OF THE PSALMS IN THE OLD TESTAMENT
AND THE CHURCH FATHERS*

Georg P. Braulik
Vienna, Austria

1. *Introduction*

The Christology of the early church could to a large extent be described as
a Christology of the Psalms, depicting Jesus Christ as being testified to in
the Psalms of Israel and also as being interpreted by them.

This same function of the Psalms can already be seen in the New
Testament writings, although they are by no means used only Christologically there (Löning 1998). To name only a few examples: the letter to the
Hebrews develops its Christology especially according to the Psalms. With
reference to Psalm 40, Hebrews 10.5-9 interprets 'the life of Jesus as one
great "psalmic prayer"' (Zenger 1997: 23). The Gospels use Psalms 22, 31
and 69 to recount the events of the passion and death of Jesus. In his
sermon on the day of Pentecost, Peter based his argumentation about
Jesus' resurrection on Psalm 16 (Acts 2.25-32). In close association with
the fate of Jesus, the experiences of his congregation are interpreted in
terms of Psalm 2 (Acts 4.25-28).

The Psalms also served the Church Fathers in their Christological
argumentation. In his fight against Christological heresies, Tertullian
already refers to the Psalms at around 200 CE. He mentions them as
biblical testimonies to the human side of Jesus:

> 'We shall also have the support of the Psalms on this point, – not the
> "Psalms" indeed of Valentinus the apostate, the heretic, and the
> Platonist, but the Psalms of David, the illustrious saint and well-known

---

* This paper is a continuation of my contribution to the liturgists' conference in Münster
1994, which was published in *Christologie der Liturgie. Der Gottesdienst der Kirche –
Christusbekenntnis und Sinaibund* (Hrsg. v. K. Richter – B. Kranemann; QD 159; Freiburg:
Herder, 1995) 57–86. However, many of the aspects which are here only briefly dealt with
because of the limitations of the framework of a lecture, were treated in greater detail there.
My appreciation to Hanneke Friedl for the English translation.

prophet. He sings to us of Christ, and through his voice Christ indeed
also sang concerning Himself.'[1]

The Christological interpretation of the Psalms in the early church also
had no small influence on the theology and spirituality of the different
liturgies, especially since the biblical Psalms had begun replacing
charismatic hymns in church services and to a certain extent became
canonized in the liturgical context (Hengel 1987). Therefore, until recently,
many liturgists accepted as a matter of course that, whoever really wanted
to understand the deepest meaning of the Psalms and wanted to use them
as such in the liturgical service, had to approach them especially 'from the
viewpoint of the Church Fathers'[2] [3].

This traditional handling of the Psalms, however, is hardly compatible
with historic-critical exegesis, at least as long as the latter merely wants to
reconstruct single Psalms in their original textual form, assign them a
specific cultic or institutional *Sitz im Leben* and, as far as the history of
religions is concerned, place them within the sphere of the Ancient Near
East. Do we Christians therefore have to accept and live with this kind of
conflict between the reception of the Psalms in the liturgy of the church on
the one hand and their interpretation within the enlightened biblical
sciences on the other? Moreover, the patristic and liturgical use of the
Psalms seem to contradict a biblical hermeneutics that tries to shun the
results of 'a self-centred disregard for Israel in Christian theology' and 'no
longer' wishes to 'interpret the Old Testament without respect for the
unbroken chosenness of Israel.' (Zenger 2000a: 243).

In the light of this dilemma, my contribution will aim at reconciling
modern exegesis of the Psalms with the interpretation of the Church
Fathers and the liturgical tradition.[4] The bridging of a gap such as this
is made possible by a reorientation in biblical studies, progressing from
'the historical formation of a single text to the text of a completed

---

1. Tertullian, *De carne Christi* 20, 3 (CSEL 70): 'Nobis quoque ad hanc speciem psalmi
patrocinantur, non quidem apostatae et haeretici et Platonici Valentini, sed sanctissimi et
receptissimi prophetae David. Ille apud nos canit Christum, per quem se cecinit ipse Christus.'
Zenger (1997: 21) already refers to this text.

2. This is true, for example, of a 'classic' in liturgical science, which has been translated
into many different languages, C. Vagaggini, *Theologie der Liturgie* (cf. Vagaggini 1959: 286).

3. See H. Buchinger's excellent article, providing an overview (Buchinger 2000: 196–199).

4. One should, however, not confine oneself to those Psalms which were cited in the New
Testament and reinterpreted Christologically, the *relecture* of which the Patristic and
Medieval theologians then took up. Rather, one should develop a hermeneutics that would be
principally valid for the whole Psalter. P. Grelot (1998) therefore falls short of this ideal when,
following on his summary of the historic-critically gleaned 'literal sense' of those Psalms cited
in the New Testament, he merely represents their Jewish, New Testament and Patristic
relecture.

biblical book to the canonical text.'[5] The methodological perspective of research on the Psalms has shifted from genre criticism of the individual psalm to the composition of the Psalter and its intertextuality, especially within the canon (cf. Janowski 2001: 161–179; Braulik 2003). For our theme, it is important that this change of perspectives opens our eyes for a deeper dimension of the Psalter already within the Old Testament, a dimension which was well-known to the New Testament and to the exegesis of the Church Fathers. Therefore I confine myself to hermeneutical convergences between modern and patristic exegesis of the Psalms. However, I want to stress: when the synagogue reads the Psalms in the context of the Hebrew Bible only, this reading of course has to lead to a different messianic-Christological interpretation than that of the church when it reads the same biblical[6] Psalms in canonical dialogue with the New Testament.[7] Yet the Jewish reading is as legitimate as the Christian, on the one hand, because the texts

5. M. Fiedrowicz (1998: XX) rightly pointed to the interest in Early Christian exegesis currently shown by modern hermeneutics: 'Die Erkenntnis, daß das Verstehen eines Textes nicht nur seine Genese, sondern auch seine Rezeption umfaßt, daß Interpretation Implizites freizulegen, verborgene Reichtümer einer Aussage ans Licht zu heben und Vergangenes in neuen Kontexten zu aktualisieren hat, läßt die Exegeten der alten Kirche zu einem ernstzunehmenden Gesprächspartner in der hermeneutischen Diskussion der Gegenwart werden.' Cf. Schwienhorst-Schönberger (2003: 415): 'Das Erstaunliche an der Diskussion ist, dass sich aus diesen manchmal als "postmodern" apostrophierten Literaturtheorien Affinitäten zur so genannten praemodernen Bibelwissenschaft ergeben. Mit Hilfe der durch die postmoderne literaturtheoretische Diskussion angestoßenen Theorien können Aporien historisch-kritischer Exegese aufgearbeitet und grundlegende Einsichten der patristischen und mittelalterlichen Schriftauslegung wiedergewonnen werden. Das Prinzip kanonischer Schriftauslegung und die Einsicht "von einer grundsätzlichen Kohärenz und Konsistenz der biblischen Aussage aus dem Universalkontext" (*Karla Pollmann*) findet sich, um nur ein Beispiel aufzugreifen, bei Augustinus, in "De doctrina christiana", dem grundlegenden Werk christlicher Bibelhermeneutik'.

6. I deliberately speak of 'biblical' and not of 'Jewish' Psalms, as is frequently done by E. Zenger especially with a view to the Christian-Jewish dialogue. The church retained the Psalms by virtue of their being part of the Holy Scriptures of early Christianity or of the Old Testament of its bipartite canon. The church however hardly 'defended' this choice, because it knew that it was confronted with 'their irrenounceable rootedness in the Jewish context' – against Zenger (1997: 22 *i.a.*).

7. This aspect may be lacking in E. Zenger's hermeneutics of the Psalms. (I do, however, otherwise generally agree with his stance.) For instance, he makes a somewhat too undifferentiated remark on Psalmic prayer, namely, 'daß die biblischen Psalmen keiner *besonderen* Verchristlichung bedürfen' (Zenger 2002: 37). The many-sided image of the Messiah that we encounter in the Psalter gains a concrete profile through Jesus as the Christ. Even Yahweh, to whom we pray our Christian psalmic prayer in concord with the tradition of the early church, thus became the God and Father of the Christ in a sense unexpectedly new compared to his fathership of the Davidic Messiah of the Psalms. In the light of the events around the Christ testified of in the New Testament, the psalmic prayer of the church has to elevate some and eliminate other of the traits of the 'incarnatory-messianic dynamics' of the

themselves are open and show multiple perspectives. This will soon be illustrated more clearly. On the other hand, it is equally legitimate because the reception of the Psalms as Holy Scripture is basically connected to the community of faith and interpretation, the canon of which they belong to (Böhler: 2002).

I will now speak about (1) the principal trend in the current exegesis of the Psalms and then (2) summarize its results concerning history and literary studies for the messianization of the Psalter, principally according to research done in the German-speaking exegetical community. Starting with the Davidic and royal Psalms, a messianic or 'Christological' understanding of the Psalms already begins to develop within the Old Testament. Their collectivization or 'democratization' then irrevocably leads to an 'ecclesiological' understanding of the Psalms. I shall conclude by (3) comparing the methodologies of the rediscovered canonical reading and the patristic interpretation of the Psalms by means of two selected examples.

2. *The principal trend in current research on the Psalms*

The methodological attention of modern Old Testament studies focuses on an aspect which can be described with the formula: '*From text to context*'. The newer exegesis of the Psalms accordingly reads any given individual psalm in the context of the entire book ('end text exegesis')[8] and of the relevant canon ('canonical exegesis')[9]. Exegesis of the *Psalms* thus

---

Psalter (Zenger 2001a: 24). This becomes especially clear when the weekly scheme of the liturgy of the hours is designed to form a Christological Easter Psalter. Cf. the outline by N. Füglister in: *Benediktinisches Antiphonale* (Münsterschwarzach: Vier Türme, 1996).

8. Cf. e.g. Zenger (2000b: 416–419). This end text exegesis does not require any reconstruction of hypothetical earlier stages. The multi-perspectivity of the end text can also be perceived and interpreted theologically without taking the diachronical detour (against Zenger 2000a: 244). On this change in the scientific-exegetical trend see, most recently, L. Schwienhorst-Schönberger (2003).

9. This canonical-intertextual interpretation takes place in such a way, that 'zunächst die im Psalm selbst explizit anwesenden Texte der Hebräischen Bibel als Prätexte (in diachroner Perspektive) oder als Hypotexte (in synchroner Perspektive) erhoben und in die Interpretation des Psalms eingebracht werden.' Then the exegete has to enquire after the explicit and implicit reception of the Psalm in the New Testament and the texts have to be correlated with each other according to the method of canonical dialogue (Zenger 2000a: 248). The enquiry into the 'Nachgeschichte der Heiligen Schriften Israels' in the Jewish reception of a Psalm, although exegetically indispensable, for the Christian Old Testament scholar no longer belongs to a canonical exegesis of the Psalms (against Zenger 2000a: 249). On the methodology of the canonical interpretation of Scripture, see the excellent recent article of G. Steins (2003).

developed into exegesis of the *Psalter*.[10] Each psalm, of course, still has to be examined according to its own literary and theological profile. However, its specific forms of speech and expression can also fulfil other functions in text pragmatics when seen within different, broader contexts.[11] They can also draw new horizons of meaning, which in turn can each be attributed with an own scheme of thought. The message of the Psalter is greater than the sum of the messages of its individual Psalms. The degree to which the Church Fathers, too, were aware of this, can for example be seen in the extensive treatise of Gregory of Nyssa, 'On the Inscriptions of the psalms' ('In Inscriptiones Psalmorum', in: GNO V [Leiden: Brill, 1962] 24–175; English translation: Heine [1995]), in which he depicts the five books of the Psalter as steps on the ascending way to blessedness. Because of this 'added value', I explicitly speak of the Psalter in the title of my paper, meaning the structured book of 150 psalms available to us today.[12] The Psalms as texts of Holy Scripture, secondly, can only be considered to be fully accessible when they are interpreted within the framework of the biblical canon. The new *canonical and intertextual reading* taught us to see a close network of diverse correspondences, connecting the Psalms with the other books of the Old and New Testaments. The phenomenon of a messianic-Christological influence which is at issue here, however already determines the Psalter in its (canonical) final form! As was said earlier, its structure and function are now looked upon in a more differentiated way than had previously been the case in exegetical circles.

10.   On the canonical-theological interpretation of the Psalter, cf. the recent works of Auwers (2003) and Zenger (2003: 126–134).

11.   F.L. Hossfeld (1998: 60) therefore rightly criticised the hermeneutical-methodological position of E. Gerstenberger (1997/2001: 212). He formulates Gerstenberger's position as follows: '"Eine flächige Auslegungsmethode, sei sie allegorisch oder christologisch, psychologisch oder historisierend, strukturalistisch oder kanonisch, verbietet sich bei der geschichtlichen Tiefendimension der P[salmen]-Texte. Die Exegese hat den Weg nachzuvollziehen, den ein Psalm von seiner Entstehungssituation und seinem ursprünglich gesellschaftlichen und gottesdienstlichem Haftpunkt an durchlaufen hat." Darauf ist knapp zu antworten: keine Einordnung der kanonischen Exegese unter die angegebenen "flächigen" Auslegungsmethoden und keine Entweder-Oder-Alternative zwischen synchron-flächiger und diachron-historischer Methode. In den nachzuvollziehenden Weg des Einzelpsalms gehören die verschiedenen Stadien seiner Existenz als Mitglied einer Teilgruppe bis hin zum Gesamtpsalter.'

12.   'First, one must understand the aim of this writing. Next, one must pay attention to the progressive arrangements of the concepts in the book under discussion. These are indicated by both the order of the psalms, which have been suitably arranged in relation to the knowledge of the aim, and by the sections of the whole book, which are defined by certain distinctive conclusions. The entire prophecy in the Psalms has been divided into five parts.' (Heine 1995: 83).

A composition and redaction-critical investigation of the (proto-Masoretic) Psalter reveals that the correspondences in form and content between the psalms had to be the result of a deliberate juxtaposition (*iuxtapositio*) and/or an intended concatenation (*concatenatio*) of psalms standing directly next to or near to one another.[13] The works of Norbert Lohfink and Erich Zenger[14] contributed fundamentally to the (re-discovery of these phenomena[15] in the Middle-European context. They observed the way in which collectors, editors and redactors used correspondences in words and contents at hand, and furthermore replaced single expressions, inserted certain additions and even entire psalms, and structured groupings of psalms to form fields of expression reaching across the whole area of the grouping.

The book of Psalms, of course, does to a large extent contain originally independent texts, this can be seen in its complex system of superscriptions. At the same time, though, the titles of the psalms illustrate that the Psalter is no unsystematic archive of individual texts out of which official liturgy or private piety borrowed one psalm or another (Zenger 1994a: 175). It has been made into a '*book of meditations*' (Füglister 1988)[16], the text of which is to be learnt by heart and is again and again to be recited to oneself. It can thus be inferred from the concatenation of the psalms and its effect,

---

13. The same techniques were applied, e.g., in systematizing legal texts within the framework of a legal corpus, cf. Braulik (1991).

14. N. Lohfink (2003b) has proved the same principles for the New Testament, too. For E. Zenger, cf. the publications listed in Zenger (2000b: 417 n. 50). These were partially prepared in cooperation with F.-L. Hossfeld. G. Barbiero (1999) even examined the whole first book of Psalms regarding the interlinkage of its individual Psalms.

15. Many of them were already represented in the commentaries on the Psalms of the 19th century, albeit in an irregular developed form. This is especially true of the (originally two-volumed) commentary on the Psalms by F. Delitzsch (1859/60). The fifth revised edition (Leipzig 1894) was reprinted in: *Die Psalmen* (Gießen: Brunnen, 1984).

16. N. Füglister also proves that, in the time of Jesus, the Psalter did not serve as the official liturgical hymn and prayerbook of the services in the Temple or synagogues of the Jewish communities. Rather, it was used as an aid to personal piety, instruction and devotion (1988: 329–352 and 380–384). The text was recited by heart, that is, it was 'meditated' on as was already required by the 'Hear Israel' for the Deuteronomic law (Deut. 6.6); also cf. Lohfink (1993). The redaction-historical arguments against the Psalter that was handed down being a collection of Psalms for the services in the Temple or synagogue were summarised by Zenger (2000b: 430–433). Also cf. the programmatic beatitude of him that 'delights in the Torah of Yahweh when he *murmurs/recites* it day and night' in the prologue to the Psalter. Zenger (2000b: 433) describes the proto-Masoretic Psalter as a 'book of Wisdom', which had retained 'seine Endgestalt im Milieu jener Weisheitsschule... die in gewisser Distanz zur Tempelaristokratie und deren hellenisierenden Tendenzen stand und die mit ihrer Verbindung von Tora-Weisheit (vgl. Ps. 1 und Ps. 147; 148), Eschatologie (vgl. besonders Ps. 2 und Ps. 149) und "Armenfrömmigkeit" (vgl. besonders Ps. 146 und Ps. 149) den Psalter als ein *Volksbuch* ausgestaltete und verbreitete, das als "konservative" Summe der Tradition gelernt und gelebt werden konnte'.

that the genre of the 'book' fits the description of the Psalter (Lohfink 2003a). A dynamics, which leads from one psalm to the next and makes the Psalter into a single, unified text, is created when keywords and motifs are taken up in successive psalms. The technique of sometimes announcing one or more following psalms at the end of a previous psalm, serves the same purpose of unifying the text of the Psalter. The announced psalm or psalms are then developed compositionally from the basis provided by the announcing psalm (Lohfink 2003a; Zenger 1997: 14–21). Apart from this unifying effect, the concatenation of psalms furthermore brings about an 'interpenetration of aspects', described by Lohfink (2003a: 83) as follows:

> 'The linking of the first three psalms already effects in those who meditatively murmur the Psalter as a whole something like an explosion of the individual statements, a sweeping obliteration of the individual levels of interpretation. One can quickly read each of these psalms on one level or another. Everything is open to insights and still further and more penetrating comprehension. The plane becomes space in which understanding can move freely. This process of understanding is typical of meditation'.

The interlinking of adjoining psalms can ultimately even change their sense, perhaps by supplying them with a new subject – for instance the nations instead of Israel. All these different 'reading instructions' are essential, not only for the genre and function of the Psalter, but especially also for its messianic *relecture*.

3. *The messianization of the Psalter*

Concerning its *total structure*[17] as delineated in the framing Psalms 1–2 and 146–150, the Psalter is directed at the praise of the universal kingship of God, which is based in creation and Torah. The book of Psalms wishes to realise this kingship through the Davidic-messianic king, appointed on Zion (cf. Ps. 2), and through his messianic people (cf. Ps. 149) in the midst of all other peoples of the world. This messianic perspective is especially made clear through the 'royal psalms' (A) and the 'Davidic psalms' (B), deliberately built in on a macro-structural level. Both of these types of psalms are to be read in connection with God's people (C). I will sketch the phenomena relevant to our theme on the synchronic level of the Psalter we have at hand.[18]

---

17. Recently summarised by Zenger (2001a: 25).

18. Today, the origin of the Psalter is explained according to three basic models: a redactional, a compositional and a collection model. All three of these are used in the commentaries on the Psalms of F.-L. Hossfeld and E. Zenger (see Hossfeld & Zenger 1996: 338). According to them, the book of Psalms that we have at hand today, originated 'in

(A) The *Royal psalms* are not arbitrarily or coincidentally distributed through the Psalter.[19] They have been inserted at certain points of compositional conjunction.[20] I will here focus only on the most important observations. Psalms 2 and 72 frame the first and second books of the Psalter, that is, Psalms 3–41 and 42–72. Psalm 89 concludes the third book, Psalms 73–89. Each of the three books that are separated by doxological formulas, thus are either introduced or concluded by a royal psalm. At the end of the first book, Psalm 41 shares a number of motifs with Psalms 72 and 89 and can therefore also be read as a royal psalm and be drawn into the framework of kingship theology.[21] Although Psalms 2, 72 and 89 are not identified as 'Davidic psalms' through superscriptions, they frame the two large collections of Davidic psalms. They are interpreted by the theme of the covenant of David: by its foundation in Psalm 2, its handing down in Psalm 72 and its failure in Psalm 89. Thus Psalms 2–89 are now to be read as 'the distressing but at the same time heartening story and theology of the Davidic reign' (Hossfeld & Zenger 1993a: 51).

The next two books, encompassing Psalms 90–106 and 107–145[22], display a different profile than that of the previous three books.[23] They now turn the Psalter into 'a great composition of theological history and creation theology – and as such, a poetical appropriation or revision of Torah and prophecy'.[24] In the last two books of the Psalter, however, the royal Psalms 101, 110 and 144 also fulfil an introductory or concluding

---

mehreren Schüben... und zwar durch Aneinanderreihung von Teilsammlungen, die teilweise ihre je eigene Entstehungsgeschichte haben. Als Faustregel kann gelten: Die Abfolge der Teilsammlungen im jetzigen Psalmenbuch entspricht auch ihrem Alter'. (Zenger 2001b: 320; Hossfeld 1998: 71). In contrast to this model of the addition of completed sub-collections, C. Rösel (1999), for instance, represents the redactional model and reckons with several redactional layers.

19.   The framing and closing function that certain royal psalms have for the groupings of Psalms or for smaller psalters, was already observed by C. Westermann (1964). It was especially G.H. Wilson (1986) that then treated this theme separately.

20.   According to M. Millard (1994: 165–167), Torah and wisdom psalms, but also Zion- and royal psalms were used in these positions by editorial preference. For the royal psalms, Millard otherwise confines himself to individual observations.

21.   On the connection of Psalm (1 and) 2 with Psalm 41 and the framing of the first book of Psalms that to a certain extent results from this, cf. e.g. Millard (1994: 125). The way in which Psalm 41 is connected with Psalms 72 and 89 under the aspect of kingship theology was illustrated by Zenger (1996: 100 n. 12.)

22.   On the demarcation of the fifth book of Psalms, cf. Wilson (1993).

23.   Cf. Zenger (1991a; 1994b; 1996), in which the structural suggestions of G.H. Wilson, K. Koch and R. G. Kratz on the fifth book of Psalms are also presented and commented critically.

24.   [Der Psalter ist nun] 'eine große geschichts- und schöpfungstheologische Komposition – und als solche eine poetische Aneignung bzw. Aktualisierung von Tora und Prophetie'. Zenger (2003: 130). On these perspectives, cf. Ballhorn (2000).

function. In contrast to Psalms 2, 72 and 89, though, they are Davidic psalms. Psalm 101 introduces a grouping of Davidic psalms, 101–104 (Zenger 1991a: 243). According to Psalm 101.1, it is the first task of David, as ruler, to sing praises to Yahweh. Psalms 110 and 144 conclude the two smaller Davidic Psalters 108–110 and 138–144. Within the fifth book of Psalms, these two minor Psalters structurally correspond and form an internal frame.[25]

Considering that every Davidic Psalter is either introduced or concluded by a royal psalm, it can be inferred that we have to reckon with a deliberate compositional scheme: Psalms 3–41 are introduced by Psalm 2 and 101–104 by Psalm 101. Psalms 51–71 end with Psalm 72, 108–110 with 110 and 138–145 with 144, followed by Psalm 145, depicting Yahweh as King above all.

The royal psalms are thus inserted in key positions of the Psalter, of groupings within the Psalter and of individual smaller Psalters. Their varying usage probably should be explained diachronically. The overall hermeneutics of the Psalter presumably was successively built up over a longer period. In these points of junction, the dimensions of meaning of the individual texts are in any event semantically transformed through compositional attribution. This in turn has an important result: In exilic and post-exilic times, Israel having lost their king, the royal psalms could hardly be understood in any other than a messianic sense. Therefore, the groupings of psalms that are framed by these royal psalms or the compositional entities to which they belong, have to be *reread from the perspective of a messianic expectation.*[26]

Concerning the compositional grouping of Psalms 2–89, Zenger (1994c: 149) speaks of a *'messianic psalter'*, which he characterises as follows:

> 'In this "messianic" psalter, on the one hand, the ambivalent experiences Israel had had with its historic monarchy are enumerated meditatively.

25. Zenger (1996). Psalm 45, where motifs of human and divine kingship meet, is to be read as God's first answer to his people's situation of need as it was sketched in the composition of lament in 42–44. It is also to be read as the hermeneutical key to the Zion theology developed in Psalms 46–48 (Zenger 1994a: 185). On Psalms 122, 127 and 132, which are characterised by kingship theology and which have a central position in the three groups of five Psalms each into which the songs of ascents can be divided, cf. Zenger 1996: 109.

26. In Psalm 45, in which the marriage ceremony of the king is celebrated, the latter is interpreted as being the Messiah. This has implications for the understanding of the woman that is extolled in the second part of the Psalm. She becomes the embodiment of Israel, which is now married to the Messianic king. Against the background of the marital bond between Yahweh and Israel, the messianic saving king vicariously steps into the role of God, wedding himself to the people. The Messiah, representing Yahweh, even appears as the bridegroom of the eschatological people of God in Psalm 45. It thus attests to a special case of the close connection between 'Christology' and 'Ecclesiology' resulting from the Messianic *relecture* of the Psalms.

Starting with David (Psalms 3ff) and moving to Solomon (Psalm 72 is a prayer of the elderly David for his son Solomon), the account leads to the end of the monarchy in the year 587 (Psalm 89). Dealing with the way the monarchy went, the "messianic" Psalter holds on to the promise given in the Davidic covenant: the programmatic opening text of Psalm 2 recapitulates the promise of Nathan in 2 Sam. 7.14 (cf. Ps. 2.7) in the context of the intimidating world of the nations. The closing Psalm, 89, brings in 2 Sam. 7.14-16 corresponding to its "historical" setting. It serves both as interpretation of the current situation and as request that opens the future (cf. Ps. 89.27, 30, 33). In its closing section, Psalm 89 in a "democratizing" way widens the messianic perspective to include Israel as a people. The faithfulness of God that "David" assures his "son" of, is meant for the "messianic" Israel, with a view to this same intimidating world of the nations. Ps. 72.17 quotes the opening passage of the story of Israel, Gen. 12.1-3 with its perspective on the nations, and thereby emphasizes: "All nations will be blessed through him, and they will call him blessed".[27]

The royal psalms are partially combined with *psalms about the kingship of Yahweh*. This can, for instance, be seen in the grouping Psalms 18–21, where the royal Psalms 18 and 20–21 frame Psalm 19, about Yahweh as universal king.[28] The royal Psalm 101 reflects on the preceding Yahweh-kingship Psalms 93–100. The fifth book of Psalms is concluded with Psalms 144 and 145, a royal and a Yahweh-kingship psalm. This combination corresponds to the programmatic opening psalm, number 2, which combines both kingship theologies. Seen from within the total

---

27. 'In diesem "messianischen" Psalter werden einerseits meditativ die ambivalenten Erfahrungen Israels mit seinem historischen Königtum abgeschritten: Von David (Psalmen 3) über Salomo (Psalm 72 ist Gebet des alten David für seinen Sohn Salomo) bis hin zum Ende des Königtums im Jahre 587 (Psalm 89). In Auseinandersetzung mit diesem Weg des Königtums hält der "messianische" Psalter aber die im Davidbund gegebene Verheißung fest: Der eröffnende Programmtext Psalm 2 rekapituliert die Natanverheißung 2 Sam. 7, 14 (vgl. Ps. 2.7) im Kontext der bedrohlichen Völkerwelt. Der abschließende Psalm 89 spielt 2 Sam. 7, 14-16, dem "geschichtlichen" Standort entsprechend, sowohl als Deutung der Situation wie auch als die Zukunft eröffnende Bitte ein (vgl. Ps. 89.27, 30–33). Psalm 89 weitet in seinem Schlußabschnitt dann "demokratisierend" die messianische Perspektive auf Israel als Volk aus. Die "David" für seinen "Sohn" zugesprochene Treue Gottes gilt einem "messianischen" Israel – gerade mit Blick auf die Völkerwelt, wie Psalm 72.17 (mit Zitat der die Geschichte Israels eröffnenden Völkerperspektive Gen. 12.1-3) herausstellt: "Und es sollen sich in ihm segnen alle Völker, ihn sollen sie glücklich preisen".'

28. If it could be proved according to literary critical criteria that the three royal Psalms were intentionally bound together into a single 'unit of expression' through redactional insertions and thus originally formed the centre of the sub-collection Psalms 15–24* – cf. Hossfeld & Zenger (1993b: 169–177) – then not only do we have an early testimony of a structurally purposed insertion, but also an example of the concatenation of Psalms, in this case, of clustered royal psalms.

perspective of the Psalter, the 'messianic concept' of the first three books with its 'dialectics of restoration and Utopia', develops into the 'theocratic concept' of the last two books, thus culminating in the universal kingship of Yahweh (Zenger 1994b: 151).

The messianic *relecture* of the royal psalms and, at that, of all other psalms in their field of tension, *partially coincides with two other new interpretations*, which I have until now more or less left out and which I now wish to introduce. These are the 'Davidization' and the 'democratization' of the 'I'-speaker of the psalms, especially the 'I' of a king or of David himself. Both interpretations, the *'historicizing'* and the *'collectivizing'*, are partially the result of redactional activity, but could also have developed from a new interpretation inherent to the Old Testament, which needs not necessarily have brought about any textual changes such as superscriptions or insertions or additions. In both cases, the psalms had been awarded a new literal meaning.[29]

(B) Jewish as well as Christian pre-critical exegetes considered David to be the author of the Psalms.[30] David, who wrote and sang them, was a prophet and archetype of Christ. He also was the David of the liturgy. This naively historical interpretation proved itself to be untenable in scientific research on the Psalms.[31] The actual value of the *Davidization*, however, namely its historical hermeneutics deeply rooted in the Old Testament, only started to be acknowledged in recent times. Today, exegetes consider David to be the canonical 'integrative figure' of the Psalter and the 'coded message' ('Chiffre-Begriff') especially pointing to Israel (Millard 1994: 231)[32]. This he became through a multi-phased process in the course of inner-Old Testament development. Apart from the Chronistic History[33],

---

29. On the nature and value of such new interpretations, see e.g. Becker (1967).

30. On the image of David in the Psalter, cf. especially Luyten (1990); Ballhorn (1995); Kleer (1996); Auwers (1999).

31. For more information in outline, cf. Becker (1975).

32. 'Das gilt einerseits lokal und sozial: für ein Israel, das – im Duktus der biblischen Geschichtsdarstellung – noch nicht in Nord- und Südreich, geschweige denn in verschiedene Diasporagruppen aufgespalten ist. Das hat andererseits aber auch eine Bedeutung in Bezug auf den Tempel:... Der Gottesdienst ohne Tempel gibt das Vorbild ab für die Wendung zu Gott in der Situation, in der der Tempel zwar als Zentralheiligtum anerkannt ist, aber faktisch unerreichbar ist. Diese situative Analogie eröffnet dem Beter, der sich mit David identifiziert, aber nicht einfach nur die Möglichkeit der gegenwärtigen Begegnung mit Gott außerhalb des Tempels, sondern zugleich die Hoffnung auf eine künftige Begegnung mit Gott im Tempel.' (Millard 1994: 231).

33. According to the Chronicles, the Psalms of the Levitical guilds of singers originated with the temple personnel appointed by David (1 Chron. 15.17, 19; 16.41-42; 25.4-6). 1 Chronicles 16.7 presents a 'snapshot' of the Chronistic Davidian Renaissance: after the Ark of the Lord was brought to the place, '... David (on that day) first committed to Asaph and his associates this psalm of thanks to the Lord'. A skilfully arranged textual collage of Psalms 105.1-15; 96.1-13a; 106.1, 47-48 then follows. It represents an excellent systematization of

the Psalms form the most important setting for the completion of this process. The canonising postscript of the Septuagint Psalter, Psalm 151, stemming from Early Judaism, proves David to be a writer and singer of psalms. The superscription even places him among the 'scriptural prophets' (Zenger 2003: 134).

David is mentioned 86 times in the Masoretic Psalter: 73 times in superscriptions, once in the colophon 72.20 and twelve times in the text of six psalms[34] in total. To this can be added a 'Davidic *relecture*' of individual psalms without explicit reference to David.[35] I will only speak about the superscriptions and the single colophon, because they are of especial hermeneutical importance and ought to be analyzed and interpreted in the end text exegesis of the Psalms.[36]

Almost half of all psalms of the Hebrew Psalter are made into 'Davidic psalms' through the superscription *l^{e}dāwid*.[37] It can also be found in cases where the speaker is a collective entity, for instance in Psalm 60. At least

important aspects of the theology of the books of Chronicles, consistently composed according to the principles of the past (a retrospect in Psalm 105), present (a praise of Yahweh from Psalm 96) and future of God's people (a prayer in Psalm 106 for liberation from the enemy). Thus Asaph acts as a singer of 'Psalms of David' (cf. 2 Chron. 29.30), which the latter, according to the Chronicles, had commissioned, but not composed himself. These Psalms cited in Chronicles neither have Davidic superscriptions nor any other remarks on the authorship of the Psalter.

34. Psalm 18.51; 78.70; 89.4, 21, 36, 50; 122.5; 132.1, 10, 11, 17; 144.10. These Psalms are neither all Davidic Psalms – Psalm 78 is attributed to Asaph and Psalm 89 to Ethan, the Ezrahite – nor do they all belong to the royal Psalms – the historical psalm, 78, describes itself as *maskil* or wisdom song and according to its superscription, Psalm 122 is a 'song of ascents'. On the image of David in Psalms 18, 78, 89, 132 cf. Luyten (1990: 209–221). He summarises this image as follows: 'On the one hand they see David as the first and very successful king of greater Israel, as the king elected by Yahweh and bearer of the dynastic and national promises. Even after the downfall of the monarchy this David-image is foremost in continuing to feed the hope of restoration and renewal and, furthermore, that expectation of a new David, an anointed "par excellence". On the other hand, these psalms reflect a growing tendency to make David the prototype of the faithful and law-abiding Israelite whom Yahweh rescues from every danger.' (1990: 225).

35. Psalms 4.3; 23.4; 31.21-22; 51.16; 52.3; 54.5; 56.4, 8; 59.16; 63.12.

36. 'Die Überschriften sind in der Regel nicht nur Reflex des Kompositionsprozesses der Teilsammlungen des Psalmenbuchs... sondern geben oft auch wichtige Hinweise zur Interpretation des jeweiligen Einzelpsalms im Kontext seiner von der Redaktion als solche intendierten "Nachbarpsalmen"' Zenger (1994c: 128).

37. For an overview, cf. e.g. Millard (1994: 251–254). The Septuagint translates *l^{e}dāwid* with τῷ Δαυίδ, that is, with the dative case: Psalm 32 (31G); 34 (33G); 35 (34G); 36 (35G); 40 (39G); 60 (59G); 61 (60G); 68 (67G); 69 (68G); 70 (69G); 144 (143G). In three superscriptions, it goes further than the Masoretic text does. Two of these additions, however, are substantiated by Qumran: Psalm 33 (32G), cf. 4QPs^q; 104 (103G), cf. 11QPs^a; 137 (136G). Four times only does the Septuagint reproduce the annotation with the genitive τοῦ Δαυίδ: Psalm 26 (25G); 27 (26G); 28 (27G); 37 (36G). Cf. the exhaustive analysis of Kleer (1996: 78–86) on the superscriptional annotation *l^{e}dāwid*.

two intentions of expression can be associated with this polysemic formula. Both Jewish and Christian interpreters usually read *lᵉdāwid* as an indication of authorship: the Psalms were considered to be composed by David. This would also agree with the biographical details given in the superscriptions and in the colophon of Psalm 72.20.[38] The 'David' of these superscriptions is a 'paradigmatic "prayer leader"' and a "figure of identification"'.[39] The 'subscript' in the colophon of Psalm 72.20, 'This concludes the prayers of David son of Jesse', extends the Davidization to include Psalms 2 to 72. Thus the preceding psalms of Korah and Asaph in the second book (Psalms 42–49 and 50) are also called 'prayers of David'. The later redaction of the Psalms brought David into connection with the entire Psalter, despite all other notes on authorship in the superscriptions of individual psalms. This by no means implies that David was the author of all psalms, since the *'lamed auctoris'* is neither philologically nor topically the only explanation for the expression *lᵉdāwid*. The superscription of Psalm 72.1 contains the note *lišlomoh*, which can only mean *'for* Solomon', since, according to the colophon in verse 20, the psalm is one of the 'prayers of David'. Thus, David composed this psalm for the enthronement of his son. The preposition *lᵉ* describes the *finality* or purpose of a psalm. Moreover, the Septuagint does not understand the *'lamed'* in the title of the psalm as *'lamed auctoris'* either, but as *'lamed relationis'*.[40]

At least since Persian times, this David of the Psalter no longer serves as historical king, but, among others, already as prototype of the 'Anointed

38. In 13 superscriptions of the Masoretic text of Psalms that, with the exception of Psalm 142, belong to the first two books of Psalms (in the first book of Psalms/Davidic Psalter these are the four Psalms 3, 7, 18, 34, in the second book of Psalms/Davidic Psalter the eight Psalms 51, 52, 54, 56, 57, 59, 60, 63), supplementary Midrash-type remarks can be found attached to the formula *lᵉdāwid*, 'of David'. These remove the Psalms from their original liturgical context and, to a certain extent countering the integration of Psalm 18 into the books of Samuel, in a mystical and ideal-typical way connect them to different events from the life of David as told in the books of Samuel. In contrast to David's appearances in the Chronicles, but also in contrast to the situation in the majority of the royal Psalms and the Psalm corpora, these mostly are situations of distress or suffering, in which David expresses his feelings through song.

39. Zenger (1991b: 407). 'Daß dabei nicht eine triumphalistische Davidfigur, sondern David als der Leidende und Büßende, aber auch als der die Tora liebende Knecht JHWHs zur messianischen Hoffnungsgestalt geworden ist, macht diese Überschriften auch für eine kanonische Auslegung der Psalmen im Horizont des Neuen Testaments kostbar' (1991b: 408).

40. Kleer 1996 translates *lᵉdāwid* with 'to David', 'referring to David', 'concerning David' and understands the superscriptional annotation 'im Sinn einer Leseanweisung oder Interpretationshilfe' (80). In 'weist den Leser/Beter des betreffenden Psalms an, bei dessen Lektüre an David zu denken' (80), it invites him to enter into 'eine Schicksalgemeinschaft mit David' (81).

One', the Messiah, who was expected for the future. In its superscriptions and even beyond them, the Septuagint further expanded on the image of David as prayer of the Psalms. It thereby strengthened this Messianic expectation (cf. e.g. Rösel 2001: especially 143).[41]

(C) The psalms of Israel do not only have an 'I'-speaker, but also the 'We' of the congregation or of the people. Principally, changes of subject are possible within a psalm and originally individual psalms and songs of praise or thanksgiving can furthermore be reinterpreted to be collectivized.[42] In this case, the Psalms would constitute a normative and formative self-portrait of Israel, especially in times of a crisis of their collective identity (Hossfeld & Zenger 1993b: 167). A *collectivizing new interpretation of the Davidic and royal psalms* 'democratized' the royal predicates, too, and thus made all Israel into an 'anointed' messianic people and the nation who prepared the way for the universal reign of God.[43] Against such a collective messianic background, the superscription

---

41.   The Psalter of the Septuagint, which was probably translated in Palestine during the second half of the second century BCE, had brought more different Messianic ideas into the Psalms. It shares its eschatological expectation with contemporary Jewish writings (Schaper 1994: 58–61). This is especially important for the New Testament and liturgical use of the Greek Psalter, although, at the time, the 'David' of the Hebrew Psalms of course had already been understood in the light of the Messiah within the Old Testament, too.

42.   Scharbert (1987). 'In dem "Wir" ist bald das Volk Israel in seinen vielen Generationen, bald die versammelte Kultgemeinde oder die Gruppe von Verwandten und Freunden, die einen der ihren zum Dankopfer geleitet, dann wieder das dem König untergebene Volk oder die Gola im Exil zu sehen. Manchmal sind es die Zuhörer eines Weisheitslehrers oder eines lehrenden Priesters, selten die sündige Menschheit, bei einer Wallfahrt auch die Wallfahrer begrüßenden oder verabschiedenden Kultdiener. Auffallend ist das seltene Sündenbekenntnis.' (1987: 308). On the level of the Psalter, Israel acts as the collective body of reference. This follows, i.a., from the doxologies concluding the books of the Psalter. The doxologies serve a number of purposes: '(Durch sie werden) Einzelpsalmen zu Bündeln zusammengefasst und in einen größeren kompositiorischen Rahmen gestellt. Über die Gottesbezeichnung wird ein weiterer Zweck erreicht: alle Psalmen werden noch einmal ausdrücklich auf den Gott Israels bezogen. Indem aber der Gott Israels gepriesen wird, ist gleichzeitig die Israeldimension angesprochen, womit auch jedes individuelle Gebet des mit der Doxologie abgeschlossenen Bündels noch einmal auf der höheren Ebene in die Gemeinschaft Israels hineingenommen wird. Das oben festgestellte Phänomen der kollektiven Relecture lässt sich also auf kompositorischer Ebene festmachen! Gerade auf der Buchebene gibt sich der Psalter als Buch Israels zu erkennen und macht damit deutlich, dass er in jeder Hinsicht das Gebet des einzelnen transzendiert' (Ballhorn 2003: 248).

43.   Cf. Becker (1977), who worked on the theme of the collectivizing reinterpretation of royal texts, especially the royal Psalms, and their Messianological setting alongside the restorative expectation of a king, resulting from the theocratic movement. The widening of horizons or the transfer of the Davidic promise to the people of Israel in the Psalms is characteristic especially for exilic and post-exilic writings and their Davidic theology. It is especially Deutero-Isaiah that transmits definite royal traits to Israel or the deportees in the exilic period. This takes place – at least within the total scheme of Isaiah 40–55 – in the texts about the 'Servant of Yahweh'. According to Isaiah 55.3-5, the proof of favour is given to

formula '*for* David' would already signalise 'that Israel' could 'internalise and realise its "Davidic-messianic" standing or mission in and with these psalms' (Hossfeld & Zenger 1993a: 16).

To summarise: On the level of the whole Psalter, the identity of the prayer of the Psalms is semantically opened up by the multiple *relecture* described here. Lohfink (1993: 280) makes an excellent résumé with a view to the canonical interpretation of Scripture:

> 'Even when originally used in a cultic context, the Psalms already were "formulas". Different prayers could use them. The reference of the words changed, depending on the person who prayed them. In the Psalter as a whole, even in the wording of individual Psalms the individuality of the "I"-speaker in prayer apparently is opened up towards Israel. The prayer is David. However, since Deutero-Isaiah, his role was given to Israel in its relationship with the nations. This is especially true where a superscription attributes a psalm to David – but not only there. Israel in prayer can of course be represented in each prayer-gathering and condensed in each individual Israelite, and all the more in the coming "messianic" David. Where all of Israel is praying, the "enemies" are the nations who threaten Israel. Where an entity within Israel is praying – so to speak, the "true Israel" – the other part of Israel can move into the position of the enemy, for instance, those groupings of rulers in Israel who oppress the "Anawim" [the poor]. Since the Theologoumenon of the eschatological flocking of the nations also is at hand, even a complete exchange of positions between the official Israel and the nations is possible. Members of the "nations" could step into the position of the prayer, and that which used to be Israel, could increasingly move into the position of the enemy. For all of these changes, the expressive structure of one psalm or the other stands waiting in the wings.'[44]

David, the 'faithful love promised to David', that is, the Davidic covenantal promise (2 Sam. 7.15-16) is also transferred to the people. They move into David's position and receive his commission as witness towards the nations.

44. 'Auch bei ursprünglichem kultischen Gebrauch waren die Psalmen schon "Formulare". Verschiedene Beter konnten sie beten. Die Referenz der Worte änderte sich je nach dem Beter. Im Psalter als ganzem wird offenbar selbst beim Wortlaut individueller Psalmen die Individualität des betenden Ich auf Israel hin entschränkt. Der Beter ist David, doch dessen Rolle ist seit Deuterojesaja auf ganz Israel in seinem Verhältnis zu den Völkern übergegangen. Das gilt noch einmal besonders, wo die Überschrift einen Psalm David zuordnet – doch nicht nur dort. Das betende Israel kann natürlich in jeder betenden Versammlung und in jedem einzelnen Israeliten verdichtet da sein, erst recht im kommenden "messianischen" David. Betet ganz Israel, dann sind die Feinde die Völker, die Israel bedrängen. Betet eine Größe innerhalb Israels, gewissermaßen das "wahre Israel", dann kann auch der andere Teil Israels in die Feindposition einrücken – etwa die in Israel herrschenden Gruppen, die die "Anawim" [die Armen] unterdrücken. Da auch das Theologumenon der endzeitlichen Völkerwallfahrt bereitliegt, ist selbst ein völliger Tausch der Positionen zwischen

This *multi-dimensionality of the Old Testament Psalms* requires of exegetes not to limit the Old Testament message of the text to the original meaning of the earliest possibly reconstructable stage of the text. The Christological reception of the Psalms in the New Testament, for example, already has to take into account the multiplicity of connotations evoked within the Old Testament. For a canonical interpretation of the Psalms, the given scriptures all are canonical writings, as one single text.

4. Canonical and patristic interpretation of the Psalms

As was just outlined, modern 'end text exegesis' as a methodological reflex first focuses on the *iuxtapositio* and on the redactionally intended *concatenatio*, secondly on the hermeneutically meant superscriptions of the psalms, especially on the 'notes on authorship' and thereby, their 'Davidization'. Thirdly, it becomes clear that this 'Davidization' oscillates between the 'king' and the people of God, and bathes all in a messianic light.[45] Crossing the boundaries of the Psalter, 'canonical exegesis' fourthly also interprets the inter-textual connections in the entire Bible, naturally within the framework of the textual repertoire of each psalm concerned. All of these principles are familiar to patristic exegesis of the Psalms, too.[46]

In 'consequence of the historical-critical analysis' as well as the 'interpretation within the entire biblical canon', Zenger and Hossfeld also consider it vitally important to take the 'history of influence (*Wirkungsgeschichte*) and reception (*Rezeptionsgeschichte*)' of the Psalms into account in a 'theologically committed and hermeneutically reflected commentary on the Psalms' (Hossfeld & Zenger 1993a: 24). This programme confirms the importance that the understanding of the early church had gained for the biblical sciences today. Equally important is the wide spectrum of questions that belongs to the background of the liturgical use of the Psalms, especially the background concerning their history of

dem offiziellen Israel und den Völkern in Reichweite. Menschen aus den Völkern könnten in die Beterposition mit eintreten, und was Israel war, könnte immer mehr in die Feindposition geraten. Für alle diese Wandlungen steht das Aussagegefüge eines Psalms parat.'

45. Old Testament Messianism thus gains a degree of relevance for the hermeneutics of the New Testament that transcends the tradition-historical observations such as were summarised and described by Gese 1995.

46. The classical work on the Church Fathers' exegesis of the Psalms is Rondeau (1982; 1985). The concept of 'Christologizing from below' had meanwhile been placed within the horizon of the 'prosopological exegesis': with Hilary of Poitier, Rondeau considers the key to the patristic interpretation of the Psalms to lie in the question, 'in whose name or referring to whom (ex cuius persona, uel in quem) that which is said, is to be understood' (1985: 7). However, neither Hippolytus nor Asterius can be found among the authors representing this prosopological process of interpretation. I will briefly present their basic exegetical principles here.

interpretation. The following two examples should illustrate some of the most important hermeneutical correspondences between patristic and modern exegesis of the Psalms – without, however, questioning either the independence of their theological profiles and of their methodical approaches or their being historically determined.

I have chosen (A) the oldest Christian homily on the Psalms, ascribed to Hippolytus, and (B) Asterius's homilies on the Psalms.

(A) *Hippolytus's Homily* 'On the psalms' (*HomPs*) is the oldest known systematic reflection on the Psalter.[47] Harald Buchinger comprehensively analyzed this explication on the Psalms, embedded in their patristic context (1995). It is one of the earliest certain records of the use of the Psalms in the Christian service. It also contains the first clear reference to the reading (!) of Psalms. The text was written in Rome at the beginning of the third century and today is only still partially preserved. It was transmitted in Greek catenae on the Psalms. From the fourth century onwards, it shows a broad history of influence. Despite its original oral rendering and fragmentary transmission, Hippolytus's homily on the Psalms formally as well as theologically represents a relatively cohesive treatise on the entire book of Psalms and on Psalms 1–2.[48] On the one hand, it expressly aims at demonstrating the inspired origin and meaning of the whole Psalter, especially the superscriptions. The actual theme of this treatise, however, is the superscriptions of the Psalms and their function in the inspired Psalter.

Hippolytus presumably considered the arrangement of the Psalms to be of hermeneutical relevance, because he reflects upon their position in the Psalter:

'Two psalms were read to us and it is necessary to state why they are the first'. (*HomPs 18*).

Thus, Psalms 1 and 2 were read and explained according to their numeric order. Hippolytus does not consider Psalms 1 and 2 to be one single text, as many Jewish and Christian sources do (Zenger 1993, especially 39–43), but he speaks of 'two psalms' (*HomPs 18*) and of a 'first' and a 'second' psalm (*HomPs 19*). Furthermore, these two psalms are not at all further explicated in their content, but, as was said, are merely treated with reference to their canonical position and to the fact that they have no superscription.

Concerning the superscriptions of the Psalms, Hippolytus first discusses the problem of the different names of the authors before he treats their

---

47. The quotations from Hippolytus are taken from the first English translation of Stewart-Sykes (2001).

48. Rondeau (1967: 15) therefore notes: '*notre homélie est justement un prologue à une exégèse des psaumes*'. He also describes it as '*le premier "Prologue au Psautier" connu*'.

further particulars. The titles of the Psalms, which naturally belong to the inspired text, not only reveal the inspired origins of the Psalter, but, concerning their content, also act as a hermeneutical key to its meaning.

Just as the redaction of the Psalter would have it, Hippolytus says:

> 'The psalms number altogether one hundred and fifty. Some think, because they have not studied with sufficient care, that all are of the blessed David, but this is not what is signified. All are attributed to David, but the titles indicate which psalm is assigned to whom. I have said that four leaders of the singers were elected, and that there were two hundred and eighty-eight accompanists. The psalms are assigned to the four leaders, as indeed the titles indicate. For when it says "A psalm of the sons of Korah", Asaph and Heman uttered it. When it says "A psalm of Asaph", Asaph himself uttered it. When it says "A psalm of Jedutun", Jedutun himself chants. When it says "A psalm of David", David himself was the speaker. But when it says "A psalm to David" it was addressed to David by another. There are, in all, hundred and fifty psalms, of which seventy-two are to David, nine of David, twelve to Asaph, twelve of the sons of Korah, one of Jedutun, one to Ethan, one to Salomon, two to Haggai and Zechariah, thirty-nine are without title and one to Moses, a total of one hundred and fifty. We must now consider the mystery of by what rationale the Psalter is attributed to David when there are different singers and when not all of the psalms are by David. We shall miss nothing out. The rationale of the attribution is this: he was himself the cause of all that came about. He chose the singers himself, and since he was himself the cause, he should be considered worthy of the honour that all the singers uttered should be reckoned to David' (*HomPs 6–7*).[49]

Hippolytus' creativeness in explicating the further elements of the psalm titles is shown in his remarks concerning the individual superscriptions. He for instance uses the superscription and introductory lines of Psalm 9 to portray Christ as prayer of the Psalms – however, not in an exclusive or typical sense:

> '"A psalm concerning the hidden things of the Son. I shall confess to you, Lord, with all my heart, I shall proclaim your marvels." Who was it who confessed the father, yet cried out and spoke with clarity of speech? "I confess to you Father, Lord of heaven and earth, because you have hidden these things from the wise and understanding and have revealed them to the simple. Yes, Father, because that it was your good pleasure in your sight." Let us see, then, beloved, the Son of God proclaimed here' (*HomPs 11*).

---

49.   The Babylonian Talmud (*BabaBatra 14b; 15a*) not only has David appearing as Psalm writer – amongst ten other authors – but also as editor of the Psalter.

The quoted words of Jesus (Mt. 11.25-26) could have lead Hippolytus to his subsequent explication of the superscription of Psalm 8, which is of especial interest for the understanding and theology of the Psalms. Here, Hippolytus formulates his basic hermeneutical principle, which he subsequently applies, as he had just done for Psalm 9: the Psalms and their titles act as mutual interpreters. Hippolytus is seldom only content with this narrow form of intertextuality, though, and applies both the Old and the New Testament in his argumentation, often starting with an association of keywords. He furthermore develops a 'trinitarian theology of prophecy': in the Psalter, David speaks to God in – and also about – the same spirit of Christ that already filled the prophets; at the same time, Christ takes up the meaning of the Psalms and deepens it. Thus the unity of the canonical scripture, too, is substantiated theologically:

> 'Another title is "Psalm of the wine-vat". What are these vats, except the blessed prophets? For just as the vat receives the sweet wine from the crushed grape, and just as therein it is boiled and fermented, likewise the Holy Spirit flows into the prophets, as Christ was crushed like a grape, and "delights the heart" just as does sweet wine. This is easy to see because the title shows the meaning of the psalm and the psalm shows the meaning of the words which are to be interpreted. For it is added "from the mouth of babies and infants you have found praise". Christ says: "You have revealed these things to suckling infants." He is speaking to the prophets, because they are partakers of the Holy Spirit, living far from evil like children, and so they build the glorious school of grace. Rightly did David sing about them' (*HomPs 12*).

As could be seen from the text cited from *HomPs 6–7*, Hippolytus considered *David* to be the originator of the Psalter, despite the differing notes on authorship (cf. *HomPs 7*). The image of David and the inspired origins of the Psalter relate to the Chronistic History, especially to 1 Chronicles 16, a key text of Old Testament Davidization, and to 1 Chronicles 25. In this context, Hippolytus interprets the number of 72 singers each that David, 'the leader of the leaders of the singers' (*HomPs 4*), allotted to each of the four chief musicians, as counterpart of the 72 nations of the world. This symbol in the sphere of the economy of grace acts as a prophecy 'that in the last times every tongue should glorify God' (*HomPs 3*).

To recapitulate: Hippolytus' Homily on the Psalms testifies to

> 'a number of fundamental perceptions on the Psalter, which the early church moreover shared with the Judaism of its time: the "total Davidization", the basically doxological understanding of psalmody, the importance of the Psalter as a revision of the rest of Scripture. These beliefs have their theological basis in the conviction that the Psalter has a (spirit-given) prophetic and messianic dimension. This conviction,

combined with the natural idea of the unity of Scripture, allows for a Christian Christological and ecclesiological reinterpretation of the Psalms. They in turn refer to the (earlier and later) history of salvation. We are, however, not dealing with arbitrary typologies and allegories here. The Psalter is the sacrament (μυστηριον) of the *one* reality of salvation, which encompasses the whole history of salvation and the road to salvation of the individual: in the Psalter, David sings about "the glorious school of grace"' (cf. *HomPs 12*).[50]

(B) Although *Asterius*[51] is no 'exegete of the stature of Origen or Diodore', he does 'have exceptional theological standing within the early exegesis of the Psalms' and is considered to be 'the rhetorician among the exegetes of the Psalms' (Kinzig 1992: 130). Wolfram Kinzig (1992) recently systematized his basic exegetic principles.[52] The *three keys* that gave Asterius access to the understanding of a psalm, almost exactly correspond with the criteria that today apply for end text exegesis (namely the arrangement of the Psalms, Davidization and messianization) as well as for canonical interpretation (that is, consideration of the whole Bible).

Firstly, Asterius always refers to the sequence of the Psalms as an indication of their interpretation (109). He clearly states: 'The sequence of the Psalms teaches us the understanding of the Psalms' ([Hom. 23:5] 110).

Secondly, the superscriptions of the Psalms play an important role:

> 'But let us look at the title! What the seals are for the testaments, the headings are for the Psalms. Just as those who (want to) open the testaments, first loosen the seals and (only) thus (can) read the

---

50.   Buchinger (1995: 298): [Hippolyt bezeugt] 'mehrere fundamentale Auffassungen über den Psalter, die übrigens die alte Kirche mit dem zeitgenössischen Judentum teilt: die "Totaldavidisierung", das grundsätzlich doxologische Verständnis der Psalmodie, die Bedeutung des Psalters als Aktualisierung der übrigen Schrift. Theologische Grundlage dafür ist die Überzeugung von seiner (geistgewirkten) prophetischen und messianischen Dimension. Diese Überzeugung, in Verbindung mit der selbstverständlichen Auffassung von der Einheit der Schrift, ermöglicht christlicherseits auch die christologische und ekklesiologische Aktualisierung der Psalmen, die ihrerseits auf die (frühere und spätere) Heilsgeschichte bezogen sind. Dabei geht es freilich nicht um willkürliche Typologien und Allegorien. Der Psalter ist vielmehr das Sakrament (μυστηριον) der *einen* Heilswirklichkeit, die die ganze Heilsgeschichte und den Heilsweg des einzelnen umfaßt: im Psalter "singt David über das schöne Lehrhaus der Gnade" (vgl. HomPs 12).'

51.   The authorship of the Homilies is disputed today. Since *Asterii Sophistae Commentariorum in Psalmos quae supersunt. Accedunt aliquot homiliae anonymae* (Ed. M. Richard; SO.S 16; Oslo: Brøgger, (1956) they are ascribed to the Arian Asterius the Sophist, also known as Asterius of Skythopolis, a student of Lucian of Antioch. This Asterius would have written them between 337 and 341 (Auf der Maur 1967). Kinzig (1990), on the other hand, holds the thesis that they could have been written by a non-Arian author of the same name who lived in Syrian Antioch in the early fourth or fifth century CE. Certain exegetical basic principles were systematized by Kinzig (1992).

52.   The following page numbers in round brackets all refer to Kinzig (1992).

document, so those who (want to) read and interpret the Psalms, first
unroll their headings and (can only) thus trace the things that are written
in them' ([*Hom. 21:3*] 112).

According to Kinzig, in Asterius' view, the titles of the Psalms determine
'whether a psalm is to be interpreted literally-parenetically or Christolo-
gically-ecclesiologically' (112). In this kind of exegesis, an allegoric-
typological (εἰκόνας καὶ; τύπους) interpretation κατα; θεωρίαν, is opposed
(119) to an interpretation κατα ἱστορίαν, which can be the starting point
and centre of the ἑρμηνεία (113).

At all times, David is the author of the Psalms (107). The notion of the
Psalms being prophetic and inspired is connected to the Davidic
authorship:

> 'Beautiful is the prophetic flute of the shepherd and king (David), for its
> reed is language, its breath is the Paraclete, its sound is the Word, its
> melody is temperate delight, its key is prophecy and its support [?] is the
> gift of the Spirit from above' ([*Hom. 26:1*] 107).

For Christian conduct, David is an example and a point of orientation
(117). In connection with the Christological interpretation, Asterius gives
an interesting reason for David's ability to write psalms that can be
explicated in the light of Christ:

> '... whence did David know the mysteries of the Son? The Son had
> revealed them to him. He himself says: "*The unknown and the hidden
> (things) you have revealed to me*" [Ps. 51.8]. He taught David the
> mysteries, because he was his father according to the flesh. And which
> are the mysteries of the Son? The mysteries of his incarnation, which
> were hidden from the beginnings of times and epochs but were revealed
> to his saints, and among them, also to David. And the prophet himself is
> a witness (to the fact) that the secret mysteries of the Son were revealed
> to David, when he says about his descent from heaven: "*And he bowed
> the heavens and came down*" [2 Sam. 22.10a]. "*Darkness covered his
> hiding-place*" [2 Sam. 22.12a]' ([*Hom. 18:4f*] 118).

Christ can also act as speaker of a psalm, especially in cases where the
Christological interpretation is given in the New Testament (107).

And this already is the *third criterion*: the interpretation is determined by
the example of the apostolic explication of scripture or of the *New
Testament* (108). Therefore, Asterius for example understands the
resurrection psalm, 16 (15G), as words of Christ, and that on account of
Acts 2.31. He justifies his Christological exegesis of Psalm 2 as follows:

> '... one should not wonder that we explained this psalm as pointing to
> the resurrection of Christ. We have followed the apostolic example and
> we have the interpretation of Paul as a guide' ([*Hom. 2:13*] 108).

Today, the cleft between an historic and literary-scientific interpretation of the Psalms on the one hand and the interpretation of the early church on the other, can be bridged. Without trying to level differences or write them off as no longer being of any consequence, it can be said that there are a number of methodical and hermeneutical similarities or convergences between the end text or canonical exegesis and the patristic or liturgical interpretation. As far as literary history is concerned, the messianic-Christological and ecclesiological understanding of the Psalms is already made legitimate by the Old Testament itself, and that against the background of the coming, the saving King Yahweh and his universal dominion.

Bibliography

Auf der Maur, H. 1967 *Die Osterhomilien des Asterios Sophistes als Quelle für die Geschichte der Osterfeier* (TThSt, 19; Trier: Paulinus): 2–10.

Auwers, J.-M. 1999 'Le David des psaumes et les psaumes de David', in L. Derousseaux & J. Vermeylen (Ed.), *Figures de David à travers la Bible* (LD, 177; Paris: Cerf): 187–224.

—2003 'Les voies de l'exégèse canonique du psautier' in J.-M. Auwers & H. J. de Jonge (Ed.), *The Biblical Canons* (BEThL, CLXIII; Leuven: University Press): 5–26.

Ballhorn, E. 1995 '"Um deines Knechtes David willen" (Ps 132,10). Die Gestalt Davids im Psalter', *BN* 76: 16–31.

—2000 *Zum Telos des Psalters. Der Textzusammenhang des vierten und fünften Psalmenbuchs (Pss. 90–150)* (Diss. Bonn).

—2003 'Zur Pragmatik des Psalters als eschatologisches Lehrbuch und Identitätsbuch Israels', in A. Gerhards, A. Doecker & Peter Ebenbauer (Hrsg.), *Identität durch Gebet. Zur gemeinschaftsbildenden Funktion institutionalisierten Betens in Judentum und Christentum* (Studien zu Judentum und Christentum; Paderborn: Schöningh): 241–259.

Barbiero, G. 1999 *Das erste Psalmenbuch als Einheit. Eine synchrone Analyse von Psalm 1-41* (ÖBS, 16; Frankfurt/M.: Lang).

Becker, J. 1967 *Israel deutet seine Psalmen* (SBS, 18; Stuttgart: Kath. Bibelwerk, 2. Aufl.): 9–39.

—1975 *Wege der Psalmenexegese* (SBS, 78; Stuttgart: Kath. Bibelwerk): 99–111.

—1977 'Die kollektive Deutung der Königspsalmen', *ThPh* 52: 561–578.

Böhler, D. 2002 'Der Kanon als hermeneutische Vorgabe biblischer Theologie. Über aktuelle Methodendiskussionen in der Bibelwissenschaft', *ThPh* 77: 161–178.

Braulik, G. 1991 *Die deuteronomischen Gesetze und der Dekalog. Studien zum Aufbau von Deuteronomium 12–26* (SBS, 145; Stuttgart: Kath. Bibelwerk).

—2003 'Psalms and Liturgy: Their reception and contextualisation', *Verbum et Ecclesia* 24/2: 309–332.

Buchinger, H. 1995 'Die älteste christliche Psalmenhomilie: Zu Verwendung und Verständnis des Psalters bei Hippolyt', *TThZ* 104: 125–144; 272–298.

—2000 'Zur Hermeneutik liturgischer Psalmenverwendung. Methodische Überlegungen im Schnittpunkt von Bibelwissenschaft, Patristik und Liturgiewissenschaft', *HlD* 54: 193–222.

Fiedrowicz, M. 1998 *Prinzipien der Schriftauslegung in der Alten Kirche* (Traditio christiana X; Bern: Lang).

Füglister, N. 1988 'Die Verwendung und das Verständnis der Psalmen und des Psalters um die Zeitenwende', in J. Schreiner (Hrsg.), *Beiträge zur Psalmenforschung. Psalm 2 und 22* (FzB, 60; Würzburg: Echter): 319–384.

Gerstenberger, E. 2001 'Psalmen (Buch)', in M. Görg & B. Lang (Hrsg.), *Neues Bibel-Lexikon* Band III (Düsseldorf – Zürich: Benziger): 209–213 [first published in fasc. 11/1997].

Gese, H. 1995 'Alttestamentliche Hermeneutik und christliche Theologie', in E. Jüngel (Hrsg.), *Theologie als gegenwärtige Schriftauslegung* (ZThK.B, 9; Tübingen: Mohr [Siebeck]): 65–81.

Grelot, P. 1998 *Le mystère du Christ dans les psaumes* (Jésus et Jésus-Christ, 74; Paris: Desclée).

Heine, R. E. 1995 *Gregory of Nyssa's Treatise on the Inscriptions of the Psalms. Introduction, Translation, and Notes* (Oxford Early Christian Studies; Oxford: Clarendon Press).

Hengel, M. 1987 'Das Christuslied im frühen Gottesdienst', in W. Baier u.a. (Hrsg.), *Weisheit Gottes – Weisheit der Welt. Festschrift J. Ratzinger zum 60. Geburtstag; im Auftrag des Schülerkreises* (St. Ottilien: Eos): 357–405.

Hossfeld, F.-L. 1998 'Die unterschiedlichen Profile der beiden Davidsammlungen Pss. 3–41 und Pss. 51–72', in E. Zenger (Hrsg.), *Der Psalter in Judentum und Christentum* (HBS, 18; Freiburg: Herder): 59–73.

Hossfeld, F.-L. & Zenger, E. 1993a *Psalmen – Psalm 1–50* (NEB, 29; Würzburg: Echter).

—1993b '"Wer darf hinaufziehn zum Berg JHWHs?" Zur Redaktionsgeschichte und Theologie der Psalmengruppe 15–24', in G. Braulik, W. Groß & S. McEvenue (Hrsg.), *Biblische Theologie und gesellschaftlicher Wandel. Für Norbert Lohfink SJ* (Freiburg: Herder): 166–182.

—1996 'Neue und alte Wege der Psalmenexegese. Antworten auf die Fragen von M. Millard und R. Rendtorff', *BI* 4: 332–343.

Janowski, B. 2001 '"Verstehst du, was du liest?" Reflexionen auf die Leserichtung der christlichen Bibel', in F.-L. Hossfeld (Hrsg.), *Wieviel Systematik erlaubt die Schrift? Auf der Suche nach einer gesamtbiblischen Theologie* (QD, 185; Freiburg: Herder): 150–191.

Kinzig, W. 1990 *In Search of Asterius. Studies on the Authorship of the Homilies on the Psalms* (FKDG, 47; Göttingen: Vandenhoeck & Ruprecht).

—1992 'Bemerkungen zur Psalmenexegese des Asterius', in J. van Oort & U. Wickert (Hrsg.), *Christliche Exegese zwischen Nizaea und Chalcedon* (Kampen: Kok Pharos): 104–131.

Kleer, M. 1996 *'Der liebliche Sänger der Psalmen Israels'. Untersuchungen zu David als Dichter und Beter der Psalmen* (BBB, 108; Bodenheim: Philo).

Löning, K. 1998 'Die Funktion des Psalters im Neuen Testament', in E. Zenger (Hrsg.), *Der Psalter in Judentum und Christentum* (HBS, 18; Freiburg: Herder): 269–295.

Lohfink, N. 1993 'Was wird anders bei kanonischer Schriftauslegung? Beobachtungen am Beispiel von Psalm 6', in *Studien zur biblischen Theologie* (SBAB, 16; Stuttgart: Kath. Bibelwerk): 263–293.

—2003a 'The Psalter and Meditation. On the Genre of the Book of Psalms', in *In the Shadow of Your Wings. New Readings of Great Texts from the Bible* (Collegeville MN: Liturgical Press): 75–90 (first published in 1992 as 'Psalmengebet und Psalterredaktion' [*ALw* 34]: 1–22).

—2003b 'The Old Testament and the course of the Christian's day. The songs in Luke's infancy narrative', in *In the Shadow of Your Wings. New Readings of Great Texts from the Bible* (Collegeville MN: Liturgical Press): 136–150.

Luyten, J. 1990 'David and the Psalms', *QL* 71: 207–226.

Millard, M. 1994 *Die Komposition des Psalters. Ein formgeschichtlicher Ansatz* (FAT, 9; Tübingen: Mohr [Siebeck]).

Rösel, C. 1999 *Die messianische Redaktion des Psalters. Studien zur Entstehung und Theologie der Sammlung Psalm 2–89* (CThM, 12; Stuttgart: Calwer).

—2001 'Die Psalmüberschriften des Septuaginta-Psalters', in E. Zenger (Hg.), *Der Septuaginta-Psalter: sprachliche und theologische Aspekte* (HBS, 32; Freiburg: Herder): 125–148.

Rondeau, M.-J. 1967 'Les polémiques d'Hippolyte de Rome et de Filastre de Brescia concernant le psautier', *RHR* 171: 1–51.

—1982, 1985 *Les commentaires patristique du psautier (IIIe – Ve siècles)*. Vol. I: *Les travaux des pères grecs et latins sur le psautier. Recherches et bilan*. Vol. II: *Exégèse prosopologique et théologie* (OCA, 219 & 220; Rom: Pont. Inst. Studiorum Orientalium).

Schaper, J. 1994 'Der Septuaginta-Psalter als Dokument jüdischer Eschatologie', in M. Hengel & A.M. Schwemmer (Hrsg.), *Die Septuaginta zwischen Judentum und Christentum* (WUNT, 72; Tübingen: Mohr Siebeck): 38–61.

Scharbert, J. 1987 'Das "Wir" in den Psalmen auf dem Hintergrund altorientalischen Betens', in E. Haag & F.-L. Hossfeld (Hrsg.), *Freude an der Weisung des Herrn: Beiträge zur Theologie der Psalmen. Festgabe zum 70. Geburtstag von Heinrich Groß* (SBB, 13; Stuttgart: Kath. Bibelwerk): 297–324.

Schwienhorst-Schönberger, L. 2003 'Einheit statt Eindeutigkeit. Paradigmenwechsel in der Bibelwissenschaft?', *HK* 57: 412–417.

Steins, G. 2003 'Der Bibelkanon als Denkmal und Text. Zu einigen methodologischen Aspekten kanonischer Schriftauslegung', in J.-M. Auwers & H. J. de Jonge (Ed.), *The Biblical Canons* (BEThL, CLXIII; Leuven: University Press): 177–198.

Stewart-Sykes, A. 2001 'Appendix: "Hippolytus'" Homily on the Psalms', in Stewart-Sykes, *Hippolytus, On The Apostolic Tradition: an English Version with Introduction and Commentary* (Crestwood, NY: St. Vladimir's Seminary Press): 175–182.

Vagaggini, C. 1959 *Theologie der Liturgie* (Einsiedeln: Benziger).

Westermann, C. 1964 'Zur Sammlung des Psalters', in ders., *Forschung am Alten Testament. Gesammelte Studien* (TB, 24; München: Kaiser): 336–343.

Wilson, G.H. 1986 'The Use of Royal Psalms at the "Seams" of the Hebrew Psalter', *JSOT* 35: 85–94.

—1993 'Shaping the Psalter. A Consideration of Editorial Linkage in the Book of Psalms', in J.C. McCann Jr. (Ed.), *The Shape and Shaping of the Psalter* (JSOT SS, 159; Sheffield: Academic Press): 72–82.

Zenger, E. 1991a 'Israel und Kirche im gemeinsamen Gottesbund. Beobachtungen zum theologischen Programm des 4. Psalmenbuchs', in M. Marcus u.a. (Hrsg.), *Israel und Kirche heute. Beiträge zum christlich-jüdischen Dialog. Für Ludwig Ehrlich* (Freiburg: Herder): 236–254.

—1991b 'Was wird anders bei kanonischer Psalmenauslegung?', in F.V. Reiterer (Hrsg.), *Ein Gott, eine Offenbarung. Beiträge zur biblischen Exegese, Theologie und Spiritualität. Festschrift für Notker Füglister zum 60. Geburtstag* (Würzburg: Echter): 397–413.

—1993 'Der Psalter als Wegweiser und Wegbegleiter: Ps. 1–2 als Proömium des Psalmenbuchs', in A. Angenendt & H. Vorgrimmler (Hrsg.), *Sie wandern von Kraft zu Kraft: Aufbrüche, Wege, Begegnungen. Festgabe für Bischof Reinhard Lettmann* (Kevelaer: Butzon & Bercker): 29–47.

—1994a 'Zur redaktionsgeschichtlichen Bedeutung der Korachpsalmen', in K. Seybold & E. Zenger (Hrsg.), *Neue Wege der Psalmenforschung. Für Walter Beyerlin* (HBS, 1; Freiburg: Herder): 175–198.

—1994b 'Das Weltenkönigtum des Gottes Israels (Ps. 90–106)', in N. Lohfink & E. Zenger, *Der Gott Israels und die Völker. Untersuchungen zum Jesajabuch und zu den Psalmen* (SBS, 154; Stuttgart: Kath. Bibelwerk): 151–178.

—1994c 'Zion als Mutter der Völker in Psalm 87', in N. Lohfink & E. Zenger, *Der Gott Israels und die Völker. Untersuchungen zum Jesajabuch und zu den Psalmen* (SBS, 154; Stuttgart: Kath. Bibelwerk): 117–150.

—1996 'Komposition und Theologie des 5. Psalmenbuchs 107–145', *BN* 82: 97–116.

—1997 '"Daß alles Fleisch den Namen seiner Heiligung segne" (Ps. 145, 21). Die Komposition Pss. 145–150 als Anstoß zu einer christlich-jüdischen Psalmen-hermeneutik', *BZ* 41: 1–27.

—2000a 'Kanonische Psalmenexegese und christlich-jüdischer Dialog. Beobach-tungen zum Sabbatpsalm 92', in E. Blum (Hrsg.), *Mincha. Festgabe für Rolf Rendtorff zum 75. Geburtstag* (Neukirchen-Vluyn: Neukirchener): 243–260.

—2000b 'Psalmenforschung nach Hermann Gunkel und Sigmund Mowinckel', in A. Lemaire & M. Sæbo/ (Eds.), *Congress Volume Oslo 1998* (VT.S, 80; Leiden: Brill): 399–435.

—2001a '"Ich aber sage: Du bist mein Gott" [Ps. 31.14]. Kirchliches Psalmengebet nach der Schoa', in A. Raffelt (Hrsg.), *Weg und Weite. Festschrift für Karl Lehmann* (Freiburg: Herder): 15–31.

—2001b 'Das Buch der Psalmen', in ders. u.a., *Einleitung in das Alte Testament* (KThSt, 1,1; Stuttgart: Kohlhammer, 4. Aufl.): 309–326.

—2002 '"Du thronst auf den Psalmen Israels" [Ps. 22.4]. Von der Unverzichtbar-keit der jüdischen Psalmen im christlichen Wortgottesdienst', in B. Kranemann & Th. Sternberg (Hrsg.), *Wie das Wort Gottes feiern? Der Wortgottesdienst als theologische Herausforderung* (QD, 194; Freiburg: Herder): 16–40.

—2003 'Der Psalter im Horizont von Tora und Prophetie. Kanongeschichtliche und kanonhermeneutische Perspektiven', in J.-M. Auwers & H. J. de Jonge (Ed.), *The Biblical Canons* (BEThL, CLXIII; Leuven: University Press): 111–134.

WORDS WITH TEETH AND CHILDBEARING MEN:
METAPHORS IN PSALM 7

Brian Doyle
Leuven, Belgium

1. *The Psalms of Imprecation*

A great deal has been written about the so-called 'cursing psalms' or the rather Victorian sounding 'psalms of imprecation'.[1] Authors and commentators in the past tended to 'Christianize'[2] and (in ecclesial contexts) even 'excise'[3] the cursing elements of such psalms, approaching them from a particularly Christian hermeneutical perspective, one which ultimately disapproved of this kind of ancient language almost in spite of scholarly focus on Ancient Near Eastern frameworks and the text in its historical context. Since the remainder of the present contribution will be dedicated to the study of one particular psalm, namely Psalm 7, we will restrict our comments at this juncture to the said psalm. Perhaps the best and most overt example in this regard can be taken from the commentary of W.O.E. Oesterley (1939). His comments on Psalm 7 are far from favourable:

> 'This psalm must be described as one of the less inspiring of the Psalter... in what follows, 12, 13, we have an illustration of the way in which a psalmist, in the bitterness of wrath against his enemy, becomes guilty of imputing to Yahweh action which is wholly human, and therefore altogether unseemly. No doubt the words are figuratively intended; but they are, none the less, distasteful... The subject-matter of the psalm does not offer material for a section on religious teaching.'[4]

---

1. The psalms of imprecation represent a heterogeneous group of psalms treated together by accident of content, namely on account of the fact that to certain readers they contain words and sentiments considered to be morally reprehensible. As such they constitute a subdivision of the psalms of lament and their cursing language is often located within the genre-specific characteristics of the laments as part of the description of the lamentable situation in which the psalmist finds himself or part of a prayer addressed to the divinity inviting him to redress some unjust situation. Traditionally the psalms of imprecation include: Pss. 7, 35, 58, 59, 69, 83, 109, 139. The present study will focus its attention on this element of the lament psalms, taking Psalm 7 as a working example, conscious of the lamenting context and the variety of forms it can take.

2. See, for example, Augustine on Psalm 7 in Coxe (1996: 20–27).

3. See the interesting and balanced survey in this regard in Holladay (1993: 304–315), especially the segment entitled *The Stance of Christians toward Enemies*.

4. Oesterley (1939: 138); see also his comments on the use of Psalms in the liturgy of the Jewish Church (sic) and Christian Church (1939: 99–110).

There can be little doubt that such comments lack any degree of objectivity and in a sense betray a negative psychological reading on the part of the commentator, which he would no doubt have vehemently denied. As a matter of fact, Psalm 7 tends only rarely to be singled out for such treatment when compared with the other so-called 'cursing psalms' and it is not the present author's primary intention to deal with this aspect at this juncture.[5]

Recent authors have sought to provide a more positive – by this we mean more acceptable to contemporary Christian/Jewish readership – hermeneutical perspective on the said texts, one which accepts their difficult character and endeavours to learn from it.[6] The pastoral-psychological reading of the cursing psalms within the context of the lament genre as offered by Walter Brueggemann might serve as an example.[7] While the present contribution might itself be located in the latter group, it will only arrive there by accident. Its primary intention is to look at the literary technique of metaphorization and the use thereof in portraying the enemy in the cursing psalms.

2. *The Enemy in the Psalms of Imprecation*

The focus of the present paper is on a particular and consistent accusation addressed against the enemy in the psalms and the specific technique (which we will designate 'non-structuring metaphorization') employed by the author not only to express and fortify that accusation, but also as a means of informing the reader about the reality of the enemy and his or her collective or individual power together with the emotional state of the psalmist. No effort will be made to try to identify the enemy in the psalms either historically or in terms of a speculated 'figure' or group thereof in the social and religious context of the psalmist, or as perceived demonic adversaries.

A considerable amount of literature has been dedicated to the study of the enemy in the lament psalms (individual and collective) and elsewhere, and those interested in such (albeit hypothetical) historical considerations

---

5. A review of older commentaries will reveal that their authors in fact make little of the psalmist's 'distasteful' words, beyond noting their difficult character for (some) contemporary readers.

6. See, for example, Laney (1981: 35–45); Althann (1992: 1–11); Zenger (1994: 11–37).

7. Brueggemann's extensive bibliography on 'confrontational' texts in the bible and in particular the lament genre includes: *The Message of the Psalms* (1984), Praying the Psalms (1995), 'Reservoirs of Unreason' (1983: 99–104), 'Psalms and the Life of Faith: a Suggested Typology of Function' (1980: 3–32), 'From Hurt to Joy, From Death to Life' (1974: 3–19), 'The Formfulness of Grief' (1977: 263–275), 'The Costly Loss of Lament', (1986: 55–71).

are free to consult them.[8] What interests us here, however, is the *literary technique* employed by the psalmist to represent the enemy. It goes without saying that use of powerful metaphorical statements to inform the reader of the character of the enemy has not gone unnoticed in the history of research into the psalms. Generally speaking, however, little is made of the significance of the metaphors in question and how they work, beyond mere reference to their presence and to their rhetorical function as comparisons or similes or simply as a more colourful technique employed by the author to say what he wanted to say in a less literal manner.[9] Before attempting to explore the literary technique of non-structuring metaphorization in the so-called cursing psalms, therefore, it will be necessary to explore the notion of metaphor itself and its workings.

3. *A Take on Metaphor*

Scholars of metaphor such as P.W. Macky are correct when they insist that metaphors are not words as such but rather 'speech acts' in which an author/speaker intentionally employs words in a metaphorical way and to a particular end, namely the intention of getting over his or her meaning, what Macky calls the 'speaker's meaning' to his or her audience.[10] Of the 'potential' uses of a word, a speaker ultimately selects an 'actual use' and it is the task of the interpreter of those words to endeavour, in our case thousands of years later, to determine the speaker's meaning by opening the various windows offered by the words he or she actually used onto the 'actual use'.

8. See, for example, Birkland (1933; 1952; 1955); Mowinckel (1934: 1–39); Ridderbos (1939); Anderson (1965: 18–29); Hauret (1967: 129–137); Schmid (1967: 377–393); Böcher (1970); Gerstenberger (1982: 61–78); Croft (1987: 15–48); Lamp & Tilly (1989: 46–57); Hobbs & Jackson (1991: 22–29); Sheppard (1991: 61–82) Rogerson (1993: 284–293); cf. also the introductions to several standard commentaries.

9. An albeit eclectic survey: Augustine in Coxe (1996: 20): the lion represents the devil; Cheyne (1904: 21): the enemy is personified as a lion; Briggs & Briggs (1906): makes nothing of the lion metaphor but notes the metaphorical use of childbirth and the pit in vv. 16–17; Dahood (1965): no reference to metaphor but notes enjambment; Jacquet (1975: 286–299): recognizes the metaphor as commonplace symbolic language of attack; Craigie (1983: 100): 'lion simile… metaphor of conception'; suggests we read 'pursuers' metaphorically and the lion as a 'dramatic simile'; Gerstenberger (1988: 66) makes no mention of the lion but does allude to the 'image of Yahweh sitting on the bench' as a judge; Kraus (1988: 170): comparison/metaphor illustrating the 'seriousness of the danger'; Limburg (2000: 19–23): comparison – more interested in an actualising reading of the psalm (petitioner is Anne Frank in her hiding place, the enemy the Nazis); Kwakkel (2001: 34): stereotypical comparison/ metaphor implying that it is the very life of the psalmist that is at stake; Terrien (2003: 116–123) makes no mention of the metaphor.

10. Macky (1990: 8–25); cf. also Kittay & Lehrer (1981: 31–63).

He also insists that this is a creative task, one in which we are invited to reconstruct a sort of 'replica' in our own minds of the speaker's meaning in an effort to understand it (the main task of exegesis?): '... understanding is a task for the imagination, guided by the store of standard word uses, standard sentence structures, and standard ways of meaning which the intellect has catalogued'.[11]

It is imperative, therefore, that we see the words employed by the author in their broader literary context. The term 'rock' is not as such a metaphor for God but it can be employed by a speaker in a metaphorical way within a larger statement in order to convey his or her meaning about God: its 'actual use' may thus differ from its commonplace literal use. We gain albeit limited access to that meaning by opening the windows provided by words and combinations thereof, by examining their potential meanings and endeavouring to determine their actual meaning in the context of a particular speech act. Ultimately, therefore, part of the task of analysing metaphorical language is rooted in word study, the close examination of the words employed by the author/speaker and their potential meanings. Since we don't have any native speakers at our disposal we are obliged to resort to the use of lexica, especially those that endeavour to determine the meanings of words from their contexts.[12]

Just such an analysis of a number of terms will constitute an important part of the present contribution. We will see that the author(s) of the cursing psalms employed a variety of words to represent the enemy that have potential associations with a particular semantic field, namely that of wild animals stalking and/or attacking their prey. At the same time, the author(s) tend to focus the crime of the enemy within a further semantic field, namely that of false witness, lying, gossiping. The encounter between both distinct semantic fields is, I would argue[13], the core of the metaphorisation process at work in the psalms and it is within this encounter that the psalmist endeavoured to express himself, to open windows into his 'speaker's meaning'.

4. *A Functioning Definition of Metaphor*

Our reading of the metaphorical language of the cursing psalms will be guided by the definition of metaphor proposed by Daniel Bourguet in his monograph *Des métaphores de Jérémie*: '... le fait de décrire intentionelle-ment, de manière médiate ou immédiate, une métaphorizé dan les termes

---

11. Macky (1990: 20–21).
12. A most useful lexicon in this regard is Van Gemeren (1997); cf. also Clines (1993–2001) as well as the standard lexica (TWAT, TDOT, HALAT etc.).
13. In line with Bourguet (1987).

d'un métaphorisant qui lui ressemble et qui appartient à une autre isotopie'.[14]

Bourguet's definition contains a number of terms that require further explanation, in particular *métaphorisé, métaphorisant*, and *isotopie*. The term *métaphorisé* is roughly equivalent to the 'tenor' or the 'principle/primary subject' as Max Black would put it. The term *métaphorisant* on the other hand is akin to the 'vehicle' or Black's 'subsidiary/secondary subject'.[15]

The term *isotopie* refers to a sector of vocabulary associated with a particular semantic field. Following Bourguet's definition, therefore, a biblical metaphorical statement must employ terminology from two distinct isotopes, two distinct domains of knowledge, two distinct semantic fields: that of the *métaphorisé* and that of the *métaphorisant*, both of which exhibit some form of resemblance, some point of similarity. Distinction in isotope is thus an essential dimension of metaphor. Where there is no distinction in isotope one is probably dealing with simple comparison or indeed simile.

Bourguet refers to the point of resemblance between the *métaphorisé* and the *métaphorisant* as the foyer or recognisable (to the recipient) cross-reference that is likewise necessary in order to ensure the adequate functioning of the metaphorical statement. An explicit point of cross-reference in one metaphorical statement, moreover, would appear to have the capacity to represent a further less explicit cross-reference with respect to a secondary metaphorical statement. In this sense different metaphorical statements can be seen to function within a said text, as we shall see with regard to Psalm 7.

Since Max Black's studies were published in the sixties and seventies, commentators have tended to speak of metaphorical speech as an 'interaction' between distinct isotopes or knowledge domains whereby one isotope (in our case the *métaphorisé*) is understood/structured in terms of the other (the métaphorisant). Exploiting his/her poetic skills, the biblical author laid down structural stylistic foundations whereby isotopes that explicitly differ yet enjoy some degree of cross-reference are allowed to encounter one another in an interaction that ultimately informs the reader/listener concerning, at least for the most part, the *métaphorisé*.

5. *Structured encounter of isotopes*

It is at this point that we have to turn our attention in brief to Biblical Hebrew Poetry (BHP) as an ancient vehicle for metaphorical speech. Research into BHP is also something of a growth industry, expanding both

---

14. Bourguet's definition is a refinement of that proposed by Ricœur (1975).
15. Cf. Black (1962: 24–27).

in quantity and complexity. Excellent and innovative manuals focusing on the variety, elegance and ultimate function of Hebrew poetical technique have been published in recent years and have become primary sources for biblical exegetes in their efforts to understand and explain the biblical texts.[16]

Few, however, deal with metaphor as an aspect of poetry in any comprehensive way. In a recent article written on the subject entitled *On Reading Biblical Poetry: The Role of Metaphor*, however, Adele Berlin[17] suggests that the study of metaphor should constitute a '"good starting-point" in the search for reading strategies...' with respect to BHP. Definitions of metaphor, albeit from exegetical sources, speak of poetry perceiving the world metaphorically 'through relations of likeness and difference'.[18] This reminds Berlin of her own understanding of parallelism in BHP, the juxtaposition of poetic 'lines that are, from a linguistic perspective, equivalent on one level while being different on another', as being rooted in 'equivalence and contrast'.[19]

In Berlin's opinion, '... the combination of likeness and difference is the essence of the relationship between parallel lines' in biblical poetry.[20] The similarity between the roots of parallelism and the roots of metaphor leads her to suggest that they are 'two sides of the same coin'. In fact, she goes so far as to say that, for her, 'the basic form of metaphor is parallelism, in the sense of the contiguous or syntagmatic arrangement of paradigmatic elements such that unlikes become alike. The inevitable conclusion is that both parallelism and metaphor are the defining characteristics of biblical poetry.'[21]

As I understand it, therefore, Berlin is suggesting that the parallel line is the location *par excellence* for the metaphorical event to take place, however one wishes to explain it. Thus distinct yet similar isotopes are introduced to one another via juxtaposition of parallel lines/expressions and allowed to interact in an event whereby a *métaphorisé* is structured in terms of a *métaphorisant*.

In her important work on parallelism in biblical poetry, Berlin describes the phenomenon under four headings: grammatical, lexical, semantic and phonological.[22] One can agree with her that parallelism in one form or another lies at the core of biblical poetic composition. It is equally fair to say, however, that virtually every stylistic technique in biblical poetry boils

---

16. Cf., for example, Watson (1995²); id. (1994); cf. also Alonso Schökel (1988).
17. Cf. Berlin (1997: 25–36).
18. Cf. Landy (1984: 61–87).
19. Cf. also Bourguet's isotopic distinction coupled with core/foyer resemblance.
20. Cf. Berlin (1997: 27).
21. Cf. Berlin (1997: 28).
22. Cf. Berlin (1985: 54–57).

down to some sort of parallel repetition based on one or other *degree* of similarity and where there is a *degree* of similarity there is also a *degree* of difference.[23]

The *métaphorisé* and the *métaphorisant*, therefore, do not have to be present in immediately parallel lines. Concentric structures[24], inclusios[25] and other structural forms of external parallelism, for example, may set them far apart yet still present both in such a way as to determine that one is read in terms of the other.[26] Another frequent feature of BHP is word-play, a non-structuring stylistic technique that has its roots in phonological (and orthographical) similarity (and semantic difference) such as assonance, consonance, rhyme, etc. In such cases, a type of parallelism is established on the basis of phonological similarity, allowing two distinct isotopes to 'meet' and 'interact', allowing a *métaphorisant* to structure a *métaphorisé*.[27]

Although non-structuring in themselves, metaphorical statements are thus evidently supported by the structuring features of biblical Hebrew poetry: distinct yet similar isotopes encounter one another in a generally highly structured poetical context, inviting the reader to explore the interaction between them and to take cognisance of what this interaction is endeavouring to say both explicitly and implicitly.

6. *Psalm 7*

In the figure below, an outline presentation is offered of the presence of the distinct isotopes of enemy verbal attack and terminology related to animals hunting or being hunted. As we have said, we will focus our attention on only one of the psalms listed in the figure, Psalm 7, endeavour to explore its use of words in the formation of metaphorical statements, and attempt to uncover the structuring poetical features upon which the non-structuring feature of metaphor rests.

23. One ought to bear in mind that repetition of one form or another (together with isotopic distinction) lies at the heart of Bourguet's understanding of the core of a metaphorical statement.

24. Cf. Berlin (1995: 187).

25. Cf. Watson (1995: 284–287).

26. See, for example, Renkema (1993) who relies heavily on 'responses' (parallelisms) at various levels (song/canto/sub-canto etc.) within and throughout a single book such as Lamentations.

27. For further information and extensive literature lists see Doyle (2000); id. (2001: 5–22); (2002b: 23–44); (2002c: 199–213); (forthcoming – *Vetus Testamentum*, 53/4 or 54/1); (2002d: 155–186); (1997: 73–193); (2002a: 77–88).

Ps.	*lying enemy*	*animals/hunting*
7	evil (v. 14)	lion (v.2)
	mischief (magic? v. 14)	tear apart (v. 2)
	lies (v. 14)	drag off as prey (v. 2)
		pursue (v. 5)
		pit (? v. 15)
	mischief (magic? v. 16)	
	violence (v. 16)	
35	malicious witness (v. 11)	net/ensnare (v. 8)
		tear at (v. 15)
		gnashing teeth (v. 16)
		ravages/lions (v. 17)
58	lies (v. 3)	snake (vv. 4-5)
		lion's fangs (v. 6)
		snail (v. 8)
59	stir up strife (v. 3)	lying in wait (v. 4)
	plot treacherously (v. 5)	howling (v. 7)
	they go unheard (v. 7)	prowling (v. 8)
	sin of the mouth (v. 13)	foaming (v. 8)
	word of the lips (v. 13)	barking (v. 8)
	curses and lies (v. 13)	
69	false accusations (v. 4)	trap/snare (v. 22)
	gossip (v. 12)	
	insults (v. 19)	
83	lay crafty plans/conspire (vv. 2-3)	
109	wicked mouths (vv. 2-3)	beset/attack (v. 3)
	lying tongues (vv. 2-3)	inhabiting ruins (v. 10)
	words of hate (v. 3)	
139	malicious speakers (v. 20)	the bloodthirsty (v. 19) – see also Psalm 59 in which bloodthirsty are related to wild animals in search of food.

There can be little doubt that the isotope of malicious words focusing the reader on the mouth of the enemy is abundantly evident in the above psalms. At the same time, the isotope of animal aggression and attack is also well represented. We shall see below how the interaction between these two isotopes forms the core of the primary metaphorical statement governing Psalm 7.

7. *Preliminary Steps*

A certain number of preliminary steps are necessary prior to the exploration of the metaphorical content of a biblical poem. Not wishing to reinvent the wheel in this regard, the present contribution casts its lot in with a number of recent (and not so recent), well-received commentaries and monographs on the Psalms in order to (i) establish the text from a text-critical perspective[28]; (ii) establish the syntactical/grammatical shape of the text[29]; (iii) establish translation and colometry to allow for parallelism and other poetical features which might indicate the presence of metaphors to emerge[30]; (iv) delimit the metaphorical statement on the basis of semantics, syntax and stylistics.[31]

Our interest lies in the first instance in the metaphorical language in the psalm. What are the metaphorical statement's outer limits? What are the structural subdivisions upon which the metaphorical statement is constructed? It should be noted that poetical features – both structuring and non-structuring – are not restricted by form-critical subdivisions. The subdivisions outlined below are rooted in structural shapes constructed on the basis of word repetition and semantics. The overall framing structure of the psalm echoes, in two chiastic segments, the lies perpetrated by the enemy and the fact that they return on their own heads (vv. 14-16) with the deeds of the psalmist who invites God to punish him if he has done wrong (vv. 1-5).

While the working translation and subdivisions provided below are essentially my own, they have been informed by a number of commentaries, particularly with regard to text-critical complications/options and basic form-critical subdivisions (see footnotes 28 & 29). Having thus gathered sufficient preparatory information we can now proceed to the exploration of Psalm 7 with a view to its metaphorical content. This is a three step procedure involving the identification of the isotope of the *métaphorisé* and that of the *métaphorisant* and thereby the presence of a functioning metaphorical statement, the determination of the point of cross-reference (*foyer*) between the distinct yet similar isotopes and the interpretation of the metaphorical statement – the creative endeavour to reconstruct the speaker's meaning.

28. See, for example, Cheyne (1904: 20–25); Briggs & Briggs (1906: 51–60); Dahood (1965: 40–57); Jacquet (1975: 86–299); Craigie (1983: 94–104); Kraus (1988: 166–176); Kwakkel (2001: 17–67).
29. See, for example, Gerstenberger (1988: 63–67); Terrien (2003: 116–123).
30. To be treated under point 1 below.
31. Likewise to be treated under point 1 below.

Psalm 7[32]

1	O LORD my God, in you I take refuge; save me
	from all my *pursuers*, and deliver me, save me[33]
2	or like a **lion** he will **tear** my נפש **apart** he will **drag**
	(my נפש) **away** as **prey**, with no one to rescue. or
3	O LORD my God, if I have <u>done</u> this, psalmist's
	if there is wrong in my <u>hands</u>, actions/hands
4	if I have <u>repaid</u> my ally with harm
	or <u>plundered</u> my foe without cause, if/or
5	then let the enemy **pursue** and overtake my נפש,
	trample my life to the ground,
	and **lay** my soul/reputation **in the dust**. don't save me

6	RISE UP, O LORD, in your ANGER; attack them
	LIFT YOURSELF UP against the fury of my enemies;
	AWAKE, O my God; you have appointed a
	judgment.
7	Let the assembly of the peoples be gathered
	around you, and over it take your seat on high.
8	The <u>LORD judges</u> the peoples; judge me, <u>O</u>
	<u>LORD</u>, according to my righteousness I am right
	and according to the integrity that is in me.
9	O let the evil of the wicked come to an end,
	but establish the righteous,
	<u>you who test</u> the minds and hearts, O righteous
	God.

10	<u>God is my shield</u>, protect me
	who saves the upright in heart.
11	<u>God is a righteous judge</u>,
	and a <u>God who has indignation</u> every day.

---

32. **Bold italics** = terminology included in the isotope of 'wild animals'; *italics* = words from the isotope of 'enemy lies' including the birthing metaphor; <u>underlined</u> = other metaphors relating to God; SMALL CAPITALS = potential association of isotope of wild animals (lion) with the divinity.

33. In the first subdivision of the psalm (vv. 1-5), the psalmist calls upon God 'to save' him (or not) on the condition that his actions have been irreprehensible; in the second section (vv. 6-9), the psalmist calls upon God to 'attack' his enemies since he (the petitioner) 'is righteous'; in the third section (vv. 10-13) the plea is 'to protect' the psalmist and 'destroy them', i.e. the enemy, on the condition that 'they' do not repent and their actions remain reprehensible; in the fourth and final section (vv. 14-16) the psalmist announces that the enemy cannot save himself, that his actions are reprehensible, and that his evil deeds will return 'upon his own head'.

12 If one does not repent, <u>God</u> will whet <u>his sword;</u>   destroy them
    <u>he</u> has bent and strung <u>his bow</u>;
13 <u>he</u> has prepared <u>his deadly weapons</u>,
    making <u>his arrows fiery shafts</u>.

14 See how he *conceives evil*,   save self
    and is *pregnant with mischief*
    and *brings forth lies*.
15   He digs a *pit, digging* it out,
      and *falls into* the *hole* that he has made.   words/actions
16 His *mischief* returns upon his own *head*,
    and on his own *head* his *violence* descends.   cannot save self

17 I will give to the LORD the thanks due to his
    righteousness, and sing praise to the name of the
    LORD, the Most High.

7.1. *Identification*

The identification of the presence of metaphorical language usually begins
with the recognition of a structure within which the terms (isotopes) of the
métaphorisé and those of the *métaphorisant* are brought into an encounter
with one another. As we noted above, this necessarily involves a degree of
word study, specifically of those employed in establishing the internal and
external parallelism upon which the structure of the psalm ultimately rests.
We limit ourselves here to the terminology of the relevant isotopes: 'wild
animals'//'lying enemies' and to that of the secondary metaphorical
statement in vv. 14-16:[34]

1   - pursuers (רדף: to set out behind a person: to pursue, persecute,
       chase)
2   - lion (אריה: the African lion)
     - tear (טרף: seize as prey, tear, rend [of wild beasts]; infrequent in
       literal sense but frequent in metaphorical sense[35]
     - me (נפש: breath, self, throat, inner person)
     - drag me (פרק: tear away from, both literal and figurative//טרף)
5   - pursue (רדף: pursue, persecute, chase)
     - me (נפש: breath self, throat, inner person)
     - trample (רמם: trample down)

---

34. The semantic alternatives are provided by the standard lectionaries, often on the basis
of contextual usage.
35. NIDOTTE #3271 (C. Van Dam)

- my life (חיי: life)
- my soul (כבודי: reputation, honour, liver [Dahood])
6   - fury (עבר: to get carried away, also used of lions roaming [Mi 5,7] /
       ערף: stiffen the neck, be stubborn [Syriac])
- awake (עורה: stir oneself, be awake) note phonetic parallel with אריה]
14   - conceive evil (חבל: labour, conception/און: magic, spoken words)
- pregnant with mischief (הרה: become pregnant/עמל: trouble,
  misfortune)
- birth lies (ילד: give birth/ שקר: lies, false words)
15   - dig (כרה: dig, hollow)
- pit (בור: hole in the ground, used for water or as prison, not used as
  trap; perhaps for giving birth)
- digging (חפר: dig for water)
- fall (נפל: fall [birth associations[36]]; death associations)
- hole (שחת: pit, grave, dwelling of the dead)
- made (פעל: make; note phonetic association with נפל)
16   - returns (שוב: return)
- mischief (עמל: labour, toil, trouble, misfortune)
- heads (ראש: head)
- foreheads (קדקד: forehead)
- violence (חמם: also false witness [Exod. 23.1; Deut. 19.16]; evokes
  psychological anguish on the part of the psalmist[37]
- descends (ירד)

The first explicit metaphorical statement is structured around the
semantically concentric stanza made up of verses 1-4. Via the concentric
structure we are invited to read the isotope of the *métaphorisé* – the enemy
pursuer – in terms of isotope of the *métaphorisant* – the lion (and its
associated commonplaces: tear at the neck, drag away as prey, trample to
the ground, to the dust). The use of pursuer and נפש in the second verse,
and the repeated use thereof in verse 5, serves to establish the boundaries
of the concentric stanza. The central segment of the concentric stanza
speaks of the actions of the psalmist in which he places his fate
conditionally in the hands of God. The presence of the comparative
particle 'like' is not necessarily (although it can be) a signal of
metaphorical language. The juxtaposition of different yet similar isotopes
is necessary.

The second explicit metaphorical statement is based on an unusual
grammatical indicator: getting pregnant in the third masculine singular and

---

36.   Although disputed (see. Beuken 2000: 139–152), potential associations of the verb נפל
with giving birth (lit. 'letting fall') have been noted, especially in relation to Isa. 13.18–19.
37.   NIDOTTE #2803 (I. Swart/C. Van Dam)

three verbs from the isotope of birthing juxtaposed with three nominal forms from the isotope of pernicious words. In an interesting parallel, it is worth paying attention to Isaiah 26.16-18[38] giving birth to wind as an endeavour to be fertile with the help of other gods, but failing to do so without YHWH. In the present instance, the external limbs of the concentric stanza allude to the conception, pregnancy and birth of evil, mischief and lies (v. 14), suggesting the completeness of the lies of the enemy, and to the fate of the enemy (v. 16) which he ultimately brings upon himself (his head and forehead) on account of his deeds. This echoes the completeness of the fate of the psalmist in verses 2 & 5 (pursuit, attack, dragged away, robbed of life). Once again the central part of the textual segment talks about actions: digging a pit and falling into it. In contrast to the first concentric stanza, in which the psalmist claims his innocence and leaves his fate in God's hands, the enemy deserves his fate and brings it upon himself. Associations with sorcery cannot be ruled out in this regard especially when one accounts for Ancient Near Eastern concepts of the power of the spoken word. In any event, the children of the enemy become their enemy: their reward is to receive something of their own medicine, their lies return to haunt them.

The use of the term 'pit' is ambiguous since it does not appear to be the usual term for a hole used for trapping an animal. It is mostly used to refer to a cistern for collecting water. On occasion it alludes to a grave and may even suggest a dugout over which a person might give birth. If the broader metaphorical statement of the psalm is inviting us to read the enemy and his lies as a lion with its savage jaws then perhaps the pit is indeed a trap/ grave in which the lion/lies are caught. On the other hand, the metaphorization of the enemy as a lion does not include aspects of consideration and premeditation. A lion might lie in wait for his or her prey but its actions are purely instinctual and thus ultimately irreprehensible. The second metaphorization of the enemy as a man giving birth, lies as offspring, is thus necessary in order to underline the calculated and thus reprehensible actions of the enemy. God responds to one of the metaphorizations as a shield and to the other as a judge.

The broader metaphorical statement involving both concentric stanzas brings four different isotopes into interaction: the psalmist and his 'irreprehensible' deeds//the enemy and his evil 'conceptions' and the attacking lion//the lies of the enemy. The psalmist is confident that he has done nothing wrong; so much so that he submits himself to God's scrutiny (v.9) and judgment and invites the lion to devour him should he be wrong and the lies of his enemy be true. The enemy conceives lies in secret and imagines himself not open to the scrutiny of God. His actions return on his own head.

38. See Doyle (2000: 307–320).

The power of the lion lies in its jaws and the power of the human enemy lies in his words. Both the present psalm and other psalms of imprecation focus the enemy's power in the mouth.[39] The enemy are liars and their lies have power to inflict damage and death. Their mischief is like the savage attack of the lion, robbing the psalmist of integrity and even life itself. The psalm thus represents a complex interweaving of terms from the isotope of wild animals, hunting and lies, falsehood. Echoes between the two isotopes serve to metaphorize the verbal attack of the enemy in terms of the physical attack of the lion. A further echo lies in the lion attacking the neck of the psalmist while the verbal 'mischief' of the enemy falls on his head/ forehead. God is metaphorized in the psalm as a protective 'shield' (v. 10) and as a 'judge' (v. 11) who *sees* the integrity of the psalmist and the evil of the enemy.[40] Armed with the weapons of defence (shielding the psalmist from the lion and the enemy) and attack (sharpening his sword, showering his fiery arrows), and metaphorized as a scrutinizing judge surrounded by witnesses, God is thereby explicitly integrated into the overall metaphorical statement.

At another level one should note the number of visceral images employed in the psalm as metaphors for conceptual/emotional states.[41] Unlike most modern languages, biblical Hebrew had not developed a set of terminology with which to express the emotional/conceptual, employing instead physical images in a process of metaphorization.[42] The author of our psalm thus made use of a series of well-known physical images to express emotional conflict.

7.2. *Points of cross-reference*
As we noted above in our reflections on the way in which metaphors function, the point of cross-reference or similarity between the distinct

39.   Psalm 35.11, 16, 20-21, 25; Psalm 58.3, 6; Psalm 59.2, 3, 7, 12; Psalm 69.4, 9-10, 12, 19-20; Psalm 83.3-5; Psalm 109.2-3, 17-18, 20, 28; Psalm 139.20. The mouth of the psalmist, on the other hand, is for praising God and speaking the truth.

40.   The metaphorization of God as a judge is also frequent in the psalms of imprecation and the laments in general. See the interesting article by Mandolfo (2002: 2751) which maintains the judge metaphor to be dominant.

41.   Pursuer (רדף: physical pursuit, emotional persecution); tear (טרף: seize as prey, tear, rend [of wild beasts], emotional attack); me (נפש: throat, breath, self); drag me (פרם: tear away from, emotional attack); trample (רמם: trample down); my life (חיי: life); my soul (כבוד: reputation, honour, liver [Dahood]); fury (עבר: to get emotionally carried away, also used of lions roaming [Mi 5,7]/ערף: stiffen the neck, be stubborn [Syriac]); the minds and hearts (לב: heart/בליה: kidneys [thoughts and feeling]); conceive evil (חבל: labour, conception/און: magic, spoken words); pregnant with mischief (הרה: become pregnant/עמל: trouble, misfortune,); bring forth lies (ילד: give birth/שקר: lies, false words); heads (ראש: head = person); foreheads (קדקד: forehead).

42.   Thus making such metaphorisation 'necessary' according to Macky (1993).

isotopes of a metaphorical statement is essential in confirming the presence of metaphor. Where do we detect the point of similarity, the cross-reference between the isotope of the enemy and his words and that of the lion? In the present instance, I would maintain, this is to be found not only in the dangerous mouth of the enemy and the equally dangerous jaws of the lion but also in the terminology for life employed by the author, especially the use of נפש, כבד and חי, which taken together signify life, breath, throat, self, physical life and moral reputation.[43]

The pursuit and verbal attack of the enemy thus represents an assault on the petitioner at every level of his being, physical, moral and psychological. The metaphorical statement takes us beyond the mere physical assault of the lion and its implied jaws/teeth. This is further elaborated in the second chiastic stanza and the second metaphorical statement in verses 14–16.

What is the point of cross-reference between the isotope of birthing and that of lies? I believe in this instance it is to be found in the temporal process of conception, pregnancy and birth. The mischief of the enemy, at least so the metaphor would imply, is not conceived alone. Their mischief is allowed to take form over time and ultimately be born as the offspring of their scheming. A lie, like a child, is conceived, formed and implemented. The point of cross-reference between the conception formation and implementation of wicked words/lies and the conception and birthing of children thus allows us to bring both isotopes into interaction. In the context of the said metaphorical statement, therefore, it is not beyond the bounds of reason that the term נפל is being used in the sense of 'birthing'/ 'letting fall' into the pit.[44]

7.3. *Author's purpose/interpretation*

We noted in the footnotes at the beginning of the present contribution that several scholars focus their comments on Psalm 7 on metaphors for God (God is a judge) and often remark that the (if recognized) metaphor of the enemy as a lion is conventional/stereotypical, thus implying that its use in the psalms of imprecation and elsewhere somehow undermines its power. Few authors make direct reference to the birthing of lies metaphor or establish any structural relationship with the enemy as a lion metaphor. The lion's attack is sudden and premeditated, the conception and birth of

43. NIDOTTE # 5883 (D.C. Fredericks); # 3877 (C.J. Collins); # 2649 (T.L. Brensinger). Indeed, it is evident that the very polysemic nature of many biblical Hebrew lexemes predisposes them for use in building metaphorical statements in this fashion.

44. Would it be stretching the metaphor too far to suggest in this regard that the text is inviting us to read the lies of the enemy's lips in interaction with the children of the enemy's labia?

lies is a longer and more deliberate process. By reading both metaphorical statements together the reader is given access to the all embracing pain of the petitioner. He is not only subject to brief physical attack, his entire person is exposed to prolonged assault and violation at the 'hands' and 'conceptions' of his enemies. The combination of metaphorical statements thus grants a degree of novelty to the otherwise conventional lion metaphor.[45]

What type of metaphorical statement are we dealing with? While Bourguet prefers to characterize metaphors according to the type of *foyer* they represent[46], Macky more appropriately endeavours to associate the author's purpose with the typification of metaphorical speech.[47] The primary purpose involved in the use of *expressive metaphors*, for example, is the pouring out of emotions, the expression of what is going on in the innermost being of the author. The fact that biblical texts abound in such metaphors is hardly surprising given the complexity of human interior life and 'expressive' may, and probably does to a degree, represent the appropriate metaphorical type present in Psalm 7. Macky also speaks of metaphors he considers *Central for Biblical Purposes*, however, the most important of which he terms *relational metaphors*.[48]

The importance of enhancing one's relationship with God and one's relationship with one's neighbour was clearly central to biblical writers. Relational speech is evident in the bible where speaker and hearer(s) are present and central to the communication which takes the form of an address. Relational metaphors introduce a level of invitation into relationship where the relationship cannot be expressed adequately with literal terms, going beyond that which literal speech can do. The three way relationship between the psalmist, his enemy and God is thus a profound communication expressing itself in metaphorical terms.

We also noted above along with Macky that metaphors provide windows into the speaker's meaning, ultimately allowing us to reconstruct the latter. How then do we go about reconstructing the speaker's meaning? The conventional exegetical process is to determine the speaker's meaning in its context and its significance for the ancient reader (leading to endeavours to identify the enemy as a military force, a judicial adversary, etc.). The expressive/relational metaphor allows the psalmist to verbalize his inner pain and at the same time test his relationship with God.

Contemporary hermeneutical approaches also see value in addressing the contemporary reader's context and the text as addressing a

---

45. See Macky (1993: 72–80).
46. Bourget (1987: 59–64).
47. Macky (1993: 260–263).
48. Macky (1993: 247ff).

contemporary reader. Psalms that address an ancient context of conflict such as Psalm 7 and the other psalms of imprecation can also address contemporary contexts of conflict (both internal and external) and, because of the frequent absence of cultural dependence and openness to contemporary actualizations, the metaphorizations they employ can thus give expression to the situation of the present-day reader.

The theme of the seminar, of which the present volume is a result, focused on the psalms and their liturgical context. We generally identify liturgical contexts as ecclesial, contexts of church and synagogue, contexts of worship. While the use and function of psalms of imprecation in such a context can also be viewed from an historical/diachronic perspective, their present day function remains of vital importance: such psalms provide language (expressive metaphor) to those threatened by the destructive force of lies and false witness, language that brings such conflict, whatever its content, into the arena of the divine encounter (relational metaphor).

It is striking that most of the so-called imprecatory psalms, in which the psalmist calls upon God to disempower his enemy in one or other evidently brutal form, employ animal metaphors encompassing a broad semantic field (including hunting for prey, trapping and ensnaring), in their portrayal of the enemy and focus their misdeeds around the telling of lies and the mouth/ lips. The power of an animal is focused in its teeth and jaws/fangs as the effect of the lies/maliciousness of the enemy is focused on their words and their mouths. In Psalm 7 God is called upon to return like for like, to rise up in his anger (באף) against the fury (עברה) of the enemy, to awake (עורה)[49] on behalf of the psalmist and disempower the enemy. In Psalm 59 God is called upon to be a wild dog to the wild dogs threatening the psalmist. The word-play[50] here suggests that God is being called to be a lion to the enemy, and as such is being metaphorized as a lion in order to confront the enemy's powerful lies with justice. The fact that the metaphorization is not explicit in this regard may have its roots in an antipathy towards the attribution of lion-like qualities to Mesopotamian deities and the frequent demonization of the enemy in the form of a lion in the psalms.[51]

---

49. Note word-play between עורה – awake, עברה – fury and אריה – lion; note also intertextual allusions to God acting as a lion: See, for example, Psalm 50, 22//7,3: טרף – subject lion//טרף – subject God, with additional repetition of אין מציל

50. According to Bourguet's (1987) typification, word-play metaphors are rare.

51. Cf. Watanabe (2002: 89–92); see also, with respect to the Psalms, Keel (1997), who points out several allusions to the enemy as a lion but appears to make no reference to the metaphorisation of the divinity as a lion; cf. similarly Janowski (1995: 155–173).

8. *Conclusion*

Gerstenberger maintains that the original *Sitz im Leben* of such laments as Psalm 7 was a liturgical one, that the words of the psalm were 'articulated within the fixed liturgical framework of a service for individuals who suffered unjust persecution (cf. Pss. 7; 17; 26).'[52] Contemporary language tends to express conflict in conceptual rather than physical terms. Yet conflict has physical consequences and this needs to be expressed in the liturgies that bring conflict into words in the ecclesial community. Instead of setting aside such language as brutal and un-Christian, contemporary liturgy might endeavour to understand its original profoundly theological purpose and use it creatively in its liturgy.

Liturgies in time of war, for example, often represent extended prayers for peace and resolution. Before peace and resolution, however, come accusation and anger, the speech of the disorientated.[53] The movement towards resolution of conflict in the ancient and contemporary reader is reflected in the form of the imprecation/lament psalms and their positive conclusions. First disorientation then orientation! Is the Church too focused on providing liturgy for the 'orientated'? According to Brueggemann,

> 'The problem with a hymnody (read: liturgy) that focuses on equilibrium, coherence and symmetry [i.e. psalms of orientation] is that it may deceive and cover over. Life is not like that. Life is also savagely marked by disequilibrium, incoherence and unrelieved asymmetry'.[54]

The poetry of Psalm 7 and other psalms of imprecation holds 'God the judge' before us as a central metaphor, as the turning point from disorientation to orientation. Embracing metaphor as a strategy for reading religious/theological poetry as we find it in the psalms and elsewhere forces us to view the other metaphorical speech employed by the psalmist(s) as theological speech, as theo-poetry, as words expressing the psalmist's inner turmoil and illustrating his relationship with God at one and the same time.

Bibliography

Alonso Schökel, L 1988 *A Manual of Hebrew Poetics* (tr. A. Graffy, Subsidia Biblica 11, Rome: Pontificio istituto biblico).

52. Anderson (1965: 64).
53. Brueggemann (1984: passim).
54. Brueggemann (1984 52); see also his recent (2003: 19–49), in which the (history of the) recovery and use of the lament in the liturgical/ecclesial community is addressed in some detail.

Althann, R. 1992 'The Psalms of Vengeance against their Ancient Near Eastern Background', *JNWSL* 18: 1–11.

Anderson, G.W. 1965 'Enemies and Evildoers in the Book of Psalms', *Bulletin of the John Rylands Library* 48: 18–29.

Berlin, A. 1985 *The Dynamics of Biblical Parallelism* (Bloomington, IN: Indiana University Press).

—1997 'On Reading Biblical Poetry: The Role of Metaphor', J.A. Emerton (ed.) *Congress Volume, Cambridge, 1995* (Leiden: Brill): 25–36.

Beuken, W.A.M. 2000 '"Deine Toten werden leben" (Jes 26,19). "Kindliche Vernunft oder reifer Glaube?"', R.G. Kratz e.a. (eds.), *Schriftauslegung in der Schrift. Festschrift O.H. Steck* (Berlin: de Gruyter): 139–152.

Birkland, H. 1933 *Die feinde des Individuums in der israelitischen Psalmenliteratur* (Oslo: Gröndahl).

—1955 *The Evildoers in the Book of Psalms* (Utgitt av Det Norske Videnskaps-Akademi, II. Historisk-Filosofisk Klasse, 1952, 2, Oslo: Jacob Dybwad).

Black, M. 1962. *Models and Metaphors: Studies in Language and Philosophy* (Ithaca, NY: Cornell University Press).

Böcher, O. 1970 *Dämonenfurcht und Dämonenabwehr* (Beiträge zur Wissenschaft von Alten und Neuen Testament, 90; Stuttgart: Kohlhammer).

Bourguet, D. 1987 *Des métaphores de Jérémie* (Etudes bibliques, 9; Paris: Gabalda).

Briggs, C.A. & Briggs, E.G. 1906 *A Critical and Exegetical Commentary on the Book of Psalms*. Vol. I (International Critical Commentary; Edinburgh: T. & T. Clark).

Brueggemann, W. 1974 'From Hurt to Joy, From Death to Life', *Interpretation* 28: 3–19.

—1977 'The Formfulness of Grief', *Interpretation* 32: 263–275.

—1980 'Psalms and the Life of Faith: a Suggested Typology of Function', *JSOT* 17: 3–32.

—1983 'Reservoirs of Unreason', *Reformed Liturgy and Music* 17: 99–104.

—1984 *The Message of the Psalms. A Theological Commentary* (Augsburg Old Testament Series, Minneapolis: Augsburg).

—1986 'The Costly Loss of Lament', *JSOT* 36: 55–71.

—1995 Praying the Psalms (Winona Lake, MN: St Mary's Press).

Cheyne, T.K. 1904 *The Book of Psalms. Translated from a revised text with Notes and Introduction*. Vol. I (London: Kegan Paul).

Clines, D.J.A. 1993–2001 *The Dictionary of Classical Hebrew* [DCH], Vols I-V (Sheffield: Sheffield Academic Press).

Coxe, A.C. (ed.), 1996 *Exposition on the Book of Psalms. By Saint Augustin (sic), Bishop of Hippo*, in P. Schaff, *A Select Library of the Nicene and Post Nicene Fathers of the Christian Church* (Vol. VIII, Grand Rapids, MI: Eerdmans, 1888 [reprint 1996]).

Craigie, P.C. 1983 *Psalms 150* (Word Biblical Commentary, 19; Waco, TX: Word).

Croft, S.J.L. 1987 *The Identity of the Individual in the Psalms* (JSOTSS, 44; Sheffield: Sheffield Academic Press).

Dahood, M. 1965 *Psalms 150* (Anchor Bible; Garden City, NY: Doubleday).

Doyle, B. 1997 'A Literary Analysis of Isaiah 25,10a', J. Van Ruiten & M. Vervenne (eds.), *Studies in the Book of Isaiah. Festschrift Willem A.M. Beuken* (BETL, 132; Leuven: Peeters): 173–193.
—2000 *The Apocalypse of Isaiah Metaphorically Speaking. A Study of the Use, Function and Significance of Metaphors in Isaiah 24–27* (BETL, 151; Leuven: Peeters/University Press).
—2001 'Metaphora Interrupta: Psalm 133', *ETL 77*: 5–22.
—2002a 'Explorations in Fertility and Infertility in Isa. 24–27', F. Postma, K. Spronk, E. Talstra (eds.), *The New Things. Eschatology in Old Testament Prophecy. Fs. Henk Leene* (Amsterdamse Cahiers Supplement Series, 3; Maastricht: Shaker Publishing): 77–88.
—2002b 'Heaven, Earth, Sea, Field and Forest: Physical Subjects – Mysterious Symbol in Ps. 96', *JNSL* 28: 23–44.
—2002c 'Just You, and I, Waiting. The Poetry of Ps. 25', *OTE* 14: 199–213.
—2002d 'How Do Isotopes Meet? A Rare Word-Play Metaphor in Isa. 25.7a-8a', K. Feyaerts (ed.), *The Bible Through Metaphor and Translation. A Cognitive Semantic Perspective* (Bern: Peter Lang).
Forthcoming 'Howling Like Dogs: Metaphorical Language in Psalm 59' (*Vetus Testamentum*, 53/4 or 54/1).
Gerstenberger, E. 1982. Enemies and Evildoers in the Psalms: A Challenge to Christian Preaching', *Horizons in Biblical Theology* 4: 61–78.
—1988 *Psalms. Part 1 with an Introduction to Cultic Poetry* (FOTL, 14; Grand Rapids, MI: Eerdmans).
Hauret, A. 1967 'Les ennemis-sorciers dans les supplications individuelles', *Rescherches Bibliques* 8: 129–137.
Hobbs, T.R. & Jackson, P.K. 1991 'The Enemies in the Psalms', *Biblical Theology Bulletin* 21: 22–29.
Holladay, W.L. 1993 *Prayerbook of a Cloud of Witnesses* (Minneapolis: Augsburg).
Jacquet, L. 1975 *Les Psaumes et le coeur de l'Homme; Etude textuelle, littéraire et doctrinale* (Gembloux: Duculot).
Janowski, B. 1995 'Dem Löwen gleich, gierig nach Raub', *EvTh* 55: 155–173.
Keel, O. 1997. *The Symbolism of the Biblical World, Ancient Near Eastern Iconography and the Book of Psalms* (tr. T.J. Hallet, Winona Lake, IN).
Kittay, E.F. & Lehrer, A. 1981 'Semantic Fields and the Structure of Metaphor', *Studies in Language* 5: 31–63.
Kraus, H.-J. 1988 *Psalms 1–59. A Commentary* (tr. H.C. Oswald, Minneapolis: Augsburg).
Kwakkel, O. 2001 *'According to my Righteousness'. Upright Behaviour as Grounds for Deliverance in Psalms 7, 17, 18, 26 and 44* (Diss. Rijksuniversiteit Groningen).
Lamp, E. & Tilly, M. 1989 'Öffentlichkeit als Bedrohung – Ein Beitrag zur Deutung des "Feindes" im Klagepsalm des Einzelnen', BN 50: 46–57.
Landy, F. 1984 'Poetics and Parallelism. Some Comments on James Kugel's *The Idea of Biblical Poetry'*, *JSOT 28:* 61–87.
Laney, J.C. 1981 'A Fresh Look at the Imprecatory Psalms', *Bibliotheca Sacra* 138: 11–37.

Limburg, J. 2000 *Psalms* (Westminster Bible Companion, Louisville, KY: Westminster John Knox).

Macky, P.W. 1993 *The Centrality of Metaphors to Biblical Thought. A Method for Interpreting the Bible* (Studies in the Bible and Early Christianity, 19; Lewiston, NY: Mellen).

Mandolfo, C. 2002 'Finding Their Voices: Sanctioned Subversions in Psalms of Lament', *Horizons in Biblical Theology* 24: 24–51.

Mowinckel, S. 1934 'Fiendene i de individuelle Klagesalmer', *Norsk Teologisk Tidsskrift* 34: 1–39.

Oesterley, W.O.E. 1939. *The Psalms* (New York: Macmillan).

Renkema, J. 1993 *Klaagliederen* (COT; Kampen: Kok).

Ricœur, P. 1975 *La métaphore vive* (Paris: Seuil).

Ridderbos, N.H. 1939 *De 'Werkers der Ongerechtigheid' in de individueele Psalmen. Een beoordeeling van Mowinckels opvatting* (Kampen: Kok).

Rogerson, J.W. 1993 'The Enemy in the Old Testament', A.G. Auld (ed.), *Understanding Poets and Prophets. Essays in Honour of George Wishart Anderson* (JSOTSS, 152; Sheffield: Sheffield Academic Press): 284–293.

Schmid, R. 1967 'Die Fluchpsalmen in christlichen Gebet', Eberhard-Karls-Universität Tübingen. Katholisch-Theologische Fakultät, *Theologie im Wandel: Festschrift zum 150 jährigen Bestehen der katholisch-theologischen Fakultät an der Universität Tübingen, 1817–1967* (Tübinger thelogische Reihe, 1; Munich: Wewel): 377–393.

Sheppard, G.T. 1991 '"Enemies" and the Politics of Prayer in the Book of Psalms', in D. Jobling, P.L. Day & G.T. Sheppard (eds.), *The Bible and the Politics of Exegesis. Essays in Honour of Norman K. Gottwald on His Sixty-Fifth Birthday* (Cleveland: Pilgrim Press): 61–82.

Terrien, S. 2003 *The Psalms. Strophic Structure and Theological Commentary* (Grand Rapids, MI: Eerdmans).

Van Gemeren, W.A. (ed.) 1997 *New International Dictionary of Old Testament Theology and Exegesis* [NIDOTTE], Vols 1–5 (Grand Rapids, MI: Zondervan).

Watson, W.G.E. 1994 *Traditional Techniques In Classical Hebrew Verse* (JSOTSS, 170; Sheffield: Sheffield Academic Press).

—1995 *Classical Hebrew Poetry. A Guide to its Techniques* (JSOTSS, 26; Sheffield: Sheffield Academic Press).

Watanabe, C.E. 2002 *Animal Symbolism in Mesopotamia: A Contextual Approach* (Wiener Offene Orientalistik, Band 1, Vienna: Institut für Orientalistik der Universität).

—2003 'Necessary Conditions of a Good Lament', *Horizons in Biblical Theology* 25: 19–49.

Zenger, E. 1994 *Ein Gott der Rache: Feindpsalmen verstehen* (Biblische Bücher, 1, Freiburg im Breisgau: Herder).

—1994 *Die Gotteszeugenschaft des 83. Psalms. Anmerkungen zur pseudotheologischen Ablehnung der sogenannten Fluchpsalmen*, in M. Lutz-Machmann & H. Vorgrimler, *Und dennoch ist von Gott zu reden. Festschrift für Herbert Vorgrimler* (Freiburg im Breisgau: Herder): 11–37.

Cult-Critical Motif in Psalm 69.32 – Does it Portray an Anti-Cultic Stance?

Alphonso Groenewald[1]
Pretoria, RSA

1. Introduction

The last stanza of Psalm 69 consists of cola 31a-37b[2]. Cola 31ab commence with the vow to praise ('Lobgelübde')[3] the name of God[4]. This stanza begins with the motive which we encounter so often in the psalms, namely the reason why God does not forsake the one who is afflicted: precisely in the midst of suffering and affliction, while even fearing that God has abandoned or, even worse, has rejected him, the supplicant is still persistent that God is with him and will give him the necessary strength to withstand his affliction[5].

The subsequent colon (32[6]) attaches syndetically a justification to this 'vow of praise' contained in cola 31ab: it elevates laudation above sacrifice. This cult-critical statement contained in colon 32 bears witness to the fact that this supplicant/these redactor(s) must have had severe criticism of the sacrificial practices prevalent during that specific time[7].

The question to be addressed in this paper is whether this cult-critical statement as contained in colon 32 portrays an anti-cultic stance. The thesis put forward can be formulated as follows: the cult-critical statement of Psalm 69.32 is to be seen against the background of the 'piety/theology of the poor'; it thus stood in service of this theology. It must therefore be stated categorically that this cult-critical statement does not aim to exclude either the sacrifice or sacrificial cult practices at all (cf. Rofé 1985: 207). It

---

1. This article is published as part of a post-doctoral fellowship programme in the Department of Old Testament Studies, Faculty of Theology, University of Pretoria.

2. Cf. Groenewald (2003: 134) with regard to the demarcation of this stanza.

3. Cf. Cartledge (1992: 150–61); Tita (2001: 105–99, 220–4) and Westermann (1977: 56–59) for a detailed discussion of this element. See also Brueggemann (1995: 71–2); Erbele-Küster (2001: 173); Gunkel & Begrich (1998: 184–6 §6 24); Ferris (1992: 100); Hieke (2000: 51–

4. Cola 31ab read as follows: 'I will praise the name of God with a song, and I will magnify it with a song of praise' (own translation).

5. Cf. Stolz (1983: 38): '*In seinem Elend* kommt der Beter zu Erhörungsgewißheit'.

6. Colon 32 reads as follows: 'and that will please Yahweh more than a bull, a young bull with horns (and) cloven hoofs' (own translation).

7. Cf. also Ro (2002: 181): 'Diese eschatologisch orientierte Erwählungs- und Demutstheologie ist sehr häufig opfer- bzw. tempelkritisch ausgerichtet'.

is not a case of the *tôdāh* vis-á-vis the sacrifice of animals: the cult without sacrifices was unimaginable[8]. However, by means of this remark the supplicant/redactors only appraised the value of the *tôdāh* higher than that of the bloody sacrifice, as well as the sacrificial practices accompanying it. They thus did not reject the sacrifice fundamentally, but instead emphasised the laudation vigorously. Noteworthy is the fact that their critical stance with regard to the cult and immolation corresponds with the view already known from the book of Isaiah (cf. Isa. 1.10-17; 66.1-6)[9].

2. *Other cult-critical statements in the Psalter*

Psalm 69.32 is, however, not the only example of a cult-critical relativisation we encounter in the Psalter. It furthermore occurs in Psalms 40, 50 and 51[10]. According to Psalm 40.7-9 the offering of sacrifice (alone) was not enough to offer to God[11]. These verses thus point to the characteristics required of the supplicant, beyond the cultic offerings and sacrifices. It is expected of the supplicant to do the will of God with delight; he/she must furthermore keep God's *Torah* within his/her being (heart). In face of Yahweh's *Torah* the supplicant offers him, instead of the sacrifice, a statement of obedience and subordination (Ps. 40.9)[12].

---

8.   In this regard Von Rad (1962: 380) infers as follows: '... muß man doch davor warnen, in diesen Sätzen die gültigste Kritik, ja die geistige 'Überwindung' des blutigen Opferkultus schlechthin zu sehen... hier aber geht es um die Frage des rechten Opfers; die Kultübung als solche wird gar nicht in Frage gestellt... '. Cf. also Berges (1999b:172): 'Wie im Falle der Fastenfrage geht es auch hier nicht um die Ablehnung gottesdienstlicher Praktiken, sondern um die persönliche Disposition derer, die am rituell-kultischen Leben des nachexilischen Israel teilnehmen'.

9.   Berges 2000a: 5, 14. Cf. also Berges (1998: 65–6): 'Es ist ein Milieu, in dem das Zittern vor dem Wort JHWHs (66.5) mehr Gewicht hat als das Blut von Böcken und Stieren (66.3–5) ... Die Kritik in 1,10–15 an der Übermenge an Opfern und am kultischen Übereifer zeigt implizit die Reaktion des nachexilischen Israel auf seinen grauen Alltag... trotz aller Opfer und kultischen Anstrengungen stand die Wende zum Besseren noch aus. Die prophetische Tora der Wir-Gruppe besteht nicht etwa in einer radikalen Ablehnung des Opferkultus, sondern im Hinweis auf den Primat der Ethik vor jedem Kult; würde JHWH Opfergaben aus Händen von Gewalttätern annehmen, dann verhielte er sich wie ein korrupter Richter, der sich der Bestechlichkeit schuldig macht!'

10.   Once again it should be stated that these texts do not intend to condemn the sacrificial cult in ancient Israel at all; to read them in such a manner is almost certainly to misinterpret them (Craigie 1983: 315).

11.   Cf. Ps. 40.7, 9: 'Sacrifice and offering you do not desire... burnt offering and sin offering you have not required... I delight to do your will, O my God; your law is within my heart' (NRSV).

12.   According to Hossfeld & Zenger 'das Tun der Tora ist die "Opfergabe"' (1993: 256). Cf. furthermore Braulik (1975: 181–2); Creach (1996: 112); Courtman (1995: 50) and Kraus (1972: 309–10).

Psalm 50 also contains cult-critical statements. This psalm can be divided into three stanzas. Stanza I (50.1-6) forms the introductory passage; the descriptive language is that of a theophany[13]. God summons the covenant people to his presence[14]. This stanza is followed by two principal sections (stanzas) which are both in the form of a divine address; both contain cult-critical statements. Stanza II (7–15) contains divine words with the theme sacrifice; stanza III (16–23) contains the second part of Yahweh's address with (primarily) a listing of individual iniquities (Hossfeld & Zenger 1993: 308). In stanza II (7–15) the true meaning of sacrifice is outlined: sacrifices and burnt offerings are legitimate when they are understood correctly as well as offered in a correct manner[15]. These verses furthermore make it quite clear: God actually does not need sacrifices; he already possesses all the animals of the world (vv. 10-11). The essence of the whole sacrificial system is rather to be seen in the song of thanksgiving (*tôdāh*) offered to God; and together with it the fulfillment of the vow (*ndr*) made to God (50:14)[16]. In stanza III (16–23) a warning is issued to those whose lives are not in accordance with the covenant stipulations. The true meaning of the law is outlined and reiterated. The concluding verse (50.23) re-emphasizes the point which has already been made in verse 14[17]: the true meaning of the sacrifice is to be found in the offering of the thanksgiving (*tôdāh*), as well as walking on the right path where the salvation of God will be revealed (cf. also Hossfeld 1991: 96).

In Psalm 51.18-19 we encounter another example of cult-critical relativization[18]. To begin with, these verses are to be seen in connection with the preceding verses[19]. They do not only serve as a justification, but

13. See Schmidt & Nel (2002: 256) with regard to theophany as type-scene in the Hebrew Bible.

14. See Ps. 50.5: 'gather to me my faithful ones, who made a covenant with me by sacrifice' (NRSV).

15. Doeker (2002: 275) infers as follows: 'Der Psalm berührt einen anderen Schwerpunkt der Thematik. Ihm geht es in den vv. 7-15 weniger um eine Kritik an der Opferpraxis, als um die Abwehr eines bestimmten, falschen Opferverständnisses und vor allem um die positive Bewertung der Toda'. Cf. also Craigie (1983: 365–6); Hossfeld & Zenger (1993: 310); Kraus (1972: 377–8); Tromp (2000: 266).

16. Ps. 50.14: 'Offer to God a sacrifice of thanksgiving, and pay your vows to the Most High' (NRSV). According to Hossfeld & Zenger (1993: 314) it is very important to interpret this verse within its context, and the context criticises 'das Opferverständnis und nicht die Opfer als solche. Er votiert also für die Interpretation von *tôdāh* als Dankopfer und nicht nur allgemein als Lob/Dank'.

17. Cf. Ps. 50.23. 'Those who bring thanksgiving as their sacrifice honour me; to those who go the right way I will show the salvation of God' (NRSV).

18. Cf. Ps. 51.18–19: 'For you have no delight in sacrifice; if I were to give a burnt offering, you would not be pleased. The sacrifice acceptable to God is a broken spirit; a broken and contrite heart, O God, you will not despise' (NRSV).

19. Cf. the particle *kî* introducing verse 18.

also as a qualification of the supplicant's praise (17) of God's salvation (16) and deliverance/righteousness (16). In verse 17 the supplicant appeals to God to open his lips and to allow his mouth to declare the praise of God. The verses 18-19 continue this prayer by giving a reason for it. The supplicant emphatically emphasizes that the merciful action of God will not be received on the basis of sacrifice alone. Actually, according to these verses the confidence of the supplicant is placed in that which God will certainly accept, namely a 'broken and contrite heart'. Rather, the point is that burnt offerings or other sacrifices, which God will accept, must express the sacrificial reality of the 'crushed' heart of the supplicant(s)[20]. Taken in this way, these verses make a powerful statement of the subordination of sacrifice to confession, as well as those personal qualities which are acceptable to God and necessary for forgiveness. The supplicant who thus offers a broken spirit as sacrifice, whether accompanied by burnt offerings or not, can be sure of divine acceptance[21]. Therefore, the psalm herewith expresses the real meaning of sacrifice: confession, forgiveness, total dependence on a merciful God and a joyful new life that emerges from that process[22]. According to Hossfeld & Zenger (2000: 54)[23] these verses actualize the prophetic cult criticism which, instead of sacrifices, requests obedience to God as well as justice and righteousness to be done[24]. Once again, it must be stated clearly that one should be cautious not to conclude that these verses (Ps. 51.18-19) point to a repudiation of cultic worship and that they encourage a kind of spirituality wholly detached from sacrifices. In this regard Leene (1996: 70) justly infers as follows: 'in that sense this psalm remains within the religious environment

20. Hossfeld & Zenger (1993: 310): 'JHWH verweigert die Schlacht- und Brandopfer wegen des kultischen Leerlaufs und der Diskrepanz von Kult und Ethos, allerdings im Urteil des Beters. Die "Schlachtopfer Gottes", auf die es ankommt, sind ein zerbrochenes und zerschlagenes Herz'. Cf. also Seybold (1996: 214) and Spieckermann (1998: 147–8).

21. Hossfeld & Zenger (2000: 54–5) states as follows: 'Nicht irgendwelche Gaben die den Geretteten "symbolisieren" sollen, sondern *sich selbst* als den an *Herz* und *Geist* erneuerten Menschen übergibt er seinem Gott'. Cf. also Dalglish (1962: 192–4); Schmidt (1994: 358).

22. Tate (1990: 26–8). Cf. also Courtman (1995: 52–6).

23. Cf. also Gunkel & Begrich (1998: 287–90).

24. Cf. for example Hos. 6.6 ('for I desire steadfast love and not sacrifice, the knowledge of God rather than burnt offerings' – NRSV); Mic. 6.6–8 ('with what shall I come before the Lord...? Shall I come before him with burnt offerings...? ... and what does the Lord require of you but to do justice, and to love kindness, and to walk humbly with your God?' – NRSV); Amos 5.21–24 ('... even though you offer me your burnt offerings and grain offerings, I will not accept them; and the offerings of well-being of your fatted animals I will not look upon... but let justice roll down like waters, and righteousness like an everflowing stream' – NRSV). Compare also Isa. 1.11-17 and Jer. 7.21-23. We even encounter this line of thought in the wisdom tradition: see Prov. 15.8; 21.3, 27; 28.9, and especially *Sirach* 34.21–35.22.

in which the Psalter originated: a world in which animal sacrifices were offered'[25].

Psalm 51 does, however, not end with these verses (18–19). In order to get a full picture of what the psalm has to say about sacrifice, it is necessary to briefly focus on the last two verses as well[26]. Verses 20-21 were most likely added by a later redactor who (re-)interpreted the psalm in terms of Israel's corporate experience[27]. A certain tension indeed exists with the first part of the text (vv. 3-19): 'Jerusalem (und Zion) ist vorher nirgends im Blick, und die opferkritischen Aussagen von V 18–19 stehen eher in Spannung zur Opfertheologie von V 21' (Hossfeld & Zenger 2000: 45). The form of these verses is that of a prayer for the restoration of Jerusalem so that sacrifices could be made on the altar in the temple. And whenever God restores Jerusalem, sacrifices on the altar there will be acceptable to him again. When the redactor thus refers to 'right sacrifices' (lit. 'sacrifices of righteousness'), he surely has sacrifices in mind in which Yahweh will find the right spirit and which are thus truly symbolic of the supplicant's complete dedication to both cult and ethos (cf. Mosis 1992: 212, 214).

3. *Psalm 69 and the 'piety/theology of the poor'*

I will now once again return to Psalm 69. It seems that according to the supplicant/redactors Yahweh will surely value the song of praise (*tôdāh*) of

---

25. Jones (1963: 30) clearly fails to recognise this fact. He therefore explains the cult-critical remarks in these psalms as the result of a total cessation of the sacrificial practices after the destruction of the temple in 587/6 BCE. Tournay (1991: 171–2) holds the same opinion. However, the destruction of the temple does not seem to have put an end to worship in Jerusalem. At all events, in Jer. 41.5 we read that some eighty men came from Shechem, Shiloh and Samaria and arrived at the 'house of Yahweh' to offer a sacrifice of cereal and incense. We are not told explicitly that the sanctuary in question was in Jerusalem; in the discussion of this text in the book of Jeremiah it is assumed, nevertheless, that this was the case (Jagersma 1994: 184). Most likely an altar was soon reconstructed on the site of the temple. It is difficult to conceive that there was no activity at all in the sphere of worship, religion and so on in Judah during the time of the exile, and it is quite clear that Jerusalem and the place where the temple had stood would have played an important role again. In this regard Willi-Plein (1999: 60) infers as follows: 'Allerdings kann auch erwogen werden, daß ein gewissermaßen inoffizieller Brandopferaltar auf dem Areal des zerstörten Tempels bereits unmittelbar nach 587 eingerichtet und während der ganzen Exilszeit von der im Land verbliebenen Bevölkerung unterhalten wurde'. Cf. also Blenkinsopp (1998: 26).

26. Psalm 51.20-21 read as follows: 'Do good to Zion in your good pleasure; rebuild the walls of Jerusalem, then you will delight in right sacrifices, in burnt offerings and whole burnt offerings; then bulls will be offered on your altar' (NRSV).

27. Hossfeld & Zenger (2000: 5) gives an outline of the process of 'Fortschreibung' which took place at the end of the text. Cf. also Becker (1966: 68); Dalglish (1962: 201–7); Schmidt (1994: 346, 358) and Tate (1990: 29–30). For contra-arguments see Leene (1996: 72–3); he regards the text as a unity.

the *anāwim* ('the poor' – 33a) and of the *dôrše Elohîm* ('the god seekers' – 33b) more than the superb sacrificial offerings of their enemies, i.e. their fellow Jewish brethren. This view indeed must have appeased the *anāwim* (33a), since they, as the ones who were seeking God (*dôrše Elohîm* – 33b), had neither the means nor the resources to partake regularly in extensive sacrificial cultic activity[28].

According to Albertz (1994: 518) the social and religious split experienced by the Judahite community in the second half of the fifth century, as the result of the economic crisis, in all probability led to the formation of a special personal piety in the impoverished classes. There is enough evidence indicating the marginalization of these poorer religious classes in the society. This caused the development of a specific kind of personal piety in these classes, viz. the so-called 'piety of the poor'[29]. The most important task of this 'theology of the poor', which was developed and practised in these communities, was to restore dignity as well as hope to the oppressed victims of the social crisis.

The marginalization of these classes indeed would have led to a situation where they celebrated their own services quite separately from the official temple cult (Albertz 1994: 520). We can only hypothesize on the exact place and time of this so-called 'community worship'. However, occasional polemics against sacrificial offerings could be an indication that these services did not take place at the temple in Jerusalem (Albertz 1994: 521). Furthermore, these would also have been services where only liturgies of the word took place. The most important task of this 'theology of the poor', which emerged from and was practised within these communities, was to restore dignity as well as prospects of life for the victims of the social crisis. They may not have had many sacrifices and offerings to contribute to the praise of Yahweh, since they could only lay their miserable existence at Yahweh's feet in order to expect deliverance and a future from him. Furthermore, they regarded themselves as the truly pious (Albertz 1994: 522).

The assumption that they formed the core actually gave them the power to assert themselves within the community of Judah despite their social marginalisation. This assumption is substantiated by the fact that they, as the 'poor', regarded themselves as the real pious, the righteous, the servants, etc. They were thus the real 'god seekers' (69.33b). They indeed even gained influence over the community as a whole with their 'theology

28. Cf. also Albertz (1994: 521); Berges (1999a: 24; 2000a: 14 and 2000b: 175).

29. Ro (2002: 181), however, differs from Albertz in this regard. He infers as follows: 'Zahlreiche Indizien, so der bisherige Befund, deuten daraufhin, daß die entsprechende Menschengruppe trotz der Selbstbezeichnung 'die Armen' etc. eindeutig nicht mit sozio-ökonomisch verelendeten Unterschichtszirkeln in Verbindung zu bringen ist, sondern aus religiös-weisheitlich interessierten und theologisch gebildeten Personen zusammensetzt'.

of the poor'. Moreover, in the later history of Israelite religion the piety of the poor constantly helped religious outsider groups to formulate their will to resist against the dominant social circles and their official theology (Albertz 1994: 522). This influence is, among other things, to be recognized in the redaction of the Psalter, namely in the 'theology of the poor'[30].

It is furthermore stated that the *anāwim* ('poor') – i.e. the real pious – will see, rejoice and their hearts will live (69.33ab) because of the fact that their songs of praise (31b) will please Yahweh more than the perfect sacrificial offering. These cola thus display features of the prophetic texts. Ro (2002: 169) infers that this section concurs with future expectations ('Zukunftserwartungen') as we encounter it in, specifically, the later texts in the *corpus propheticum*. According to these later texts in the *corpus propheticum* it was not anymore the whole of Israel which would survive the final judgement, but only the 'poor' (Isa. 66.2; Zeph. 2.3; 3.12[31]); and then specifically the 'poor' as the real pious (Isa. 66.2), as the righteous (Zeph. 3.13) and as the servants (Isa. 66.14)[32].

4. *Conclusion*

It is thus not surprising that the Psalter is regarded more and more as the prayer and meditation book[33] of the small man/person – i.e. the marginalized – who had a critical view of the post-exilic temple aristocracy

30. We have also come to see their influence in the book of Isaiah. According to Berges (1999b: 175) 'der Gang durch die Armenbelege des Buches Jesaja und des übrigen *corpus propheticum* hat gezeigt, daß sich gerade dieses Buch mit den Armen in besonderer Weise auseinandersetzt...' See also Berges (1999a: 14–27).

31. With regard to these last two texts Ro (2002: 193) infers as follows: 'In der hellenistischen Zeit des 4./3. Jh. v. Chr., in der die an der Armenfrömmigkeit orientierten Texteinheiten des Zefanjabuches verfaßt wurden, war schließlich der Bruch zwischen den unterschiedlichen Strömungen so tiefgreifend, daß die eschatologisch orientierten Kreise nun davon ausing und propagiert, daß die verhaßten Repräsentanten des Temples incl. der in Jerusalem herrschenden Führungsschicht als ganzer wegen ihres hochmütigen, aggressiven und rücksichtslosen Verhaltens aus Jahwes Heilsplan herausgefallen waren (vgl. Zef 2.1–3; 3.11–13)'.

32. Cf. also Ro (2002: 204): '... ist eine nachexilische Frömmigkeitsrichtung zu veranschlagen, die mit ihrem Demuts- und Niedrigkeitsbewußtsein immer wieder und je länger je mehr auf Ablehnung und Feindseligkeit stößt und als Reaktion darauf sich theologisch zunehmend eschatologisch orientiert. Man steht über längere Zeiträume in einer Frontstellung zu politisch maßgeblichen Gruppierungen des judäischen Gemeinwesens, zumal der Tempelführung, denen man diverse Fehlhaltungen vorwirft. In dieser Hinsicht stehen sie ganz eindeutig jenen Gruppierungen sehr nahe, deren ähnliche Konfliktlage in Jes 66 und Zef 3 sowie in bestimmten Texten der Qumran-Essener angesprochen ist'.

33. Braulik (2003: 316). See especially Braulik (2003: 317): 'Knowledge about the Psalter and its popularity is to be explained by the fact that it had been a book of life..., nurturing a

as well as their position of power[34]. The Psalter thus rather functioned as a '*Volksbuch* für Laien..., das als "fromme" und "konservative" *Kurzfassung* von Tora und Nebiim gelesen, gelernt und gelebt werden konnte' (Zenger 1998a: 323). The perception that the Psalter functioned as the cultic songbook of the second temple has thus finally been rejected[35]. The supplicants (redactors) of the psalms thus did not find protection in the cult, first of all, but rather in the praises of the psalms which ascended to Yahweh, the king of the world, who had established his just rule on mount Zion (Berges 1999a: 15). No wonder that it is made clear in this actualizing inscription in Psalm 69 that to praise the name of God (31ab) will please Yahweh more than a perfect sacrificial animal (32).

Bibliography

Albertz, R. 1994 *A history of Israelite religion in the Old Testament period. Vol. I: From the beginnings to the end of the monarchy. Vol. II: From the exile to the Maccabees* (Old Testament Library; London: SCM Press).

Becker, J. 1966 *Israel deutet seine Psalmen* (SBS, 18; Stuttgart: Katholische Bibelwerk).

Berges, U. 1998 *Das Buch Jesaja – Komposition und Endgestalt* (HBS, 16; Freiburg i.B.: Herder).

—1999a *De armen van het boek Jesaja. Een bijdrage tot de literatuurgeschiedenis van het Oude Testament* (Inaugural speech; 5 March 1999; Katholieke Universiteit Nijmegen).

personal and individual piety both before and after the beginning of the Common Era... Modern biblical reasearch has proved that the Psalter is to be understood as a text meant for meditation'.

34.   Cf. also in this regard Ro (2002: 187): 'Auf Grund ihres spezifischen Charackters sind diese Psalmen mit einer nachexilischen Frömmigkeitsrichtung in Verbindung zu bringen, die mit ihren religiösen Überzeugung in eine Frontstellung zu anderen Kreisen des nachexilischen judäischen Gemeinwesens geraten war. Wie diese Frommen diese Frontstellung verstehen, machen sie u.a. auch mit Hilfe der Armentermini als Selbstkennzeichnung deutlich ... Für die Mitglieder dieser Frömmigkeitsrichtung sind die Armentermini eine Art Ehrenzeichnung bzw. 'Markenzeichen', womit sie aus ihrer Sicht einen Sonderstatus vor Gott und der Welt signalisieren wollen: Anders als die Gegenseite, Gruppen der Jerusalemer politischen Spitze und der Tempelführung, halten sie sich wirklich und ausschließlich an Jahwe, als diese 'Armen' sind sie die wirklich 'Gerechten', die 'Knechte' Jahwes; nur diese so praktizierte Haltung der Demut und Selbsterniedrigung wird vor Jahwe Bestand haben und Anerkennung finden'.

35.   Füglister (1988: 337). In this regard Zenger (1998b: 35) infers 'der Psalter als Ganzer (und im übrigen bereits die meisten Teilsammlungen, die in ihm integriert sind) hat *originär* einen nicht-liturgischen und kultunabhängigen "Sitz im Leben"'. See furthermore Braulik (2003: 316): '... it is important to realise that, apart from only a few individual psalms, the Psalter has been used liturgically neither in the Second Temple nor in the early synagogue...'.

—1999b 'Die Armen im Buch Jesaja. Ein Beitrag zur Literaturgeschichte des AT', *Biblica* 80 (2): 153–177.

—2000a Who were the servants? A comparative inquiry in the book of Isaiah and the Psalms, in J.C. de Moor and H.F. van Rooy (eds.), *Past, present, future. The Deuteronomistic history and the prophets* (OTS, XLIV; Leiden: Brill): 1–18.

—2000b 'Die Knechte im Psalter. Ein Beitrag zu seiner Kompositionsgeschichte', *Biblica* 81(2): 153–178.

Blenkinsopp, J. 1998 The Judaean priesthood during the Neo-Babylonian and Achaemenid periods: a hypothetical reconstruction', *CBQ* 60(1): 25–43.

Braulik, G. 1975 *Psalm 40 und der Gottesknecht* (FzB, 18; Würzburg: Echter Verlag).

—2003 'Psalms and liturgy: their reception and contextualisation', *Verbum et Ecclesia* 24/2: 309–332.

Brueggemann, W. 1995 *The Psalms and the life of faith* (Edited by P.D. Miller; Minneapolis: Fortress Press).

Cartledge, T.W. 1992 *Vows in the Hebrew Bible and the Ancient Near East* (JSOT SS, 147; Sheffield: Sheffield Academic Press).

Courtman, N.B. 1995 Sacrifice in the Psalms, in R.T. Beckwith & M.J. Selman (eds.), *Sacrifice in the Bible* (Carlisle: Paternoster Press): 41–58.

Craigie, P.C. 1983 *Psalms 1–50* (WBC, 19; Waco, Texas: Word Books Publisher).

Creach, J.F.D. 1996 *Yahweh as refuge and the editing of the Hebrew Psalter* (JSOT SS, 217; Sheffield: Sheffield Academic Press).

Dalglish, E.R. 1962 *Psalm fifty-one in the light of ancient near eastern patternism* (Leiden: E.J. Brill).

Doeker, A. 2002 *Die Funktion der Gottesrede in den Psalmen. Eine poetologische Untersuchung* (BBB, 135; Berlin: Philo).

Erbele-Küster, D. 2001 *Lesen als Akt des Betens. Eine Rezeptionsästhetik der Psalmen* (WMANT, 87; Neukirchen-Vluyn: Neukirchener Verlag).

Ferris, P.W. (jr). 1992 *The genre of communal lament in the Bible and the Ancient Near East* (SBL DS, 127; Atlanta, Georgia: Scholars Press).

Füglister, N. 1988 Die Verwendung und das Verständnis der Psalmen und des Psalters um die Zeitenwende, in J. Schreiner (Hrsg.), *Beiträge zur Psalmenforschung. Psalm 2 und 22* (FzB, 60; Würzburg: Echter Verlag): 319–384.

Groenewald, A. 2003 *Psalm 69: Its structure, redaction and composition* (Altes Testament und Moderne, 18; Münster: Lit-Verlag).

Gunkel, H. & Begrich, J. 1998 *Introduction to Psalms. The genres of the religious lyric of Israel* (Mercer Library of Biblical Studies; Macon, Georgia: Mercer University Press). (Translated by J.D. Nogalski from the fourth edition of 'Einleitung in die Psalmen: die Gattungen der religiösen Lyrik Israels'. 1. Auflage 1933; [4]1985).

Hieke, T. 2000 Schweigen wäre gotteslästerlich. Klagebete – Auswege aus dem verzweifelten Verstummen, in G. Steins (Hrsg.), *Schweigen wäre gotteslästerlich. Die heilende Kraft der Klage* (Würzburg: Echter Verlag): 45–68.

Hossfeld, F.-L. 1991 Ps 50 und die Verkündigung des Gottesrechts, in F.V. Reiterer (Hrsg.), *Ein Gott eine Offenbarung. Beiträge zur biblischen Exegese, Theologie und Spiritualität* (FS. N. Füglister; Würzburg: Echter Verlag): 83–101.

Hossfeld, F.-L. & Zenger, E. 1993 *Die Psalmen I: 1–50* (NEB, 29; Würzburg: Echter Verlag).

—2000 *Psalmen 51–100* (HThKAT; Freiburg i.B.: Herder).

Jagersma, H. 1994 *A history of Israel to Bar Kochba* (Translated from the Dutch; this edition first published in one volume; London: SCM Press).

Jones, D. 1963 'The cessation of sacrifice after the destruction of the temple in 586 B.C.', *Journal of Theological Studies* 14:12–31.

Kraus, H-J. [4]1972 *Psalmen 1–63* (BKAT, XV/1; Neukirchen-Vluyn: Neukirchener Verlag).

Leene, H. 1996 Personal penitence and the rebuilding of Zion. The unity of Psalm 51, in J. Dyk (ed.), *Give ear to my words. Psalms and other poetry in and around the Hebrew Bible. Essays in honour of Prof. N.A. van Uchelen* (Kampen: Kok Pharos Publishing House): 61–77.

Limbeck, M. 1977 'Die Klage – eine verschwundene Gebetsgattung', *Theologische Quartalschrift* 157:3–16.

Mosis, R. 1992 Die Mauern Jerusalems. Beobachtungen zu Psalm 51,20f, in J. Hausmann & H.-J. Zobel (Hrsg.), *Alttestamentlicher Glaube und biblische Theologie* (FS. H.D. Preuß; Stuttgart: Kohlhammer): 201–15.

Ro, J.U. 2002 *Die sogenannte 'Armenfrömmigkeit' im nachexilischen Israel* (BZAW, 322; Berlin: Walter de Gruyter).

Rofé, A. 1985 Isaiah 66:1-4. Judean sects in the Persian period as viewed by Trito-Isaiah, in A. Kort & S. Morschauser (eds.), *Biblical and related studies presented to Samuel Iwry* (Winona Lake, Indiana: Eisenbrauns): 205–17.

Schmidt, N.F. & Nel, P.J. 2002 'Theophany as type-scene in the Hebrew Bible', *Journal for Semitics* 11(2): 256–81.

Schmidt, W.H. 1994 Individuelle Eschatologie im Gebet – Psalm 51, in K. Seybold & E. Zenger (Hrsg.), *Neue Wege der Psalmenforschung* (FS. W. Beyerlin; HBS, 1; Freiburg i.B.: Herder): 345–60.

Seybold, K. 1996 *Die Psalmen* (HAT, I/15; Tübingen: J.C.B. Mohr [Paul Siebeck]).

Spieckermann, H. 1998 Psalmen und Psalter. Suchbewegungen des Forschens und Betens, in F.G. Martínez & E. Noort (eds), *Perspectives in the study of the Old Testament and early Judaism* (FS. A.S. van der Woude; Supplements to Vetus Testamentum, 73; Leiden: Brill): 137–53.

Stolz, F. 1983 *Psalmen im nachkultischen Raum* (Theologische Studien, 129; Zürich: Theologischer Verlag).

Tate, M.E. 1990 *Psalms 51–100* (WBC, 20; Dallas, Texas: Word).

Tita, H. 2001 *Gelübde als Bekenntnis. Eine Studie zu den Gelübden im Alten Testament* (OBO, 181; Freiburg, Schweiz: Universitätsverlag).

Tournay, R.J. 1991 *Seeing and hearing God with the Psalms. The prophetic liturgy of the second temple in Jerusalem* (Translated by J.E. Crowley; JSOT SS, 118; Sheffield: Sheffield Academic Press).

Tromp, N. 2000 *Psalmen 1–50* (Belichting van het Bijbelboek; 's-Hertogenbosch: Katholieke Bijbelstichting).

Von Rad, G. [4]1962 *Theologie des Alten Testaments. Band I: Die Theologie der geschichtlichen Überlieferungen Israels* (München: Chr. Kaiser Verlag).

Weber, B. 2001 *Werkbuch Psalmen I. Die Psalmen 1 bis 72* (Stuttgart: W. Kohlhammer).

Westermann, C. 1964 Struktur und Geschichte der Klage im Alten Testament, in C. Westermann, *Forschung am Alten Testament. Gesammelte Studien* (Theologische Bücherei, 24; München: Chr. Kaiser Verlag): 266–305 (First published 1954: *ZAW*, 66:44–80).

—1974a Die Rolle der Klage in der Theologie des Alten Testaments, in C. Westermann (Hrsg. R. Albertz & E. Ruprecht), *Forschung am Alten Testament. Gesammelte Studien II* (Theologische Bücherei, 55; München: Chr. Kaiser Verlag): 250–68.

—1974b 'The role of the lament in the theology of the Old Testament', *Interpretation* 28:20–38.

—[5]1977 *Lob und Klage in den Psalmen.* (5. erweiterte Auflage von *Das Loben Gottes in den Psalmen*; Göttingen: Vandenhoeck & Ruprecht).

Willi-Plein, I. 1999 Warum mußte der zweite Tempel gebaut werden?, in B. Ego *et al.* (Hrsg.), *Gemeinde ohne Tempel. Community without temple. Zur Substituierung und Transformation des Jerusalemer Tempels und seines Kults im Alten Testament, antiken Judentum und frühen Christentum.* (Wissenschaftliche Untersuchungen zum Neuen Testament, 118; Tübingen: J.C.B. Mohr [Paul Siebeck]): 57–73.

Zenger, E [3]1998[a] Das Buch der Psalmen, in E. Zenger *et al.* (Hrsg.), *Einleitung in das Alte Testament* (Studienbücher Theologie, 1,1; Stuttgart: W. Kohlhammer): 309–326.

—1998b Der Psalter als Buch, in E. Zenger (Hrsg.), *Der Psalter im Judentum und Christentum* (HBS, 18; Freiburg i.B.: Herder): 1–57.

PSALM 136:
A LITURGY WITH REFERENCE TO CREATION AND HISTORY

Dirk J. Human
Pretoria, RSA

1. *Introduction*

In the late Jewish tradition, according to the Talmud and other rabbinical writings, the picturesque Psalm 136 with its profound content is known as the *Hallel ha-Gadôl*, the Great Hallel (Oesterley 1939: 542)[1]. Due to the introductory (1–3) and concluding (26) imperative summons to praise and give thanks to Yahweh, Psalm 136 participates in the gallery of five 'Hôdû-psalms' (Pss. 105–107; 118; 136) in order to portray appreciation for the character and deeds of Yahweh, the God of Israel.

Among other hymnic collections, like the Egyptian Hallel (Pss. 113–118) and the final Hallel (Pss. 146–150) this poem surpasses the number of exaltations or thanksgiving proclamations of other collections by the repetition of its exclamatory and monotonous refrain: 'for his steadfast love endures forever'. Twenty six times these praise utterances become audible in the voices of appreciative Yahweh believers[2].

With a predominantly hymnic character in a litany-fashioned structure, Psalm 136 tends to reflect imitations of similar praise songs in Qumran[3] and in deutero-canonical texts, like the Song of the three youths in the fiery furnace (Dan. 3.52-90) or the praise litany in the prayer of Ben Sirach (Eccl. 51.12). Other extra-biblical parallels with similar refrains are visible in a hymn dedicated to El (Obermann 1936: 21–44) or praises sung to the Babylonian god Marduk, the god Ninurta or to the Egyptian pharaoh Sesostris III (Van der Ploeg 1974: 417). These litanies of praise, petition or lament contain constant and repetitive refrains that are uttered in reciprocal interaction between an officiant and a group or between various congregant groups. Like Psalm 136, they were probably part of liturgical rituals during religious worship.

In Psalm 136, the enumeration of Yahweh's extraordinary qualities and his wondrous deeds (miracles) in the first half of every verse alternates with an antiphonal refrain in the second part of the verse. This refrain renders a

---

1. According to the Talmud and Midrash three possibilities on the compass of the Great Hallel are given: 1) Psalm 136 alone; 2) Psalms 135–136, because of their close literary and theological interrelationship, see also König (1927: 451); and 3) Psalms 120–136.

2. In Psalm 118.1-4 this phrase only appears four times.

3. See the refrain after each verse in Psalm 145 (IIQPs[a]).

unique compositional and artistic character to the psalm. It tends to be the text's most outstanding and dominant stylistic feature. Despite similarities with the pattern of the previous psalm, Psalm 136's structure is unparalleled in the Psalter.

What seems to be a wearisome repetition of an antiphonal refrain ultimately binds the various depictions of Yahweh into a coherent whole. The phrase 'for his steadfast love endures forever', in combination with a preceding description functions like an illuminated, revolving diamond, that gradually radiates the multifaceted image of Yahweh's acts and attributes from different angles. Every addition of the refrain builds up a series of experiences that contribute to the everlasting character of Yahweh's 'steadfast love'.

2. Text and structure

2.1 Introduction

The Hebrew text of Psalm 136 is well preserved and transmitted. It offers intelligible text readings. With the exception of verses 4, 9, 12 and 15, a constant metrical pattern is apparent. It is only verses 9 and 15 which could be subjected to text-critical revision, when considering metrical reasons.

It is suggested that וכוכבים ('and stars') in verse 9 should be omitted because of the verse's unbalanced metre in comparison with the rest of the poem. Moreover, the plural form לממשלות ('for dominion/to govern') should accordingly be altered to the singular form לממשלת. A further argument for this textual alteration is that 'the stars' might be a later addition to the text because they are not indicated as co-regents of the night in Genesis 1.16, to which Psalm 136.9 probably alludes. The stars are only mentioned in the Genesis text (1.16) in addition to the moon, which is noted as the sole governor of the night. In the same manner, suggestions prevail that the noun וחילו ('and his army') in verse 15 should be omitted for metrical reasons. However, as it is impossible for the reader to ascertain the author's intention in his application of metrical patterns, I am prevented from accepting any of the above-mentioned text-critical suggestions. The Masoretic text is clear without any text-critical intervention and therefore need not be altered.

2.2 Translation

The following translation offers a possible understanding of the text and also suggests a possible structure in the discourse:

1   Give thanks to the LORD, for he   *for his love endures forever.*
       is good,

2	Give thanks to the God of gods,	*for his love endures forever.*
3	Give thanks to the Lord of lords,	*for his love endures forever.*
4	to him who alone does great wonders,	*for his love endures forever.*
5	who by his understanding made the heavens,	*for his love endures forever.*
6	who spread out the earth upon the waters,	*for his love endures forever.*
7	who made the great lights,	*for his love endures forever.*
8	the sun to govern the day,	*for his love endures forever.*
9	the moon and stars to govern the night;	*for his love endures forever.*
10	to him who struck down the first-born of Egypt,	*for his love endures forever.*
11	and brought Israel out from among them,	*for his love endures forever.*
12	with a mighty hand and outstretched arm,	*for his love endures forever.*
13	to him who divided the Reed Sea,	*for his love endures forever.*
14	and brought Israel through the midst of it,	*for his love endures forever.*
15	but swept Pharaoh and his army into the Reed Sea,	*for his love endures forever.*
16	to him who led his people through the desert,	*for his love endures forever.*
17	who struck down great kings,	*for his love endures forever.*
18	and killed mighty kings,	*for his love endures forever.*
19	Sihon king of the Amorites,	*for his love endures forever.*
20	and Og king of Bashan,	*for his love endures forever.*
21	and gave their land as an inheritance,	*for his love endures forever.*
22	an inheritance to his servant Israel;	*for his love endures forever.*
23	to the One who remembered us in our low estate,	*for his love endures forever.*
24	and freed us from our adversaries,	*for his love endures forever.*
25	who gives food to every creature.	*for his love endures forever.*

26   Give thanks to the God of   *for his love endures forever.*
      heaven.

2.3 *Structure*

2.3.1 *Introduction*. The stylistic structure of Psalm 136 has been widely debated[4]. Several suggestions have been made to divide the text into smaller units. My own literary analysis will show that the poem can be divided into three-verse strophes, with the exception of verses 16-22 and the concluding summons in verse 26. The strophes link together to form larger or smaller stanzas. An imperatival frame (1–3; 26) embraces the central body (4–25) of the psalm.

Besides the regular occurrence of the refrain 'for his steadfast love endures forever' throughout the text, the other most prominent characteristic features are the repetition of *Leitworte* and the participle finite verbs. Several words and phrases are repeated in order to establish cohesion or to enhance the theological meaning of certain key concepts in the psalm. Prominent examples include: 1. הודו ('give thanks to' in 1–3; 26); לעשה ('to him who does' in 4; 5; 7); למכה ('to him who struck' in 10; 17); השמים ('the heavens' in 5; 26); הארץ/ארצם ('the earth/their land' in 6; 21); גדלים/גדלות ('great' in 4; 7; 17); ישראל ('Israel' in 11; 14; 22); ים־ סוף ('Reed Sea' in 13; 15); מלכים/מלך ('kings/king' in 17; 18; 19; 20); and נחלה ('inheritance' in 21; 22).

Both the literary and the cultic traditions make their presence felt in the text. A traditio-historical analysis illuminates how cultic and literary motives are shared with other psalms. In addition, similar motives fashioned by Deuteronomy or the deuteronomists[5] seem to be evident, while the content of Pentateuchal[6] and Priestly texts[7] was also known to the text's composer(s).

Mythological allusions[8] function subtly, albeit sporadically and mostly to contribute to the polemic character that sometimes prevails in the text. Striking resemblances are apparent between Psalms 136 and 135 regarding

---

4. Allen (1983: 231–232) gives an outline of important contributors in the discussion.
5. Compare verse 2 with Deuteronomy 10.27; verse 11 with Deuteronomy 1.27; 4.20; 5.15; verse 12 with Deuteronomy 4.34; 5.15; 7.19; 9.29; 11.2; 26.8; 1 Kings 8.42; 2 Kings 17.36; verse 16 with Deuteronomy 8.15; 32.10; verse 19 with Deuteronomy 2.33; verse 22 with Deuteronomy 32.36; verses 17-18 with Joshua 12, see also Keil & Delitzsch (1973: 329).
6. Compare verse 10 with Exodus 11–12; verse 11 with Exodus 7.5; 18.1; 20.1; verse 12 with Exodus 6.1, 6; verse 13 with Exodus 14.16-31 (especially 16-17 and 21); verse 14 with Exodus 14.22; verse 15 with Exodus 14.27; verses 17-22 with Numbers 21.21-24, 33-35.
7. Compare verses 7-9 with Genesis 1.14-16.
8. Compare verses 2-3; 5-6; 13 and 15.

structure and subject-matter[9]. It should be determined individually, whether or not a motive or a verse of Psalm 136 is in each instance directly dependent on traditions outside these psalms. In most instances, the probability of direct dependence is questionable, but a dependence on common traditions is more likely to be the case (Weiser 1979: 547; Loretz 1979: 313–314).

Psalm 136 purports various hymnic descriptions that extol Yahweh's endless steadfast love (חסדו). This descriptive praise of Yahweh, which is in all instances connected to his חסד, constitutes the basic theme of the psalm, the thanksgiving praise of Yahweh for his qualities and deeds in creation and history. Apart from the summons in the introductory (1–3) and concluding (26) parts of the psalm to give thanks to this most High God, the central parts comprise of motivation(s) for the summons (4–22) as well as a concrete application (23–25) of God's deliverance in the current community of believers.

The first stanza, which motivates the initial call for hymnic thanksgiving addresses God's universal activities, especially his deeds during the creation (4–9). In the following stanza (10–22), descriptions of Yahweh's particular involvement in the history of Israel motivate the same summons from a different viewpoint, while the last stanza (23–25) describes how Yahweh delivered the current generation of believers, the 'we', from a similar life-endangering situation. A resumption of God's universal activities culminates in a reference to his provisional care for all creatures. Ultimately a renewed call to thank Yahweh as the God of the heavens is uttered (26).

To summarise, the extraordinary deeds of Yahweh during creation and throughout Israelite history provide enough reason for the worshipping community to revere him and give him thanksgiving praise. Through a cultic re-enactment and remembrance of Yahweh's past performances in ritual or in exclamatory response and narration, Yahweh's goodness is relived and revived in the communion of Israelite believers.

2.3.2 *Text analysis*
2.3.2.1 *Introit: Summons for hymnic thanksgiving (1–3).* In resonance with the threefold acclamation of reverence in Isaiah 6, the psalm commences with a threefold summons. With a typical liturgical formula (Ridderbos 1950: 15; Anderson 1972: 894; Seybold 1996: 507)[10], 'Give thanks to the

---

9. The structure of Psalm 135 also follows a pattern of Psalm 136: An introduction and conclusion form a framework consisting of calls for praise of Yahweh (1-3; 19-21), while the body part provides reasons why Yahweh should be praised. Regarding the content, compare Psalm 136.10 with 135.8; 136.15 with 135.9; 136.17-22 with 135.10-12.

10. See also 1 Chronicles 16.34; 2 Chronicles 5.13; 20.21; Psalms 100.4-5; 105.1; 106.1; 107.1; 117.2; 118.1, 29; Ezra 3.11; Jeremiah 33.11.

LORD, for he is good, for his love endures forever', the Israelite
worshipping community is called to render hymnic thanksgiving to
Yahweh. Even the motivation for this challenge כי טוב ('for He is good')
was most probably a cultic shout (Gerstenberger 2001: 384)[11]. Then a
liturgical interplay between a precentor and community or between a
(Levitical) choir and the congregation might be assumed[12]. In response to
the challenge of the calling voices, the repetitive refrain builds a gallery of
witnesses to give expression to Israel's collected experiences of Yahweh's
חסד.

Psalm 136 reflects the typical structure of a hymn[13]. Three imperatives of
the same verb (ידה), in each instance followed by the dative preposition ל
('for/to') with the particle כי[14] and a further description, link verses 1-3
syntactically together as a strophic unit. Yahweh is the object of the
congregation's response in verses 4-25, but his name does not appear
again, until the final hymnic summons. The preposition ל in combination
with the finite verbs in the rest of the poem (4-7; 10; 13; 16-17) links the
imperative summons syntactically with Yahweh as the described object of
praise. Verses 4-22 are governed by these imperatives. Both the imperative
forms and divine titles in verses 1-3 and 26 position the content of the
psalm within a hymnic framework, by means of an inclusion.

The two epithets 'God of the gods' and 'Lord of the lords' (2-3) most
probably allude to polytheistic polemics in the earlier developmental
phases of these expressions. Against the interpretation of this polytheistic
background, these titles appear to proclaim the supremacy of Yahweh as
the Highest God. Since several indicators in the psalm suggest a post-exilic
date for its final composition, the absolute monotheistic nature of the
Yahweh faith during this epoch of Israelite history gives a superlative
function to these titles. While alluding to the mythological image of an
ancient Near-Eastern pantheon, these titles might have been part of the
Jerusalem cult traditions in order to describe Yahweh as the undisputed,
incomparable and only reigning God[15]. His power and the domain of his
reign are soon unveiled in the psalm.

11.   See also Psalms 52.11; 54.8; 69.17; Nahum 1.7.
12.   Because of the uncertain identity of the liturgical participants, the ambiguity of
possibilities should be respected. Either the whole congregation or all the representatives
(choir) could have responded to the call of a priest or the Levitical representatives (choir).
Time and circumstances could have varied the scene and voices. In Babylonian texts the
second part of the verse was usually sung by a priestly choir, see König (1927: 452).
13.   Spieckerman (2003: 144) prefers the notion of an antiphonic hymn.
14.   This particle could either be interpreted as a causal indicator ('for') or with an
emphatic assertive meaning ('yes/indeed').
15.   See also Deuteronomy 10.17; Psalm 50.1; 95.3; 96.4; 97.9; 135.5. The Babylonian god
Marduk was also honoured with the title 'Lord of lords', see Gunkel (1926: 577).

2.3.2.2 *Yahweh, the God of creation (4-9)*. In two separate strophic units (4-6; 7-9), each introduced with the hymnic participle clause לעשה ('to him who does/make') and the adjective גדול ('great') the extraordinarily wondrous deeds of Yahweh during the creation are listed. Both strophes are syntactically and stylistically bound in a three-verse pattern. A descriptive introductory phrase on Yahweh's creative performances (4 and 7) is followed by a depiction of two opposites or pairs – the heavens and earth, sun and moon, day and night. Hence, this stanza (4-9), as a whole, is a eulogy (Gerstenberger 2001: 384) to the creative powers of Yahweh, while the verb עשה ('to make') and participle descriptions constitute literary cohesion in the stanza.

The 'great wonders' or miracles (נפלאות) for which Yahweh is responsible (4) describe both his creative and redemptive activities[16] according to Old Testament traditions. It is further a *Leitbegriff* of the hymn (Seybold 1996: 507) and tends to be a summation of all the forthcoming divine deeds depicted in verses 4-25. In relation to the polytheistic allusions in verses 2-3, the indication that Yahweh performs these deeds alone (לבדו)[17] expresses his unique character in comparison to the other (heavenly) powers and gods. He, alone, created the heavens and earth, including the astral bodies like the sun, moon and the stars. A polemical atmosphere can be detected in the stanza, as the attributes of Yahweh are depicted in contrast with ancient Near-Eastern beliefs in the power of deified heavenly bodies. Psalm 136 devalues the latter as being mere creations of the Supreme God, Yahweh, and lacking his power.

The mythological tripartite world-view of a three-story building with the heavens, the earth and water under the earth comes to the fore in verses 5-6. A different creation account of the earth occurs in verse 6, which is in contrast to the priestly writings of Genesis 1.9. In the former the earth is spread out over the subterranean waters[18], while the latter describes the appearance of the dry land as a result of the waters that Yahweh has gathered together under the sky. Allusions to the priestly narrative of Genesis 1.14-16 also appear to reflect the authors' independent use and application of other literary and cultic traditions in the text. For example, the expression 'lights' (אורים) in verse 7 is a *hapax legomenon* in the Old Testament and differs from the המארת in Genesis 1.16. Moreover, in Psalm 136 the stars become co-regents of the moon, while in Genesis 1.16, however, the small light alone governs the night. Nonetheless, Yahweh's

---

16. See Exodus 34.10; Joshua 3.5; Job 5.9; 37.5, 14; 42.3; Psalms 72.18; 78.4,11; 86.10; 96.3; 98.1; 105.5; 106.7, 22; 107.8, 15, 21, 24, 31; 119.18; Daniel 11.36; Micah 7.15.
17. See Psalms 72.18; 86.10 and Isaiah 2.11.
18. See Psalm 24.2; Isaiah 42.5; 44.24.

dominion, greatness and power over space and time are underscored in the references to his creative endeavours.

Echoes of cultic formulas are apparent in verses 5-6. In liturgical and prophetical contexts, the formula 'Yahweh, maker of heaven and earth' was probably used as part of a blessing formula, or a confession to celebrate God's power (Habel 1972: 333)[19]. In a similar way, the description 'to him who spread out the earth' in verse 6 stems from a cultic hymnic tradition in which praise is given to Yahweh (Ludwig 1973: 347–349)[20]. Ultimately, the undertone of both verses adds a hymnic element to Yahweh's inequitable power of creation.

In verses 4-9, this creative power thus underpins Yahweh's steadfast love and serves as the motivation as to why believers should give thanks via the hymn.

2.3.2.3 Yahweh, the God of Israel's history (10–22). Verses 10-22 consist of two stanzas (10-15; 16-22) that can further be divided into four strophic units (10-12; 13-15; 16-18; 19-22). Each strophe becomes a pit stop alongside the racing track of Israel's salvation history, where Yahweh's powerful involvement in his servant's life is upheld, e.g., Israel's exodus from Egypt (10-12), the deliverance at the Reed Sea (13-15), Yahweh's guidance and protection in the desert (16-18), as well as Yahweh's donation of the great kings' land as inheritance to Israel (19-22).

God's salvation activities during the Egyptian exodus and the entry into the Promised Land constitute the foundational pillars of this history. Emphasis on these two tradition historical themes amid the absence of the Sinai tradition alludes to the course of events described in the so-called 'small historical credo' of Deuteronomy 26.5 and 6.20. Our psalm's additional references to the creation (4-9) and the desert wanderings (16) are characteristic of its own style, yet also reminiscent of other texts that breathe a hymnic or confessional character[21].

The relationship between Psalms 135 and 136 becomes particularly evident in these two stanzas[22]. Suggestions that both psalms stem from one author (Van der Ploeg 1974: 418), or that Psalm 135 is dependent on Psalm 136, seem rather unconvincing in view of the obvious literary and context-based differences between the two psalms. The dependence of 136 on 135 is more possible, but also dubious. Instead, it is likely that both psalms

19.   Genesis 14.19; Psalms 115.15; 121.2; 124.8, 134.3; 146.5, 6a.
20.   The formula was preserved only in Deutero-Isaiah (Isa. 40.22; 45.12; 51.13) and in Psalm 136.
21.   See Psalms 78; 105; 135; Exodus 15; Joshua 24.
22.   Compare Psalm 136.10 with 135.8; 136.15 with 135.9; 136.17-18 with 135.10; 136.19-20 with 135.11; and 136.21-22 with 135.12.

developed independently, based on a common oral or written tradition[23].

The first strophe of this stanza (10-12) recalls with eclectic descriptions, the wondrous deeds of Yahweh during Israel's deliverance from Egyptian slavery. The descriptions are reminiscent of the narrative in Exodus 11–12. As with the commencement in previous strophes, verse 10 is introduced by the preposition ל and a participle description. Verses 10 and 11 are not only syntactically bound by a conjunction particle *waw*, but, from an Israelite perspective, Yahweh's redemptive deeds are first described in relation to Egypt (10) and then to Israel (11) – he struck down the enemy, but then led Israel out of distress and danger. In the deuteronomic-deuteronomistic tradition, verse 12 describes the means by which these powerful deeds were accomplished – with a strong hand and an outstretched arm. These are anthropomorphic symbols expressing Yahweh's power and protection.

In the second strophe of this stanza (13-15), the division of the Reed Sea and Yahweh's victory over Pharaoh and his army are proclaimed. Commencing with the preposition ל and a participle verb, the unit forms a coherent whole. Cohesion is created via an inclusion featuring the term ים־סוף ('Reed Sea') in verses 13 and 15, while the two *waw*-conjunctive particles in verses 14 and 15 bind all three verses together syntactically. On a poetic or synchronic level, Israel's safe journey through the life-endangering waters is given a picturesque depiction with the two references to the Reed Sea (13, 15) surrounding Israel's name (14). Traditio-historically, all three verses allude to Exodus 14, the Pentateuch's narration of Israel's journey through the Reed Sea[24].

In this context, the expression גזר ים־סוף לגזרים (13) deserves to be mentioned. In comparison with texts like Genesis 15.17 and 1 Kings 3.25 where the verb גזר occurs, one can infer that the verb means 'to cut into pieces'. The interpretation that Yahweh has divided the Reed Sea by cutting it into pieces has both polemical and theological implications. The presentation clearly alludes to the mythological *Drachenkampf* struggle in Ugarit (Deissler 1964: 529; Kraus 1978: 1080) or the cutting of Tiamat's body into pieces by the god Marduk, according to the Babylonian Enuma Elish epic[25]. Immediately, a polemic between the powers of the Canaanite and Babylonian gods on the one hand and Yahweh on the other is at stake. The author(s) of Psalm 136 are in no doubt that Yahweh has supreme power. In Israel's primary salvation experience at the Reed Sea, his power exceeds all other chaos powers, as well as the power of other ancient Near-

23. Cf. Loretz (1979: 313–314) for a synopsis of the differences and his similar conclusion.

24. Compare 136.13 with Exodus 14.16-31 especially 16ff. and 21; 136.14 with Exodus 14.22; 136.15 with Exodus 14.22.

25. Cf. Hallo & Younger (1997: 398) for the Enuma Elish epic on Tablet IV/135.

Eastern gods. Hence, Yahweh deserves thanksgiving praise from the
congregation for this victorious power.

   In the first strophe of the unit's second stanza, verses 16-18 portray
God's guidance of Israel in the desert and his wars with the kings. The
wandering of Israel through the desert was, as in the case of the Reed Sea,
similarly endangered by threatening powers, namely the kings of the other
nations. Repetition of the plural noun מלכים ('kings') and the parallel
descriptions of Yahweh's slaying actions relate verses 17-18 to each other.
Again, the hymnic participles with the preposition ל and a participle verb,
link verses 16 with 17.

   In verses 19-22, a detailed focus on the warlords and on the result of the
wars are presented. These verses appear to have a strong relationship to
the previous strophe (16–18), given the repetition of the noun מלך ('king')
in both verses and because of the tradition-historical relationship of these
verses to Psalm 135. Both Sihon, king of Heshbon and Og, the king of
Bashan are exemplary prototypes of enemies in Israel's history and serve as
defeated legendary adversaries[26]. They might even be interpreted as
legendary heroes or mythological figures with superhuman powers[27], but
Yahweh's victory over them in the Trans-Jordanian region illustrates his
power over these endangering historical forces. It further confirms his
supreme divine lordship in consecutive hopeless and life-threatening
situations throughout his people's existence.

   Through the author's use of stylistic features like anadiplosis and
repetition of the noun נחלה ('inheritance'), verses 21 and 22 are linked to
focus on the land Yahweh granted Israel as an inheritance. The psalmist's
application of the term הארץ at this point in the text is significant. The ארץ
('earth') that God has established with his creative powers (6) has been
taken from the kings (21) by this warrior God, using his powers of
salvation. He did this in order to give ארצם ('their land') to Israel. Israel
received the land from Yahweh, but, in their relationship to him, the final
depiction of Israel in verse 22 as עבדו ('his servant'), describes their role in
this land[28]. It is here that they should exercise their servitude to Yahweh,
the Creator and Giver of the land[29]. In the context of the psalm, this
servitude implies a demeanour of giving praise, because Yahweh has
turned their Egyptian slavery into a situation where they can serve him as
servants. Therefore, the liturgy calls on believers to give Yahweh
thanksgiving and praise.

---

   26.   Gerstenberger (2001: 387) portrays these figures as 'examples for the multitude of
other local kings' (Deuteronomy 1.4; 2.26–3.11; 29.6; 31.4; Judges 11.19-22).
   27.   Gerstenberger (2001: 387) also refers to Joshua 13.12 for this.
   28.   Seybold (1996: 508) regards verse 22 as the climax of the hymn.
   29.   See Israel as servant in Isaiah 41.8; 44.1, etc.

2.3.2.4 *Contemporary application (23-25)*. In the last strophic unit of the psalm (23-25) the reader encounters a sudden change in language and style. Previous third person descriptions make room for the first person plural ('we'). A relative clause introduced by verse 23 and a lack of the usual preposition ל as introduction to the participle finite verb נתן (25) characterize these three verses in distinction to previous strophes. A syntactic continuation between verses 23 and 24 is therefore apparent because of the first person plural references.

Both verses reflect a contemporary experience for believers from a later period in Israel's history, probably from a late post-exilic[30] date. If these verses bear witness to a later addition to the text, they are probably an application confirming the current believers' salvation experience of the same God of creation and history, but at a later stage. If the verses were part of the original psalm they testify to a later date for the text as a whole.

It follows that the 'low estate' (23) in which the present generation finds itself in, expresses a life-threatening situation where the 'we' are endangered by adversaries[31]. Obvious wordplay between מצרינו ('our adversaries') of 24 in relation to מצרים ('Egypt') in verse 10 suggests that the current danger is similar to the suffering of the slavery in Egypt and the submission to the Pharaoh. The primary danger of Israel's experience in Egypt is repeated, and the enemies are defeated again. This ensures that Yahweh's deeds of salvation show a continuous (everlasting) character. Yahweh has delivered his congregation from their Egyptian-like situation. The chiasm between verses 23 and 24 not only underscores the changing fate and circumstances of the present believers, but Yahweh's remembrance of his people also finds a parallel description in his acts of deliverance.

Verse 25 resumes in a hymnic fashion the description of the universal role of Yahweh as the One who cares and provides for all creatures. After his particular involvement in Israelite history (10-22), Yahweh now provides for all flesh[32], an indication of his concern for the entire creation and not only for the people of Israel. He is not only the God of Israel, but the universal God of All.

---

30. Evidence for such a late date might be sought in the late relative clause ש (23); the term שפל (23) that is only known from the late text of Ecclesiastes 10.6; and the verb פרק (24) which was a well-known term in Aramaic, see Delitzsch (1973: 331) and Allen (1983: 231).

31. Different suggestions are made to allocate this 'low state' of the so-called 'we'. Possibilities include events from the Judges period; happenings during the reign of David; the Babylonian exile and return (Lam. 5.8); or events from the occupation of the land Canaan to the Persian period.

32. See Psalms 104.27-28; 145.15; 146.7.

2.3.2.5 *Final summons to bring thanks (26)*. The last verse of the Psalm 136 (26) repeats the summons of 1-26 to give Yahweh thanks. It is part of the imperative framework of the text. The divine epithet 'God of the heavens' is a *hapax legomenon* in the Psalms and originates from a relatively late date, probably from the Persian period[33]. Such a late date could support the assumption that the verse might be linked to the previous strophe as a later addition to the text. By using this epithet, the exalted nature and supreme divinity of Yahweh are emphatically emphasized.

2.4 *Cultic setting*
From the textual analysis it is evident that the *Sitz im Leben* of Psalm 136 belongs to the cult. Definite traces of liturgical elements in Israelite worship can be seen. Cultic formulas like the summons to praise (1-3, the liturgical shouts or interruptions (1), a liturgical *responsorium* (1-26), the change from summons to compliance (1-26) and the alternation between speakers of two groups, or between an officiant and the congregation are all indications of the psalm's cultic function (Mowinckel 1962: 83; Westermann 1989: 271). Especially the so-called *Wechsellieder* (alternating songs) with the *Kehrvers* (response) were characteristic of Israelite liturgy (Gunkel & Begrich 1933: 404).

Although the alternation of voices in the Israelite cult was an artistic, intentional, and artificial means of expression in a psalm, it entails more than mere poetic strategy to the addition of aesthetic value. In the liturgy, the participation of the congregants expresses a relationship bound to divinity and a way of communion and communication with Yahweh, who gives life. In the lively re-enactment of the liturgy's content, the believer's experience of the divine is revived, while the hope and faith in Yahweh, the God of creation and history rekindled.

The exact ceremonies of cultic worship service or festive occasions for the recital of Psalm 136 remain ambiguous. Various suggestions only state possibilities for the performance of this liturgy. They include the following:

The Hallel was traditionally associated with the Jewish Passover Feast (Anderson 1972: 893; Kraus 1978: 1079), because of the text's commemoration of the Exodus events. These events include the killing of the first-born Egyptian sons (10), the redemption and protection of Israel (11-12), the division of the Reed Sea (13) and the defeat of Pharaoh and his army (14-15). Although the exodus events and Yahweh's salvation acts play a crucial role in the psalm, it might be problematic to fix this liturgical celebration of Yahweh's power of creation and salvation to the cultic setting of the Passover alone. It was certainly not the only venue for the

---

33. The title 'God of heavens' appears in Ezra 1.2; 5.11; 6.9; 7.12; Nehemiah 1.4; 2.4; 2 Chronicles 36.23; Jonah 1.9; Daniel 2.18 which allude to a Persian period.

recital of this liturgy, but sincerely a very important cultic *Sitz im Leben* in terms of the cultic tradition, to celebrate Yahweh's supreme divine power and his victory over other threatening powers.

Another suggestion (Oesterley 1939: 543) is the New Year festival in autumn. With the beginning of the New Year Yahweh's activities in creation and in Israel's history are commemorated. His capabilities and his power serve as a source of hope and trust in God, should dangerous situations arise in the coming year. After the exile this feast was celebrated by the Israelites, probably in spring and autumn.

The Feast of the Tabernacles is another possibility. According to 2 Chronicles 7.3 and 6 the recital of the formula 'for he is good, for his love endures forever' is accompanied by cultic gestures like prostration[34]. Along with elements such as God's guidance, protection and provision (aspects that can be traced in the text), the re-enactment of Psalm 136 could well find a suitable cultic *Sitz* during this festival of the Booths.

Some scholars (Schmidt 1934: 240; Weiser 1962: 793) are convinced that this psalm, because of its close relationship to Psalm 135 and a climactic emphasis on verse 25 ('he who gives food to every creature'), belongs to the liturgy of the harvest festival in autumn. It is questionable, though, to assign special emphasis to verse 25 alone if the structure of the psalm does not require it. Aspects of creation and salvation history like the Exodus and Yahweh's bestowal of the land, deserve equal importance in the interpretation of the psalm and its structure.

The character of the psalm probably allows for the liturgy to be recited on the morning of the Sabbath (Deissler 1964: 529). As a hymn with a thanksgiving character this is quite possible.

Despite all these possibilities there is no thrust for fixing the text to a single cultic *Sitz im Leben* in terms of the cultic tradition. To give thanks to Yahweh by means of praise, especially where his character and deeds are concerned, anticipates many cultic occasions where he could be exalted with this litany-structured liturgy. This life-bringing recitation and re-enactment of Yahweh's deeds of creation and salvation should not in any way be restricted to single events. The various above-mentioned suggestions confirm this.

2.5 *Possible date for Psalm 136*

To date a psalm as a whole is always problematic. Psalm 136 is no exception. Even if parts of a psalm allude to an early or to a later date it is not imperative to date the whole text accordingly. The oral tradition or gradual growth of the written text is dated with great difficulty.

---

34. See also Psalms 95.2; 99.5.

However, several indicators in Psalm 136 allude to a post-exilic date. Although older cultic and literary traditions (5-6) are audible in the psalm the final text might have been fixed at the end of the fifth, beginning of the fourth century BC. The text's allusions to the Pentateuch, especially to the priestly writings and the Exodus tradition, are obvious. The contemporary reliving of the primary Israelite salvation experience (23-24) speaks for a later post-exilic dating of the psalm. Even the epithet in verse 26 alludes to descriptions that belong to the Persian period. In view of this, but with the awareness that the entire psalm should not be dealt with in a homogenous way, a possible date for the text might be the end of the fifth or beginning of the fourth century BC.

3. *Concluding remarks*

Psalm 136 is a litany in which elements of the thanksgiving hymn give expression to the celebration of the character and deeds of Yahweh. If this static poem is translated and transferred into a vivid and lively situation it becomes intelligible as a liturgy in the cult. It is here, where a responding voice continuously replies to voices that call on believers to give Yahweh praise and to describe his character and wondrous deeds. As a basic attitude reflected by Old Testament theology's understanding of man's destiny, the praising of God forms the kernel of the relationship between Yahweh and Israel, or between God and man (Janowski 2003: 126–127).

In the liturgy a series of experiences emphasize the perpetual or everlasting character of Yahweh's חסד ('loyal love'). In a polemical way, Yahweh is being portrayed as the God of the gods, who displays incomparable power throughout creation and history. His deeds in creation and history emphasize that he is the supreme God, who delivered his people from dangerous and life-threatening situations.

For Israel this deliverance did not remain a mere fact of the past. Time and again the Israelites have experienced God's power in consecutive situations of hopelessness. Even a contemporary application of the present congregation confirms that Yahweh has turned their current Egyptian-like experience on its head. Israel has repeatedly experienced the primary salvation deed of Yahweh that he performed at the Reed Sea. To use the conceptualized words of the psalm itself (23-24), it was through his remembrance of 'us' that He rescued 'us' in a 'low estate'.

God's remembrance of Israel calls for the remembrance of him by his people, the servants of Israel. Because they have experienced Yahweh's love in creation and in history they owe him a special service. This service can in various ways and in various traditions be kept alive and brought to the fore through repetitive and hymnic thanksgiving. All God's remembrances relate to the bundle of חסד experiences for which all believers should show gratitude.

Today, a reinterpretation of the psalm and the cultic circumstances might result in various creative ways to praise God in the liturgy and to keep his wondrous deeds in creation and history alive. These deeds, which, for the Christian congregation, are confirmed in and through the life of Jesus Christ, should be enumerated in creative ways through the various elements of worship. Then Yahweh's servants will not only express their gratitude as a result of his חסד which they always experience, in addition, they will keep alive the faith in the incomparable God of gods.

Bibliography

Allen, L.C. 1983 *Psalms 101–150* (Word Biblical Commentary, 21; Waco, Texas: Word).

Anderson, A.A. 1972 *The Book of Psalms* (Vol. II. The New Century Bible Commentary. Grand Rapids, MI.: WB Eerdmans).

Baethgen, D.F. 1904 *Die Psalmen übersetzt und erklärt* (Göttingen: Vandenhoeck und Ruprecht).

Bazak, J. 1985 'The geometric-figurative structure of Psalm CXXXVI', *Vetus Testamentum* 35: 129–138.

Burden, J.J. 1991 *Psalms 120–150* (Kaapstad: NG Kerkuitgewers).

Crüsemann, F. 1969 *Studien zur Formgeschichte von Hymnus und Danklied* (WMANT, 32; Neukirchen-Vluyn: Neukirchener Verlag).

Deissler, A. 1964 *Die Psalmen* (Düsseldorf: Patmos Verlag).

De Liagre Böhl, F.M.Th. & Gemser, B. 1968 *De Psalmen* (Tekst en Uitleg; Nijkerk: Callenbach).

Duhm, D.B. 1922 *Die Psalmen* (Kurzer Handkommentar zum Alten Testament. Bd. XIV Tübingen: Mohr [Siebeck]).

Gerstenberger, E.S. 2001 *Psalms Part 2 and Lamentations* (The Forms of the Old Testament Literature. Volume XV. Grand Rapids, MI.: WB Eerdmans).

Gunkel, H. 1926 *Die Psalmen übersetzt und erklärt* (Göttinger Handkommentar zum Alten Testament. Göttingen: Vandenhoeck & Ruprecht).

Gunkel, H. & Begrich, J. 1933 *Einleitung in die Psalmen. Die Gattungen der religiösen Lyrik Israels* (Göttingen: Vandenhoeck & Ruprecht).

Habel, N.C. 1972 '"Yahweh, Maker of heaven and earth": A study in tradition criticism', *JBL* 91: 321–337.

Hallo, W.W. and Younger, K.L. (eds.) 1997 *The Context of Scripture. Canonical Compositions from the Biblical World* (Vol. 1; Leiden/New York/Köln: Brill).

Janowski, B. 2003 Dankbarkeit. Ein antropologischer Grundbegriff im Spiegel der Toda-Psalmen, in E. Zenger (Hrsg.) *Ritual und Poesie* (Freiburg/Basel/Wien: Herder): 91–136.

Keil, C.F. & Delitzsch, F. 1973 *Psalms* (Commentary on the Old Testament in ten volumes. Vol. V. Grand Rapids, MI.: WB Eerdmans).

Kirkpatrick, A.F. 1903 *The Book of Psalms* (The Cambridge Bible for Schools and Colleges. Cambridge: University Press).

Kittel, R. 1922 *Die Psalmen* (Kommentar zum Alten Testament. Bd. XIII. Erlangen: W. Scholl).

König, E. 1927 *Die Psalmen* (Gütersloh: Bertelsmann Verlag).

Kraus, H.J. 1978 *Psalmen* (BKAT XV/2; Teilband 2; Neukirchen-Vluyn: Neukirchener Verlag).

Loretz, O. 1979 *Die Psalmen II* (Beitrag der Ugarit-Texte zum Verständnis von Kolometrie und Textologie der Psalmen. Alter Orient und Altes Testament. Veröffentlichungen zur Kultur und Geschichte des Alten Orients und des Alten Testaments. Neukirchen-Vluyn: Neukirchener Verlag).

Ludwig, T.M. 1973 'The traditions of establishing the earth in Deutero-Isaiah', *JBL 92*: 345–357.

Miller, P.D. 1995 'Between text and sermon. Psalm 136:1-9, 23–26', *Interpretation* 49: 390-393.

Mowinckel, S. 1962 *The Psalms in Israel's worship* (Vol. II; Oxford: Basil Blackwell).

Obermann, J. 1936 'An antiphonal psalm from Ras Shamra', *JBL 55*: 21–44.

Oesterley, W.O.E. 1939 *The Psalms* (New York: Macmillan Company).

Ridderbos, N.H. 1950 *Psalmen en Cultus* (Kampen: Kok).

Schedl, C. 1986 'Die alphabetisch-arithmetische Struktur von Psalm CXXXVI', *VT* 36: 489–494.

Schmidt, H. 1934 *Die Psalmen* (Handbuch zum Alten Testament. I/15. Tübingen: Mohr [Siebeck]).

Seybold, K. 1996 *Die Psalmen* (Handbuch zum Alten Testament. I/15. Tübingen: Mohr [Siebeck]).

Spieckermann, H 2003 Hymnen im Psalter. Ihre Funktion und ihre Verfasser, in E. Zenger (Hrsg.) *Ritual und Poesie* (Freiburg/Basel/Wien: Herder): 137–162.

Stoebe, H.J. 1984 'חסד – Hæsæd Güte', in E. Jenni & C. Westermann (Hrsg.) *THAT* (Bd I.). München: Kaiser Verlag: 600–621.

Van der Ploeg, J.P.M. 1974 *Psalmen, Deel II* (Psalms 76–150). (Roermond: Romen & Zonen).

Weiser, A. 1979 *Die Psalmen* (Das Alte Testament Deutsch. Teilband 14. Göttingen: Vandenhoeck & Ruprecht).

Westermann, C. 1977 *Lob und Klage in den Psalmen* (Göttingen: Vandenhoeck & Ruprecht).

—1989 *The living Psalms* (Translated by J.R. Porter; Edinburgh: T & T Clark).

Zenger, E. (Hrsg.) 2003 *Ritual und Poesie. Formen und Orte religiöser Dichtung im Alten Orient, im Judentum und im Christentum* (Freiburg/Basel/Wien: Herder).

WORSHIP AND THEOLOGY IN THE PSALMS

Jörg Jeremias
Marburg, Germany

Introduction

My choice of subject has a biographical element. For more than 20 years I have been a member of a small theological commission that was formed to promote dialogue between the Romanian Orthodox Church and the Protestant Church of Germany. The responsibility of leading debates within this theological commission lay with the church historians and the systematic theologians, and I have found these sessions to be highly informative as far as Orthodox theology is concerned[1].

One discovery in particular, has been significant to me. In continuity with Eastern Church Fathers, theology for the Orthodox Churches is defined as a reflection on worship. The celebration of the Liturgy takes priority over and above theology. The Liturgy is not a result of theology, but conversely, theology would not be possible without the Liturgy, that is its subject. Theology in the Orthodox Churches tries to understand and interpret what the Liturgy means.

In my opinion, this definition of the relationship between worship and theology is unmistakably biblical. The praising of Yahweh usually preceded any attempt to come to terms with the experience of God.

The older I have grown the more important has become the realisation that the oldest texts of both the Old and New Testaments are hymns. The apostle Paul often refers to old Christian hymns as fundamental to his theology. Most biblical scholars consider the hymn of Miriam to be the oldest text in the Old Testament, and I would like to begin my discussion with this text.

The superlative – the oldest hymn – is not as important as the fact that hymns (at least in the beginning) are not the product of theology, but a source thereof. And another fact is just as important to consider: There is no hymn in the Old Testament without the tendency to portray knowledge, without the tendency to theologize. There is no hymn in the Old Testament that merely enumerates experiences of God without reflecting on what they mean for humanity. Let me elaborate by using the following three examples:

---

1. A useful summary is found in Felmy (1990).

I.

The first example is *Exod. 15.21*, which is perhaps the oldest text of the Bible. (According to some authors, it is not a separate hymn, but a repetition of Exod. 15.1)[2].

> And Miriam sang to them this song:
> Sing to the Lord, for he is highly exalted;
> the horse and his chariot he has hurled into the sea.

Two observations provide the main reason for confirming the antiquity of this text: 1) In terms of form, the main characteristic of typical Israelite and Canaanite poetic texts, the *parallelismus membrorum*, is lacking. Instead, the rhythm of two forms of stress within each poetic section divides the poetic lines. 2) In terms of content, the event itself is described very briefly, making it difficult to understand what occurred. Not even the Egyptians are mentioned. Instead, the emphasis is placed on the horses and chariots, the main military power against which the early farmers and shepherds of later Israel had no chance to defend themselves.

The form of our hymn is straightforward. It starts with an imperative plural, a call to praise, directed at a group of people by a female leader. It follows a dative mentioning the one who is to be praised. Of most importance is the particle כי followed by a perfect; it gives the reason as to why the call to praise is of great consequence at that very moment. At the same time, the כי marks the where the praise begins (Crüsemann 1996: 32–35). What follows, is a second, perfectly explaining the first, short sentence.

In terms of my subject matter, the relationship between the last two sentences is important. Grammatically, the second sentence explains the first one ('this is shown by the fact that . . .'). Logically, however, the first sentence is the consequence of the second one ('by hurling horse and war chariot into the sea, Yahweh has shown himself highly exalted'). Three formal elements are constitutive: first, a leader calls a group to praise. Then, the contents of praise are given in the כי-sentence. Finally, and interestingly, it is not the fact of hurling the enemy into the sea that is given priority; it is the *conclusion* drawn from this deed, i.e. 'he is highly exalted'. The reason for the praise is clearly an experience. However, not the description of the fact of this experience is mentioned in the first place, but the knowledge of God gained by the people who were present.

In this old hymn, we come to know a kind of praise that is specifically Israelite. Yahweh is praised by telling of his deeds (cf. the perfect), while the deeds themselves are not stressed, rather the conclusions drawn by the

2.   For the first opinion cf. Crüsemann (1969: 19–24), for the second, cf. Cross-Freedman (1955).

people and the effects of God's deeds on them. Compared to the hymns of the great nations in Mesopotamia and Egypt, biblical Israel was rather hesitant to use adjectives for God in hymns. Rather, the people would tell of what they had experienced of God. However, these experiences were not reduced to mere facts but to those facts that led to knowledge.

This basic hymn of the Old Testament led later generations to three logical conclusions: First, no deed of God has been praised as often as the salvation at the Reed Sea. It was this act of God that became the reference point for any subsequent praise, and in the reiterations of salvation experiences in later hymns, this deed very often stands at the beginning. The following experiences, namely, the guidance through the wilderness, the giving of the land, victory over enemies, etc., were proofs of the truth of the basic salvation at the Reed Sea. Historically, it was an absurd confrontation. The enemy's modern weapons were pitted against nothing more than the fear of farmers and shepherds, who were militarily inexperienced. The salvation at the Reed Sea became the source for speaking of God's miracles[3]. It therefore sparked a continued reference to God's miracles in hymns, where it often states 'You are a God who creates miracles' (Pss. 77.12, 15; 78.12; 88.11, etc.). The experience at the Reed Sea was the foundational miracle.

The second important theological subject which evolved from this experience in later times was the subject of faith. In the prosaic narrative just preceding our hymn, Moses says to the people, 'Have no fear, stand firm and see the deliverance that the Lord will bring to you this day; for as sure as you see the Egyptians now, you will never see them again. The Lord will fight for you, you should remain silent.' (Exod. 14.13f.). This clear difference between the human act ('be silent and look') and the function of God ('fight for Israel') is a precise description of what was meant by faith during the Old Testament times. There is no allusion to synergism. God acts, Israel looks on. Later texts call this kind of expectation of God's deeds, which, by definition, are exclusive of human deeds: faith (Exod. 14.31; Isa. 7.9, etc.).

The third important subject which is rooted in the salvation of the Reed Sea is election. Later Israel did not expect that the basic experience of salvation at the Reed Sea could be surpassed by subsequent experiences. Rather, Israel understood it as an experience in which God bound himself to Israel. According to the prophet Hosea, God presents himself by merely saying, 'I am your God from the land of Egypt.' (Hos. 12.10; 13.4). Anybody who knows of this experience of salvation knows enough of the special characteristics of Yahweh. Because of the experience at the Reed

---

3. The term 'miracle' does not mean the violation of natural laws. In biblical times, a miracle referred to the help of God in situations, where human beings had no hope left.

Sea, God is Israel's God, he is 'your God'. Therefore, in the Decalogue,
Israel's experience in Egypt is the sole reason underlying the First and
Second Commandment: 'I am the Lord, your God who brought you out of
Egypt, out of the land of slavery. You shall have no other God to set
against me' (Exod. 20.2f.; Deut. 5.6f.). The salvation in Egypt signals an
exclusive commitment on the part of God to Israel, and it calls for an
exclusive worship of this one God.

Of course, the conclusions just enumerated result from reflections of
later times. But they follow the first conclusion of praising God as 'highly
exalted' in Exod. 15.21. 'Highly exalted' was not merely a momentary
exclamation; it was intended to praise the king of the world. This sentence
confesses that there is no power equal to that of God.

As a second example, I have chosen *Ps. 136*. The connection between the
praise of God and human knowledge of God becomes more obvious here.
In terms of form, Ps. 136 is clearly a variation of the basic form of the
hymn in Exod. 15.21. I cite verses 1-6, 23-26[4]:

Give thanks to Yahweh, for he is so good
for his loyal love is everlasting.
Give thanks to the God of gods
for his loyal love is everlasting.
Give thanks to the Lord of lords
for his loyal love is everlasting.
To him who alone has performed great wonders
for his loyal love is everlasting,
to him who made the heavens with wisdom
for his loyal love is everlasting,
to him who spread out the earth over the waters...

Who remembered us when we were down
for his loyal love is everlasting,
and rescued us from our foes
for his loyal love is everlasting,
who gives food to all living creatures
for his loyal love is everlasting.
Give thanks to the God of heaven
for his loyal love is everlasting.

In v. 1, the imperative is followed by a dative (naming the addressee) and
the particle כִּי, giving the motive for praise. Yet, there are a number of
peculiarities; I shall mention the most important ones:

---

4. The quotations of the Psalms are taken from Craigie (1983). – Tate (1990) – Allen
(1983).

Psalm 136 is a litany; the congregation answers the different sections of the poem with a refrain.

It comprises a long list of God's deeds, which are enumerated by the grammar of the participles. Thus, the psalm consists of one single sentence.

These different deeds of God belong to the category of miracles (v. 4); v. 4 forms a kind of hermeneutic superscription.

A noticeable polemical atmosphere is present in the poem; vv. 2-3 provides it in the form of a superlative, while v. 4 stresses God's incomparability ('he alone'). The First Commandment with its differentiation of powers forms the basis of this sentence (Schmidt 1969: 40–42).

More important than these observations, is the theological knowledge out of which the refrain evolves. This refrain dares to say: 'his love is everlasting'. This is new knowledge compared to Exod. 15.21. The refrain implies that it is possible to say things about God that will remain valid forever, based on the experiences, which the psalm enumerates. The refrain implies that Israel did not experience Yahweh's kindness only on some occasions, but always and continuously, even when the people did not notice anything. This is a rather keen assertion and it is clear that it cannot be supported by a single experience of God, but only by a chain of experiences (which are given in the canonical order: exodus-desert-land, vv. 10-22). This chain of experiences reaches even into the present (vv. 23-25). It starts with creation (vv. 6-9), which qualifies as the first-ever act of God in history. Each of these experiences is in itself a 'miracle'; each of these experiences bears witness to the truth of the First Commandment (v. 4). Yet, according to the hymn, only these experiences together can have 'everlasting' consequence. This consequence is emphasized as special, given the specific undertones of the term חסד, which denotes not only the kindness of God, but also implies an element of the unexpected and of an abundance in the experience of God (Stoebe 1952: 244–254; Jepsen 1961: 261–271).

In this context it seems important that the knowledge that 'his love is everlasting' is not limited to the hymns of the Old Testament. When people in need confess that they not only trust Yahweh as a person, but specifically his חסד – as in Pss. 13.6 and 52.10 – they are referring to the truth of the hymn that Yahweh's kindness is not merely an experience of good and happy days. It is an experience that is 'everlasting', even when nothing is felt and Yahweh seems silent to the person praying to him.

My third example is taken from a hymn, which is very unusual due to its form. *Ps. 118* is well known, because it is part of the Easter liturgy. The psalm starts and ends much like a typical hymn (vv. 1, 29). The difference, however, is apparent in that the elements of a collective hymn are almost absent, while elements, which are usually part of a song of thanksgiving, form the centre of the psalm. In her own praise, the congregation is reacting to the experiences of an individual. Since the songs of thanksgiving tend to include didactic elements, the congregation is instructed to learn about God through the salvation of the individual. Hence, the connection between the praising of God and the congregation's knowledge of God can be easily grasped.

> Give thanks to Yahweh for his goodness,
> for the everlastingness of his loyal love.

> From my narrow straits I called Yah(weh):
> Yah(weh) answered me with spacious freedom.
> Yahweh is on my side, I need not fear.
> What can men do to me?
> Yahweh is on my side as my helper,
> and so I can look in triumph at my enemies.
> It is better to take refuge in Yahweh
> than to trust in men.
> It is better to trust in Yahweh
> than to trust in rulers. (Ps. 118. 1, 5–9)

I would like to concentrate upon this single group of verses: vv. 5-9. Verse 5 contains the narrative of the salvation of an individual in need. This narrative is extremely short – there is no biographical detail. The author limits his report to an experience which he wants to generalise. Yet, it contains some of the most beautiful imagery in the entire Old Testament. The individual's need is likened to confinement; salvation to a large and free space in which movement in all directions is possible.

In greater detail, the consequences are given in vv. 6-9, i.e. the knowledge, which the congregation can glean from the individual's experience. Two pairs of verses are used – the first (v. 6) is written in first person ('I'-style), the second (v. 8) already in a generalised didactic style. This second pair of verses takes up a common subject in the discourse of the Old Testament, namely the difference between trusting Yahweh and trusting human power.

With regard to the latter, influential persons are named, whereas 'horses' (Isa. 31.3 etc.) or 'young men' in their prime (Isa. 40.30f.) usually fulfil this role. Here, the usual values of life are exchanged with the hymn of festival worship. Circumstances that are seemingly evident – the use of power, the idealisation of youthful strength, the relationship with important people – all these appear as failure. Trusting in God, though seemingly uncertain, is presented as the true foundation of life.

II.

The connection between the praising of God and human knowledge of God becomes even more evident when the nations are the subject of praise, i.e. when nations are called upon to praise God. In this context, the connection between the two becomes more explicit, because the nations themselves are not really present in the worship of Israel; they are present only according to the ideal. Herewith four examples:

First is *Psalm 117*, the shortest psalm in the Old Testament. It evidently corresponds to the basic form of biblical hymns, namely the imperative, the addressee, the vocative, the particle כי and the verb in the perfect.

> Praise Yahweh, all nations,
> extol him, all you peoples,
> because his loyal love has towered over us
> and Yahweh's faithfulness is everlasting.
> Hallelujah   (Ps. 117)

There are three important digressions from the usual form:

The imperatives at the beginning are no longer liturgical in a realistic manner. The people called upon to praise God are not present; they are represented by Israel. Implied is that the whole world should worship Yahweh, because he is the king of the world. But this is an eschatological perspective; for the time being, the congregation is worshipping in a representative way.

The nations themselves did not personally experience the God of the Bible, but the experiences of Israel suffice to call upon the nations to join in the praising of God. The people who are called upon to praise God and the people who know the reason for the praise are two different groups. Of course, the question is raised of how the nations should come to their own knowledge of God. I will examine this question shortly.

Since the psalm is touching on a basic problem, instead of an enumeration of deeds of Yahweh, as is the case in Ps. 136, only the essential knowledge derived from his deeds is mentioned, namely Yahweh's kindness and trustworthiness. The nations can participate in worship only when they possess a basic knowledge of these attributes of Yahweh. For the time being, his kindness is only being experienced by Israel and will only be experienced by the nations at a later stage.

How are the nations expected to attain this salvific knowledge of God? According to Deutero-Isaiah, they will witness Israel's expected acts of salvation ('All the ends of the world see [observe] the victory of our God', Isa. 52.10). The psalms, however, provide a different reason. In these texts it is expected that Israel's worship will have a particular effect on the nations. I cite the first verses of *Ps. 96* as my second example:

Sing to Yahweh a new song;
Sing to Yahweh, all the earth.
Sing to Yahweh; bless his name;
Tell of his salvation from day to day.
Declare his glory among the nations,
His wondrous deeds among all peoples.
For great is Yahweh, most worthy of praise;
He is to be feared above all gods. (Ps. 96.1-4)

Again we notice the basic form of a hymn – the imperative, the addressee, the vocative (v. 1) and the particle כי (v. 4). But the imperatives are liturgical only in part (three times 'sing'). They are followed by verbs which characterize the form of speech directed at people outside the community of worship. The first verb (בשר pi.) refers to a messenger of victory, who informs people who have not yet known anything of the positive outcome of a battle. More importantly, the second verb ספר pi. stands for the narrative of an individual, who has been saved, in a worshipping community, to which he or she invites relatives and friends. At such a casual gathering to worship God, it is fitting to express gratitude towards him. This involves as well thanking him (addressing the second person) as ספר pi., i.e. telling of the salvation to the 'brothers' (Ps. 22.23) who should learn this for themselves.

Also, the term 'new song' belongs to the context of a song of thanksgiving (cf. Pss. 40.10; 144.9, etc.)[5]. This song is 'new', because it tells of God's new act of salvation. In this way, in the context of worship, the narrative of an individual who has experienced salvation, becomes an exemplary model for reporting God's deeds to the nations. The psalm is not thinking of missionary action on the part of Israel but is concerned with the effect of Israel's speech about God in the context of worship. The main content of this speech revolves around Yahweh's 'glory' (קבוד), because this glory is reflected in his deeds. Once again, the relating of these deeds as mere facts is not the aim of Israel's speech, but rather the imparting of theological knowledge to the nations.

Most important, in terms of my subject matter, are the two psalms, Pss. 100 and 46, which I quote as my third and my fourth examples. They summon the nations to attain specific knowledge of God. In *Ps. 100*, the plural imperative of the basic form of the verbs is used to invite the nations to participate in Israel's worship (twice, 'enter', vv. 2, 4). They are not invited to just any form of worship, but to a festival of worship ('raise a shout' is a technical term for festival worship).

---

5.   For more details Jeremias (1987: 126) should be consulted.

> Raise a shout to Yahweh, all the earth!
> Serve Yahweh with gladness;
> come before him with joyful songs.
> Acknowledge that Yahweh, he is God.
> He made us, and we are indeed
> his people and the flock he shepherds.
> Enter his gates with thanksgiving,
> his courts with praise;
> give thanks to him, and bless his name!
> For Yahweh is good; his loyal love is forever,
> And from generation to generation is his faithfulness. (Ps. 100.1-5)

The effect of such participation is formulated in the central imperative, which is placed between the two invitations (v. 3):

> Acknowledge that Yahweh, he is God.
> He made us, and we are indeed
> his people and the flock he shepherds.

This verse is very unusual, in so far as it dares to broaden the old covenant formula, which is the central theme of Old Testament theology, to the nations. Verse 3 cites the famous covenant formula according to Ps. 95.7 (and Ps. 79.13), and then modifies it:

> For he is our God,
> and we are the people of his pasture,
> a flock under his care. (Ps. 95.7)

> Then we, your people,
> the flock of your pasture,
> will give you thanks forever,
> to every generation we will declare your praise. (Ps. 79.13)

The covenant formula can be applied to the nations, because it is founded on the basis of a theology of creation. Ps. 95 assured Israel of its election and stressed the necessity of obedience. In contrast to election and obedience, Ps. 100 hints at creation and aims at the knowledge of the nations who are part of the worshipping congregation. Yet this knowledge affords the basis that is formulated in v. 3a: 'Only Yahweh is God'.

As in the famous confession of the nations in Isa. 45.23, the First Commandment is broadened to relate to the nations. The First Commandment – in the form of a propositional sentence, not a commandment – becomes the basis for the nations' knowledge of God. This they gain within the context of worship and from their knowledge of their own existence as beings of Creation. The decisive fact in all of this is, according to Ps. 100, that knowledge is not a prerequisite for participation in worship; it is gained during the course of such acts of worship (Jeremias 1998: 609–615).

By this invitation to the nations to worship and to gain knowledge, Ps. 100 probably presupposes Ps. 46. The beginning of *Ps. 46* – one of the so-called Zion Psalms – is marked by a reference to the unshakeable trust of the congregation and the belief that no danger will threaten it, because God is in its midst.

> A river! Its streams cause rejoicing for the city of God,
> the holy dwelling place of the Most High.
> God is in its midst – it will not slip!
> God will help it at the break of dawn.
> The nations roared!
> The kingdoms slipped!
> He gave forth his voice,
> the earth melts!
> The Lord of Hosts is with us;
> the God of Jacob is our stronghold.
>
> Come, see the Lord's deeds,
> the desolation he has caused on the earth.
> He makes wars cease to the ends of the earth;
> he breaks the bow and shatters the spear,
> and burns chariots in the fire.
> "Relax, and know that I am God;
> I will be exalted among the nations, exalted on the earth."
> The Lord of Hosts is with us;
> the God of Jacob is our stronghold. (Ps. 46.5-12)

This idea is conveyed by a very subtle play on words: While Jerusalem cannot 'slip' (מוט, v. 6) in Yahweh's presence, a potential attack of the nations in itself is just such a 'slipping' (v. 7), i.e. its failure cannot be prevented.

In the last strophe of the psalm (vv. 9-12) this concept is still emphasized. Now, the psalm takes up the ideas of the prophets (Bach 1971). It dares to say that Yahweh will not only defend Jerusalem from all the nations attacking Zion, but that he will also remove the possibility for nations to attack Zion by destroying all their weapons (v. 10)[6]. Then, knowledge of Yahweh among the nations will become a reality. What Israel already presently knows, because Yahweh is dwelling in Zion, the nations will learn by the destruction of their weapons: 'Yahweh alone is God' (v. 11).

---

6. Note the contrast to Isa. 2 and Mic. 4, according to which the nations, during their pilgrimage to Zion, will realise how meaningless their weapons are.

This knowledge is the basis for the integration of the nations into the worship of Israel in Ps. 100. When the nations are freed from their trust in weapons and their own power, they will be prepared for the truth of the worship of Israel: a trust in God alone.

III.

The theological knowledge which results from Israel's hymns is comprehensive. It starts with Yahweh's superiority over all powers of the world, which is the reason for his kingship ('he is highly exalted', Exod. 15.21). This proceeds towards the truth that God's kindness lasts forever (Ps. 136). It comprehends the principles for the organisation of one's life (in abandoning the reliance on human beings, for trust in God, Ps. 118). It builds up to God's binding relationship with the congregation (in the so-called covenant formula) and with all nations (Ps. 100), to the expectation of a time when all wars will cease (Ps. 46).

This knowledge is fundamental. Therefore, for biblical Israel, a life without such knowledge is as impossible as a life without giving praise to God. The Old Testament reiterates the following sentence ten times: 'The dead people do not praise God'. It has long been observed that this sentence is not primarily concerned with dead people, but with those still living (Westermann 1963: 120–123). If there is no giving of praise, there is no life. If no praises are sung, the power of death penetrates life. Therefore, giving praise is the meaning of life:

> May I have life so that I may praise you
> and may your rulings help me. (Ps. 119.175)

> I did not die, but survived
> to recount Yah(weh)'s acts. (Ps. 118.17)

Giving praise, according to these texts, becomes the most elementary characteristic of being alive. It is not something, which *may* be existing in life or *may* be lacking, but it forms the basis of any life. However, human beings have to be wary of one particularly dangerous situation:

> Bless Yahweh, I tell myself:
> every part of me, bless his transcendent name.
> Bless Yahweh, I tell myself,
> and do not forget any of his benefits.
> He is the one who has forgiven all your iniquity,
> who has cured all your ailments. (Ps. 103.1-3)

People who 'forget' to praise God, lose their complete life. 'Forgetting', –
in contrast to 'remembering' – is not merely an intellectual act, but it
involves a loss of orientation towards life.[7] A good example of this
orientation on God's part can be found in Ps. 25.6-7:

> Remember your acts of mercy and loving kindness,
> 　for they are from old.
> Do not remember the sins of my youth or my transgressions;
> 　please remember me according to your loving kindness.

If God were to remember all the guilt of youth, nobody will survive. But
the congregation hopes that instead God will remember them with mercy.

'Remembering' (זכר) God's deeds on the part of humanity is so decisive
for the hymns of the Bible that later hymns in the Old Testament combine
the call for praise with the call to remember. The beginning of Ps. 105 may
serve as an example:

> Give thanks to Yahweh, proclaim his name,
> make known his actions among the peoples.
> Sing to him songs, celebrate him with music,
> 　make all his wonders your theme.
> 　Praise with pride his sacred name.
> Let those who seek Yahweh rejoice in heart.
> 　Come to Yahweh and his might,
> 　Seek his presence always.
> Remember the wonders he has performed,
> his portents and the judgements from his mouth,
> 　You descendants of his servant Abraham,
> 　his chosen sons of Jacob.　　(Ps. 105.1-6)

This psalm combines the necessity to impart to the nations knowledge of
Yahweh's deeds during worship (v. 1), with the importance of reflection (v.
2), and 'remembering' (v. 5) God's miracles. 'Reflection' and 'remembering' are ideally practised within the community of worship (v. 4), rather
than in the privacy of one's own home. Such worship helps to prevent
human beings from 'forgetting'.

I would like to close with one of the most magnificent words found in the
Psalter. As I have mentioned before, Ps. 136 and many similar psalms,
confess that God's kindness lasts forever. It lasts always and does not occur
only from time to time. Ps. 63.4 intensifies this motif the most. It dares to use
an expression, which seems to surpass the thoughts of the Old Testament:

---

7. The prophet who referred most often to this danger of 'forgetting' God's deeds is
Hosea. He drew out the implications of such forgetfulness, which, according to him, cannot be
prevented: Yahweh becomes Baal.

> For your loyal love is better than life (itself),
> my lips have praised you.

In the majority of the psalms, God's kindness is experienced in life itself, in a complete life, which is characterized by a good relationship between God and humanity. In contrast to this majority view, Ps. 63 knows of an experience of God's kindness outside such a fulfilled life, i.e. an experience during the darkness of suffering, during loneliness, during disaster. The psalm maintains that Yahweh's kindness is more important than all the experiences of this kind of darkness and imminent death. Here, the knowledge of the everlasting kindness of God has gained a new dimension, which leads to many utterances in the New Testament.

Bibliography

Allen, L.C. 1983 *Psalms 101–150* (Word Biblical Commentary 21; Waco, Texas: Word).

Bach, R. 1971 'Der Bogen zerbricht, Spieße zerschlägt und Wagen mit Feuer verbrennt', in H. W. Wolff (ed.), *Probleme biblischer Theologie* (München: Chr. Kaiser): 13–26.

Craigie, P.C. 1983 *Psalms 1–50* (Word Biblical Commentary, 19; Waco, Texas: Word).

Cross, F.M. and Freedman, D.N. 1955 'The Song of Miriam', *Journal of Near Eastern Studies* 14: 237–250.

Crüsemann, Frank 1969 *Studien zur Formgeschichte von Hymnus und Danklied in Israel* (Wissenschaftliche Monographien zum Alten und Neuen Testament, 32; Neukirchen: Neukirchener Verlag).

Felmy, K.C. 1990 *Die Orthodoxe Theologie der Gegenwart. Eine Einführung* (Darmstadt: Wissenschaftliche Buchgesellschaft).

Jepsen, A. 1961 'Gnade und Barmherzigkeit im Alten Testament', *Kerygma und Dogma* 7: 261–271.

Jeremias, J. 1987 *Das Königtum Gottes in den Psalmen*. Israels Begegnung mit dem kanaanäischen Mythos in den Jahwe-König-Psalmen (Forschungen zur Religion und Literatur des Alten und Neuen Testaments, 141; Göttingen: Vandenhoeck und Ruprecht).

—1998 'Ps 100 als Auslegung von Ps 93–99', *Skrif en Kerk* 19: 605–615.

Schmidt, W.H. 1969 *Das erste Gebot: Seine Bedeutung für das Alte Testament* (Theologische Existenz heute, 165; München: Chr. Kaiser).

Stoebe, H.J. 1952 'Die Bedeutung des Wortes häsäd im Alten Testament', *Vetus Testamentum* 2: 244–254.

Tate, M.E. 1990 *Psalms 51–100* (Word Biblical Commentary, 20; Dallas, Texas: Word).

Westermann, C. 1963 *Das Loben Gottes in den Psalmen* (3rd edn; Göttingen: Vandenhoeck und Ruprecht).

REVISITING THE PSALM HEADINGS:
SECOND TEMPLE LEVITICAL PROPAGANDA?[1]

Louis C. Jonker
Stellenbosch, RSA

1. *Introduction*

'The titles have often been given little importance in the contemporary study of the Psalms.' This is the observation of Craigie in his 1983-commentary on the Psalter (Craigie 1983: 32). He observes furthermore (1983: 31) that, because '... the titles do not appear to form an integral part of the psalm to which they are attached', and because they '... represent the work of the editors of the early collections, or of the Book of Psalms as a whole', the titles '... are frequently of more importance for understanding the role of particular psalms in the context of the Psalter and in the historical context of Israel's worship than they are for understanding the original meaning and context of the individual psalms.'

Since Craigie's commentary was published twenty years ago, Psalm studies have indeed called for more attention to the psalm headings. In different studies the psalm superscriptions are used in support of theories about the composition of the Psalter, indicating certain borderlines between the different books identified in the Psalms, or showing relationships between certain Psalms or groups of Psalms. However, Craigie's indication that the Psalm titles are of 'importance for under-standing the role of particular psalms ... *in the historical context of Israel's worship* (my italics – LCJ)' (1983: 31) has not been given enough attention in the past two decades. Still, many modern commentators follow in the footsteps of older studies by merely indicating that the Psalm headings are later additions that were attached to individual psalms by certain editors, probably during the post-exilic era[2].

However, there are also certain commentators and studies that have attempted to indicate that the superscriptions are more than just 'neutral' titles. Sigmund Mowinckel in his *The Psalms in Israel's worship* (1962: 100), as well as Brevard Childs in an article (1971: 137–150) that picks up Mowinckel's argumentation, have described the Psalm headings as

---

1. A shortened version of this article was delivered as a paper at the *Pro Psalm* conference in Pretoria on 22 August 2003.

2. Cf. Craigie's remark (1983: 32): 'Though the date of the titles cannot be determined with precision, some may come from the post-exilic period and the final stages in the process of compiling the Psalter.'

midrashic (Mowinckel 1962: 100). Kraus (1966: xxx), in his discussion of the origin of the superscriptions, indicates that 'Bei einem Vergleich zwischen den Psalmenüberschriften und den kultisch-liturgischen Traditionen des chronistischen Geschichtswerkes hat sich immer wieder eine überraschende Uebereinstimmung gezeigt. Es kann kein Zweifel bestehen, daß hier Traditionsbeziehungen vorliegen.'[3] Kraus then continues to ask the all important question: 'Aber welcher Art sind diese Traditionsbeziehungen?'[4] He tries to answer his own question by proposing that the Psalm titles were the work of the Levitic priesthood during the post-exilic era, the same circles that produced the Chronistic History.

The observations that I want to offer in this article, link up Kraus's line of thought. However, in answering his question 'Welcher Art sind die Traditionsbeziehungen?', I will view the data from a pragmatic-rhetorical, or even ideological, angle. My intention is to associate the discussion about the Psalm headings with views I have expressed elsewhere about the pragmatic-rhetorical function of the Books of Chronicles (cf. Jonker 2002; 2003). In pursuing this, I will limit myself to the different personal names mentioned in the Psalm titles.

2. *Some observations on the Psalms and the Chronistic Literature*

My first task is to look at the data involved. This will be done in two steps: Firstly, I will present the statistical data about the distribution of the different names in the Psalm headings, and secondly, I will look at the distribution of these names in other parts of the Hebrew Bible.

Table I indicates the different names that occur in the Psalm headings. The following observations should be emphasized:

- The following names[5] occur in the titles: David, Solomon, Moses, Asaph, The Sons of Korah, Heman the Ezrahite, Ethan the Ezrahite and Jeduthun[6].
- 'David' occurs in 73 titles, the majority in Book I (37 times), but also 18 times in Book II, once in Book III, twice in Book IV and 15 times in Book V. The LXX has added the name to another 14 Psalm titles, mainly in Books IV and

---

3. 'When the Psalm superscriptions are compared with the cultic-liturgical traditions of the Chronistic history, some surprising similarities always emerge. There can be no doubt that some sort of a transmission relationship is apparent here.'

4. 'But of what type is this transmission relationship?'

5. I do not consider the indication in many superscriptions, למנצח, here. Although this refers to a person, probably the chief musician (the translation of the KJV), it is rather a technical indication that does not provide information about the association with certain groups in the post-exilic era. However, it may provide us with some information on the cult organization during this period.

6. Jeduthun is regarded as a person here, in contrast to the view of Gese (1974: 152–153) who regards it as a nomen from the verb ידע ('to know').

V of the Psalter. However, in two cases (namely Pss. 122 and 124) the name 'David' was omitted by the LXX.

- 'Solomon' occurs twice, in Psalm 72 as the closing of Book II, and again in one of the Songs of Ascent, Psalm 127 in Book V.
- 'Moses' occurs in the heading of Psalm 90, the introductory psalm of Book IV.
- 'Asaph' occurs 12 times, mainly as a group in Book III, namely Psalms 73–83, but also once in Book II in Psalm 50.
- The name 'Korah' occurs always in the construct combination 'The Sons of Korah'. This expression occurs 11 times in two groups: at the beginning of Book II (Pss. 42, 44–49) and the end of Book III (Pss. 84–85, 87–88).
- 'Ethan the Ezrahite' occurs only once, namely in the closing psalm of Book III (Ps. 89).
- 'Heman the Ezrahite' appears once in the heading of a Korahite psalm, namely Ps. 88, also at the end of Book III.
- 'Jeduthun' does also not occur on its own, but twice in combination with 'David' (Pss. 39 and 62) and once in combination with 'Asaph' (Ps. 77).

To summarize: when 'David', 'Solomon' and 'Moses' are for a moment ignored, all the other Levitical names[7] (with the exception of Jeduthun in Ps. 39) occur exclusively in Books II–III. 'Moses' stands at the junction between Books III and IV.

The next step is to determine where these Levitical names occur in other parts of the Hebrew Bible, and Table II provides the overview in this respect. The following comments should be made here:

- The names Asaph, Heman (with the exception of 1 Kgs. 4.31), Ethan (also with the exception of 1 Kgs. 4.31) and Jeduthun occur exclusively in the Chronistic literature of the Hebrew Bible[8].
- The kings with whom Asaph, Heman, Ethan and Jeduthun are associated according to the Chronistic version of history, are David, Solomon, Hezekiah and Josiah. The names do not occur in the narratives about the other kings. The only exception is in the Jehoshaphat narrative (2 Chron. 20.14) where reference is made to the 'sons of Asaph'.
- Apart from the 'neutral' genealogical references to Asaph, Heman, Ethan and Jeduthun, all the other references are in positive contexts, namely the participation in some or other way in the cult, or in the rebuilding of the temple community after the exile.

The pattern that evolves from the distribution of the name 'Korah' is, however, different.

---

7. This term will be explained below.

8. The term 'Chronistic literature' is used here to refer both to Chronicles and Ezra-Nehemia, without presupposing certain theories about dating and authorship.

- Apart from the genealogical references to Korah in 1 Chronicles 6 and 9, the name does not occur elsewhere in the Chronistic literature.
- The name occurs in the Pentateuch in numerous instances, in genealogical references, as well as in a narrative.
- The portrayal of Korah in the narrative (Num. 16) is negative. It tells the story of Korah's revolt against Moses and Aaron. The reference in Numbers 27 refers back to this incident, indicating that it was actually revolt against Yahweh.

Before making any conclusions from the data at this stage, it is necessary to examine the Levitical perspective in the Chronistic literature, to look at the probable developments in Levitical circles, and to consider certain theories about the formation and closing of the Psalter.

3. *Levitical perspective in Chronistic Literature*

The discussion in this section will deal mainly with the Books of Chronicles, as it is my opinion that our conclusions with regard to Chronicles can also be extrapolated for Ezra-Nehemiah. I agree with the authors that take Chronicles and Ezra-Nehemiah to be separate works (Williamson 1982; Japhet 1993), but I also agree with those who argue that they could possibly be ascribed to the same author(s) (cf. Welten 1973 and Willi 1995). The term 'Chronistic literature' in my heading therefore refers to the perspective in these books, and not so much to its structural unity. It is accepted here that the Chronicles originated in the late Persian era in the province Yehud.

The following research results with reference to the Levitical perspective in the Chronistic literature are of importance for the argument in this article:

1. Dennerlein (1999: 238), along with many other commentators, mentions that almost all the references to the Levites in Chronicles are part of the writers' own material, and was not found in the Deuteronomistic *Vorlage*. 'Diese Tatsache läßt keine Zweifel an der außergewöhnlichen Bedeutung, die der Chr den Leviten beimisst[9]', according to him[10].

2. The Levites are associated in the Chronicles with the 'main' kings in history, namely David, Solomon, Hezekiah and Josiah. I have

---

9. 'This fact leaves no doubt that the Chronicler regarded the Levites to be of extreme importance.'

10. Much has already been written about the position of the Levites in the Persian period, as well as on their portrayal in the Biblical literature from this period. Apart from the often-cited work by Cody (1969) on the history of Old Testament priesthood (cf. chapter 8, 175 in particular), the following more recent works could be cited: Nel (1987), Hanson (1992), Laato

indicated elsewhere that the narrative line running from David to
Solomon, and which is paralleled by the line running from Hezekiah
to Josiah, is crucial for establishing the pragmatic-rhetorical
function of the Chronicles as a whole. These kings are discussed
within the context of two prominent themes, namely temple
construction/inauguration and celebration of the Passover. According to the Chronicler's picture, the Levites played important roles in
both these cultic activities[11].

3. Knoppers has, however, argued that it cannot be proved that the
Chronicler was exclusively pro-Priestly or pro-Levitical. The picture
portrayed by Chronicles is that 'both the priests and the Levites are
essential to the success of the Temple cult. ... There is no firm
evidence to suggest that the Chronicler holds to an absolute equality
between priests and Levites. Nevertheless, the author does not
emphasize hierarchy' (1999: 70–71). Although Hanson's view, which
was expressed earlier than that of Knoppers, agrees that there is no
attempt to put the Levites on top of the priestly hierarchy, he
indicates that 'the Chronicler is fond of seizing opportunities to
extol the virtues of the Levites. ... In the temple cleansing/
restoration of both Hezekiah and Josiah, the Levites occupy centre
stage... While the *de facto* superior status of the priests is not
denied, the most significant action revolves around the Levites. They
are the ones the Chronicler seems excited about' (1992: 74–75).
Hanson (1992: 75) therefore regards the Chronicles '... as a
monumental effort to bring reconciliation into a community
threatening to destroy itself through bitter infighting.' According
to him, '... the Chronicler composed a history that acknowledged
the role of Davidic prince and Zadokite priesthood, but above all
demonstrated the important role that was to be accorded to the

(1994), Blenkinsopp (1995: 87–98), Albertz (1997: 605–623), Dyck (1998), Nurmela (1998) and
Knoppers (1999). The following studies provide broader overviews: Schulz (1987), O'Brien
(1990), Ulrich *et al* (1992) and Grabbe (1995).

11. Many commentators have, for e.g., indicated that the designation for the Levites in 2
Chronicles 35.3 (לכל־ישראל הקדושים ליהוה...ללוים המבינים) reflects the new position that they
took up in the Second Temple period. Cf. for e.g. Japhet (1993: 1047): 'The Levites are
identified with two appellations: "the teachers of... all Israel", and "holy to the Lord", both
relevant to the present situation. The view of the Levites as teachers betrays the late date of
the address; the role of "teaching" had originally been that of the priests, who are almost by
definition "teaching priests" (2 Chron. 15.3); ... This role is also evidenced during the Persian
period... It seems, however, that in this realm as well as the cultic sphere, a new class – a class
of "teachers" (*mᵉbinim*) – gradually emerged, mediating between "the teaching", i.e. the Law,
and the people. ... Rather than replacing the priests..., the Levites become an auxiliary class
in this role, too; the priests keep the law and study it, but the Levites are the teachers of "all
Israel".

threatened Levitical families in the restored temple cult and community' (1992: 75).

4. In order to advocate the reconciliation that Hanson is referring to, the Chronicler amalgamated different traditions to portray a picture of co-operation and complementarity. This point is confirmed, for example, in the amalgamation of Deuteronomic and Priestly legal terminology in the Passover descriptions in Chronicles. Another example is the way in which the Deuteronomistic *Vorlage* is used. Continuity with various older historical traditions was established, but a Levitical perspective was then imposed on this material[12].

5. If the above view is accepted, it seems most likely that the intended audience of Chronicles was not broader society in the first place[13], but rather those in society that endangered or suppressed the position of the Levites. That means that the discourse in this literature was mainly directed inwards towards the religious establishment in the province of Yehud in Jerusalem. The pragmatic function would then be to counter the values of mainstream society, and to argue for (at least) an equal position among the clergy in Jerusalem. The Books of Chronicles can therefore be seen as a form of propaganda, putting forth the case of the Levites.

4. *Developments within Levitical circles*

The next step in my argument is to describe the developments that have taken place in Levitical circles. The importance of this discussion for the identification of the different stages during which the superscriptions with Levitical names were attached to certain Psalms, is obvious.

A study that has established a broad consensus on the history of the Levites, is that of Hartmut Gese that was published already in 1963[14]. Gese has pointed to several stages in the evolution of the Levites. (1) After the return from exile, the cultic singers are simply called 'sons of Asaph' and are not yet reckoned as Levites (cf. Ezra 2.41 = Neh. 7.44). (2) At Nehemiah's time, the singers are reckoned as Levites and divided into two

---

12. Laato indicates that, although there is no reason to doubt that many of the cultic institutions/offices described in the Chronistic literature were already in operation in the First Temple period, older genealogical traditions were used by the Chronicler '... to argue for the cultic practice of his own time when the sons of Heman, the seer of the king and the sons of Ethan (=Jeduthun), the leading gatekeeper of David's time, acted as singers in the Second Temple after the time of Nehemiah' (1994: 92).

13. It could, however, also have been possible that broader society might be intended as a 'secondary' audience, i.e. as those who should also hear about this strife in order to support the argument advanced in the text.

14. Cf. Braun's summary of this aspect (1986: xxxi–xxxii).

groups, the sons of Asaph and the sons of Jeduthun (cf. Neh. 11.3-19; 1 Chron. 9.1-18). (3a) The Levitical singers are in three groups, Asaph, Heman, and Jeduthun (cf. 1 Chron. 16.37-42; 2 Chron. 5.12; 29.13-14; 35.15). (3b) Three groups remain, but Jeduthun has been replaced by Ethan, and Heman has become more prominent than Asaph (cf. 1 Chron. 6.31-48; 15.16-21).

Although these stages[15] have been generally accepted, there is no agreement upon the dates of stages 3a and 3b. Gese himself assigned stage 3a to the Chronicler (hence dating him post-Nehemiah), and 3b to a subsequent stage. Williamson[16], seeking to preserve a greater part of the text for the Chronicler, argues that the Chronicler stood at stage 3b and incorporated older strata into his work. Whatever the case may have been with regard to Chronicles is not so important for the present argument. However, it is important to note that the Asaphites were more important at an earlier stage, and that the distinction of three Levitical families was a later development.

5. *The formation and closing of the Book of the Psalms*

At this stage we may return to the Book of Psalms. Crucial for the argument that I want to advance in this article are certain theories about the formation and closing of the Psalter. It is important to look at the origin of the Korahite and Asaphite psalms respectively. The stages at which the different books of the Hebrew Psalter reached stability, should also be considered.

5.1. *The Korahite and Asaphite collections*
Scholars are in agreement that certain collections of psalms, and even certain individual psalms, originated already at an early, that means pre-exilic, stage, but were only later on incorporated in bigger psalm collections. Two of these earlier collections are the so-called Korahite and Asaphite psalms. Gary Rendsburg (1990) has concluded on account of linguistic evidence that 35 psalms are of northern Israelite origin. Among these are all the Korahite (42–49, 84–85, 87–88) and Asaphite (50, 73–83) psalms. These psalms contain many references to geographical features or tribes of the north, and also exhibit northern dialect in their language use. It is also significant that these two collections make up the majority of the so-called Elohistic collection (42–89) that is often identified as another grouping in the Psalter.

---

15. Clines (1984: 219), however, holds a different view.
16. Laato (1994) agrees with Williamson that stage 3b reflects the thinking of the Chronicler's own time.

Michael Goulder (1982 and 1996) has done two extensive studies on the Asaphite and Korahite psalms respectively. Goulder believes that the Korahites had become the Levitical priesthood at the northern sanctuary at Dan. Once their shrine became the centre for the national festival, they developed a set of psalms suited to the occasion. After Dan was lost, the Korahites moved southwards, first to Bethel, and from there to their permanent home, Jerusalem. According to Goulder the Asaphite psalms were also composed in the North during circumstances of danger. When the priests from Bethel fled to the South after the fall of the North, they brought along this collection of psalms. They were taken up into the cult in Jerusalem and became suitable expressions in the phase after 597 BCE when Jerusalem also was threatened. The collections from the north were used in conjunction with those psalm collections that originated in Jerusalem within the Zadokite priesthood under David and Solomon.

Although not many scholars accept Goulder's elaborate liturgical theory for the origin and composition of the Psalter, there is general agreement that the Korahite and Asaphite psalms have a northern origin, probably in Levitical priestly circles[17].

Although one could agree with Goulder on the prominence of the Korahites at an early stage in the North, it seems as if this prominence within the Levitical context diminished with time. The genealogical note in Numbers 26.58 probably reflects a relatively early tradition, listing the family of Korah as one of the five major Levitical families. However, the Korahites are already here understood to be the major representatives of the Levitical families of Gershon, Kohath and Merari who have established themselves as dominant phratries. The genealogy in Exodus 6 indicates that Korah was the grandson of Kohath. The same position is reflected in the genealogies in 1 Chronicles 6 and 9. However, in 1 Chronicles 23 where another genealogy of Kohath is listed, Korah is conspicuously absent. The prominence of the Kohathites, and therefore also of Korah, has diminished, it seems. Hutton (1992: 100–101) argues that the 'reduction of the Kohathites to oblivion is likely the subject of the polemic underlying the major story of Korah and his followers in Numbers 16. It is generally acknowledged that the narrative in Numbers 16 is a composite of at least two stories.' One of these comes from the Zadokite 'priestly tradition concerning the cultic/religious conflict between the Korahites and Aaron over the exclusive claims of Aaron to the priesthood.' According to Hutton 'this priestly narrative is certainly to be understood as attesting to the intense struggle for the control of temple prerogatives in the post-exilic community.' Hutton continues: 'Whether the Korahites were among former groups of Levitical priestly groups who

---

17. Cf. Holladay's (1993) chapter on 'Psalms from the north'.

went into exile or whether they were a prominent Levitical group which functioned in Palestine during the exile, is unclear. What is clear, however, is that the Korahites were among the major losers in this power struggle.'

5.2 *Stabilization of the Psalter*

At this point it becomes important to enquire as to the date when the Psalter took on a stabilised form. The significance of what has been described earlier in this article will only become clear when viewed against the background of the development of the Psalter as a whole.

Gerstenberger (1988: 29) suggests that the genesis of the Psalter took place roughly in four stages. In the *early pre-exilic phase* certain individual psalms and liturgies, as well as small, unidentified collections for liturgical use, originated. In the *later pre-exilic phase* the following collections originated: the Korahite collection (42–49), the Asaph collection (78–83), the Yahweh enthronement psalms (96–99), the Hallelujah psalms (111–118) and the Psalms of Ascent (120–134). *During the exile* a few Davidic collections (3–41; 51–72; 108–110; 138–145) were added. The Korahite and Asaphite psalms, as well as a group of the Davidic psalms, were grouped as Elohistic psalms, and another group of Elohistic psalms (84–89) were added. In the *post-exilic phase* the five books of the Psalter were formed and provided with a frame (1–2 and 150). At this stage many of the superscriptions were added or rephrased. According to Gerstenberger (1988: 30) 'the superscriptions had been growing continuously with the collection of psalms, replacing perhaps ritual titles such as were customary in Mesopotamian incantations. ... Most ... superscriptions betray only later theological and liturgical interests, without heeding the original intentions of the psalm.'

Gerald Wilson (2000), in an article in which he argues for a first-century CE closing of the Book of the Psalms, provides valuable information for the present argumentation[18]. He states (2000: 102): 'Traditionally, it has been generally accepted that the Book of Psalms reached its final, fixed form and arrangement by late in the fourth century BCE. In the last 15 years, however, investigation of the more than 35 scrolls of psalms discovered at Qumran near the Dead Sea has raised the possibility that final closure of the Book of the Psalms was not completed until the middle of the first century CE! The Qumran psalms manuscripts – which date from the second or third century BCE through the late first century CE – demonstrate almost complete stability for the arrangement of Psalms 2–89, suggesting this portion of the canonical collection may have been fixed by

---

18. Cf. also some of his other publications that deal with the composition of the Psalter (Wilson 1985, 1993a and 1993b).

the traditional fourth century BCE date. For Psalms 90–150, however, the situation is much different.'

Without evaluating Wilson's argument on the stabilization of Psalms 90–150, his indication with reference to the Qumran evidence that Psalms 2–89 might have been stabilized at an earlier stage than the rest of the Psalter, proves to be quite important for my argument. It seems as if the occurrence of Levitical names in Psalm superscriptions only in Books II and III of the Psalter is no coincidence.

But this point brings me to the core of my argument about the Psalm headings.

6. *The Psalm headings as Levitical Propaganda?*

Before I try to answer the question in this heading, certain conclusions with reference to the history of the origin of the Psalm headings and the Psalter should be made here:

1. Although scholars are probably correct that the origin of the Korahite and Asaphite psalms should be sought in the pre-exilic era, their headings are probably the product of the (early) post-exilic era. My theory is that these collections were both known and in liturgical use throughout the exile, and that they were therefore used in the post-exilic formation of a liturgical hymn book. Because of their association with northern and Elohistic circles, these Psalms were given superscriptions by the Levitical singers in order to identify/ proclaim them as authoritative for the post-exilic cult. This adding of superscriptions to the Korahite and Asaphite psalms took place during the phase in which the Levitical singers were known as 'Asaphites' (i.e. Gese's phase I), and during which the Korahites still had some influence in the cult (i.e. before the final decline of the Korahites).

2. The Korahite and Asaphite psalms were used as 'backbone' by the early Levites to construct the post-exilic liturgical hymnbook. Gerstenberger is probably correct that the Davidic psalm collection in Psalms 3–41 originated during the exile. It might even be that these psalms received their superscriptions and historical notes during the exilic period. This Davidic collection from the exile probably formed the first part of the hymnbook (today known as Book I). The second part (today known as Books II and III) was formed with the insertion of another Davidic collection (Pss. 51–72) into a Levitic framework. This framework was formed by means of a Korahite collection (Pss. 44–49, excluding Psalm 43) and an Asaphite psalm (Ps. 50) at the beginning, and an Asaphite collection

(Pss. 73–83) and Korahite collection (Pss. 84–88, excluding Ps. 86) at
the end.

3. At a later stage, probably during the phase within which the Levite
    families (Asaphites, Hemanites, Ethanites) were already differen-
    tiated, a further reworking of the hymn book took place. Only
    minor additions were made in order to reflect the contemporary
    situation with regard to Levitical influence. Psalm 89 was probably
    added at this stage, and additional names were added to the
    superscriptions of four psalms, namely Psalms 39 and 62 (Jeduthun
    attached to David headings), Psalm 77 (Jeduthun attached to an
    Asaphite heading), and Psalm 88 (Heman the Ezrahite attached to a
    Korahite heading). At this stage the headings would have reflected
    the earlier phase in Levitical influence, as well as the later phase
    during which the three families were prominent. The addition of
    names at this stage made the psalms representative of the Kohathite
    family (Heman came from the Kohathite branch via Korah –
    according to 1 Chron. 5.33-38), the Gersonite line (Asaph was a
    Gershonite – according to 1 Chron. 6.39-43), and the Merarite
    family (Ethan came from the Merari branch – according to 1 Chron.
    6.44-49).

4. After this phase, which coincided more or less with the Chronicler's
    era (i.e. Gese's phases 3a and 3b), the first part of the Psalter (Books
    I to III in present-day language) reached relative stability. Certain
    individual psalms were probably still slipped into the greater
    collection. However, at the end of the Persian era or beginning of
    the Hellenistic period, Books I to III of the Psalter probably
    functioned as a unity in the cultic communities[19].

5. During a next phase the further development of the Psalter took
    place. This was probably at a later stage when the Levitical influence

---

19. Holladay (1993: 75) comes to a similar conclusion: 'The superscriptions occur in both
the Hebrew text that has come down to us and in the Greek Septuagint translation, which was
probably made about 150 BCE, though… there are some variations in the details between the
two traditions. The activity of adding the notations, then, took place at some time before 150
BCE. Such classifying and annotating must have been a part of the activity of collecting that
took place in this period. And it must have taken place well after the close of the period of
active composition of the Psalms. The activity of collecting and annotating, perhaps the work
of the Levites, must have taken place during the fourth and third centuries BCE, that is, in the
last part of the Persian period and in the Ptolemaic period, two centuries for which we have
very little historical information. It was a time in Jerusalem not of innovation but of
consolidation. The notations that cite the circumstances of David's life when he is presumed
to have uttered a given psalm are expressions of the same kind of view of David as that which
gave rise to the present books of Chronicles: David as organizer of worship in Jerusalem. And
again and again in the books of Chronicles we have found references for this or that detail of
the superscriptions.'

had declined altogether. This could be deduced from the fact that Levitical names are no longer used in Psalm titles in Books IV and V of the Psalter. The name of David, as well as Solomon (once) and Moses (once) are used in many of the titles of Psalms 90–150. This reflects the practice that can also be seen in the psalm titles of the LXX. Throughout Jewish history the figure of David remained a national and cultic symbol. The Levites, however, lost their influence and significance and were no longer mentioned in the titles. This would imply that it was not Levites who were responsible for the formation of the later part of the Psalter (as was the case with Pss. 2–89). The frame of the Psalter was also added at this late stage of composition. The view expressed in this point confirms Wilson's theory that the closing of the Psalter with Psalms 90–150 took place much later than the closing and stabilization of Psalms 3–89.

I have argued in favour of a strong Levitical influence in the formation and closing of Books I to III of the Psalter (Books II and III in particular). However, the reasons for my suspicion that these Levitical headings are not neutral, but are in fact Levitical propaganda[20] must still be stated. The following points in that direction:

- The Levitical names used in the Psalm headings are the same names that function as symbols/representatives of Levite influence in the Chronistic literature. The only exception is Korah, but it was shown above that the Korahites were probably no longer influential during the time of origin of the Chronistic literature.
- The very strategic linking of Levitical names to the one prominent name in the Psalm titles, namely David, seems to be in line with the linking of Levitical activity to specific kings in the Books of Chronicles. Those kings who were responsible for the temple building and institution (David and Solomon), as well as the kings that cleansed the temple and celebrated the Passover (Hezekiah and Josiah) are portrayed in Chronicles as the kings who involved the Levitical families in cultic activities. Of all these kings David is the one that initiated the rehabilitation of the Levites in the cult (according to the Chronicler's version). It seems as if the same strategic linking takes place in the grouping of Psalm superscriptions.
- The main argument is, however, that the same strategy of amalgamating and complementing different earlier traditions that is characteristic of the Chronistic literature, can also be seen in the formation of Books I to III of the Psalter. The fact that the Levites used cultic traditions from both the North (Korahite and Asaphite) and the South (Davidic) to form a cultic hymn book, shows the same tendency that was detected in Chronicles.

---

20. Berquist (1995: 147) describes the dynamics of the Persian era under the heading 'the priesthood's capture of religion'.

TABLE I

Bk	Ps.	Name 1	Name 2
I	1	0	0
I	2	0	0
I	3	David	0
I	4	David	0
I	5	David	0
I	6	David	0
I	7	David	0
I	8	David	0
I	9	David	0
I	10	0	0
I	11	David	0
I	12	David	0
I	13	David	0
I	14	David	0
I	15	David	0
I	16	David	0
I	17	David	0
I	18	David	0
I	19	David	0
I	20	David	0
I	21	David	0
I	22	David	0
I	23	David	0
I	24	David	0
I	25	David	0
I	26	David	0
I	27	David	0
I	28	David	0
I	29	David	0
I	30	David	0
I	31	David	0
I	32	David	0
I	33	0	0
I	34	David	0
I	35	David	0
I	36	David	0
I	37	David	0
I	38	David	0
I	39	David	Jeduthun
I	40	David	0

Bk	Ps.	Name 1	Name 2
I	41	David	0
II	42	Sons of Korah	0
II	43	0	0
II	44	Sons of Korah	0
II	45	Sons of Korah	0
II	46	Sons of Korah	0
II	47	Sons of Korah	0
II	48	Sons of Korah	0
II	49	Sons of Korah	0
II	50	Asaph	0
II	51	David	0
II	52	David	0
II	53	David	0
II	54	David	0
II	55	David	0
II	56	David	0
II	57	David	0
II	58	David	0
II	59	David	0
II	60	David	0
II	61	David	0
II	62	David	Jeduthun
II	63	David	0
II	64	David	0
II	65	David	0
II	66	0	0
II	67	0	0
II	68	David	0
II	69	David	0
II	70	David	0
II	71	0	0
II	72	Solomon	0
III	73	Asaph	0
III	74	Asaph	0
III	75	Asaph	0
III	76	Asaph	0
III	77	Asaph	Jeduthun
III	78	Asaph	0
III	79	Asaph	0
III	80	Asaph	0

Bk	Ps.	Name 1	Name 2
III	81	Asaph	0
III	82	Asaph	0
III	83	Asaph	0
III	84	Sons of Korah	0
III	85	Sons of Korah	0
III	86	David	0
III	87	Sons of Korah	0
III	88	Sons of Korah	Heman the Ezrahite
III	89	Ethan the Ezrahite	0
IV	90	Moses	0
IV	91	0	0
IV	92	0	0
IV	93	0	0
IV	94	0	0
IV	95	0	0
IV	96	0	0
IV	97	0	0
IV	98	0	0
IV	99	0	0
IV	100	0	0
IV	101	David	0
IV	102	0	0
IV	103	David	0
IV	104	0	0
IV	105	0	0
IV	106	0	0
V	107	0	0
V	108	David	0
V	109	David	0
V	110	David	0
V	111	0	0
V	112	0	0
V	113	0	0
V	114	0	0
V	115	0	0
V	116	0	0
V	117	0	0
V	118	0	0

Bk	Ps.	Name 1	Name 2
V	119	0	0
V	120	0	0
V	121	0	0
V	122	David	0
V	123	0	0
V	124	David	0
V	125	0	0
V	126	0	0
V	127	Solomon	0
V	128	0	0
V	129	0	0
V	130	0	0
V	131	David	0
V	132	0	0
V	133	David	0
V	134	0	0
V	135	0	0
V	136	0	0
V	137	0	0
V	138	David	0
V	139	David	0
V	140	David	0
V	141	David	0
V	142	David	0
V	143	David	0
V	144	David	0
V	145	David	0
V	146	0	0
V	147	0	0
V	148	0	0
V	149	0	0
V	150	0	0

The Levitic superscriptions alongside the numerous Davidic titles, probably indicate again that an amalgamation of traditions was attempted, but then with the portrayal of the Levites in an equal position with the Zadokite priesthood (who probably were the tradents of the Davidic collections). What the Chronicler did for the historical traditions of the Jews, the Levitical redactors of the Psalter did for their cultic traditions. With the strategy of amalgamation the Levites (in the early post-exilic stages, but also in the late Persian stages) claimed their (at least equal) position in the Jewish cult.

TABLE II

NAME	REFERENCES	CONTEXT
Asaph[21]	1 Chron. 6.39 1 Chron. 9.15	Genealogy
	1 Chron. 15.17, 19	David appoints cultic singers
	1 Chron. 16.5, 7, 37	David appoints Levites to minister before the ark, and delivers a psalm in the hand of Asaph
	1 Chron. 25.1, 2, 6, 9	David appoints Levites to prophecy
	1 Chron. 26.1	Porters during David's time
	2 Chron. 5.12	Participate as singers in the inauguration of Solomon's temple
	2 Chron. 20.14	Reference to 'sons of Asaph' during Jehoshaphat's days
	2 Chron. 29.13, 30	Hezekiah orders the cleaning of the temple
	2 Chron. 35.15	Celebration of the Passover during Josiah's days
	Ezra 2.41	Later generation that returned from exile
	Ezra 3.10	Later generation that served in the rebuilt temple after the exile
	Neh. 7.44	Later generation that returned from exile
	Neh. 11.17, 22	Later generation (singers and porter) who dwelt in
	Neh. 12.35, 46	Jerusalem after the return from exile, and restored the cultic organization like in the time of David and Solomon

21. The name 'Asaph' also occurs in 2 Kings 18.18, 37 and Nehemiah 2.8. However, according to Rogers (1992), these verses refer to other persons also called by the same name. In Kings, reference is made to Asaph, the father of Joah the recorder under Hezekiah, while Nehemiah refers to someone called Asaph who was the 'keeper of the forest' under the Persian king Artaxerxes. These references are therefore left out of the discussion in this article.

NAME	REFERENCES	CONTEXT
Korah[22]	Ex. 6.21, 24	Genealogy
	Num. 16.1, 5, 6, 8, 16, 19, 24–27, 32, 40, 49	Revolt against Moses and Aaron
	Num. 26.9, 10, 11	Genealogy
	Num. 27.3	Referring back to the revolt of Korah
	1 Chron. 6.22, 37 1 Chron. 9.19	Genealogy
Heman	1 Kgs 4.31	Comparison of Solomon to certain wise men
	1 Chron. 2.6 1 Chron. 6.33	Genealogy
	1 Chron. 15.19	David appoints cultic singers
	1 Chron. 16.41, 42	David appoints Levites to offer together with the Zadokite priests
	1 Chron. 25.1, 4, 5, 6	David appoints Levites to prophecy
	2 Chron. 5.12	Participate as singers in the inauguration of Solomon's temple
	2 Chron. 29.14	Hezekiah orders the cleansing of the temple
	2 Chron. 35.15	Celebration of the Passover during Josiah's days
Ethan	1 Kgs 4.31	Comparison of Solomon with certain wise men
	1 Chron. 2.6,8 1 Chron. 6.44	Genealogy
	1 Chron. 15.17, 19	David appoints cultic singers
Jeduthun	1 Chron. 9.16	Genealogy
	1 Chron. 16.38, 41, 42	David appoints Levites to offer together with the Zadokite priests

22. The name 'Korah' also occurs in Gen. 36.5, 14, 16, 18 and 1 Chron. 1.35 where it refers to a son of Esau, as well as in 1 Chron. 2.43 where it probably refers to a town (cf. Hutton 1992). These references are therefore left out of the discussion in this article.

NAME	REFERENCES	CONTEXT
		The sons of Jeduthun were appointed by David as porters
	1 Chron. 25.1, 3, 6	David appoints Levites to prophecy
	2 Chron. 5.12	Participate as singers in the inauguration of Solomon's temple
	2 Chron. 29.14	Hezekiah ordering the cleansing of the temple
	2 Chron. 35.15	Celebration of the Passover during Josiah's days
	Neh. 11.17	Later generation (singers and porters) who dwelt in Jerusalem after the return from exile

These observations would lead me then to answering the question in the title in the affirmative. The headings of the Psalms, at least those of Books II and III, were probably part of Second Temple Levitical propaganda.

Bibliography

Albertz, R. 1997 *Religionsgeschichte Israels in alttestamentlicher Zeit. Teil 2: Vom Exil bis zu den Makkabäern* (Göttingen: Vandenhoeck & Ruprecht).

Barnes, W.H. 1992 'Jeduthun', *Anchor Bible Dictionary III*: 655–656.

Berquist, J.L. 1995 *Judaism in Persia's Shadow. A Social and historical approach* (Minneapolis: Fortress Press).

Blenkinsopp, J. 1995 *Sage, Priest, Prophet. Religious and Intellectual Leadership in Ancient Israel* (Louisville, Kentucky: Westminster John Knox Press).

Braun, R. 1986 *1 Chronicles* (WBC; Waco TX: Word Books).

Childs, B.S. 1971 'Psalm titles and Misrashic exegesis', *JSS* 16/2:137–150.

Clines, D.J.A. 1984 *Ezra, Nehemiah, Esther* (NCBC; Grand Rapids, MI.: Eerdmans).

Cody, A. 1969 *History of Old Testament priesthood* (Rome: Pontifical Biblical Institute).

Craigie, P.C. 1983 *Psalms 1–50* (WBC; Waco TX: Word Books).

Dennerlein, N. 1999 *Die Bedeutung Jerusalems in den Chronikbüchern* (Frankfurt: Peter Lang).

Dyck, J.E. 1998 *The theocratic ideology of the Chronicler* (Leiden: Brill).

Gerstenberger, E.S. 1988 *Psalms. Part I with an introduction to cultic poetry* (FOTL, 14; Grand Rapids, MI: Eerdmans).

Gese, H. 1974 'Zur Geschicte der Kultsänger am zweiten Temple', in H. Gese, *Vom Sinai zum Zion. Alttestamentliche Beiträge zur biblischen Theologie* (BevTh; München: Chr. Kaiser Verlag).

Goulder, M.D. 1982 *The Psalms of the Sons of Korah* (JSOTS, 20. Sheffield: JSOT Press).

—1996 *The Psalms of Asaph and the Pentateuch* (*Studies in the Psalter, III.* Sheffield: Sheffield Academic Press).

Grabbe, L. 1995 *Priest, Prophets, Diviners, Sages. A Socio-historical study of religious specialists in Ancient Israel* (Valley Forge, Pennsylvania: Trinity Press International).

Hanson, P.D. 1992 '1 Chronicles 15–16 and the Chronicler's views on the Levites' in M. Fishbane & E. Tov (eds.), *'Sha'arei Talmon'. Studies in the Bible, Qumran, and the Ancient Near East. Presented to Shemaryahu Talmon.* (Winona Lake, Indiana: Eisenbrauns): 69–77.

Holladay, W.L. 1993 *The Psalms through three thousand years. Prayerbook of a cloud of witnesses* (Minneapolis: Fortress Press).

Hutton, R.R. 1992 'Korah (Person)', *Anchor Bible Dictionary IV*: 100–101.

Japhet, S. 1993 *I and II Chronicles* (London: SCM Press).

Jonker, L.C. 2002 'Completing the temple with the celebration of Josiah's Passover?', *Old Testament Essays* 15(2): 381–397.

—2003 *Reflections of King Josiah in Chronicles. Late stages of the Josiah Reception in 2 Chr 34f* (Gütersloher: Gütersloh Verlag).

Knoppers, G.N. 1999 'Hierodules, priests, or janitors? The Levites in Chronicles and the history of the Israelite priesthood', *Journal of Biblical Literature* 118/1: 49–72).

Kraus, H.-J. 1966 *Psalmen. I. Teilband.* (BKAT, 15/1; Neukirchen-Vluyn: Neukirchner Verlag).

Laato, A. 1994 'The Levitical genealogies in 1 Chronicles 5–6 and the formation of Levitical ideology in Post-exilic Judah', *JSOT 62*: 77–99.

Mariotinni, C.F. 1992 'Ethan', *Anchor Bible Dictionary II*: 644–645.

Mowinckel, S. 1962 *The Psalm's in Israel's worship II* (Translated by D.R. Ap-Thomas. Oxford: Blackwell).

Nel, H.W. 1987 *Die Leviete in die kronistiese geskiedwerk* (Unpublished MA (Judaica) thesis, Pretoria: University of South Africa).

Nurmela, R. 1998 *The Levites. Their emergence as a second-class priesthood* (Florida: University of South-Florida Press).

O'Brien, J. 1990 *Priest and Levite in Malachi* (Atlanta, Georgia: Scholars Press).

Rendsburg, G.A. 1990 *Linguistic evidence for the northern origin of selected Psalms* (SBLMS, 43. Atlanta, Georgia: Scholars Press).

Rogers, J.S. 1992 'Asaph (Person)', *Anchor Bible Dictionary I*: 471.

Schulz, H. 1987 *Leviten im vorstaatlichen Israel und im Mittleren Osten* (Munich: Chr. Kaiser Verlag).

Ulrich, E. *et al* (edd.) 1992 *Priests, prophets and scribes. Essays on the formation and heritage of Second Temple Judaism in honour of Joseph Blenkinsopp* (Sheffield: JSOT Press).

Welten, P. 1973 *Geschichte und Geschichtsdarstellung in den Chronikbüchern* (WMANT, 42. Neukirchen-Vluyn: Neukirchner Verlag).

Willi, T. 1995 *Juda – Jehud – Israel. Studien zum Selbstverständnis des Judentums in persischer Zeit* (FAT, 12; Tübingen: Mohr, Siebeck).

Williamson, H.G.M. 1982 *1 and 2 Chronicles* (NCBC; Grand Rapids, MI: Eerdmans).

Wilson, G.R. 1985 *The editing of the Hebrew Psalter* (Chico, California: Scholars Press).

—1993a 'Understanding the purposeful arrangement of the Psalms in the Psalter: Pitfalls and Promise', in J.C. McCann (ed.), *The shape and shaping of the Psalter* (JSOTS 159. Sheffield: Sheffield Academic Press): 42–51.

—1993b 'Shaping the Psalter: A consideration of editorial linkage in the Book of Psalms', in J.C. McCann (ed.), *The shape and shaping of the Psalter* (JSOTS, 159. Sheffield: Sheffield Academic Press): 72–82.

—2000 'A first century CE date for the closing of the Book of Psalms?', *JBQ* 28/2: 102–110.

Augustine, Gadamer and the Psalms
(or: The Psalms as the Answer to a Question)

Jurie H. le Roux

Pretoria, RSA

1. *Introduction*

Von Rad depicted the psalms as Israel's answer. An answer to the two
great interventions of Yahweh in Israel's history. The first was the
canonical salvation history (from Abraham to Joshua) described in the
Hexateuch. The second was the confirmation of David and his throne for
all times which found literary expression in the historical works of the
Deuteronomist and the Chronicler. These interventions shaped Israel into
Yahweh's people and laid the foundation for the constant experience of
Yahweh's presence.

Israel's very personal reaction to these great interventions is expressed
especially in the psalms. They did not only often recall these events but also
viewed them as the basis for their relationship with Yahweh. In their
answer they praised Him but also complained about their suffering. Their
reaction also showed how Israel interpreted these great deeds of God and
how they were affected by them (Von Rad 1958: 352–353).

In this article the psalms are also depicted as an answer but we are
following a totally different route. The psalms are not primarily a reaction
to the '*Heilsgeschichte*' but rather an answer to a question. At one point in
Israel's history, a question was asked and an answer (which the text of the
psalms reflects) was given. However, this answer is incomplete and cannot
be understood in terms of linguistic and literary devices alone. Something
is lacking: the initial question to which the psalm was the answer. To
accomplish this the reader must become engaged in the endless task of
asking historical questions. Consequently the historical embeddedness of
the answer (the text of the psalms) is highlighted and the questions
(arguments, views, perspectives) which prevailed at that specific time in
Israel's history are emphasized. Below, this view is elaborated with
reference to the views of Augustine and Hans-Georg Gadamer.

In the hermeneutics of the twentieth century, Augustine's view of the
verbum cordis received much attention (Von Balthasar 1936: 9–13; Adam
1965: 278–284; Reventlow 1994: 85–104; Grondin 1995: 99–110; Van Oort
1995: 214–219). Typical of western hermeneutics is the so-called
forgetfulness of language ('*Sprachvergessenheit*'). This forgetfulness
implies the severing of the link between language and its life context as
well as the emphasis on its instrumentalist nature. Any proposition is thus

viewed as complete in itself because it can be understood through the linguistic signs in the text. The linguistic expressions are thus sufficient to determine the meaning of the text (Gadamer 1990: 422). Due to Augustine's views of the *verbum cordis,* this forgetfulness of language in the West has not been completed. According to him, each text is incomplete because the *verbum cordis* or inner word has not been emptied in the text; the words in the text do not reflect the *verbum cordis* in its full meaning; something has been withheld. To the exegete, however, the *verbum cordis* is extremely important and one must constantly try to understand this inner word of the (psalm) text (cf. Altaner 1951: 377–378, 380–381; Bakhuizen van den Brink 1965: 258–265).

2. *Difference between the 'inner' and 'outer' word*

Words are the most important of all signs: 'Words have gained an altogether dominant role among humans in signifying the ideas conceived by the mind that a person wants to reveal... an incalculable number of the signs by which people disclose their thoughts consist in words' (*De doctr. chr.* II.3.6-7). And since words disappear the moment they are uttered, and their sound fades away, writing was invented in order to rescue these words (Drobner 1994: 355–357). In this way, 'words are presented to the eyes, not in themselves, but by certain signs peculiar to them' (*De doctr. chr.* II.8). Augustine, however, clearly distinguished between a *verbum cordis* or inner word on the one hand and a *verbum exterior* or outer word on the other. The written or spoken word is only a partial reflection of the inner word. This distinction has great consequences for our understanding of the psalms.

First, something on the inner word. It refers to that 'word' before it is uttered in sound (Drobner 1994: 352–354). This word belongs to no language or tongue (*De trin.* XV.10.19). The word which we utter or write is only a sign of the inward word; this inner word is more authentic and it is the real true word and it never looses its quality as the ineffable inner word. Each word that we utter is therefore not the true word. Thus: the word that sounds outwardly is only a sign of 'the word that gives light inwardly' (*De trin.* XV.11.20). However, in order to communicate with others this inner word must, however, become an articulate sound which makes an appeal to the senses. Although this inner word becomes an articulate sound, it is not changed into sound (*De trin.* XV.11.20).

All words of all the languages which are expressed in sound are therefore also thought silently. The mind is thus full of words, unuttered words. Even songs live silently in the mind before they assume a corporeal form. As Augustine said: 'the mind runs over verses while the bodily mouth is silent'. The word in the mind thus precedes all the signs by means of which it is signified. And this word comes from and is begotten from knowledge which resides in the mind; this knowledge is only spoken inwardly. And whenever this knowledge becomes a word, this word does not contain the knowledge of the mind as it really is. Seen from the perspective of the reader or the listener, one could say the sound that one hears and the words that one reads are not the expression of the full knowledge of the mind: 'For when it is uttered by sound, or by any bodily sign, it is not uttered according as it really is, but as it can be seen or heard by the body' (*De trin*. XV.11.20).

Something similar happened to the Word of God: it became flesh in order that people might understand Him. Our words become an articulate sound of an inner word in order that it may appeal to the senses of others; in a similar way the Word of God became flesh in order that people might understand Him. Although our word becomes a sound it is not changed into sound as such. The Word of God became flesh without being changed into flesh: 'For both that word of ours became an articulate sound, and that other Word became flesh, by assuming it, not by consuming itself so as to be changed into it'. Thus: never must a link be forged between the outer and the inner word; never must a likeness between the outer word and the inner word be sought for (*De trin*. XV.11.20).

There is, however, a great difference between our word and the Word of God. Our word is born from our knowledge but the Word of God is born from the essence of the Father. And whatever knowledge might be in the Father is also in Him, 'in all things like and equal to the Father, God of God, Light of Light, Wisdom of Wisdom, Essence of Essence, is altogether that which the Father is' (*De trin*. XV.14.23). Although He is not the Father the Word is however of the same essence as the Father; He is equal to the Father in all things. And when the Father spoke through the word it was as if the Father was uttering Himself. And the Father uttered Himself wholly and perfectly in the Word because of this sameness (*De trin*. XV.13.22).

It is extremely important to understand this difference between a human word and the Word. God was fully present in the Word; God uttered Himself through the Word. However, there is never a similar sameness between one's inner thoughts and the words endeavouring to express those thoughts. No one is ever fully present in the words he/she utters; human words very seldom reflect a certain knowledge. Thus, behind each word uttered or written lies an inner word or a *verbum cordis*. This refers to the original speech of thought which can never be fully expressed. This inner word is purely intellectual or universal and is never uttered in a material form and never fully expressed in any language (*De trin*. XV.10.19; cf. Gadamer 1976: 276–291; Grondin 1995: 102–104; 1999: 119–122; 2000: 210–215).

3. *A loss of reality*

All words expressed in sound or in written form thus always have something contingent, uncertain and accidental about them. Only one aspect of what is said is illuminated; not the whole *verbum* is expressed; not everything is expressed by means of language in the text before us. Thus, we must never take the linguistic sign in speech or writing as final. What we have is incomplete and partial. No text exhausts what the author had in mind (cf. Gadamer 1970: 184–198; Grondin 1999: 2002: 36–51).

There is an inner word 'behind' the expressed word in the text which cannot be expressed by any word: '*Was ausgesagt ist, ist nicht alles*' (Gadamer 1973; 504). Thus, the words in the psalms are not the full expression of the psalmists' inner word; there is not a similar 'sameness' between *verbum interior* and *exterior* as in God and the Word; the inner words of the psalmists were therefore not fully emptied in the 'final text' (cf. *De trin*. XV.11.20); something remained 'behind' and even the final text of the psalms seems to be imperfect; it does not 'contain' what it asserts to contain (cf. Grondin 1995: 107–110).

This feeling of loss can also be illustrated with the loss of historical reality (cf. Le Roux 1997: 401–423). A well-known Afrikaans author, Karel Schoeman, begins his work, '*Verliesfontein*', with a moving statement that the past is another country and then poses the question, 'How will we ever reach that country?' (Schoeman 1998: 7). History is like a far-off 'country' which can never be reached, entered or described. When toiling historically, this elusiveness of the past must be taken into account (cf. Derrida 1997: 102–107). This is due to the nature of the past event: it denies us access; it keeps us at bay; it always escapes critical investigation. In short: we have lost something and no historical investigation can ever retrieve it (Thiselton 1992: 103–113). Put differently: we have lost the inner word of the psalmists forever and no outer word can ever recover it.

Not even dates in the text can regain the past fully. When Paul Celan dated his poems he endeavoured to preserve the uniqueness of the event but the moment he inscribed it into the poem it 'loses what it wants to keep. It burns what it wants to save'. All historical experience is the experience of singularity and the desire to keep this singularity is just natural. But when it is written down it is effaced right away (Derrida 1995: 378).

4. *Dialogue: a different way of understanding a text*

Although ineffable, the *verbum cordis* (of the psalmists) nevertheless remains important and the reader must be engaged in a constant endeavour to understand this inner word of the text (Figal 2002: 102–

125). Put differently: it is always important to transcend the physical words in order to determine the meaning of the inner word (of the text), that *verbum cordis* (of the psalmists) which was not fully emptied in the 'final text' (cf. *De trin.* XV.11.20). How is that to be accomplished?

It is important to note that no method can enter this world of the *verbum cordis*. A method is usually related to the ideal of control and knowledge which is only gained through the mastering of a text. The understanding of a text can, however, never be reduced to the intellectual grasp of objectifiable and isolated contents (cf. Bernstein 2002: 267–282). Understanding can never be equated to the control of a text (Grondin 1995: 107). This, however, does not exclude the importance and significance of a method. If one builds a house, one needs a plan of the structures as well as of the procedures. Without these the house cannot be built. But plans, structures and procedures (the method) are not the house. The same applies to the humanities and to Biblical scholarship: a method is important, but a method does not provide entrance into the world of the inner words of the psalmist (Grondin 2000: 32–39). Gadamer protested against the idea of a method that would provide conclusive evidence which is beyond all doubt (Gadamer 1976: 276–291). According to Gadamer, this positivist method-ideal went just too far: it was setting its foot on soil where it did not belong, and it was making unfair demands on knowledge and on truth (Gadamer 1990: 9–15).

However, there must be another way out and that is dialogue. According to Gadamer, Augustine's ideas regarding the *verbum cordis* gave rise to a 'dialogical' understanding of language: '*Die Sprache vollzieht sich also nicht in Aussagen, sondern als Gespräch*' (Gadamer 1985: 359). Over and against the primacy of method, Gadamer emphasized the importance of a dialogue in the form of question and answer. According to him, understanding is 'a participation in meaning, in tradition and, finally, in dialogue' (Grondin 1995: 107). And this dialogue does not comprise of propositions but of questions and answers which always give rise to new questions and different answers (cf. Taylor 2002: 126–142).

There is 'information' in the text which are not expressed and this can only be 'recovered' in the dialectic of question and answer. We must always ask 'which answers to which questions fit the facts'. This phrase 'is in fact the hermeneutical "*Urphänomenon*": No assertion is possible that cannot be understood as an answer to question, and assertions can only be understood in this way' (Gadamer 1966: 224). The question thus has the primacy: '*Nicht das Urteil, sondern die Frage hat in der Logik den Primat*' (Gadamer 1957: 52).

In all exegetical endeavour this dialogue between question and answer must be heard because each discourse is embedded in a dialogue. The truth of a text lies not in the accidental signs of the given moment but in what it opens up. One must therefore become aware of everything that the text carries with it. No proposition can ever be understood in terms of the content that it presents; every proposition is motivated and has presuppositions that are not expressed (Gadamer 1957: 55). Thus: '*Was ausgesagt ist, ist nicht alles. Das Ungesagte erst macht das Gesagte zum Wort, das uns erreichen kann*' (Gadamer 1973: 504). These unsaid things can be called, with Augustine, the *verbum cordis*.

Although the inner world of words (of the psalmists) will always remain a no-man's-land, it does not exclude the possibility of an endless dialogue. It is, however, important to take cognisance of the questions and answers of others and of previous generations. No-one can escape the '*Wirkungs-geschichte*' of these questions and answers. Since the explanation of a text is never complete, new generations pose different questions and supply different answers. And these questions and answers can help us to understand. They provide many unknown or forgotten interpretations and shed new light on the text. Gadamer calls this continuing process of interpretation and re-interpretation (by means of questions and answers) '*Wirkungsgeschichte*' (Gadamer 1990: 305–312). This '*Wirkungsgeschichte*' is a historical movement that influences the reading and understanding consciously or subconsciously. The history of the questions and answers of a text co-determine its understanding. A text cannot be understood on its own and detached from previous interpretations (Gadamer 1990: 124; Grondin 2000: 32–39).

5. *Conclusion*

A psalm does not contain the final meaning of the author; it is imperfect and its meaning limited because the *verbum cordis* of the author was not fully 'emptied' in the psalm itself; there never was a similarity between the psalmist's inner thoughts and the words he used to express these thoughts; the final text of a psalm is thus never final in the sense that it contains a complete and adequate expression of the psalmist's *verbum cordis* or inner thoughts. The psalms are anwers to questions; at a specific juncture in Israel's history certain questions were posed and the psalms are the answers to these questions; traces of the original questions and answers are reflected in the psalms and the exegete must endeavour to determine the original question to which the psalm is the answer. No method can unlock the true meaning of a psalm; meaning is linked to the 'dialogical' process of question and answer; the exegete must become engaged in the endless process of asking (historical) questions: What was the original question? What were the circumstances? To what is this psalm an answer? To whom was it directed? How did the psalmist interpret and formulate the answer? etc. (cf. Zenger 2000: 399–435).

Bibliography

Adam, A. 1965 *Lehrbuch der Dogmengeschichte* (Gütersloh: Gerd Mohn).

Altaner, B. 1951 *Patrologie* (Freiburg: Herder Verlag).

Augustinus, A. 1968 *De trinitate* (Corpus Christianorum, Corpus Latina, 50–50A; 2 vols; Turnhout: Typographi Brepols editores pontificii).

—1995 De doctrina Christiana, in R.P.H. Green (ed.), *Augustine – De doctrina Christiana* (Oxford: Clarendon Press).

Bakhuizen van den Brink, J.N. 1965 *Handboek der kerkgeschiedenis* (Den Haag: Bert Bakker).

Bernstein, R.J. 2002 The constellation of Hermeneutics, critical theory and deconstruction, in R.J. Dostal (ed.), *The Cambridge companion to Gadamer* (Cambridge: University Press): 267–282.

Derrida, J. 1995 *Points...* (Stanford: University Press).

—1997 *Limited Inc.* (Evanston, Illinois: Northwestern University Press).

Drobner, H.R. 1994 *Lehrbuch der Patrologie* (Freiburg: Herder).

Figal, G. 2002 The doing of the thing itself: Gadamer's hermeneutic ontology of language, in R.J. Dostal (ed.), *The Cambridge companion to Gadamer* (Cambridge: University Press): 102–125.

Gadamer, H-G. 1957 Was ist Wahrheit, in H-G. Gadamer, *Gesammelte Werke* 2 (Tübingen: J.C.B. Mohr): 44–56.

—1966 The universality of the hermeneutical problem, in H-G. Gadamer, *Philosophical hermeneutics* (Berkeley: University of California Press).

—1970 Sprache und Hermeneutik, in H-G. Gadamer, *Gesammelte Werke* 2 (Tübingen: J.C.B. Mohr): 184–198.

—1973 Selbstdarstellung, in H-G. Gadamer, *Gesammelte Werke* 2 (Tübingen: J.C.B. Mohr): 479–508.

—1976 Rhetorik und Hermeneutik, in H-G. Gadamer, *Gesammelte Werke* 2 (Tübingen: J.C.B. Mohr): 276–291.

—1985 Grenzen der Sprache, in H-G. Gadamer, *Gesammelte Werke* 8 (Tübingen: J.C.B. Mohr): 350–361.

—1990 *Wahrheit und Methode* (Tübingen: JCB Mohr).

Green, R.P.H. 1995 *Augustine – De doctrina Christiana* (Oxford: Clarendon Press).

Grondin, J. 1995 *Sources of Hermeneutics* (Albany: State University of New York).

—1999 *Hans-Georg Gadamer* (Tübingen: JCB Mohr).

—2000 *Einführung zu Gadamer* (Tübingen: JCB Mohr).

—2002 Gadamer's basic understanding of understanding, in R.J. Dostal (ed.), *The Cambridge companion to Gadamer* (Cambridge: University Press): 36–51.

Haddan, A.W. 1887 St. Augustine: On the holy Trinity, in P. Schaff (ed.), *A select library of the Nicene and post-Nicene fathers* 3 (Edinburgh: T&T Clark).

Le Roux, J.H. 1997 'Our historical heritage', *Old Testament Essays* 10(3): 401–423.

Reventlow, H.G. 1994 *Epochen der Bibelauslegung* (München: C.H. Beck).

Schoeman, K. 1998 *Verliesfontein* (Kaapstad: Human & Rousseau).

Taylor, C. 2002 Gadamer on the human sciences, in R.J. Dostal (ed.), *The Cambridge companion to Gadamer* (Cambridge: University Press): 126–142.

Thiselton, A.C. 1992 *New horizons in hermeneutics* (Grand Rapids: Zondervan Publishing House).

Von Balthasar, H.U. 1936 *Aurelius Augustinus – Über die Psalmen* (Leipzig: Jakob Hegner).

Van Oort, J. 1995 *Jeruzalem en Babylon* (Zoetermeer: Uitgeverij Boekcentrum).

Von Rad, G. 1958 *Theologie des Alten Testament* (1. Vol.; München: Chr Kaiser Verlag).

Zenger, E. (ed.) 2000 Psalmenforschung nach Hermann Gunkel und Sigmund Mowinckel, in A. Lemaire & M. Saebø (eds), *Congress Volume* (Supplements to Vetus Testamentum, 80; Leiden: Brill): 399–435.

THE JUDEAN LEGITIMATION OF ROYAL RULERS IN ITS ANCIENT NEAR EASTERN CONTEXTS

Eckart Otto
Munich, Germany

In Psalm 2, Egyptian and Assyrian motifs of the legitimation of rulers of the Davidic dynasty were combined and mixed in a complex way. It is not only of importance that we should ask about the cultural influences of the fertile-crescent on Judean religion in order to reconstruct the Judean reception of these Ancient Near Eastern (ANE) motifs in the royal psalms. It is even more important, if we want to date the literary history of these psalms.

The royal psalms do not only have a key-function in post-exilic literary structuring of the book of the psalms but also in our dating of literary history. If we can detect dated motifs of Egyptian, Assyrian, Babylonian or Persian royal ideology in the royal psalms, this can hint at the *terminus a quo* of their Judean reception. If, as will be shown in this article, such ANE motifs lost their function in Egypt or Mesopotamia and were at a certain time no longer used, this could deliver *a terminus ad quem*. A Judean reception of motifs, which came out of use in the countries of their origin, was rather improbable.

As for Psalm 2, the mixture of Egyptian and Assyrian motifs is especially complicated so that we may take this psalm as a test case and begin with the Egyptian background of the royal protocol (*ḥoq*) in Psalm 2.7b-8:

> 'I will declare the decree: YHWH has said unto me. You are my son. This day I have begotten you. Ask of me, and I shall give you the nations for your inheritance and the uttermost parts of the earth for your possession.'

That the motif of the king as 'son of God' was derived from Egyptian royal ideology is well known since Gerhard von Rad's article of 1947: *'Das judäische Königsritual'*. Therein, he detected the Egyptian influence on the royal protocol in Psalm 2.7-8. New Egyptian mythical material, published by Helmut Brunner (1986), delivers an even more precise insight into the process of the Judean reception of motifs of Egyptian royal ideology of the eighteenth and nineteenth dynasty (Koch 1999). A cycle of drawings called 'Birth of the Divine King' in the temple of queen Hatchepsut in Deir-el-Bahri and in the temple of Amenophis III in Luxor, which was connected with interpretative inscriptions, explains the Egyptian legitimization of the King, showing the procreation, birth and breeding of the crown prince as 'son of God':

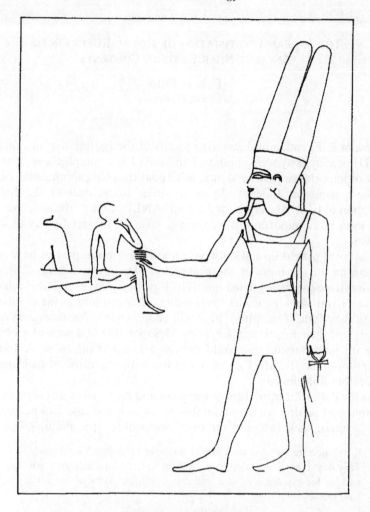

Amun acknowledges his son

The god Amun arrives to see the newborn crown prince for the first time and to acknowledge him as his son. The goddess Hathor stretches out her hand to pass his son over. The drawing was connected with the inscription of his divine acknowledgment:

'My son (Hatchepsut: my daughter) of my flesh, my shining image, coming out of me.'

In the following scene of the cycle Amun is putting the crown prince on his knees to welcome his son as the inscription shows:

Amun and Thot clothe the crown prince

'Welcome in peace my beloved son. You are the king.'

In the next scene Amun and Thot present the crown prince to the public and clothe him as a sign of his investiture:

In the corresponding inscription Amun declares:

'My beloved son of my flesh, whom I have begotten as my image.'

In the eighteenth Egyptian dynasty, the legitimation of the ruler by the motif of divine sonship was underlined and completed by the performative divine speech acts that realise the idea of divine procreation, birth and breeding of the crown prince. This development to supplement the royal ideology by performative acts continued during the nineteenth Egyptian dynasty as the blessing of the God Ptah-Tatenen shows, which was preserved in an inscription at the temple of Abu-Simbel dated to the reign of Ramses II (Görg 1975: 237–250):

> 'I am your father, who has begotten you as God and all your limbs as Gods.'

The divine status of the king was underlined by the idea that each limb of the king was a God of his own. In the cycle 'Birth of the Divine King' the formation of the divine baby by the God Chnum was connected with the promise of his universal dominion over all the nations of the world:

> 'You will be king of Egypt and ruler of the Red Land; all the nations will be under your dominion and the nine bows under your feet.'[1]

Also the scene of the divine acknowledgement of the crown prince was connected with a promise of his universal dominion.

> 'Welcome in peace my beloved son. You are the king, who will conquer the world.'

Psalm 2.7b-8 is construed in a way analogous to the ideology of the drawings and the inscriptions of the cycle 'Birth of the Divine King'. As in this cycle the Davidic king was legitimized by the idea of divine sonship, which was also connected with the promise of his universal dominion over the nations proleptically realized by a divine performative speech act:

> 'You are my son. This day I have begotten you. Ask of me, and I shall give you the nations for your inheritance and the uttermost parts of the earth for your possession.'

These Egyptian motifs underwent an *interpretatio iudaica* by integrating the typical Judean motif of inheritance (*nah^{a}lāh*) of the nations, which had no parallels in Egyptian or Canaanite royal ideology.

There is no doubt, that this royal protocol in Psalm 2.7-8 was not derived from a Mesopotamian background. The son-of-God-motif was well known in Mesopotamia but it had an entirely different function. Everybody was son or daughter of his or her personal God (mar ilišu), so that this motif equalized all the people instead of separating the king from all the other human beings as in the royal ideology of Egypt and Judah. Only when the Judean royal ideology was democratized during the exilic and post-exilic period did it integrate aspects of the Mesopotamian son-of-God idea.

---

1. For the ritual-iterative character of Egyptian foreign politics as a consequence of royal ideology cf Otto (1999: 28–37).

When were the Egyptian motifs taken over in Judah? The history of the Egyptian religion and its royal ideology delivers some clear hints to answer this question. After the break down of the New Kingdom in the eleventh century BCE not only the structure of the Egyptian state underwent dramatic changes but also the religion. As the state developed into a theocracy under priestly rule the royal ideology of the New Kingdom lost its function. The motive of the divine Son of God got a new context as part of the idea of a divine triad of father, mother and son.

Psalm 2 shows the features of the Egyptian royal ideology of the second but not of the first millennium BCE. This means that the reception of these motifs cannot be dated late in the first millennium without answering the question of their transmission history after they came out of use in Egypt at the end of the New Kingdom. Most probable is the assumption that the royal ideology of the New Kingdom was taken over in Jerusalem during the eighteenth or nineteenth dynasty. During this period, Egypt was the overlord in Jerusalem and these motifs of royal ideology were used in Egypt.

But this does not at all mean that Psalm 2 was an early Judean psalm but only that the royal protocol of Psalm 2.7–8 contains traditional motifs that were going back to the Jebusite Jerusalem of the second half of the second millennium BCE and had their roots in the Egyptian royal ideology. What makes the interpretation of Psalm 2 so complicated is the fact that with the traditional motifs of Egyptian background of the second millennium BCE others were connected, which were going back to a neo-Assyrian background of the eighth and seventh century BCE (Otto 2002). The promise of the king's dominion over the nations continued in Psalm 2.9a:

'You shall pasture[2] them with a rod of iron.'

The motif of the king as shepherd was very common in the ANE, but in connection with the motif of an iron rod very specific. Composite-sceptres with iron parts dated to the Iron Age II of the eighth and seventh century BCE were excavated in Tel Dan, Ta'anach and Nimrud (Lemaire 1986). Such sceptres were unknown in Egypt.

The connection between shepherdship and military functions of the king was well documented in the Assyrian royal inscriptions. Assurbanipal's coronation hymn was connected with a list of divine gifts to the Assyrian king (Livingstone 1989: 27), which is a good example for the connection of shepherdship and military tasks of the king[3]:

---

2. Read with LXX the root *r'h* (Emerton 1978). The assumption of an Aramaic root *r"* is as an argument for dating the psalm late without any basis.

3. For the influence of Assurbanipal's coronation hymn on the biblical royal psalms especially Psalm 72, cf Arneth 2000.

The Assyrian King with the ḫattu-sceptre

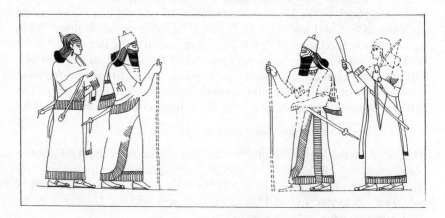

The Assyrian King with the staff of a shepherd

'Place in his hand the weapon of war and battle, give him the black-headed people [i.e. mankind], that he may rule as a shepherd.'

A wall-relief in the north-west palace of Kalhu shows Assurbanipal II with a *ḫattu*-sceptre framed by two horncap-*apkallū* (Adam 2001: 237):

The outer frame of this relief shows the king with the staff of a shepherd and a sword. Behind him two porters of his weapons are standing:

Psalm 2.9b too shows neo-Assyrian influence:

'Smash them in pieces like a potter's vessel.'

To smash the enemy like potsherds (*kīa hasbattī/hasbattiš daqāqu*) or like a potter's vessel *(karpāniš/kīma karpāt hēpû/kīma karpāt pahāru)* is a well-documented motif in neo-Assyrian royal inscriptions (Borger 1956: 57) and a close parallel to Psalm 2.9b (Becking 1990). Psalm 2.9 actualized the traditional promise of the universal dominion of the old royal protocol in the eighth or seventh century BCE using typical neo-Assyrian motifs.

This reformulation of the royal protocol of Psalm 2.7-8 in Psalm 2.9 was written by the author of the *introitus* of this psalm in Psalm 2.1-6:

> 'Why do the foreign people rage and the nations make plans in vain? The kings of the earth set themselves and the rulers take counsel together, against YHWH and against his anointed, saying: Let us break their fetters asunder and cast away their cords from us. He who is sitting in the heaven laughs about them, YHWH mocks at them. He speaks to them in his wrath and vexes them in his anger: I have set my king upon my holy hill of Zion.'

The motif of a conspiracy (*rikiltu*) of nations against the king and his god has close parallels in the neo-Assyrian royal inscriptions. A typical example is the rebellion of Egyptian princes against Assurbanipal (Onasch 1994: 91; Borger 1996: 21, 213). Also the motif of enemies making plans in vain (*kapadū lemuttu*; CAD/K: 599; Psalm 2.1b: *hgh rîq*) is typical for neo-Assyrian royal inscriptions:

> 'Their hearts make bad plans (*libbašunu ikpud lemuttu*), they tell lies, an unsuccessful plan they planned among themselves' (*milik lā kušīri imliku ramanšun*; Borger 1996: 22).

In neo-Assyrian inscriptions opposition of foreign princes against the king also meant rebellion against the gods of the Assyrian empire (Borger 1996: 21). As in Psalm 2.3 the princes intended to throw off the yoke of the god Assur (*nir^D Aššur*; CAD/N II: 262–263)[4].

Psalm 2.1-9 was formulated in the eighth/seventh century BCE during the neo-Assyrian period. The authors of this psalm used a much older piece of Davidic royal legitimization by a royal protocol in Psalm 2.7-8 as literary kernel of the psalm, which was already rooted in the Jebusite Jerusalem of the second millennium BCE. They framed this traditional core section in Psalm 2.7-8 by Psalm 2.1-6, 9 and it was used to formulate an anti-Assyrian royal psalm integrating motifs of neo-Assyrian royal inscriptions but turning them into a kind of subversive reception against their Assyrian authors: Not the god Assur but YHWH should be the overlord of the

---

4. For parallels of the motif of the ropes, see the neo-Assyrian version of an *emesal*-prayer from Kalhu (Maul 1998: 170) and a relief on a stele, which shows Esarhaddon as conqueror, who keeps the subdued kings by a rope (Porter 1993, Table 1 [frontispiece])

nations and his tool should not be the Assyrian but the Davidic king in Jerusalem.

In the post-exilic period, Psalm 2.10-12 was added to the pre-exilic psalm as a cramp between Psalm 2 and Psalm 1 (Hossfeld & Zenger 1993: 50). The intention of this redactional connection of the royal psalm 2 with the wisdom psalm 1 as the entrance hall for the book of psalms was the idea that everybody who lived according to the Torah (Psalm 1) became a 'son of God'. The democratisation of the pre-exilic royal ideology after the exile contrasted with the opposite development in the Egyptian religion. There the figure of the king as 'son of God' became part of the divine triad and member of the pantheon without direct connection with the human realm. In Israel's creation theology every human being was looked upon *sub specie Dei* as a king (Psalm 8; Genesis 1.26-28).

The Egyptian religion broke down and left the stage of the universal history of religions because it lost its contacts with its worshippers. The Israelite democratization of the royal ideology, which implied the disconnection of religion and state, was the precondition for the fact that the Jewish religion, and with it Christianity and Islam, survived up to now. The theology of democratization in the Hebrew Bible had its roots in the subversive reception of motifs of the neo-Assyrian royal ideology in the eighth/seventh century BCE turning them against their own origins.

The same development but even more consequent than in Psalm 2 can be detected in the late pre-exilic Deuteronomy, which had its literary core section in the subversive reception of Esharraddon's loyalty oath (Deuteronomy 13; 28; Otto 1999). If we want to answer the question of the theological meaning of the royal psalms today we must go back to their original religious intention as subversive literature against the superpowers of their time. They could have become like Deuteronomy a cradle for a history of liberation and freedom. But the Christian reception history of these psalms lost their original intention using them to legitimize the rulership of Christian kings, because the original historical contexts of the psalms were forgotten.

Only in our days are we getting them back by excavating the Egyptian and Mesopotamian culture. Now we can see again for the first time after many centuries how critical the biblical authors were with the so-called 'modern' ideas of their political overlords, who seemed to be politically and economically so successful – but, in the end, were not.

Bibliography

Adam, K.-P. 2001 *Der königliche Held. Die Entsprechung von kämpfendem Gott und kämpfendem König in Psalm 18* (WMANT, 91; Neukirchen-Vluyn: Neukirchener Verlag).

Arneth, M. 2000 'Sonne der Gerechtigkeit'. *Studien zur Solarisierung der Jahwe-Religion im Lichte von Psalm 72* (Beihefte zur Zeitschrift für Altorientalische und Biblische Rechtsgeschichte, 1; Wiesbaden: Harrassowitz).

Becking, B. 1990 '"*Wie Töpfe sollst du sie zerschmeißen*". Mesopotamische Parallelen zu Psalm 2.9b', *Zeitschrift für die Alttestamentliche Wissenschaft* 102: 59–79.

Borger, R. 1956 *Die Inschriften Asarhaddons, Königs von Assyrien* (Archiv für Orientforschung. Beihefte, 9; Graz [repr. 1967, Osnabrück: Biblio]).

Borger, R. 1996 *Beiträge zum Inschriftenwerk Assurbanipals. Die Prismenklasse A, B, C = K, D, E, F, G, H, J und T sowie andere Inschriften.* Mit einem Beitrag von Andreas Fuchs (Wiesbaden: Harrassowitz).

Brunner, H. 1986 *Die Geburt des Gottkönigs. Studien zur Überlieferung eines altägyptischen Mythos* (Wiesbaden: Harrassowitz).

Emerton, J.A. 1978 'The Translation of the Verbs in the Imperfect in Psalm II,9', *Journal of Theological Studies* 29: 499–503.

Görg, M. 1975 *Gott-König-Reden in Israel und Ägypten* (BWANT, 105; Stuttgart: Kohlhammer).

Hossfeld, F.-L. & Zenger, E. 1993 *Die Psalmen. Psalmen 1–50* (Neue Echter Bibel, 29; Würzburg: Echter Verlag).

Koch, K. 1999 'Israel im Orient', in: B. Janowski/M. Köckert (Hg.), *Religionsgeschichte Israels. Formale und materiale Aspekte* (Gütersloh: Gütersloher Verlag): 242–71.

Livingstone, A. 1989 *Court Poetry and Literary Miscellanea* (State Archives of Assyria, 3; Helsinki: University Press).

Maul, S.M. 1997 'Marduk, Nabû und der assyrische Enlil. Die Geschichte eines sumerischen Šu'ilas', in S. Maul (Hg.), *tikip santakki mala bašmu*. Festschrift für Rykele Borger (Cuneiform Monographs, 10, Groningen).

Onasch, H.-U. 1994 *Die assyrischen Eroberungen Ägyptens* (Ägypten und Altes Testament, 27; 2 vols; Wiesbaden: Harrassowitz).

Otto, E. 1999a *Das Deuteronomium. Politische Theologie und Rechtsreform in Juda und Assyrien* (BZAW, 284; Berlin/New York: W de Gruyter).

—1999b *Krieg und Frieden in der Hebräischen Bibel und im Alten Orient. Aspekte für eine Friedensordnung in der Moderne* (Theologie und Frieden, 18; Stuttgart: Kohlhammer).

—2002 'Die Herrscherlegitimation in den Psalmen 2 und 18 in ihren altorientalischen Kontexten', in: E. Otto, E. Zenger (Hg.), *'Mein Sohn bist du' (Ps. 2, 7). Studien zu den Königspsalmen* (Stuttgarter Bibelstudien, 192; Stuttgart: Katholisches Bibelwerk).

Porter, B.N. 1993 *Images, Power, and Politics. Figurative Aspects of Esarhaddon's Babylonian Policy* (Memoirs of the American Philosophical Society Held at Philadelphia, 208; Philadelphia: American Philosophical Society).

Von Rad, G. 1947 'Das judäische Königsritual', *Theologische Literaturzeitung* 72: 211–15.

PASCHAL LITURGY AND PSALMODY IN JERUSALEM 380–384 CE: SOME OBSERVATIONS AND IMPLICATIONS

Niek A. Schuman
Amsterdam, the Netherlands

1. *Introduction*

In the present contribution I want to bring together the two theological disciplines in which I have personally taken an interest in during the past forty years: Old Testament exegesis and Liturgics. More specifically, I am interested in the place and function of the psalms in the liturgy of Sunday and festival celebrations, i.e. which psalms are chosen in a fixed arrangement on the day of Scripture readings, prayers and preaching, and what the theological implications of that choice may be.

I feel quite unable to find a comprehensive answer to this question. By way of a random test, I shall focus on the liturgy of the Holy Week in Jerusalem of about 380–384 CE, with some special emphasis on the liturgy of the Pascal or Easter Vigil.

We are rather well informed about that liturgy thanks to the so-called *'Diary of a Pelgrimage'* of Egeria (sometimes: Aetheria). First, therefore, I shall pay some attention to fragments of the diary in question. We will get an impression of the liturgical ceremonies in general, in and about Jerusalem, on every Sunday, at Epiphany, on the occasion of the bishop's instruction of the *catechumens* in the week after Easter, and, finally, of the meetings during the Holy Week before Easter in Jerusalem.

Then we have at our disposal the so-called *'Armenian Lectionary of Jerusalem'*. Indeed, this liturgical document is supposed to have originated during the twenties or thirties of the fifth century CE, in its written form anyway. Actually, the data of the Armenian Lectionary will be older, as is generally assumed. So we may use it as liturgical data on the one hand, alongside with the corresponding notices of Egeria's diary on the other hand.

Next, we can take a closer look at these arrangements with regard to their contents. What exactly is the nature of the 'appropriateness' of the liturgy Egeria is speaking about? To find a (part of an) answer we will pay attention to fragments of those psalms which are mentioned in the Armenian Lectionary of Jerusalem. Some emphasis will be laid on the Paschal Vigil, more specifically, on the psalms of the opening ceremony, i.e. the *Lucernarium*.

Finally, I shall make some provisional remarks about the theological implications of our findings.

2. *Egeria's Diary of a Pilgrimage (EDP)*

At present there exists a continuing debate concerning the precise date of Egeria's travels in the Ancient Near East (especially to Edessa, Syria, and to Egypt, including Mount Sinai) during the three years of her proper stay in Jerusalem and the surrounding territory. The arguments for dating those years from 381 up to 384 seem rather convincing to me, although a dating in the early fifth century remains possible too (see Maraval 1982: 29, resp. Gingras 1970: 12). So, probably, she will have been a witness to the public appearance of bishop Cyrill of Jerusalem (*circa* 313–386/387 CE.), the author of the *'Mystagogical Catecheses'*, a text which offers us a deeper understanding of the theological insights within the Christian community of those days in Jerusalem. Cyrill was succeeded by bishop John of Jerusalem (387–417 CE).

In her notices, Egeria mentions a lot of churches and holy places in and around Jerusalem. The most important are respectively those on Golgotha (*'Martyrium or Major church'* and *'Anastasis'*) and those on the Mount of Olives (*'Eleon' and 'Imbonon'*). Here and elsewhere she has participated in a lot of ceremonies of which she provides accounts in her diary.

It may be useful to get a first impression of the liturgy of those animated ceremonies in general by reading some of the first hand reports of it. (The mentioned animation is clearly brought out by Egeria in her description of the daily services in Jerusalem, see § 24:1-7). Four examples will be sufficient to show a common characteristic trait: the way Egeria describes the liturgy in amazement at the appropriateness of Scripture-readings and the singing of psalms and hymns alongside during the celebration. The quotations are taken from Gingras (1970).

With regard to the Sunday service Egeria writes:

> 'Among all these matters this takes first place, that proper psalms and antiphons are always sung. Those sung at night or towards the morning, those sung by day at the sixth and ninth hours or at the vespers, continually they are proper and have a meaning pertinent to what is being celebrated' (§ 25:5).

Shortly after, in the textual edition of her diary (but see below!), Egeria gives an impression of the great celebration of Epiphany in the major church on Golgotha. Here she notes that:

> 'On the first day, then, the service takes place in the major church on Golgotha. Whatever sermons are preached, whatever hymns are sung, everything is appropriate to the day' (§ 25:10).

This fragment forms part of a more comprehensive description of a procession to Jerusalem after the Epiphany vigil in the Church of the Nativity in Bethlehem. During that procession, all participants were singing the 'Benedictus' of Psalm 118.26 and Matthew 21.9: 'Blessings on him who comes in the name of the Lord'. It may be presumed that the vigil itself was described by Egeria in a missing sheet of the text of her diary. Possibly she also may have presented an introduction to the liturgical year as such, in the same way she did in the preceding chapter about the Sunday celebrations in general.

Anyway, again Egeria underlines the appropriateness of the liturgical components of the ceremony. The same recurs in her description of the solemn meetings in the *anastasis* of the '*neophytes*' (newly baptized at Easter) and those faithful who wish to hear the mysteries, led by the bishop himself. 'For he explains all these mysteries in such a manner that there is no one who would not be drawn to them, when he heard them thus explained' (§ 47:2)! Then, some lines further down:

> 'But this above all is very pleasing and very admirable here, that whatever hymns and antiphons are sung, whatever readings and prayers are recited by the bishop, they are said in such a manner as to be proper and fitting to the feast which is being observed and to the place where the service is being held' (§ 47:5).

With this fragment we are taken back to Jerusalem in the days immediately after Easter. With the last example we find ourselves in the days before, 'which are called here the Great Week' (§ 30.1). Egeria gives a description of the liturgical ceremonies on every day of that week, more specifically of Good Friday and the Paschal Vigil (see below). On Monday, she writes, at first the same things are done as usually in the fourty days before Easter. But on the ninth hour there is a very prolonged meeting in the Martyrium:

> 'At the ninth hour everyone comes together in the major church. And until the first hour of the night they continually sing hymns and antiphons, and read passages from the Scripures, fitting to the day and the place, interrupting them with prayers' (§ 32:1).

Now we turn to some more extensive fragments of Egeria's diary with regard to the celebrations in the Holy Week ('the Great Week'). We may start on the Saturday before:

> 'When a prayer has been said and a blessing given to all, everyone continues on to the Lazarium (in Bethany), chanting hymns. And by the time they have come to the Lazarium, such a multitude has gathered that not only the place itself, but all the surrounding fields are filled with people. Hymns are sung as well as antiphons appropiate to the day and the place [cf. above!]. Various scriptural readings, also fitting to the day, are read. Just before the dismissal is given, the Pasch [Passover/Easter] is proclaimed, that is to say, a priest mounts to an elevated spot and reads the passage from Scripture where it is written: 'When Jesus came into

Bethany six days before the Pascha'. When this has been read and the Pascha has been proclaimed, the dismissal is given' (§ 29:5).

Then, on Sunday, there is the beginning of the 'Great Week'. During that time, the Sunday itself is not yet called 'Palm Sunday'. It is not until the evening that the entry of Jesus in Jerusalem is celebrated:

'As the eleventh hour draws near, that particular passage from Scripture is read in which the children bearing palms and branches came forth to meet the Lord, saying: "Blessed is he who comes in the name of the Lord!" The bishop and all the people rise immediately, and then everyone walks down from the top of the Mount of Olives, with the people preceding the bishop and responding continually with "Blessed is he who comes in the name of the Lord!" to the hymns and antiphons' (§ 31:2).

In the next paragraphs Egeria briefly describes several ceremonies on the following days of that special week. After having mentioned in passing the celebration of the Last Supper on Maundy Thursday, she continues with an elaborate account of what happens on Good Friday. I quote a fragment of it:

'When the sixth hour is at hand, everyone goes before the Cross, regardless of whether it is raining or whether it is hot. This place has no roof, for it is a sort of very large and beautiful courtyard between the Cross and the Anastasis. The people are so clustered together there that it is impossible for anything to be opened. A chair is placed for the bishop before the Cross, and from the sixth to the ninth hours nothing else is done except the reading of passages from Scripture. First, whichever psalms speak of the Passion are read. Next, there are readings from the apostles, either from the Epistles or the Acts of the apostles, wherever they speak of the Passion of the Lord. Next, the texts of the Passion from the Gospels are read. Then there are readings from the prophets, where they said that the Lord would suffer; and then they read from the Gospels, where He foretells the Passion. (. . .) And so, during those three hours, all the people are taught that nothing happened which was not first prophesied; and that nothing was prophesied which was not completely fulfilled' (§ 37:4-6).

Proportionately, Egeria pays little attention to the Paschal or Easter Vigil itself. See her explanation:

'The Easter Vigil is observed here exactly as we observe it at home. Only one thing is done more elaborately here. After the children [the neophytes!] have been baptized and dressed as soon as they came forth from the baptismal font, they are led first of all to the Anastasis with the bishop. The bishop goes within the railings of the Anastasis, a hymn is sung, and he prays for them. Then he returns with them to the major

church [the Martyrium], where all the people are holding the vigil as is
customary. Everything is done which is customarily done at home with
us, and after the sacrifice has been offered, the dismissal is given. After
the vigil service has been celebrated in the major church, everyone comes
to the Anastasis singing hymns. There, once again, the text of the
Gospel of the Resurrection is read, a prayer is daid, and once again the
bishop offers the sacrifice. However, for the sake of the people,
everything is done rapidly, lest they be delayed too long [!]. And so the
people are dismissed. On this day the dismissal from the vigil takes place
at the same hour as at home with us' (38:1-2).

3. *The Armenian Lectionary of Jerusalem (ALJ)*

Actually, how fascinating the lecture of Egeria's diary may be, it leaves us
in ignorance of the very data of the liturgical arrangements. We remain
wondering what psalms and hymns, readings and sermons Egeria meant in
her repeated notices about their 'appropiateness to the day'. Fortunately,
we can try to insert those gaps by consulting the so-called Armenian
Lectionary of Jerusalem. The Greek original of this oldest proper
lectionary has been lost. It is transmitted in three Armenian versions,
now accessible to us in the magnificent edition of Athanase Renoux.

It is not my intention to go further in detail on the Armenian Lectionary
as such. I restrict myself to the data we find in this lectionary relating the
same special days as reported by Egeria in her EDP. So we can start at the
feast of Epiphany, that is to say: the beginning of the liturgical year at the
time (cf. Renoux 1969: 182). The information of the ALJ is more
interesting because of the missing part of Egeria's diary exactly pertaining
to this particular Christian festival.

Now then, thanks to the ALJ we get more information about the place
and the liturgical order of a great and solemn celebration of Epiphany. The
community came together at a place called 'Poimnion' or 'Poimenion' near
Bethlehem ('Field of the shepherds', Renoux 1969: 202). The service
included a lot of Scripture-readings taken from Old Testament prophecies
(like Isa. 7.10-17; 11.1-9; 40.10-17; Mic. 5.1-6) as well as some significant
couples of psalms and New Testament readings. Regarding the psalms
mentioned by ALJ, we note that it regularly indicates the first psalm by
means of an antiphon taken from that psalm. That antiphon is supposed to
be the refrain, while the entire psalm or at least a greater part of it was
sung.

Now, the service started with the well-known Psalm 23, obviously
chosen in direct relation with the following reading of the narrative
passage (we would say 'the Christmas narrative') of Luke 2.8-20. Next,
directly linked up with the narrative of the shepherds, the passage of the
wise men of the East is read, immediately followed by (parts of) Psalm 2.

Then, in a similar way, we find the combination of another 'messianic' psalm and a Scripture-reading about the birth of Jesus Christ: Psalm 110 and (in that order) Matthew 1.18-25.

Later on, I will point out some striking elements and theological implications of these liturgical arrangements at the feast of Epiphany. First, we take a look at the data of the ALJ with regard to the ceremonies in the Holy Week as noted down by Egeria. Indeed, the service on the Saturday before took place at 'the Lazarium'. Two psalms are mentioned, alongside with two Scripture-readings: Psalm 30 with 1 Thessalonians 4.13-18 and Psalm 40 with John 11.55–12.11, the last one being the proper narrative of Lazarus' resurrection by Jesus.

On Sunday at the beginning of the 'Great Week', before the procession to the Mount of Olives mentioned in EPD, there was a great celebration which is shortly reported by Egeria. ALJ gives us further particular information. Again we find two arrangements of psalms and Scripture-readings: respectively Psalm 98 with Ephesians 1.3-10 and Psalm 97 with Matthew 21.1-10.

The lectionary continues with a lot of data for liturgical meetings on Monday, Tuesday, Wednesday and Thursday of the Holy Week. The last one, especially, offers a lot of celebrations with their respective arrangements, all concentrated around the institution of the Last Supper and the beginning of the Passion narratives. Many psalms are recited in that context, among which once more we find Psalm 23 (verse 5: 'Thou spreadest a table for me in the sight of my enemies'!) and no less than five groups of three psalms each during the Vigil on the Mount of Olives. Again we find Psalm 2, along with, among others, Psalm 41, 59 or 109. To anticipate for a moment of that which will be illustrated more elaborately in section III: These psalms are good examples of what Egeria meant by her mention, once more, of 'hymns, antiphons and readings which are appropriate to this day and this place', § 31:1):

> 'The kings of the earth stand ready,
> and the rulers conspire together
> against the Lord and his anointed king (Ps. 2.2).
>
> Even the friend whom I trusted,
> who ate at my table,
> exults over my misfortune (Ps. 41.9).
>
> Savage men lie in wait for me,
> they lie in ambush ready to attack me,
> for no fault or guilt of mine, O Lord (Ps. 59.4).
>
> They have attacked me without a cause
> and accused me though I have done nothing unseemly' (Ps. 109.2).

Likewise for the service at Good Friday, the ALJ prescribes a great number of psalms and readings. Among the last ones are famous prophetic passages like Isaiah 50.4-9 and 53.1-12, speaking of the destiny of the Servant of the Lord. The use of such passages are accompanied by reciting, for example, Psalm 35 or 88, and obviously Psalm 22. In the next section we shall take a closer look at some parts of those psalms.

Finally there is the abundant liturgical arrangement of the Paschal (Easter) Vigil, taking place in turn in the *Anastasis*, in the *Martyrium* and again in the *Anastasis*. The series of Scripture-readings, Old and New Testament, is a great deal similar to that which we practise in our own days. Among the psalms we notice (after the entrance of the neophytes!) Psalm 65 and 30, before the reading of, respectively, 1 Corinthians 15.1-11 and Matthew 28.1-20 together with John 19.38–20.18. But most interesting, I think, are the two psalms which feature in the first part of the Paschal Vigil: Psalm 113 (antiphon verse 2) and Psalm 118 (antiphon verse 24). The utilization of these two psalms occurs respectively during the opening and closing of the light ceremony (the *lucernarium*).

4. *The liturgical appropriateness in question*

To get a deeper understanding of the liturgical 'appropriateness' Egeria is talking about so repeatedly, we have to 'zoom in' on the very themes and texts of the arrangements mentioned above. Once more I shall restrict myself to the psalms which form part of those arrangements. When there are striking correspondences between words or themes in the psalms on the one hand, the Scripture-readings on the other hand, I will indicate them in italics.

The arrangement at the feast of the Epiphany of the indicated psalms and the New Testament passages about the birth of Christ speaks for itself:

'The Lord is my *shepherd*,
I shall want nothing.
He makes me lie down in green pastures
and leads me beside the waters of peace (Ps. 23.1-2).

Now in this same district there were *shepherds* out in the fields, keeping watch through the night over their flock, when suddenly... (Lk. 2.8).

Jesus was born at Bethlehem in Judea during the reign of *king* Herod. After his birth, see, wise men of the East arrived in Jerusalem, asking: 'Where is the child who is born to be *king* of the Jews?' (...) *King* Herod was greatly perturbed when he heard this... (Mt. 2.1-3).

The *kings* of the earth stand ready,

and the rulers conspire together
against the Lord and his anointed *king* (Ps. 2.2).

When the Lord from Zion hands you the *sceptre*,
the symbol of your power,
march forth through the ranks of your enemies (Ps. 2.2).

She (Mary) will bear a son. And you will give him the name Jesus
(Saviour), for he will save *his people* from their sins' (Mt. 1.21).

So this liturgical arrangement underlines the kingship of the annunciated
and new born child Jesus. At the same time it evokes in a particular way
the tension bewteen this kingship and that of 'the kings of the earth' (of
whom Herod figures here as the representative).

The reading of Paul's first letter to the Thessalonians, about the
resurrection of all who have died 'in Christ', results in that of Jesus' stay at
Bethany after the resurrection of Lazarus.

'*Six days before the Passover festival* Jesus came to Bethany, where
Lazarus lived whom he had *raised* from the dead. There a supper was
given in his honour, at which Martha served, and Lazarus sat among the
guests with Jesus' (Jn 12.1).

The two readings are flanked by two significant psalms:

'O Lord my God, I cried to thee
and thou didst heal me.
O Lord, thou hast *brought me up* from Sheol
and *saved my life* as I was sinking into the abyss.
Thou hast turned my laments into dancing,
thou hast stripped off my sackcloth
and clothed me with joy (Ps. 30.3, 12).

I waited, waited for the Lord,
He bent down to me and heard my cry.
He *brought me up* out of the muddle pit,
out of the mire and the clay;
He set my feet on a rock
and gave me a firm footing' (Ps. 40.2).

Who is the 'I' of Psalm 30 and 40 in this very context? Apparently it applies
to Lazarus. However, the coincidence with the 'I' of Jesus himself,
immediately before the Holy Week, seems obvious to me. This connection
recurs, albeit in a different way, in Luke 16: Lazarus here has the features
of Jesus, risen from the dead; compare for instance Luke 16.31 and Luke
24.27 and 44. I shall shortly return to the subject below.

In the service of 'Palm Sunday', the reading of Ephesians 1.3-19 and
Matthew 21.1-10 are accompanied by the two psalms we know as 'Yhwh is
King'-psalms:

> 'Let the rivers clap their hands,
> let the hills sing aloud together
> before the Lord; for He comes to *judge* the earth.
> He will judge the world with righteousness
> and the peoples in justice (Ps. 98.8).
> The Lord is *king*! Let the earth be glad,
> let coasts and islands all rejoice' (Ps. 97.1).

It is quite obvious that the choice of these psalms intends to stress Paul's
accent on the cosmological impact of the reign of Christ (Eph. 1.10!), who
is welcomed in Jerusalem by the crowd as the great king (Mt. 21.1-10).

Above, we already had a look at some fragments of psalms featuring
during the night right before Good Friday. A great number of psalms are
sung, and what they have in common is the theme of conspiring, treason
and accusation of the innoccent. Again the 'I' of those psalms evidently is
taken as the 'I' of Christ himself.

If possible, this seems even more to be the case with regard to the Psalms
recited on Good Friday:

> 'Malicious witnesses step forward,
> they question me on matters of which I know nothing.
> They return me evil for good,
> *lying* in wait to take my life (Ps. 35.11).
>
> I have had my fill of woes,
> they have brought me to the threshold of Sheol.
> I am numbered with those who go down to the abyss,
> I have become like *a man beyond help*.
> Will thy wonders be known in the dark,
> thy victories in the land of oblivion? (Ps. 88.4, 13).
>
> My God, my God, why hast thou *forsaken* me
> and art so far form saving me,
> from heeding my groans?
> They share out my garments among them
> and cast lots for my clothes' (Ps. 22.2, 19).

Besides these psalms of suffering, once more also Psalm 109 is sung. It
needs no argument that continually the 'I' is identified with the 'I' of Christ
in his agony. [Apart from that, I am of the opinion that verses 9-19 of
Psalm 109 must be understood as a long quotation out of the mouth of the
enemies, and that verse 20 can be read as: 'This, the acting of those who are

prosecuting me by the Lord' (corresponding to the version of the Septuagint).]

Before turning to the psalms which figure in the opening of the Pascal Vigil, we take a look at two other psalms sung later on. It applies to Psalm 65 and 30:

'We owe thee *praise*, O God in Zion,
thou hearest prayer,
vows shall be paid to thee (Ps. 65.1).

I called unto thee, O Lord [or: '*Lord*!']
and I pleaded with thee, Lord, for mercy:
'What profit in my death if I go down into the pit?
Can the dust confess thee or proclaim thy truth?' (Ps. 30.9).

Psalm 30 also appeared in the 'Lazarus-service' a week before. So the psalm functions as an inclusion of the octave of the Holy (Great) Week. Again we may see how the 'I' of the crying Lazarus becomes the 'I' of Christ, who is finally 'brought up from Sheol' by God – to whom is directed the praise of Psalm 65.

Now I would like to mention the two psalms of the *lucernarium*-rite as opening of the Pascal Vigil. In fact, the light ceremony is flanked by Psalm 113 and 118 respectively, with Psalm 113.2 and 118.24 as antiphons. The psalms are reproduced here in whole, with numbered verses and a main division as proposed by me:

1. 'Halleluiah! Praise, you that are his servants,
    praise the name of the Lord.
2. *Blessed be the name of the Lord*
    now and evermore.
3. From the rising of the sun to its setting
    may the Lord's name be praised.
4. High [Elevate] is the Lord above all nations,
    his glory above the heavens
5. Who is like the Lord our God
    who sets his throne so high,
6. who deigns to look down so low
    in heaven and on earth?
7. Who lifts up the weak out of the dust
    and raises [elevates] the poor from the dunghill,
8. giving him a place [throne] among princes,
    among the princes of his people;
9. who makes [let throne] the woman in a childless house
    a happy mother of children. Halleluiah!' (Ps. 113)

A (1–4)

1. 'It is good to give thanks to the Lord,
   for his love endures for ever.
2. Declare it, house of Israel:
   his love endures for ever!
3. Declare it, house of Aaron:
   his love endures for ever!
4. Declare it, you that fear the Lord:
   his love endures for ever!

B (5–21)

5. When in my distress I called to the Lord,
   his answer was to set me free.
6. The Lord is on my side, I have no fear;
   what can man do to me?
7. The Lord is on my side, He is my helper,
   and I shall gloat over my enemies.
8. It is better to find refuge in the Lord
   than to trust in men.
9. It is better to find refuge in the Lord
   than to trust in princes.
10. All nations surround,
    but in the Lord's name I will drive them away.
11. They surround me on this side and on that,
    but in the Lord's name I will drive them away.
12. They surround me like bees at the honey,
    they attack me, as fire attacks brushwood,
    but in the Lord's name I will drive them away.
13. They thrust hard against me so that I nearly fall,
    but the Lord has helped me.
14. The Lord is my refuge and defence,
    He has become my deliverer.
15. Hark! Shouts of deliverance
    in the camp of the righteous!
16. With his right hand the Lord does mighty deeds,
    the right hand of the Lord raises up.
17. I shall not die, but live,
    to proclaim the works of the Lord.
18. The Lord did indeed chasten me,
    but He did not surrender me to Death.
19. Open to me the gates of righteousness;
    I will enter by them and praise the Lord.

20. 'This is the gate of the Lord:
    the righteous shall make their entry through it!'
21. I will praise thee, for thou hast answered me
    and hast become my deliverer.

    C (22–27)

22. The stone which the builders rejected
    has become the chief corner-stone.
23. This is the Lord's doing,
    it is marvellous in our eyes.
24. *This is the day which the Lord has made,*
    let us exult and rejoice in it.
25. We pray thee, O Lord, deliver us (Hosannah),
    we pray thee, O Lord, send us prosperity.
26. Blessed in the name of the Lord are all who come;
    we bless you from the house of the lord.
27. The Lord is God, He has given light to us,
    the ordered line of pilgrims by the horns of the altar.

    D (28–29)

28. Thou art my God, and I will praise thee,
    my God, I will exalt thee.
29. It is good to give thanks to the Lord:
    yes, his love endures for ever!'

I take it for granted that what we have here are the two psalms which open and close the so-called 'Hallel' (Ps. 113–118). In Matthew 26.30/ Mark 14.26 we read:

> 'And having sung the *Hallel* they left unto the Mount of Olives'.

We know that in Jewish tradition the same group of psalms has been linked with the *Pesach* as well as with the feast of Leaves. In the light of everything, it seems to be a very interesting datum that the Armenian Lectionary of Jerusalem just relates these 'corner-psalms' of the 'Hallel' with the celebration in the Paschal Vigil.

Let us take a further look at these two psalms. Psalm 113 can be seen as the basic Creed of the entire Old Testament. The most characteristic quality of Yhwh is that he, the *Elevate*, with his *throne* so immensely high settling, *elevates* the poor from the dunghill, giving him a *throne* among princes, while enthroning the unfruitful among her children! Indeed, we meet here the very message of the Old Testament in a nutshell: the highness of Yhwh is demonstrated in the lives of the most humble men. The songs of Miriam and Hannah, alongside with that of Mary in the New Testament, are hymnic affirmation of that very faith. In Psalm 113, the same motif finds expression once more in another way: he who sets his throne *so high*, he also looks down *so low* (verse 5). And when Yhwh looks down, he looks after the oppressed ones, we learn of Exodus 2.23–25.

Psalm 118 can be divided into four main parts (A–D). In A we find an appeal to the liturgical community for praise. Also at the end, in D, there is a similar appeal, now from the mouth of a single person, whose 'I' is expressed in verse 28. This person appears in part B, telling his story of deliverance to the assembly. The essence of his story is summarized at the beginning of this part B, in verse 5:

> 'I called (for help), he answered (by setting me free)'.

They, the many, had already reacted to this particular story of deliverance, in verse 20:

> 'This (properly: *here*) is the gate of the Lord: the righteous shall make their entry through it!'

Indeed just that happens in part C, where the astonished assembly sings of the rejected stone that had become the chief corner-stone. And the many react in verse 24 like they did in verse 20:

> 'This (properly: *here*) is the day which the Lord has made, let us exult and rejoice in it!'.

There too we find the famous text of the 'Benedictus', quoted in Matthew 21.9 (verse 26).

All in all, both psalms give evidence of great amazement about what can be called 'the impossible possibility' which has been experienced as reality. That is to say: a reality in confession, or rather, the type of reality celebrated in a liturgical way at Passover. And it is the 'I' and the 'He' respectively of all the psalms which have passed the revue, who stay in the centre of this reality.

5. *Some theological implications*

With that we have arrived at an answer to our initial question that is, theologically speaking, very relevant indeed. Thanks to the data of the Armenian Lectionary we now know what exactly could be meant by Egeria speaking of the appropiateness of Scripture-readings, psalms and hymns in the fourth-century Christian community of Jerusalem. Anyway, we have seen in sections 3 and 4 above which psalms feature in the ALJ.

The appropiateness of those psalms is found in their direct application to Christ, his deepest humiliation and his most exalted glorification. Bishop Cyril and John of Jerusalem, their catechumens and their entire community, heard in the 'I' of so many psalms the voice of Christ (*vox*

Christi ad Patrem). Likewise, they heard in some other psalms the voice of prophecy about Christ (*vox prophetae de Christo*). Finally, they heard their own cries to Christ in yet another type of psalm (*vox ecclesiae ad Christum*; cf. Fisher 1982: 31).

With that they were in line with a similar approach to the psalms in former times as well as later on.

Concerning the former times I would like to point out the way in which Luke describes how the 'Law and Prophets' have spoken of the Messiah. We have already found an allusion to that in the parable of the rich man and Lazarus (Lk. 16.19-31). We can find the same, yet more explicitly in the last chapter of the third gospel. On their way to Emmaus, there suddenly appears a stranger who is astonished at the disciples' lack of insight:

> 'How dull you are!', he answered. 'How slow to believe all that the prophets said! Was the Messiah not bound to suffer thus before entering upon his glory?' Then he began with Moses and all the prophets, and explained to them the passages which referred to himself in every part of the scriptures (Lk. 24.25-27).

Some verses later, the risen Christ appears amidst his disciples:

> 'And he said to them: "This is what I meant by saying, while I was still with you, that everything written about me in the Law of Moses and in the Prophets *and Psalms* was bound to be fulfilled". Then he opened their minds to understand the scriptures' (Lk. 24.43b-45, italics mine).

Some decades after Egeria's travels, and more or less during the same time the ALJ appeared in its written form, it is Augustine who fully continues the messianic reading and interpretation of the psalms. To give just a very small impression of it, I note a few sayings of Augustine taken from his *Enarrationes in Psalmos*. The following quotations deal with the pronouncements of Psalms 42.1 and 43.1 (in a free rendering of the original Latin text):

> 'Who is speaking here? If we want to, we ourselves are speaking here. Not as one single human person, but as one single body, the body of Christ, the church (. . .) That is to say: that one omnipresent human person, with the head in heaven, the limbs here below. That voice, now rejoicing, now lamenting (. . .) that voice appears to be well-known: it is our own voice' [sit unusquisque in Christi corpore, et loquetur hic].

Finally, I would like to mention a particular utterance along the same line of interpretation, but now set in and grown out of our own contemporary context. Dietrich Bonhoeffer who, writing about the great sufferings, the expressions of innocence, but no less the curses and impassioned cries for justice in the psalms, ultimately concludes that:

'We are going to suppose that it is here someone else who is praying. That one who is expressing his innocence, who is evoking the divine judgement, or has descended into such a massive suffering, is nobody else than Jesus Christ himself. He himself is praying here. And not only here, but in the whole Psalter. The *human* Jesus Christ, to whom distress, illness or sorrow are not strange, who yet was the Righteous one, he is praying in the Psalter through the mouth of his community. The Psalter is the prayerbook of Jesus Christ in its most proper sense' (Bonhoeffer 1987: 39; italics mine).

This line of thinking, profound as it is, offers a very fruitful broadening of something like the multi-perspectivism of the psalms. I personally think it is really significant to continue reflecting in this way on the psalms, in line with the Jerusalem community back during the celebration of the Pascal Vigil of 380–384 CE.

Bibliography

Bonhoeffer, D. 1987 *Gemeinsames Leben. Das Gebetbuch der Bibel* (DBW, 5; G.L. Müller / A. Schönherr (eds.), München).

Gingras, G.E. (ed.) 1970 *Egeria: Diary of a Pilgrimage* (ACW, 38; New York).

Fischer, B. 1982 *Die Psalmen als Stimme der Kirche. Gesammelte Studien zur christlichen Psalmenfrömmigkeit* (Trier).

Maraval, P. (ed.) 1971 *Égérie: Journal de voyage (Itinéraire)* (Paris: SC 296).

Renoux, A. (ed.) 1969 [1971] *Le Codex Arménien Jérusalem 121*, Turnhout I 1969, II 1971 (PO 165/168).

Scriptural quotations are mostly taken from the New English Bible.

PSALM 32 – STRUCTURE, GENRE, INTENT AND LITURGICAL USE

Stephanus D. Snyman
Bloemfontein, RSA

1. *Introduction*

Psalm 32 is an interesting psalm. It was one of the church father Augustine's favourite psalms and Luther called it one of the Pauline psalms (according to Luther the other Pauline psalms are Psalms 51, 130 and 143), and the psalm is in fact quoted in Rom. 4.7-8. This psalm is also the second of the seven penitential psalms of the early church (Pss. 6, 32, 38, 51, 102, 130 and 143). It is somewhat surprising that there is relatively little published on a psalm with such a rich tradition in the church, and therefore it would be worthwhile to investigate the psalm anew.

2. *Structure*

2.1 *Demarcation of the psalm*

Before any investigation into the structure of the psalm in question can be made, it first needs to be demarcated. The heading of the psalm (משכיל לדוד) is an indication of the start of a new psalm. It scarcely needs to be argued that לדוד appears prominently in the headings of several psalms (thus for example Pss. 26, 27, 28, 29, 30, 31, 34 in the immediate vicinity of the Psalm) and that משכיל is also found in the headings of several other psalms (Pss. 42; 44; 45; 52; 53; 54; 55; 74; 78; 88; 89; 142). Psalm 32 is also characterized by a unique vocabulary that differs from that of Psalm 31. The אשרי in verses 1 and 2 also serve as an indication of a new pericope.

The conclusion of the psalm is not so easily determined. Psalm 33 contains no heading, which leads to the question as to where Psalm 32 ends and Psalm 33 begins, if indeed these are two psalms.

A comparison between verse 11 of Psalm 32 and verse 1 of Psalm 33 clearly illustrates that significant similarities exist between these two verses:

32:11 שמחו ביהוה וגי לו צדיקים והרנינו

33.1 רננו צדיקים ביהוה לישרים נאוה תהלה:

'Rejoice in the Lord and be glad, you righteous, sing, all you who are upright in heart!' (NIV Ps. 32:11).

'Sing joyfully to the Lord, you righteous; it is fitting for the upright to praise him.' (NIV Ps. 33:1).

The righteous צדיקים (32:11 and 33:1) and upright ישרים (32:11 and 33:1) must rejoice רננו (32:11 and 33:1) in the Lord ביהוה (32:11 and 33:1). There might even be the possibility of a chiastic construction between verse 11 of Psalm 32 and verse 1 of Psalm 33. The first hemistich of 32:11 forms a chiasm with the first hemistich of 33:1 and similarly the second hemistich of 32:11 and the second hemistich of 33:1 form a chiasm:

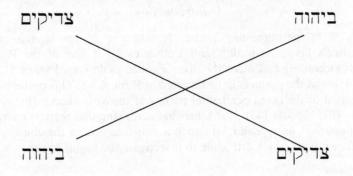

Also compare:

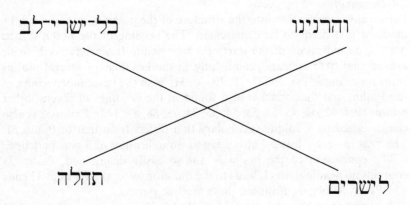

There is also the possibility of a chiastic construction between these two verses: שמחו (A rejoice, at the beginning of the verse); והרנינו (B sing); רננו (B sing); תהלה (A praise, at the end of the verse).

The syntactic and stylistic correlation between the concluding verse of Psalm 32 and the first verse of Psalm 33 is too conspicuous and prominent to be ignored. The imperatives of 32.11 are continued in 33.1; the common vocabulary shared by the two verses and the common addressee – the

righteous – indicate a connection between the two verses (Willmes 1996: 10). There are different possibilities to be considered:

The *first possibility* is to maintain the traditional division of the two psalms. It would be possible to argue that the praise that concludes Psalm 32 does not necessarily imply that it originally belonged together with Psalm 33. The praise that concludes Psalm 32 and the praise that forms the beginning of Psalm 33 could indeed have been the reason why the two Psalms were placed one after the other. It often happens in the Psalter that lament changes to praise at the end of a psalm. One could also point out the ביהוה which occurs in both verses 10 and 11 and which serves as an indication of the connection between verse 11 and the rest of Psalm 32. As far as Psalm 33 is concerned, the Psalm consists of 22 verses, which is the exact number of letters in the Hebrew alphabet, and which gives the impression of an own complete unit. Moreover, the common features of the last verse of Psalm 32 and the first verse of Psalm 33 may indeed form the basis of an argument for the division of the two Psalms (Willmes 1996: 10). Another argument in favour of the traditional standpoint is that if Psalm 33:2 were to be the opening verse of the psalm, the imperative of 33:2 would have no addressee (Willmes 1996: 10).

The *second possibility* is the exact opposite of the first. Psalms 32 and 33 must be regarded as one psalm, especially as Psalm 33 has no heading and simply seems to proceed from Psalm 32. Text-critically there is also support for this standpoint. There are indeed a few manuscripts that have Psalms 32 and 33 reading as one psalm. The praise of Yahweh expressed in verse 11 of Psalm 32 is elaborated on in Psalm 33. However, Psalm 33 approaches the theme of praise for Yahweh from a totally different perspective than that of Psalm 32. In Psalm 33 the reason for the praise of Yahweh is his care for his creation. The theme of forgiveness of sins that forms the basis for the praise of Yahweh in Psalm 32 does not play a role again in Psalm 33. Psalms 32 and 33 should therefore preferably be read as two separate psalms.

The *third possibility* would be to add Psalm 32:11 to Psalm 33:1. Psalm 32:10 could serve as a good conclusion for Psalm 32, while the element of praise in verse 11 could join up effortlessly with Psalm 33 due to the syntactic and stylistic connection between the two verses. The imperative plural forms in verse 11 also result in a break with the preceding 10 verses of Psalms 32. Yet it is also true that it is not strange to find a psalm ending with praise of Yahweh. There are also links between verse 11 and the rest of Psalm 32, which serve as an indication that verse 11 indeed belongs to the rest of Psalm 32. ביהוה is encountered in both verses 10 and 11, and רני in verse 7 once again occurs as הרנינו in verse 11. The possibility of regarding Psalm 32:11 as part of Psalm 33 therefore does not convince. The last verse of Psalm 32 is part of the psalm.

The *fourth possibility* is to add Psalm 33:1 to Psalm 32:11. As already mentioned above, the conspicuous syntactic and stylistic links between the two verses make this a possibility. The occurrence of ביהוה in Psalm 32:10; 32:11 and 33:1 supports the argument that Psalm 33:1 rather belongs with the conclusion of Psalm 32:11. Psalm 33:2 contains ליהוה which differs from the ביהוה of the preceding verses. The 22 verses of Psalm 33 correspond with the number of letters of the Hebrew alphabet, but this is not a decisive argument, for it does not make of Psalm 33 an acrostic psalm like, for example, Psalm 34 where every line of verse starts with the next letter of the Hebrew alphabet.

Choosing between the possibilities is not easy. In this contribution a provisional choice is made for the standpoint that the traditional division between Psalms 32 and 33 should be maintained. The subtle wordplay between אשרי in verse 1 and ישרי in verse 11 tips the scale in favour of the traditional division.

2.2 *Text-critical considerations*

In verse 2 the Sexta Manuscript has a reading meaning 'to forget' and accordingly reads the נשא (carry, forgiven) as נשה which means 'to forget' in Hebrew. There are no other Hebrew manuscripts that contain this reading and, for this reason, the reading of the Masoretic text should be retained. The phrase ואין ברוחו רמיה (and in whose spirit there is no deceit), is sometimes regarded as a possible addition to the text. There is, however, no manuscript evidence that supports the omission of the phrase. The Greek translation (LXX) also reads 'in his mouth' instead of 'in his spirit' in the case of the phrase ואין ברוחו רמיה. If one were to accept the reading of the Septuagint, it would amount to a changing of the consonant text from ברוחו to בפיו, something which is usually avoided. The Syrian translation reads בלבו as 'in his heart', which is also a deviation from the consonant text, without any textual evidence.

In the case of verse 3 some manuscripts read כלו as a third person masculine singular perfect, qal, of כלה the sense of 'destroyed', 'finished' instead of בלו as the third person masculine singular perfect qal of בלה in the sense of 'decrepit', 'eroded', 'emaciated', 'grown old'. In the context of the psalm the reading of the Masoretic text nevertheless makes more sense. The psalmist was not yet completely destroyed by his silence as the alternative reading suggests, but he was indeed decrepit and emaciated as the Masoretic text implies.

In the case of verse 4, the Septuagint has a reading which can be translated as 'through hard work' or 'by suffering' instead of 'my vitality'. There is, however, no compelling reason to change the text on the basis of the reading of the Septuagint. The idea of vitality that drains away is a powerful metaphor used by the poet to express his condition before Yahweh. There are also manuscripts that read כתרבני instead of בחרבני with the result that the text reads 'my vitality was turned into the drought of summer' in order to express the comparison even better and, for this reason, this reading is preferred to that of the Masoretic text. The New International Version (NIV) and the 1933/53 as well as the 1983 translation of the Bible into Afrikaans also accepted this version in preference to that of the Masoretic text.

In the case of verse 5 there are a few manuscripts and a version of the Septuagint that read פשעי as פשעי, the concept 'my iniquities' (plural) is changed to 'my iniquity' (singular). It is better to retain the Masoretic text in this instance, as the context makes it clear that more than one transgression is at stake here.

In verse 7 there is a *hapax legomenon* רני that because of dittography should, according to BHS, rather be replaced with מגני in the sense of 'shields'. In this case the translation would have to read 'with saving shield You surround me'. It is, however, unnecessary to change the text in this way.

The variant readings proposed for the rest of the psalm are either unimportant or result in changes that are too drastic for the Masoretic text (cf. Kraus 1972: 254; Willmes 1996: 10–14).

2.3. *An analysis of the structure of the psalm*

A quick overview of some relevant publications on Psalm 32 reveals how little agreement exists between scholars regarding the structure of the psalm. Auffret (1988: 257, 262) and Ridderbos (1972: 233) distinguish a dichotomy of verse 1-5 and 6-11. According to quite a number of scholars the psalm should be seen as consisting of three parts. Ridderbos (1955: 273–278) distinguishes a tripartition in the psalm consisting of vv. 1-2; 3-5 and 6-11, a division also encountered in the work of Van Uchelen (1979: 214–215). Lamparter (1962: 163–166) also works with a tripartition, but

differs from Ridderbos in the sense that the division he arrives at consists
of verses 1-5; 6-10 and 11. Brinkman (1995: 152–153) divides the psalm
into verses 1-2; 3-9 and 10-11. Weiser's (1975: 282) division of the psalm
consists of verses 1-2; 3-7 and 8-11, thus also dividing the psalm in three
parts. Following an in-depth analysis, Willmes (1996: 27) arrives at the
following division of the psalm: verses 1-2; 3-7; 8; 9-11 creating a four-part
division.

Craigie (1983: 265) sees a chiastic structure in the psalm: Wisdom (vv. 1-
2) A; Thanksgiving (vv. 3-5) B; Thanksgiving (vv. 6-8) B and Wisdom (vv.
9-10) B, after which verse 11 follows as the conclusion of the psalm. Kraus
(1972: 255–258) works with a division of verses 1-2; 3-5; 6-7; 8-9; 10 and 11,
distinguishing no less than six units in the psalm. Anderson's (1972: 255–
259) division corresponds with that of Kraus, but differs regarding the
division of the last two verses of the psalm, which Anderson regards as a
unit. Hossfeld (1993: 203–205) also detects a six part division in the psalm
consisting of 1-2; 3-5; 6; 7-8; 9-10 and 11.

A fresh look at the structure of the psalm yields the following results:

1 לדוד משכיל

1.1 אשרי נשוי־פשע כסוי חטאה:

2 אשרי אדם לא יחשב יהוה לו עון

2.1 ואין ברוחו רמיה:

3 כי החרשתי בלו עצמי בשאגתי כל־היום

4 כי יומם ולילה תכבד עלי ידך

4.1 נהפך לשדי בחרבני קי סלה:

5 חטאתי אודיעך ועוני לא־כסיתי

5.1 אמרתי אודה עלי פשעי ליהוה

5.2 ואתה נשאת עון חטאתי סלה:

6 על־זאת יתפלל כל־חסיד אליך לעת מצא רק

6.1 לשטף מים רבים אליו לא יגיעו:

7 אתה סתר לי מצר תצרני רני פלט תסובבני סלה:

8 אשכילך ואורך בדרך־זו תלך איעצה עליך עיני:

9 אל־תהיו כסוס כפרד אין הבין במתג־ורסן עדיולבלום

9.1 בל קרב אליך:

10 רבים מכאובים לרשע והבוטח ביהוה חסד יסובבנו:

11 שמחו ביהוה וגילו צדיקים והרנינו כל־ישרי־לב:

Stich 2 and stich 2.1 must be connected because of the *waw* copulative
that stich 2.1 starts with. The אשרי with which both stich 1.1 and 2 start and
which also occurs only here in the psalm, necessitates the joining of the two
stichs (Willmes 1996: 15). In addition the stichs are characterized by an
accumulation of words from the semantic field of sin / transgression / guilt:
עון חטא פשע.

Stichs 3 – 4.1 are connected. The causal כי in stich 4 and the references to human body parts ('my bones' in stich 3, 'my vitality' in stich 4.1 and 'your hand' in stich 4) serve as arguments for the connection. Stichs 3 and 4 are also unified by the occurrence of first person singular forms, and the occurrence of יום in stichs 3 and 4 serves as a further basis for their connection.

The stichs of verse 5 are linked together by the first person singular forms in stichs 5, 5.1 and 5.2. The occurrence of words used to describe sin also forms an interesting pattern:

חטא (stich 5)
עון (stich 5)
פשע (stich 5.1)
עון (stich 5.2)
חטא (stich 5.2)

The pattern forms an unmistakable *inclusio*.

Stichs 6 and 6.1 are connected as a result of the ל, which functions as a connecting particle. Stich 7 connects with stichs 6 and 6.1. via the על-זאת with which stich 6 commences, and a connection is also made with the preceding stichs 5–5.2. The occurrence of אתה reinforces this connection even further. Stichs 3–7 are further characterized by the occurrence of סלה at the end of the stichs 4, 5 and 7. This also serves to connect the stichs with one another, while simultaneously placing them in an exceptional position in terms of the rest of the Psalm.

The כי of stich 3 establishes a connection with stichs 1–2.1, with the result that stichs 1–7 are connected. It is also noteworthy that exactly the same word used for 'sin' in stich 5 is also used in stichs 1–2. There is also an interesting chiastic relation between stichs 1–2 and 5: כסה נשא in stich 1 and נשא כסה in stichs 5 and 5.2.

Stich 8 introduces a new section of the psalm. For the first time since verse 1 the stem form שכל is used. There is no mention of a confession of sins. Also, the image or metaphor used of a horse and/or mule does not have any conspicuous connection with the preceding passage. Stichs 9 and 9.1 are connected by the unity of the image of a horse that must be controlled with a bit and a bridle. Stichs 9 and 9.1 are connected to stich 8, as the stich forms the introduction to what is said in stich 9. Stich 10 forms the conclusion of stichs 8 – 9.1 and is therefore connected to them. Stich 10 forms a chiasm (Hossfeld 1993: 200): over against the woes of the wicked (ארבים מכאובים) are those surrounded by Yahweh's love (חסד יסובבנו) and the wicked is contrasted with those who put their trust in Yahweh. It is notable that the stem form סבב appears at the end of both stichs 7 and 10, creating a connection between stichs 1–7 and 8–10.

Stich 11 distinguishes itself from the rest of the psalm through the
occurrence of the plural imperatives in the form of a call to praise. The
occurrence of ביהוה in both stichs 10 and 11 further creates a connection
between stichs 8–10 and 11. The psalm forms a unit with the wordplay
between אשרי in verses 1 and 2 and ישרי-לב in verse 11.

Schematically the result of the analysis can be presented as follows:

Verses (stichs) 1–2	Two benedictions	A
Verses (stichs) 3–4	The effect of remaining silent	B1
Verse (stich) 5	Confession	B2
Verses (stichs) 6–7	The effect of confession	B3
Verses (stichs) 8–10	Wisdom advice	C
Verse (stich) 11	A Call to praise	D

The six strophes which comprise the psalm therefore form four stanzas: A
(vv. 1-2); B (vv. 3-7); C (vv. 8-10), and D (v. 11). In addition it is clear that
stanza B (strophes B1, B2 and B3 – vv. 3-7) forms the centre of the psalm
with strophe B2 (v. 5) as the core of that strophe. Seybold (1996: 134–136)
arrives at the same conclusion, but without offering any reasoned
argument for the division of the psalm.

Another interesting stylistic feature of the psalm is the amount of times
that specific words appear in it. A significant number of words occur twice
in the psalm:

- אשרי occurs twice (vv. 1, 2).
- נשא occurs twice (vv. 1, 5).
- יום occurs twice (vv. 3, 4).
- כסה occurs twice (vv. 1, 5).
- ידה occurs twice (v. 5).
- רבים occurs twice (vv. 6, 10).
- אתה occurs twice (vv. 5, 7).
- רנן occurs twice (vv. 7, 11).
- סבב occurs twice (vv. 7, 10).
- שכל occurs twice (vv. 1, 8).
- חסד occurs twice (vv. 6, 10).

Ridderbos (1972: 233–234) and Hossfeld (1993: 200) draw attention to
the role played by the number three in the psalm. In verse 1 three words are
used to describe sin: חטא עון פשע. The same three words are repeated in the
confession of verse 5. Verses 1-2 also use three words (יחשב תנשוי כסוי)
to describe the forgiveness of sins. Three words are used to describe the
poet's confession of sin (אודה אודיעך לא-כסיתי). Verse 8 contains three
expressions for 'teach' (אשכילך אורך איעצה). Verse 9 uses three
concepts for 'bridle' (במתג-ורסן לבלום). In verse 7 three words are used
to describe Yahweh's protection (סתר נצר סבב). The word סלה occurs three

times (vv. 4, 5 and 7) and in verse 11 three concepts are used as a call to rejoice (שמחו וגילו טוהרנינו). The name of Yahweh (יהוה), however, occurs four times.

3. Genre

3.1 *Gattung and Sitz im Leben*

The psalm exhibits the typical characteristics of an individual song of thanksgiving (Weiser 1962: 281; Ridderbos 1972: 231; Kraus 1972: 254; Craigie 1983: 265; Hossfeld 1993: 200; Mays 1994: 145). Kraus (1972: 254) distinguishes a range of other *Gattungen* in the psalm: a *Glückwünsche* or benediction in verses 1-2, a narrative in verses 3-5, a didactic statement in verses 6-7, a *Gottesspruch* in verses 8-9, a *'lehrhafte Formulierung einer Grunderfahrung'* or a didactic formulation of a basic experience (of deliverance) in verse 10 and a call to thanksgiving and rejoicing in the style of a hymn in verse 11.

Without repeating the debate concerning the *Gattung* of the psalm, it is clear that two distinguishing elements are prominently present in the psalm. On the one hand, the psalm exhibits the typical characteristics of an individual song of thanksgiving (a situation of distress, deliverance, an expression of trust, and a call to praise). On the other hand, there are undeniably also wisdom elements present in the psalm (counsel; teaching and instruction offered; the way one should go; and the distinction between the righteous and the wicked).

For Ridderbos (1955: 270–271), the psalm is a thanksgiving song with a didactic paranetic character. In this regard Weiser (1982: 281) remarks: 'The juxtaposition of the two motives of thanksgiving and instruction causes a mixed style, so that the prayer of thanksgiving is interspersed with fragments which are closely connected with the Wisdom Literature.' Dahood's summary (1972: 194) points in the same direction: 'A psalm of thanksgiving for recovery from illness... Because of the several didactic elements, some would label this a Wisdom psalm.' (cf. also Anderson 1972: 254). For Hossfeld (1993: 200) the psalm contains elements of both a thanksgiving song as well as typical characteristics of a wisdom song. Seybold (1996: 134) characterizes the psalm as *'ein Danklied mit einem starken weisheitlichen Einschlag'* or a thanksgiving song with a strong orientation to wisdom in it. The determination of the *Gattung* shows that the psalm cannot be read only as a penitential psalm. Psalm 32 concludes with a call to praise the Lord.

What is the *Sitz im Leben* or typical setting of the psalm? There are few, if any indications in the text itself that could lead one to a specific *Sitz im Leben* for the psalm. Kraus (1972: 254) considers an event in the life of a believer that involved such a person experiencing salvation and now sharing it with other believers, presumably in the temple as a place of worship (Hossfeld 1993: 204). There is speculation about whether the psalmist was cured of a deadly disease, but this is improbable. The psalm is about an experience of forgiveness of sins rather than an experience of healing from illness.

The psalm contains no historical markers, with the result that an exact dating is impossible. However, the absence of the mentioning of any offerings or sacrifices, the personal nature of the psalm and the influence from wisdom circles point towards a late (exilic or even post-exilic, cf. Buttenwieser 1969: 654ff.) dating (*contra* Ridderbos 1955: 272 who attributes the psalm to David).

3.2 *Investigation into possible traditio-historical material*
There is no reference to the stereotypical salvific traditions in the history of the people of Israel (creation, the Patriarchs, the Exodus, Sinai, wilderness, land and Zion). The reference to 'a flood of great waters' in verse 6 must not be understood as referring to the Flood (*contra* Lamparter 1961: 165), but rather as a metaphor expressing danger, as is the case elsewhere in the Old Testament (Ps. 66:12; Isa. 43:2). The heading, the benedictions in verses 1 and 2 (cf. Ps. 1) and the שכיל in verse 8 suggest influences from the wisdom tradition. The absence of reference to the prominent salvific traditions in the history of the people of Israel enhances the personal – even intimate – nature and style of the psalm (*contra* Willmes 1996: 48, who mentions the possibility of the psalm having been composed by temple personnel for liturgical purposes).

3.3 *Some remarks on possible redactional activity*
The mixture of two different *Gattungen* (an individual song of thanksgiving and the influence of wisdom elements) gives rise to the suspicion that Psalm 32 possibly did not originate from the hand of one poet as one complete unit at one specific time. Verses 3-7 are probably the original part of the psalm, which was later provided with a wisdom framework (vv. 1-2; 8-10). When the psalm found its place in the temple and cult, verse 11 was probably added as an appropriate call to the community of believers to praise Yahweh for his deed of forgiveness. It therefore seems that at least three stages in the development of the psalm may be distinguished.

4. *Intent*

Nearing the end of this investigation, it should be clear that Psalm 32 is rich in theological insights. Weiser (1962: 281) summarises the psalm as a psalm of thanksgiving reminiscing about the poet's personal experience of confession of sin and the consequent forgiveness he received, and the vital lesson every God-fearing person can learn from his experience. For Kraus

(1972: 255, 259), the broken (as a result of sin) and restored (as a result of forgiveness received) relationship between a human being and God is the crucial theme of the psalm.

Starting with the core of the psalm, strophe B1 (vv. 3-4) describes the negative effect of a failure to confess sin ('my bones wasted away... For day and night your hand was heavy upon me; my strength was sapped as in the heat of summer' NIV). At a theological level, one should not make too much of the fact that three different words for sin are used in verses 1 and 5. In the psalm the words are probably used as synonyms (Anderson 1972: 255; Hossfeld 1993: 203). The use of three different concepts serves to emphasize the extent of sin and consequently also the radical nature and extent of the forgiveness received by the poet (Ridderbos 1972: 234). Lamparter (1962: 163) observes that it is not only the moral-ethical dimension of sin that is of importance here, but especially the fact that sin obstructed the poet's relationship with God. The poet relates his psychological and physical suffering due to his failure to confess his sins to God: it was God's hand that was heavy upon him (Weiser 1975: 284; Seybold 1996: 135; cf. also Ps. 38:3). In turn, strophe B3 (vv. 6-7) describes the positive consequences of his confession of sin (the godly shall pray to the Lord; a flood of great water shall not come near him; the Lord is a hiding place and he enjoys the protection of the Lord).

Stanza C (vv. 8-10) also describes a negative and positive aspect but from a different perspective. Negatively, the reader is admonished not to be like a horse or a mule that must be harnessed with a bit and a bridle (v. 9). The woes of the wicked people are many (v. 10a). Positively, the consequence of people putting their trust in the Lord is pointed out: they will be surrounded by his unfailing love (v. 10).

A further question posed to the exegete of Psalm 32 concerns the identity of the speaker in verses 8-10. Some scholars suggest that it may be Yahweh (Lamparter 1961: 165; Kraus 1972: 257; Brinkman 1995: 153; Dahood 1974: 196), while others consider the possibility of it being a wisdom teacher, the poet himself or somebody else (Weiser 1975: 286; Ridderbos 1955: 277; Anderson 1972: 258; Van Uchelen 1979: 216; Seybold 1996: 136; Ridderbos 1972: 233; Craigie 1983: 267). In light of the wisdom elements typical of the psalm, it is proposed here that the speaker in verse 8 should be seen as the poet acting as a wisdom teacher. There are no explicit indications in the text that Yahweh is speaking here. Furthermore, the reference to Yahweh is in the third person singular instead of in the first person singular, as would have been the case if He was speaking in verses 8-10.

The image of the horse or mule that has to be harnessed with a bit in the mouth in order to be controlled by its owner (v. 9), reminds one of the poet's experience narrated in verses 3-4. The reader of the psalm receives the counsel not to make the same mistake as the poet, namely to stubbornly refuse to confess his or her sin. A human being will eventually have to arrive at a confession of sin due to the unbearable burden of Yahweh's hand, which is heavy upon the sinner (Weiser 1975: 287; Lamparter 1962: 166; Ridderbos 1955: 278; Anderson 1972: 259).

Two positive statements frame the psalm: It opens by proclaiming as blessed those people whose sins are forgiven (A, vv. 1-2), and concludes with a call to praise the Lord (D, v. 11). This frame is reinforced by the wordplay between שרי) in verses 1 and 2 and כל־ישרי־לב in verse 11.

The poet confesses his sins with remarkable openness and frankness, and the accumulation of concepts for sin used in the confession indicates the totality with which this is done. The personal nature of the confession is also striking. When the poet gets to the point of confessing his sin, the Lord forgives immediately and completely. Hossfeld (1993: 204) remarks in this regard: 'Divine forgiveness follows immediately after the penitential exercise'. After the confession and forgiveness of sin in strophe B2 (v. 5), the concept of sin is not mentioned again and no further reference is made to it in the remainder of the psalm. This serves as a further indication of Yahweh's complete and immediate forgiveness. What is expressed as a general truth in verse 1 becomes the poet's personal experience in verse 5. Also remarkable, is that forgiveness of sin is received without any mention of sacrifices or offerings. The wordplay between verses 1 and 5 is significant: confessing sin is better than attempting to keep it covered (v. 5). Sin that is uncovered and confessed openly is covered by the Lord (v. 1). Where a human being no longer tries to cover his or her sin, the Lord himself covers it (Ridderbos 1972: 235).

5. *Psalm 32 and liturgy*

According to Hossfeld (1993: 201), Psalm 32 found its place in the worshipping community of exilic / post-exilic Judah. However, it may also find a useful place in current liturgies. Possessing a rich theological content which can be exploited in a sermon, Psalm 32 may be used in a worship service. Verses 1, 2 and 11 may serve as a *votum* or benediction at the beginning or end of such a service. The confession of sin forms part of the liturgy in at least liturgies followed in the reformed tradition. Psalm 32 serves as a prime example of a true confession of sin, and the confession. Forgiveness is proclaimed in a traditional reformed liturgy. Once again Psalm 32 may be put to use in a meaningful way showing that complete forgiveness follows immediately after a true confession of sin.

6. *Conclusion*

Psalm 32 is a psalm with a rich content. In a world where the idea of sin has almost become an embarrassment, the psalm once again focuses on the importance of a consciousness of sin and the eventual confession thereof. It is the disruption of the relationship between God and human beings that renders the confession of sin so essential. More important is the immediate and complete forgiveness on the part of the Lord after the poet's prayer. In the New Testament the theological message of the psalm is echoed in 1 John 1.9: 'If we confess our sins, He is faithful and just to forgive us our sins and to cleanse us from all unrighteousness'.

Bibliography

Anderson, A. A. 1972 *The Book of the Psalms* (Vol. I; New Century Bible; London: Marshall, Morgan & Scott).

Auffret, P. 1988 'Essai sur la structure litteraire du Psaume xxxii', *Vetus Testamentum* 38(3): 257–285.

Brinkman, J. M. 1995 *Psalmen I: Een praktischse bijbelverklaring* (Tekst en Toelichting; Kampen: Kok).

Buttenwieser, M. 1969 *The Psalms chronologically treated with a new translation* (New York: Ktav Publishing House).

Craigie, P. C. 1983 *Psalms 1–50* (WBC; Waco, Texas: Word Books).

Dahood, M. 1974 *Psalms I (1–50)* (AB; New York: Doubleday & Co.).

Hossfeld, F-L. & Zenger, E. 1993 *Die Psalmen I (Psalm 1–50)* (Neue Echter Bibel; Würzburg: Echter).

Kraus, H.-J. 1972 *Psalmen I (Psalmen 1–63)* (BKAT XV/I; Neukirchen-Vluyn: Neukirchener).

Lamparter, H. 1962 *Das Buch der Psalmen I (Psalmen 1–72)* (Die Botschaft des Alten Testaments, 14; Stuttgart: Calwer).

Mays, J. L. 1994 *Psalms* (Interpretation; Louisville: John Knox).

Ridderbos, J. 1955 *De Psalmen I (Psalm 1–41)* (Commentaar op het Oude Testament; Kampen: Kok).

Ridderbos, N. H. 1972 *Die Psalmen. Stilistische Verfahren und Aufbau. Mit besonderer Berücksichtigung von Ps. 1–41* (BZAW, 117; Berlin: Walter de Gruyter).

Seybold, K. 1996 *Die Psalmen* (HAT I/15; Tübingen: Mohr).

Van Uchelen, N. A. 1979 *Psalmen deel I (1–40)* (Nijkerk: Callenbach).

Weiser, A. 1975 *The Psalms: A Commentary* (OTL; London: SCM).

Willmes, B. 1996 *Freude über die Vergebung der Sunde: synchrone end diachrone Analyse von Ps. 32* (Frankfurt am Main: Josef Knecht).

TRACES OF LITURGIES IN THE PSALTER:
THE COMMUNAL LAMENTS, PSALMS 79, 80, 83, 89 IN CONTEXT

Hans Ulrich Steymans
Jerusalem, Israel.

1. *Introduction*

Formal comparison of Mesopotamian prayers and biblical psalms started in the twenties and thirties of the twentieth century.[1] But some developments in both Assyriology and biblical scholarship cast shadows on such attempts at correlation. Benno Landsberger (1926) expressed the need to understand the Babylonian world from its own system without input of biblical ideas and interests. Walter G. Kunstmann (1932: 1) applied this to the investigation of Mesopotamian prayers explicitly reproaching any comparison with biblical material.

Herman Gunkel applied his form-critical or form-historical method to the investigation of psalms. Gunkel saw that psalm poetry as such was ancient in Israel, and that many Psalms must be dated to pre-exilic times. But he mainly kept to the opinion ruling at the beginning of the twentieth century, that the greater number of extant psalms were post-exilic and came from small, more or less private 'conventicles' of pious laymen. The majority of extant psalms were in Gunkel's opinion not real cult psalms; they were 'spiritualized' imitations of the old, now mostly lost, cultic psalm poetry (Mowinkel 1962, vol. I: 29).

Sigmund Mowinckel added to the form-historical method his cult-functional method.

> 'Scientifically speaking, the historical viewpoint from which I regard the psalms is that of form history – or, as it may better be termed, type history (*Gattungsgeschichte*) – a method of approach introduced by Hermann Gunkel. But when I began my *Psalmenstudien* I-VI (1921–24) it had become apparent to me that that point of view was not sufficient. In order to understand the psalms in their relationship to the religious life of Israel and of Judaism it is necessary also to use in addition the cult functional approach. (...) One result of my work in connection with the psalms – which has even surprised myself – is to see to how great an extent the piety and image of God which grew up within the official cult religion in the Temple at Jerusalem is presupposed by, and not a result of, the activity of the great classical prophets' (1962, vol. I: xxiii).

---

1. Stummer (1922); Begrich (1928); Widengren (1937).

Mowinckel had not only drawn a clear distinction between himself and Gunkel but also between himself and the so-called Myth and Ritual School[2] (1962, vol. I: 50–61). Criticism of the Myth and Ritual School and a move from cult and history to literature and canon as horizons for psalm interpretation led to the fact that the main stream of biblical scholarship is not inclined to compare Babylonian prayers with biblical psalms. Gunkel's sociological setting (*Sitz im Leben*) yielded to settings in wisdom and redaction (*Sitz in der Literatur*).[3] Nevertheless some exceptions exist, but nowadays the comparison with ANE material focuses more on the biblical book of Lamentations and Sumerian City Laments than on the Psalter (Dopps-Allsopp 1993; Edelman forthcoming; Berges 2002).[4] The treatment of Mesopotamian laments in studies on Psalms often consists only in an overview of the genres and their structure with the citation of some examples. A ritual or liturgical use of those laments is sometimes mentioned but never taken into account in order to compare the sequence of prayers and their motifs in rituals with those of psalm groups.

The ritual calendar of the New Year Feast at Asshur for the lamentation priest (gala/*kalû*) allows insights in liturgical procedures exercised on special days in the months of *Šabâtu*, *Adaru* and *Nisanu* during the Neo-Assyrian period. Some of the prayers prescribed in this role book for the New Year rituals still exist and so it is possible to reconstruct the liturgy for some days. We are able to witness the liturgical actions as they were celebrated including the words sung or recited. In order to do this one has to combine the role book that only indicates the incipit of the prayers and the editions of those prayers, which arrange the texts according to catalogues, dating or the gods implored.[5]

The collection of prayers used on specific days in a special liturgical setting shows how these texts interacted. For the comparison with biblical material I have selected the third book of the Psalter, because it shows a high percentage of communal laments and most of the psalms belong to two collections with outstanding characteristics (Zenger 2000: 425), the Asaph and the Korah collections.

---

2. Cf. Hooke (1933); Widengren (1937); Engnell (1969: 89–98, 102–106, 180–184); on Ps. 89 Ahlström (1959).

3. Cf. e.g., on Psalm 89, Volgger (1994). For the methodological move from *Psalmenexegese*, which treats each psalm as an individual poem, to *Psalterexegese*, which considers the context of a psalm and the composition of the Psalter, cf. Zenger (2000: 416–435; 2001). For the composition of the third book of the Psalter (73–89) cf. Cole (2000).

4. Dalglish (1962); Ferris (1993); Gerstenberger (1980, 1988, 2001), Bouzard (1997), Emmendörffer (1998).

5. Ebeling (1953); Mayer (1976); Cohen (1981, 1988); Maul (1988); Volk (1989). For the use of *balags* on days 10 and 11 of the *akîtu* festival at Uruk cf. Bouzard (1997: 150).

The last five psalms of the Asaph-collection, Psalms 79–83, show striking resemblances to the remains of certain prayers used during the New Year celebration at Asshur in both form and sequence.[6] A modern approach that focuses on Psalter-redaction sees a border between Psalm 78 and Psalm 79. Psalms 79 and 80 are lamentations, in Psalm 81 an oracle follows, and Psalm 82 tells about God's judgment over other gods. This structure resembles Psalm 74, which is a lament, 75 as an oracle and 76 in the form of a hymn praising God's judgment (Millard 1994: 89; Hossfeld/ Zenger, 2000: 451). Psalm 78 separates those two sequences. But why does the second sequence (Pss. 79–83) contain two laments (Pss. 79, 80)? Why does the whole Asaph collection end in a lament in Psalm 83?

Already Mowinckel (1962, vol. I: 150, vol. II: 63) suggested that Psalms 81 and 82 belong to the New Year celebrations in Jerusalem. Michael D. Goulder (1996) assigned all the psalms of Asaph to several days of the New Year festival. Neither Mowinckel nor Goulder considered the Mesopotamian festival calendar.

In comparing a series of psalms with a series of Mesopotamian prayers used in one specific liturgical context we will become aware that the form and content of prayers do not necessarily reflect their liturgical use. The use of lamentations in Mesopotamia is not restricted to penitential liturgies, as is commonly proposed for the *Sitz im Leben* of laments in biblical scholarship. As a matter of fact, they were used in New Year celebrations, rituals during the restoration of temples and temple walls, war rituals, rituals for the consecration of divine statues, etc. I shall argue that Psalms 79–83, i.e. the final psalms of the Asaph collection, present us with psalms used on one single day of the New Year celebration in exactly the sequence they presently exhibit in the collection and the Psalter. The sequence of psalms in the Psalter, therefore, is not only the outcome of redactional activity, but may sometimes be a reminder of their liturgical use. Evidence for this is given by the sequence of Psalm 70, a psalm for the offering of incense, followed by Psalm 71 which lacks a superscription and thus is distinguished from the preceding psalm in the manuscripts only by an intermediate free space. In manuscript 4QPs[a] from Qumran, Psalm 71 is attached to Psalm 38 bearing a superscript that appoints Psalm 38 to the offering of incense (Flint 1997: 147). Thus the sequence of Psalm 70 and 71 in the canonical Psalter most probably does not result from mere redactional arrangement, but reflects the use of both psalms in the ritual of offering incense.

In asking for the ritual use of Psalms 79–83, I combine both of Mowinckel's approaches, the form critical one, by investigating the

---

6.   For a bibliography and research history on Asaph psalms cf. Seybold (1994: 142 n. 1); Weber (2000b: 521 n. 1); Hossfeld/Zenger (2000: 330–507); Zenger (2000: 425 n. 63).

common and different structures, vocabulary and motifs in Mesopotamian and biblical laments, and the cult functional one, by drawing conclusions from the cultic evidence at Asshur for the cult of Israel.

2. *The Form Critical Approach: Communal Laments*

2.1 *Structure and Motifs*

There is a general lack of agreement as to just which of the biblical psalms are indeed communal laments.[7] Nevertheless, the majority of alleged communal laments belongs to the Korah (Pss. 43, 44, 85) and Asaph (Pss. 74, 77, 79, 80, 83) collections. Moreover, all psalms but 44 and 60 are embodied in the third book of the Psalter. This concentration of communal laments in the third book of the Psalter becomes still more evident when, with many scholars, we include Psalm 89 in this genre (Ferris 1993:16).

According to Mowinckel (1962: 195–219) and Thomas Hieke (1997: 260) the structure of communal laments contains the following elements, which can be correlated to the basic structure of *balags* (Akkadian lament songs) as given by Paul Wayne Ferris (1993: 42).

Psalm	44	60	74	79	80	83	85	balag
Invocation of Yhwh's name	2a	3aV	1aV	1bV	2aV	2aV	5aV	Praise
Imperative Lament	-	-	2–3	-	2–3	2a–c	5ab	
	10–17 18–23	3a–c 4ab.5	1ab 4–9	1b–4	5–7 13–14	3–9	-	Accusatory Complaint
Complaining Question	24b.25	12	10–11	5	5.13a	-	6–7	*adi mati*
Prayer	24–27	3d.4cd. 6–7.13	18–23	6–12	4.8.20 15–18 19b	10–19	8	Appeal
Vow	-	-	-	13	19a.c	-	-	Lament Proper

7. Ferris (1993: 14–16) includes passages from Psalms 31, 35, 42, 43, 44, 56, 59, 60, 69, 74, 77, 79, 80, 83, 85, 89, 94, 102, 109, 137, 142. Hieke (1997: 212–399) treats only Psalms 44, 60, 74, 79, 80, 85 and Lamentations 5 in his thorough linguistic and form critical study of the *Klagelied des Volkes*.

Peculiarities: Divine discourse: Pss. 60.8–10, 85.9–14
                  Yhwh's deeds: Pss. 44.2–4, 80.9–12
                  Hymn: Ps. 74.12–17
                  Confidence: Pss. 44.5–9, 60.14
                  Question: Ps. 60.11

Mowinckel and Ferris use different terms in order to name similar features
and both Hiecke and Ferris state that their table only shows a basic outline
and that the sequence of elements in a particular poem may differ
considerably. Nevertheless, the basic pattern of both the biblical and
Mesopotamian lament is identical. The *invocation of Yhwh's name* may be
developed into a complete hymn of praise, in which the psalm gets a
hymnal introduction. This corresponds to the *praise* in the *balags*, which
does not necessarily start the poem. Such a laudatory element may follow a
lament section. When the *balag* praises the power of the divine word or
strength it can be compared with the mention of Yhwh's deeds in Psalms
44.2-4, 80.9-12, 85.2-4 or the hymn in 74.12-17. Imperatives such as
'Hear!', 'Look here!', 'Appear!', and 'Arise!' have their counterpart in
balags as 'Arise!', 'Go about!', 'Watch!'

> 'The lament may be directed at Yahweh himself, because he has allowed
> such things to happen.... (...) But as a rule, the lamentations are
> directed against the enemies of the people. The *evil and audacious words*
> of the enemies play a distinct part in the lamentations and descriptions
> of distress.' (Mowinckel 1962: 198).

The *accusatory complaint* in Ferris's terminology points to the deity as the
prime cause of the calamity. The question 'Why?' becomes a big issue, as
likewise the impatient 'How long?', which is, in Akkadian, *adi mati* and in
Hebrew *ad matay* (Pss. 74.10; 89.5).

The *appeal* emphasizes that Yhwh's own cause is at stake: 'thy people',
'thine inheritance', 'thy possession', 'thy congregation', 'the sheep of thy
pasture', 'thine anointed', 'thy sanctuary', 'thine enemies', and so on (Pss.
74.1; 79.13; 83.4; 89.39, 52; cf. 94.5; Isa. 69.18). *Balags* use personal
pronouns in order to connect the gods with the suffering people. There are
e.g. 'her – the goddess's – destroyed cattle pen', and 'your sheep with bent
legs' (Cohen 1988: 59).

In order to illustrate the similarities and differences between biblical and
Mesopotamian laments I juxtapose existing texts, thus avoiding the
possible rebuttal that I present only corresponding elements and neglect
the complete structure of each composition. Mesopotamian prayers
compared with biblical laments are *balags*, i.e. laments (Sumerian ér,
Akkadian *taqribtu*) sung to a musical instrument called *balag*, *eršemmas*,
i.e. laments sung to a drum, *eršahungas (Herzberuhigungsklagen)*, i.e.

prayers for the pacification of the allegedly angry divine heart, and *šuillas* (*Handerhebungsgebete*), i.e. prayers said while raising a hand.[8]

The first examples are two laments, which do not totally fit the structure given in the table above. The typical form of a genre is an abstraction hardly ever fitting exactly the real form of a single text (Fohrer 1989: 86). During the New Year liturgies in Asshur, the *balag Nir-gál lú è-dè* is sung on the 26th of *Šabâtu*. There are some parts missing in the extant text copies and I insert into these lacunas passages from other *balags* which show closer resemblance to the biblical counterpart, i.e. Psalm 89. **The common elements are stressed in bold script.** A double line in the *balag* indicates the end of a *kirugu*, a subsection after whose recitation the supplicants probably bowed down.[9]

Balag: Nir-gál lú è-dè	Psalm 89
Praise	Praise
	2 I will sing of your loving kindnesses, O Yhwh, forever; with my mouth I will proclaim your faithfulness to all generations. 3 For you said: 'Loving kindness is established forever.' The heavens – your faithfulness is made firm therein. 4 For you said, 'I have made a covenant with my chosen one, I have sworn to my servant David: 5 'I will establish your descendants forever, and build your throne for all generations.' Selah.

8. Cohen's editions of *balags* and *eršemmas* are far from being available in every library of institutions for biblical studies. Therefore I quote many texts entirely, thus enabling the reader to get an impression of the Mesopotamian laments. For more information about the different genres of Mesopotamian laments cf. Falkenstein (1953: 9–12); Dalglish (1962: 18–40); Cohen (1974, 1981); Maul (1988: 1–72); Dobbs-Allsopp (1993: 30–96); Bouzard (1997: 71–99); Emmendörffer (1998: 22–38). All psalm references in this paper follow the Hebrew Bible, not the King James or NRSV.

9. 'In regard to content each *kirugu* is an independent literary entity of varying length, unrelated to the preceding and subsequent *kirugu's*. On the Old Babylonian texts, with the exception of a find of texts provenience unknown, each *kirugu* is separated from the other by the words "1st (2nd, 3rd, etc.) *kirugu*". (. . .) In the collection of *balag*-tablets of unknown provenience, the *kirugu's* are separated by a heavy line drawn horizontally between the units, the actual term *kirugu* rarely appearing. This latter procedure was also observed in all the first millennium BCE copies of *balag*-lamentations. In some compositions using the horizontal line procedure there also occurs the *gišgigal*, a one line unit situated between some *kirugus's* of the *balag*, this unit likewise being set off form the *kirugus's* by a heavy line drawn horizontally above and below it.' (Cohen 1974: 8). The gesture of bowing down at the end of a *kirugu* seems to be comparable to the inclination during the recitation of the Trinitarian doxology at the end of a psalm or psalm section (Ps. 119) in Roman Catholic monastic tradition.

Expression of Inscrutability

Respected one, manifest one, **what can one know about you?** Bison, respected one, manifest one, what can one know about you? Bison, lord, great hero, **great hero,** ensi of Enlil, bison, lord of Urash, great hero, lord of the Eninnu, bison, heir to the Eshara, great hero, lord of the Eshumesha, bison, lord of the Eshamah, (10) great hero, lord of the Emeurur, great hero, lord of the Emahdi, bison, lord of Kish, great hero, lord of the Ekishiba, bison, lord of the Emeteursag, great hero, lord of the Eunirkitushmah, bison, lord of the house of Kutha, great hero, lord of the Emeslam, bison, lord of Dilbat, (20) great hero, lord of the Eibianum, bison, lord of Dikumaham, great hero, lord of Erabiri,

The Mighty Arm

bison, **the mighty arm** of Enlil, great hero, the child, **the faithful one of 'The Great Mountain',** bison, **lord with overpowering strength,** great hero, son who avenges his father, bison, **reared in the Ekur,** great hero, whose word is joyous, bison, foremost of the Ekur, (30) **great hero, lofty hand of heaven,** bison, surpassing as the heavens, great hero, **as wide as the earth,** (*break in the composition*)

Appeal

May a prayer be said to you, **who knows** his heart!
May a prayer be said to you, **who knows** the heart of An! May a prayer be said to you, who knows the heart of the **Honoured One!** May a prayer be said to you, who knows the heart of great An! May a prayer be said to you, who knows the heart of Enlil! May a prayer be said to you, who knows the heart of the great mountain, father Enlil! (a + 40) May a prayer be said to you, who knows the heart of the great hero! May a prayer be said to you, who knows the heart of the ensi of Enlil! May a prayer be said to you, who knows the heart of the lord of Urash! May a prayer be said to you, who knows the heart of the hero Zababa! May a prayer be said to you, who knows the heart of the lord Dikumaham! May a prayer be said to you, who

Expression of Incomparability

6 Let the **heavens praise** your wonders, O Yhwh, your faithfulness in the assembly of the holy ones. 7 For **who** in the skies **can be compared to** Yhwh? Who among the **heavenly** beings **is like** Yhwh, 8 a God feared in the council of the holy ones, great and awesome above all that are around him?

The Mighty Arm

9 O Yhwh God of hosts, who is as **mighty** as you, O Yhwh? Your faithfulness surrounds you. 10 **You rule** the raging of the sea; when its waves rise, you still them. 11 You crushed Rahab like a carcass; you scattered your enemies with **your mighty arm.** 12 The **heavens** are yours, the **earth** also is yours; the world and all that is in it — you have founded them. 13 The north and the south — you created them; Tabor and Hermon joyously praise your name. 14 **You have a mighty arm; strong is your hand,** high your right **hand.**

knows the heart of Ursaggal! May a prayer be said to you, who knows the heart of Nusku! At the time **the gods go out with harps and laments,** may a prayer be uttered to you! May the great ensi, Umungurusha, utter a prayer to you. May the clamoring one, Ninnibru, utter a prayer to you. (a + 50) May the holy lady, Gashanmagia, utter a prayer to you. May the great princely son, Nanna-Suen, utter a prayer to you. May the hierodule of heaven, Inanna, utter a prayer to you. May the he-man, Utu, the lord, the great hero, utter a prayer to you. May the shining lady, Shuzianna, utter a prayer to you. May the mother of the house of the chief city, Nintinuga, utter a prayer to you. May the land registrar, Ninisina, utter a prayer to you. May Nusku, the mighty arm, the genie of the Ekur, utter a prayer to you. May Kalkal, the great doorkeeper of the Ekur, utter a prayer to you. May the lofty lieutenant, Enlilazi, utter a prayer to you. (a + 60) May Ur-Suena, the herald of the outer shrine, utter a prayer to you. May each utter 'You should not abandon your city!' May each utter a prayer to you. May each utter a prayer to you over Nippur, over his Ekur! May each utter a prayer to you over the Kiur, over his Enamtila! May each utter a prayer to you over his Eshumesha! May each utter a prayer to you over Sippar, over his Ebabbar! May each utter a prayer to you over the brickwork of his Tintir! May each utter a prayer to you over the Esagil, over his Borsippa! May each utter a prayer to you over the Ezida, over his Emahtila! May each utter a prayer to you over his Etemenanki! (a + 70) May each utter a prayer to you over his Edaranna! May each utter a prayer to you over Kish, over his Ekishiba! May each utter a prayer to you over his Emeterursag! May each utter a prayer to you over Kutha, over his Emeslam! May each utter a prayer to you over Dilbat, over his Eibianum!

'Indeed, you are its lord! You should not abandon it' may each utter to you. May each utter a prayer to you

'Indeed, you are its shepherd! You should not abandon it' may each utter to you. May each utter a prayer to you

'A storm locked in a house! You should not abandon it' may each utter to you. May each utter a prayer to you

15 **Righteousness and justice** are the foundation of your throne; **loving kindness and faithfulness precede** into you.

16 Happy are the people **who know** the festal shout, who walk, Yhwh, in the light of your countenance; 17 they exult in your name all day long, and extol your righteousness.

18 For you are the glory of their strength; by your favour our horn is exalted.

19 For our shield is in Yhwh, in the **Holy One** of Israel, our king.

Divine Discourse

I, the great hero who has destroyed the mountains, ... against its Lord.
(*break of a few lines*)
(from E turgin niginam:)
e-130 (In) the princely place [my me's are rightly entrusted me's]. My me's are rightly entrusted me's. No one (else) dares wish for them. My numerous me's are me's for which no one (else dares) wish.
I am *Enki!* My numerous me's *are me's for which no one (else dares) wish. No (one else) dares wish. No one (else dares) wish for* my me's.
My utterance! *My me's for which no one (else dares) wish!* My...!
The me's for which no one (else dares) wish!
... presented as a gift... wise... precious...[10]
(from A urumu ime:)
I, the great light, I, the great light, I, the great light which is surpassing in the land, I, the great light of the gods, I the leader of the Anunna, I, the... person of the princes, I, the horned bison of the mountain, I... the silt, I, the lord of heaven, I, the lady of earth, am the surpassing one of the gods. (a + 10) I am the surpassing one of the Anunna. My raised hand *skims the heavens. My lifted foot treads upon the earth. As for me, the lady, no* hand *is equal to mine. As for me, the lady, no foot is equal to mine. Who (can run) ahead of me? Who can (follow) behind me? Who can escape my raised glance? Who can escape my pursuit? I, the* exalted *child of Enlil, I, the elevated one of my father Suen, (a + 20)* I, *the lady, the cared for of Nudimmud,* install *the en-priest. And after I have installed him,* I install him *for the* king *in accordance with the me's. It is I who gives the crook to the shepherd.* I adorn *the lord* with lordship. *I adorn the lady with ladyship.*[11]

Divine Discourse
Great Divine Deeds in the Past

20 Then you spoke in a vision to your faithful ones, and said: 'I have set the crown on a hero, I have exalted one chosen from the people. 21 I have found my servant David; with my holy oil I have anointed him; 22 my hand shall always remain with him; my arm also shall strengthen him. 23 The enemy shall not outwit him, the wicked shall not humble him. 24 I will crush his foes before him and strike down those who hate him. 25 My faithfulness and loving kindness shall be with him; and in my name his horn shall be exalted. 26 I will set his hand on the sea and his right hand on the rivers. 27 He shall cry to me, 'You are my Father, my God, and the Rock of my salvation!'

28 I will make him the firstborn, the highest of the kings of the earth. 29 Forever I will keep my loving kindness for him, and my covenant with him will stand firm. 30 I will establish his line forever, and his throne as long as the heavens endure.

---

10.   Cohen (1988: 87). A second discourse of Enki's exists in the same *balag* ll. f + 187–189: 'I am... I am Enki, the lord! I am... I am the Lord... on the earth, I am the lord.' See 218 ll. c + 153–163 the divine voice speaks: 'Let (this) lament be sung to me in its fury! Let the populace sing (this) to me! I am the ruler! I am the king! Right and left I will pillage like a storm! ... am I. I am the son of Asarluhi! I, the hero! I, the... ! The mighty heir of... am I! The ruler who instills life... am I! c + 160 He who bundles together the yield... am I! ... hero... storm... am I! A storm... heaven and earth... am I!' Cf. 496 and the divine self-praise which stresses Yhwh's triumph over different lands in Psalm 60:8–10.

11.   Cohen (1988: 646 cf. 648). Or compare ll. a + 20–26 with Psalm 89: 20b-21. Both texts tell of divine distribution of power to chosen human beings.

Praise
Great Divine Deeds in the Past

God's Deeds in Future

The lord, the great hero, **has destroyed** the mountains. The *ensi* of Enlil has destroyed the mountains! The lord of Uras has destroyed the mountains! The lord of the Eninnu has destroyed the mountains! The **firstborn** of the Eshara has destroyed the mountains! The lord of the Eshumesha has destroyed the mountains! The hero, Zababa, has destroyed the mountains! The lord of the Ekishiba has destroyed the mountains!
(a + 90) The lord of the Emeteursag has destroyed the mountains! The lord of the Emeslam has destroyed the mountains! The lord of the Eibianum has destroyed the mountains! The lord Dikumaham has destroyed the mountains! The lord of the Erabiri has destroyed the mountains! ... has destroyed the mountains! The mighty arm of Enlil has destroyed the mountains! The child, the faithful one of 'The Great Mountain' has destroyed the mountains! The lord with overpowering strength has destroyed the mountains! The **son** who avenges his father has destroyed the mountains! The one reared in the Ekur has destroyed the mountains! He whose word is joyous has destroyed the mountains! The foremost of the Ekur has destroyed the mountains! The **lofty hand of heaven** has destroyed the mountains!...has destroyed the mountains! The one surpassing as the heavens has destroyed the mountains! The one as wide as the earth has destroyed the mountains!

31 If his **sons** forsake my law and do not walk according to my ordinances, 32 if they violate my statutes and do not keep my commandments, 33 then I will punish their transgression with the rod and their iniquity with scourges; 34 but I will not remove from him my loving kindness, or be false to my faithfulness. 35 I will not violate my covenant, or alter **the utterance of my lips**. 36 Once and for all I have sworn by my holiness; I will not lie to David. 37 His line shall continue forever, and his throne endure before me like the sun. 38 It shall be established forever like the moon. The witness in the skies endures.' Selah.

(break in the composition)
Lament
(b + 110) ... lies down ...
(break of a few lines)
... gored ... He cried out over ...
(from utugin eta:)
a + 207 In the city **he has cursed its lord.** *He causes its lady to sit down in sickness.* **That city** *which is being neglected by its lord a + 210* **has Enlil turned into a haunted place.** *The (professional) mourner weeps there. The sayer of laments laments there. The cowherd... there. The shepherd plays the reed-of-mourning there. The gudu-priest no longer speaks happily there. The gala-priest no longer chants there 'O, your heart!' The gudu-priest has left... The en-priest has left the gipar-building. The gala-priest has left in sighs.*

Lament
39 But now you have spurned and rejected him; **you are full of wrath** against your anointed. 40 **You** have renounced the covenant of your servant; you have defiled his crown to the netherworld. 41 **You** have broken through all his walls; **you have laid his strongholds in ruins.** 42 All who pass by plunder him; he has become the scorn of his neighbours. 43 **You** have exalted the right hand of his foes; you have made all his enemies rejoice. 44 Moreover, you have turned back the edge of his sword, and you have not supported him in battle. 45 **You** have caused his purity to end, and hurled his throne to the netherworld. 46 **You have cut short the days of his youth;** you have covered him with shame. Selah.

*a + 220 Its lord is no longer present. Its lady is no longer present. **Its lord... has gone to the netherworld**. Its lady... has gone with him to the netherworld. The fox drags his tail there. The frencolin cries out from there with uplifted voice. Its interior is haunted; its environs are haunted. He silences and destroys its interior. He destroys its front, which is **ruined**. Inside, the singer of dirges causes men to leave. Its large shovel is standing in the pit.*

*a + 230 In that place where oxen are slain **men are slain**. In that place where sheep are butchered **men are butchered**.*[12]

(from Utugin eta:)

*b + 250. **What** does the lord have in his heart? **What** does he have in his mind? **What** does he have in his holy mind? He has destroyed the land. He has poured the waters of destruction into the canals. ... Enlil's wife, Ninlil, his older sister, the lady of the Emah, and holy Ninnibru utter a wail to him. ...*

*You have exceeded everything you have promised. The place you have cursed has been destroyed. You have placed a shepherd who never stoops over the sheep. You have placed on watch a shepherd who never sleeps. ... **inspect!** It has been written on his favourable tablet.*[13]

47 **How long**, O Yhwh? Will you hide yourself forever? **How long** will your wrath burn like fire? 48 **Remember** how short my time is – for what vanity you have created all mortals! 49 **Who** can live and never see death? **Who** can escape the power of Sheol? Selah.

III. Appeal

[May the heart be pacified! May the heart be calmed! Urash, the place of motley grain, father Enlil, his spouse Ninlil, your older sister, the lady of Kesh, the clamouring one, the lady of Nippur, the great princely son, Nanna-Suen, the beloved child, Inanna, the great ensi, Umungurusha, (b + 140) the holy lady, Gashanmagia, the **lord** Nanna, the lord Ashimbabbar, the he-man Utu, the **lord**, the great hero, the hierodule, the lady of the Eturkalama, the destroyer of the land, the lady of Eanna, the faithful princess, my lady Nanâ, Lillaenna, Gasjgunisura, Ishur, the bull who mounts the storm, the **lord** of the netherworld, Meslamtaea, the great hero, the **lord** of Urash, Martu, the man of the mountains, Enki, the bull of Eridu, the mother of the lofty shrine, Damgalnuna, Ilurugu, the judge of the land, the faithful lady, Kisha, the beautiful woman, your father begetter, Asarluhi, your

Appeal

50 **Lord**, where are your loving kindnesses of old, which by your faithfulness you swore to David?

---

12. Cohen (1988: 112). An almost identical text exists, 171 ll. b + 225–249.
13. Cohen (1988: 113).

mother progenitress, Panunanki, your beloved spouse, Gashangutesahasgia, the vizier of heaven, Ninshubur, the lofty vizier, the head of the assembly, Nusku, Umunug, Umunbar, the *sangamal*priest of the Apsu, the great hero, Dugabshuggi, the advisor, the princess of advice, the advisor, Gashanshudde, the advisor, whose utterance is joyous, the mother of the chief city, Nintinugga, the great hero, the lord Dikumaham, the lord of the secrets of heaven and earth, **the gods of heaven and the gods of earth, utter a prayer to you**[14]

51 Remember, O Lord, how your servants are taunted; how **I lifted unto my bosom the multitude of peoples**, 52 while your enemies taunt, O Yhwh, while they taunt the footsteps of your anointed.

[A supplication that the brickwork of the Eshumesha should be restored.]

53 Blessed be Yhwh forever. Amen and men.

It is noteworthy that the sequence of themes in both poems is roughly the same though some sections of the *balag* show characteristics that differ from Psalm 89, e.g. two praise and two appeal sections, but no lament or accusatory complaint proper. The comparison follows the outline of Psalm 89.

2.1.1 *Self-invitation to praise (Ps. 89.2-5)*. Psalm 89 begins with a self-invitation of the singing voice to praise. The *balag* chosen for comparison lacks this element, but the *balag Elum didara* starts:

> Thus let me sit down with the honoured one who wanders about! With him who wanders about, thus let me sit down with the honoured one who wanders about! With the lord, great An, who wanders about, with the lord of the lands, who wanders about, with the lord whose pronouncement is true, who wanders about, with Enlil, the father of the nation, who wanders about, with the shepherd of the black-headed, who wanders about, with him who witnesses everything first-hand, who wanders about, with the bull who causes the troops to wander, who wanders about, (10) with him who sleeps a false sleep, who wanders about! Let me libate beer from the vessel for him! Like a bull, may I submit to him! (Cohen 1988: 181).

14. A similar passage exists in Cohen (1988: 422 ll. a + 36–41): 'In the house the gods spend the day with the *balag*-instrument and laments. The gala-priest sings to him. The gala-priest sings a song of lordship to him. The gala-priest sings a song to him accompanied by the *balag*-instrument. He plays the holy *uppu*-drum and the holy *lilis*-drum. He plays the *shem*-drum, the *meze*-drum and the *balag*-instrument for him.' This section shows how gods and men join into the supplication using the *balag*-instrument. 475 l. 47 reads: 'At the time the gods go out with harps and laments, may a prayer be uttered to you!' Thus the terrestrial liturgy, when men utter the prayer, attempts to be synchronous with the celestial liturgy, when gods go in procession with instruments.

The singing voice summons itself to sit down with the supreme god An/ Enlil in order to venerate him by libations and submission. This resembles the psalm's voice which summons itself to sing and praise Yhwh's loving kindness and faithfulness. In Psalm 89.3a the translation follows the Septuagint rendering a divine speech, while the Masoretic text has the singing voice speaking. The *balag* praises the true divine pronouncement in l.5.

Both poems praise God using traditional formal elements. The *balag* starts with a section that expresses the inscrutability of the god and goes on listing divine epithets. Probably the phrase 'what can one know about you' was repeated after every epithet. The position of such a section is not fixed, in the *balag Gudnim ekura* a similar section starts the *balag* (Cohen 1988:450). In the *balag Elum gusin* a section that is similar but has a complaining overtone builds the second *kirugu*.[15]

2.1.2 *Expression of Inscrutability or Incomparability (89.6-19).* While the *balag* expresses the inscrutability of the divinity, the psalm expresses Yhwh's incomparability. There are also *balags* stressing the incomparability, as e.g. *Agalgal buru susu* ll. 24-36. This section has a lot of parallels with the praise in Psalm 89. I give the comparable verses in brackets.

> Great hero, king whose word is steadfast, (89.19 the Holy One of Israel, our king)[16]
> broad of wisdom, wise in matters,

---

15.   A flood which drowns the harvest, what can one know of you? Honoured one, a flood which drowns the harvest, what can one know of you? Father Enlil, lord of lands, father Enlil, lord whose pronouncement is true, father Enlil, father of the nation, father Enlil, shepherd of the blackheaded, father Enlil, he who witnesses everything first-hand, father Enlil, bull, who causes the troops to wander, father Enlil, he who sleeps a false sleep, bison, hero Asarluhi, great hero, lord Enbilulu, bison, hero Muzebbasa, bison… a flood which drowns the harvest, what can one know of you? (Cohen 1988: 312, ll. 47–61). Calling Enlil a flood recalls the deluge which Enlil caused to come over the earth. The flood story was told in the epics of Gilgamesh and Atrahasis and was similarly told in Israel (Gen. 8). It is also referred to in Cohen (1988: 436 ll. a + 10–26). Thus the divine destructive power has been experienced in times of old before recorded history. The flood motifs are a further hint that destruction motifs do not necessarily point to historical events, though floods may have caused devastation in Mesopotamia time and again, sometimes even man made as Sennacherib's attempt to destroy Babylon by making the Euphrates flow over the city. But the *balag* does not refer to one single historical flood, it uses a topic. It even states in l. a + 100 'The land is devastated', which was probably neither the historical truth whenever this *balag* has been sung nor when it was composed. It is literary truth or religious truth, because the land is feeling as if devastated whenever the benevolence of the god turns away.

16.   In the MT 'king' may refer to either the terrestrial or the celestial king, but the Septuagint and the Vulgate (vers. Hebr.) both translate 'our king' as epithet of Holy One, thus meaning the celestial king.

masterfully clever (*var.* exceedingly wise), he who is unfathomable, (*var.* incomparable) fitting for the golden throne of Sumer, (89.15 the foundation of your throne)
raised upon the silver throne of Sumer.
Lord, who is like you? Who can compare (favourably) to you?
(89.7 who in the skies can be compared to Yhwh? Who among the heavenly beings is like Yhwh?)
Great hero, who is like you? Who can compare (favourably) to you?
Nergal, who is like you? Who can compare (favourably) to you?
When you mount... like a storm, (who can compare (favorably) to you?)
When you care for the shepherd and the herdsman, (who can compare (favourably) to you?)
Who can escape your raised glance?
Who can escape your pursuit? (89.11 you scattered your enemies with your mighty arm)
Your word is a huge net stretched over the lands.
Cow, right arm..., bull...[17] (89.14 You have a mighty arm... high is your right hand)

The themes divine kingship, throne, incomparability, warfare (pursuit, enemies) and mighty right arm/hand are motives, which were at the disposal for both Mesopotamian and Hebrew poets in order to create the praise section of a communal lament. Nevertheless this part of the *balag* also shows the remarkable differences between the Mesopotamian and biblical prayer. The *balag* elaborates the incomparability theme into a litany, which repeats the same antiphonal phrase several times. This does not exist in biblical communal laments.

A second difference exists on the theological level. Hebrew psalms do not use animals as metaphors for Yhwh.[18] Nergal is called cow and bull here, other deities are called lion, ox, etc., in both individual and communal laments of Mesopotamia. In biblical laments, on the contrary, animals serve as metaphors for the enemies of the supplicant. Nevertheless, there is one idea in common: the animal metaphor for divinities in Mesopotamia often also stresses their hostile behaviour against the supplicant or the praying community. The characteristic of biblical laments in comparison with the ANE is therefore that, though Yhwh can behave like an enemy as Psalm 89.39-46 states, only demonic and

17. Cohen (1988: 512).
18. It is a sin to represent Yhwh in the image of an animal as says Psalm 106.20: They exchanged the glory of God for the image of an ox that eats grass. The only metaphor, which uses animal imagery in connection with Yhwh, is the mention of his wings (Psalms 17.8; 36.8; 57.2; 63.8). But this may rather be influenced by the winged sun disc depicting the supreme god in Mesopotamian art or else a metonymy of the cherub's wings, which surround the throne on which Yhwh is believed to sit (Ps. 80.2).

human hostile powers are disguised in animal metaphors, while other religions of the ANE apply this also to hostile divine power. Up to a certain extent, however, the Akkadian translation often added to the *Emesal balags* shares the Hebrew practice of avoiding animal images as metaphors for God.[19] This is one example – others will follow – where the Akkadian translation of the *balag* is closer to Hebrew psalm language than to its Sumerian *Vorlage*.

Strikingly enough, the inscrutability/incomparability motif is followed in the *balag Nirgal lu ede* and Psalm 89 by the motif of the divine mighty arm. Thus, we encounter motif combinations in both Mesopotamian and biblical laments. The mightiness of Yhwh is shown in his victory over chaotic powers, a motif that is not prevalent in Mesopotamian laments but has a counterpart in Mesopotamian myths, e.g. *Enuma Elish*.

The *kirugu* line in the *balag* starts a new section, an appeal in which a lot of gods are summoned to utter a prayer on behalf of the praying community. Though Psalm 89 goes on with the praise, there are affinities to the *balag*. Suddenly the scene changes to a heavenly setting where personified ideas, namely righteousness and justice, loving kindness and faithfulness, appear as members of Yhwh's entourage who support his throne and proceed unto him. Such a heavenly procession is also mentioned in the *balag*, where the gods go out with harps and laments. While Enlil/An is the Honoured One, Yhwh is the Holy One, and while the psalm's human worshippers know the festival shout, the *balag's* praying gods know the heart of the god they pray to.

2.1.3 *Divine Discourse (89.20-38)*. The horizontal line which indicates the end of a *kirugu* separates the long appeal from a divine discourse in the first person singular. Such a divine discourse can be long in *balags* such as Inanna's speech in Uru amirabi (Cohen 1988: 594–598; Volk 1989). Taking the Mesopotamian *balags* into account, Hieke (1997: 242) is not correct in cutting out the divine discourse in Psalms 60.8-10 and 85.9-14 as elements not properly belonging to the genre. A divine discourse can be an

---

19. 'In the Akkadian interlinear translations added to Sumerian literary compositions during the latter half of the second millennium BCE, when Sumerian was a dead language, or during the first millennium, and in the bilingual lexical vocabularies either derived form the translations or on the basis of which the translations were made, the translation of Sumerian *gud* "bull" as Akkadian *qaradu* "hero" may imply… that the word had lost its imagic significance, raising the possibility that *gud*, referring in literary compositions to gods or heroes, was no more than an epithet and no longer a vivid image. The same may be true of Sumerian *amar* "bull-calf" or in general "male offspring" of an animal or bird, translated as Akkadian *maru* "son"; of *uz-sag* = "lead-goat" (that is, the goat who leads the herd) translated as *ašarittu* "foremost", and of *am* "wild bull" translated as *belu* "lord"' (Black 1998: 17).

integral part of communal laments both in Mesopotamia and in Judah.[20] The content of the divine speech differs from text to text. In the *balags* it contains mostly a self praise of the deity, but the deity can also tell a story as in the *balag* Uru amirabi (Cohen 1988: 588f, 591, 592), where Inanna/ Ishtar refers to her love-story with Dumuzi and comments on the sin of her maidservant. This resembles Yhwh's discourse in Psalm 89.20-38, where he tells about his love-story with David and foretells his reaction to the possible misbehaviour of David's sons. The self-praising divine discourse, in which the divinity may tell about his or her deeds in the past must be distinguished from another sort of divine discourse in first person singular in *balags*, where the lamenting goddess complains of her misery or the misery of her city and temple.[21]

Some motives show striking similarities. Yhwh excludes explicitly that he will be false or lie to David (89.34, 36), thus just bringing the idea of doubting his trustworthiness to the fore. There was a tradition of untrustworthy deities spread through the ANE (Steymans 1998). Yhwh's statement belongs to this tradition and so does a statement of Inanna/ Ishtar in the *balag Uru amirabi* (Cohen 1988: 595):

> To him who says 'She is deceitful!' I, the lady, bring a deceitful person
> into (his) home.

Also Inanna/Ishtar has to struggle with the human assumption that she might deceive and lie. In a prophecy to the Assyrian king Esharadon she excludes that she might lie as explicitly as Yhwh does in Psalm 89 (Parpola 1997: 7 l. 31; Steymans 2002: 236).

Even Yhwh's threatening words in Psalm 89.31-33 which predict punishment of David's rebellious sons by means of blows find their counterpart in *balags*. Thus, in the *Uruhulake of Gula*, Enlil predicts that the rebellious land will invoke his name after he has overthrown it (Cohen 1988: 269f):

> (Rev. col v)... Invoking the name of the built house, invoking my name,
> it invokes my name. Invoking the name of the built city, invoking my
> name, it invokes my name. I destroy the land and overthrow the land. It
> invokes my name. After I have caused the land in its entirety to quake, it
> invokes my name. I pile up the lands into heaps. It invokes my name. I
> strew the rebellious land into heaps. It invokes my name. After I have...
> the sweet waters into bitter waters, it invokes my name.

---

20. This may shed new light on the so-called prophetic psalms, i.e. psalms which contain a divine discourse, in the collection of Asaph (cf. Millard 1994: 44; Hossfeld 1998: 237–243). Is the divine discourse in Asaph psalms an imitation of prophetic oracles or a typical element of the prayer genre as in the Mesopotamian *balag*, or even both?

21. Such a lament one finds e.g. in *Immal gudede* ll. c + 226–250, Cohen (1988: 629).

From the *balag Nirgal lu ede* only one line of the divine discourse is preserved. The god praises himself for having destroyed the mountains. This motif is taken over in a following litany that praises the god speaking of him in third person and always repeating the refrain 'has destroyed the mountains'. It is noteworthy that both the first person self praise and the third person litany speak of the god's deeds in the past. The mountains mean the enemy country, the Sumerian word sign *lú kúr* 'enemy' meaning literally 'man of the mountain'. Thus the god's destructive activity against the hostile mountains has at the same time protective power for the city and its praying community. There is a slight thematic parallel in Yhwh's foretelling of his behaviour against David's rebellious sons. The god has to overcome unsubmissive and hostile opponents from royal line or from enemy country and the Mesopotamian god gets the epithet 'son who avenges his father'. This epithet alludes to the idea, that Nergal's divine father has to be avenged, thus has experienced offence and disobedience, as Yhwh foretells about David's sons. The difference consists mainly in a different concept of the pantheon. In Mesopotamia several gods interact and human beings play rather marginal roles, in the psalms Yhwh alone interacts with human beings and vice versa.

But the divine discourse does not always contain allusions to the god's aggressive power – an idea by the way also extant in Psalm 89.23-24. The portion inserted from *E turgin niginam* depicts Enki proud of his *mes* – divine instruments – as Yhwh is proud of his chosen one, David.

2.1.4 *Accusatory Complaint or Lament (Ps. 89.39-46)*. Hieke (1997: 241f) points to the address to God in second person singular as a typical feature of laments. God is seen responsible for the calamity even when he only gave way to enemies doing their disastrous work (Pss. 44.10-15.20; 60.3-5.12b; 80.6-7.13). The *balag Utugin eta* describes the god's hostile activity in a third person account. But there are *balags* which address the destroying god in second person:

> Your eye never tires from gazing about. Your neck doesn't straighten up from bending. When will your heart tire from thinking? You have handed over the ewe and its own lamb to the foreigner. You have handed over the goat and its own kid to the foreigners. You have destroyed the property of the wealthy. Enlil, (even) those wearing much clothing have been killed by cold. Your eye never tires.[22]
> Lord of the Nation, Enlil, unfathomable one, how long will your heart not be soothed? Father Enlil, who gazes about, how long will your eyes

---

22. *Udam ki amus* ll. 120–126, Cohen (1988: 139). Cf. the handing over of animals to the foreigners who plundered the country with Psalm 89.42-43, and the destruction of the property with Psalm 89.41, 45.

not be tired? How long will you keep your head covered with a cloth? How long will you keep your neck in (your) lap? How long will you keep your mind covered like a reed box? Important one, how long will you lean your ear against (your) lap? (30) Father Enlil, you have smitten the land until you have (completely) destroyed it. Lord of the nation, the ewe has abandoned (her) lamb. The goat has abandoned (her) kid. Oh your city is faithful! ... Father Enlil, you called forth to the corner; the people at the corner have been killed. (40) Lord of the nation, you called forth to the side; the people at the side have been killed. You called forth to every clay pit; they have been filled with blood. You called forth to the treasure-house of the land; it has been turned into ruins.[23] You have killed by your spoken word. You have spoken (at) a place and you then accomplish it. Whatever you have said you have excelled. You have destroyed the place you have cursed. You have stationed a shepherd who never relaxes over the sheep, a shepherd who never sleeps at the watch.[24]

In the *balag Utugin eta* the lord and lady of the city are gone to the netherworld. The terms may refer to the divine patron and patroness of the city, but they may also refer to king and queen. In the section from *A urumu ime* quoted above, the words 'lord' and 'lady' mean most probably human beings. The mentioning of the netherworld has some affinity to the ארץ appearing twice in Psalm 89.40, 45. The anointed's royal attributes are humiliated to the ground or thrown into the 'underground, netherworld' (Dahood 1968: 202).

The plundering enemies (Ps. 89.42) are also extant in *balags* as e.g. in *Mutin nunuz dima* ll.a + 192–202:

She approaches the *Eibianumm*. ... come! (The enemy) has plundered it. She who goes around the house, she who goes around the city, my lady, in the *Esapar* how long will you wander about? They carry off my house and my city from me. They carry off the lady (of) my house from me. They carry off my cella, my treasure house from me. They carry off

---

23. *Ameamashana* ll. 24–42, Cohen (1988: 166). Cf. l. 26 – the covering of the god's head – with Psalm 44.25 and l. 27, 29 – the god's head and ear in the lap, which is a sleeping position – with Psalm 44.24, and l. 32 the faithful city with Psalm 44.18-19. Thus this *balag* contains motifs similar to one biblical communal lament, namely Psalm 44, and forms similar to another, namely the questions 'how long' as in Psalm 89.47.

24. *Aabba huluha* of Enlil ll. a + 31–36, Cohen (1988: 393). The last two lines show that the shepherd who never sleeps or sleeps a false sleep seems to be a threatening motif not the consoling one of the Bible's good shepherd. This threatening shepherd does not give rest to the sheep, his watching is felt like oppression. Such an always watching shepherd seems to be the contradiction of the ones described in Jeremiah 23.1-4; Ezekiel 34.1-7; Zechariah 11.4-17, but not to the better. The latter ones are neglecting the sheep, the always watching one oppresses them, perhaps a metaphor for too severe a king.

> my property, my possessions from me. ... They carry off my throne,
> my seat from me.

Two different I-voices seem to speak here. One voice addresses the goddess
as 'my lady' (l. 195) and complains of the deportation of the goddess's
statue from the temple (l. 197). The voice complaining of the deportation
of house, city, temple, cella, property, throne belongs most probably to the
goddess.[25] Thus the city and her divine patroness mingle in their lament.
The different roles played by the *dramatis personae* in Mesopotamian and
biblical laments will be discussed later. But it may be noticed that there
exists a similarity to the praying I-voice in Psalm 89, because it is one
singing human lamenting in intercession as the goddess laments in
intercession. This single human is part of the collective of Israel as the
goddess's voice mingles with that of the city's collective.

The question 'how long' (Ps. 89.47) is typical of both Mesopotamian and
biblical laments.[26] In the *balags* the interceding goddess often asks the
question, in Psalm 89 it is the singing I-voice. Typical are also other
questions starting with 'what' or 'who'. While the *balag* chosen for
comparison asks the god to inspect, the psalm asks Yhwh to remember.
Identical and typical of the genre is the imperative address.

The lament of Psalm 89 focuses less on the people than on the anointed,
who is more probably the king than Israel. Yhwh brings his anointed to
the realm of death by desecrating his royal coronation covenant (cf. 1 Kgs.
11.4; Levin 1982: 93), his crown, his purity and his throne (89.40, 45), by
cutting short his possibility and potency of procreation (89.46; Dahood
1968: 319) and by giving him away to military defeat and plundering
(89.42-44), ruining his strongholds and city walls (89.41). Such individual
traits of calamity have close parallels in *eršahungas*.[27] Prayers of this type
were recited in liturgies together with *balags* on behalf of and sometimes
even by the king. The Hebrew word ארץ translated 'earth' in 89.40, 45 has
been translated 'netherworld', because it is used in this meaning in Ugarit
and can adopt this meaning in Hebrew too. Similar expressions referring to

---

25. The *balag Uruhulake of Gula* makes it explicit that the goddess is speaking in ll. a + 37–
40: *Ninashte*, the lady of Larak, the mother of the house, *Ezinu-Kusu*, (says) 'My cella, my
shrine of the Egalmah!' She feels humiliated. 'My treasure house, my shrine of the Erabriri!'
She feels humiliated.

26. Cf. in *Enemani ilu ilu* ll. 71–73: [Lifting up] his head covering, she inquires about him.
How long will the sleeping one sleep? How long will the great mountain Enlil sleep? (Cohen
1988: 193).

27. Cf. Maul 1988: 109 l. 38: *la tab-ba-ak belum arad(IR)-ka la tab-ba-ak* 'Verstoße nicht,
o Herr, deinen Diener verstoße nicht' and l. 42 *re-e-ka bi-bil libbi-ka la tabbak* 'den von dir
erwählten Hirten verstoße nicht' with Psalm 89.39-40: Aber du, du hast verstoßen, hast
verworfen, hast gezürnt mit deinem Gesalbten, hast zu Boden entweiht seine Krone, hast
entehrt den Bund deines Dieners.

the temple in Psalm 74.7 and to the monarchy and its princes in Lamentations 2.2 (Veijola 1982: 79) do not contradict this, because the expression always focuses on desecration. For the temple building desecration finds its harshest form in tearing down the building to its foundations, for the abstract monarchy the expression can only mean a metaphor, for living beings like princes and kings the zenith of desecration is death which brings total impurity.[28]

The simultaneous destruction of several cities and temples alluded to in lists of city and temple names in *balags* hardly depict a historical fact and when the *balag* was sung in liturgies it was not the historical background for the prayer. Thus it is a mere inner-biblical prejudice that one can trace the date of a communal lament from alleged hints to historical events like destruction or national calamity. The words of the poem describe a virtual scene of calamity either to avoid a situation as described or to draw the god's attention and sympathy to the praying community by exaggerating the calamity.[29] It can by no means be excluded that the allusions to calamity, plundering and destruction in the communal laments of the Psalter have the same purpose. They cannot be used beyond doubt for the dating of the psalm by looking for a period of Israel's history that fits the calamities mentioned in the prayer.

2.1.5 *Appeal.* The second appeal of the *balag* begins with the heart pacification motif, which we also find in *eršemmas* and *eršahungas*. Then a lot of gods are asked to intercede through their prayer on behalf of the praying community. In the psalm it is the praying I-voice who comes to the fore in an interceding manner on behalf of the anointed and Yhwh's

---

28. The anointed carries attributes of holiness similar to a sanctuary. He is sanctified by Yhwh's oil of holiness (Ps. 89.21b). The rejection of his covenant is similar to the rejection of the temple (in Ps. 89.40 and Lam. 2.7). His ruin is connected with the end of purity (Ps. 89.45b).

29. The lack of historicity can clearly be seen in the *balag Aabba huluha* of Enlil ll.a + 13–28, where the destruction is referred to as having taken place long ago afflicting at the same time Nippur and Tintir/Babylon and allegedly has not been overcome in the moment of the prayer: 'on that day, on that day long ago, in that night, in that night long since, in that year, in that year long ago, when the spouse was handed over to the foreigner, when the child was handed over to the foreigner, when the girlfriend... the spouse was killed, when the spouse was killed, the spouse was killed, (a + 20) when the child was killed, the child was killed, your city being destroyed, weapons slaughtering the cella like a bull, Nippur being destroyed, weapons slaughtering the cella like a bull, Tintir being destroyed, weapons slaughtering the cella like a bull, when the temple was enshrouded in a reed mat, its lord, 'Oh, my house!' he says. 'Oh, my city!' he says. Its lord, 'Oh, my little ones!' he says. 'Oh, my older ones!' he says. As in days of yore, sore-hearted, he spends the day in woe, in woe! How long, Enlil? How long shall the prayers not pacify (you)?' (Cohen 1988: 393).

servants. The function of intercession is the same, but the form differs, praying gods *versus* praying individual.

Both the catalogues and the New Year Feast ritual join the balag Nir-gál lú è-dè with the *eršemma* Ur-sag ut-u₁₈-lu.

> (1) Warrior, south-storm, verily a flood! Honoured one, warrior, south-storm! Nergal, warrior, south-storm!
> Lord (of) Kish, lord of the Ekishibba!
> (5) Lord (of) the Emeteursag, lord (of) the Eunirkitushmah! Igalimata-tra! Iggunu! Lord Sukkalmah! Vizier Papsukkal! Warrior who alone is exalted! Warrior who is Luhush! *Honoured One*, warrior, southstorm!
> (10) When you are as surpassing as heaven and earth, (verily a flood)! When you are the warrior goring the rebellious land, (verily a flood)!
>
> So that the heart (of) the storm be pacified; so that the exterior (of) the storm be pacified! So that the heart (of) the great warrior be pacified! So that the heart (of) Utulu be pacified! (15) So that the heart (of) Dikumah be pacified! So that the heart of Baba, the beautiful woman, be pacified! So that the heart of Ninitinugga be pacified! So that the heart (of) Ninisina be pacified! (20) So that the heart (of) my lady Nanâ be pacified! So that the heart of the lady (of) Hursagkalama be pacified! So that the heart (of) the lady (of) the Eturkalama be pacified! So that the heart (of) the lady of Tintir be pacified!
>
> It is an ershemma of Ninurta.[30]

As the quotation shows, an *eršemma* consists of only two (sometimes three) units. The division of prayers into units and tablets and their combination in a fixed sequence reminds us of the fact that the division of psalms is by no means certain (Auwers 2000: 96–108). There are psalms divided in the Hebrew Psalter that form one poem in the Greek one and vice versa. There are psalms without heading that are enclitic to the preceding psalm like the above mentioned Psalm 71 joined to Psalm 70 or Psalm 2, which is sometimes regarded as an appendix to Psalm 1.

The lack of a superscript and the position of Psalm 2 at the beginning of that part of the Psalter whose superscripts predominantly mention David may witness a liturgical use of Psalm 89 and Psalm 2 in immediate sequence during royal ceremonies. If there had been a messianic edition of the Psalter, going from Psalm 2–89, as Christoph Rösel's study (1999) makes most probable, then after reading Psalm 89, the final psalm of this edition, one continued with Psalm 2, the first psalm of this edition, as soon as one recommenced the reading of the

---

30. Cohen (1981: 143), *Eršemma* No. 45, preserved only in the first millennium BCE copy.

messianic Psalter. Psalm 2 can be understood as a divine answer to the appeal of Psalm 89. This setting may reflect a former liturgical use of previous versions[31] of both psalms as a lament for the deceased king (Ps. 89) and a prayer for his successor (Ps. 2). KTU 1.161 combines the lament for king Niqmaddu III of Ugarit with the prescription of offerings for the new king Ammurapi III and his queen Tharyelli. Hence lament for the late and intercession for the new king formed one single liturgical complex in Ugarit.

The italics in the *eršemmas* indicate vocabulary shared with the preceding *balag*. There is thematic coherence, the prayers being directed to Nergal and his brother Ninurta, or in the Assyrian ritual probably rather to Asshur in his warrior-like manifestation resembling Nergal and Ninurta. *Balags* and to a certain extent *eršemmas* and *eršahungas* share specific lexical and formal elements, as the heart pacification theme in the second part of Ur-sag ut-u$_{18}$-lu.

2.2 *Vocabulary*

Veijola (1982: 54–59, 79–82, 120–133) and Hieke (1997: 241–244) base their qualification of Psalm 89 and Psalm 80, the psalms they study, as communal laments (*Volksklagelied*) on lists of vocabulary typical for this genre. Much of this vocabulary has its counterpart in *Emesal* prayers. In order to show this we quote Hieke's lists, add the words Veijola gives focusing on Psalm 89.39-52, and join as far as possible the corresponding Akkadian and Sumerian words. The Emesal quotations come from the *balags* of Cohen's edition (1988). The purpose of this inquiry is to show a common pool of vocabulary, motifs and patterns, from which a poet in Mesopotamia could draw, and obviously a poet in Israel too. If the typical vocabulary of communal laments comes from a pool of forms, this vocabulary cannot be used for dating a psalm.[32]

---

31. For previous forms of both psalms cf. Koch 2002: 11; Rösel 1999: 137, 139, 142. In liturgical use Psalm 2 and Psalm 89 would not yet contain the passages added in successive redactions in order to link both poems with the growing Psalter (cf. Hossfeld/Zenger 2000: 35–37).

32. Against Veijola (1982:79): 'Ein starkes Argument zugunsten der *exilischen* Datierung von Ps 89,4-5.20-46 liefern die sprachlichen Beziehungen zu exilischen Klageliedern, die zum Teil ganz singulärer Art und deshalb von einem besonders hohen Stellenwert sind.' It is noteworthy that the vocabulary which Veijola estimates the most significant refer to the anointed in Ps. 89 but to the temple in their other occurrences and are thus part of the language that describes the destruction of temple and city that is extant in Mesopotamian laments too as will be demonstrated below. לדר ודור כסאך refers to David in Psalm 89.5, but to God in Lamentations 5.19 as e.g. in Cohen 1988: 452, l. 80 quoted below as counterpart to עזר (for Assyrian parallels to the Hebrew phrase cf. Steymans: 2002: 194). חלל לארץ 'to defile unto the ground' refers to the royal crown in Psalm 89.40; the state and its officials in Lamentations 2.2, but the temple in Psalm 74.7 as e.g. Cohen 1988:59, l. 58: 'She walks about (aimlessly) in

Hieke focuses mainly on verbs and groups them in two semantic fields: 2.2.1) God's alienation (*Abwendung*) in opposition to 2.2.2) God's benevolent return (*Zuwendung*) and 2.2.3) construction (*Aufbau*) in opposition to 2.2.4) destruction (*Zerstörung*).[33]

her defiled *cella*. She cries bitterly. She walks about (aimlessly) in her levelled treasure house. She cries bitterly.' For זנח (often) and נאר (Ps. 89.40; Lam. 2.7) see the table below. The rest of the examples given by Veijola do not point to a common genre at all, because כל עברי דרך in Psalm 89.42 (cf. 80.13; Lam. 1.12; 2.15) may be a later interpolation into Psalm 89, not Yhwh being the agent of destruction in this verse as in the context; הקציר ימים (89.46) does not really appear in 102.24 and is nothing else than the desire for long days turned into a curse (cf. the desire Maul 1988: 298, l. 25 and the curse 153, l. 22). אבי(נו) אתה in 89.27 does not at all fit to Isaiah 63.16; 64.7; Jeremiah 34.19 because in Psalm 89 it is the address that Yhwh longs to hear from David's lips at the peak of the love story told in the divine oracle (89.20-38), but in the prophetic texts these words are uttered by imploring supplicants or ironically used in a divine reproach against disobedient humans.

33. The table does not include Hieke's and Veijola's quotations from the book of Lamentations, because these city laments have their counterpart in the Mesopotamian city laments and lie beyond the outline of this inquiry. For a comparison of Lamentations with the Mesopotamian city laments see Berges (2002), Dopps-Allsopp (1993), Edelman forthcoming.

2.2.1 *Alienation (Abwendung)*.

Hebrew	Pss.	Emesal	Akkadian	Cohen 1988 page, line
זנח G 'reject, exclude'[34]	44.10,24; 60.3,12 (// 108.12); 74.1; 77.8; 89.39	gur[35]	*sakâpu* cf. CAD S (1984) 70–74.	225, a + 32[36] = 101, 158 99, 90–98 refrain ta-ra-ab-du$_{11}$ ta-aš ba-da-gur-re[37] 169, c + 24-257 refrain ba-da-gur-ra-en-na me-na-šè ì-g[i$_4$$^?$][38]

34. The Hebrew verb זנח and the Akkadian verb or adjective *zenû* 'to be angry' or 'angry' (CAD Z 1961: 84–87) which are both also said of gods, may be linked etymologically. I owe this correlation to an oral remark of Joan Goodnick Westenholz.

35. Note that the Sumerian verb *gur* means 'to turn away' but it is idiomatically rendered in Akkadian by the verb *sakâpu*, 'to reject'. Both Semitic languages Akkadian and Hebrew are thus semantically closer in the meaning 'to reject' than the Sumerian prayer that is translated into Akkadian not literally but in an idiomatic way. Cf. Krecher (1966: 183f, note 524): 'gur wird schon altbabylonisch mit *sakapu* wiedergegeben, s. CAD ilu lex. ("OB Lu"); ferner in 4 R 10 Rs 35f. und K. 1353 Rs. 12–23 (BA 5, 640, dann OEC 6 Tf. 21), s. S. LANGDON, OEC 6, 43 und 23. Sumerisch entspricht wenigstens in SBH 46:46 = BL 18:5 das bekannte gur "sich abwenden", wenn jedenfalls mu-lu = ša. "Den Menschen niederwerfen" ist demnach idiomatische Wiedergabe von "sich vom Menschen abwenden". Zu gur "sich abwenden" vgl. in unserem Zusammenhang Urklage 234 und TU 55: 22.'

36. Krecher 1966: 245 a + 32: The lord has turned away from the nation. He has made it haunted = 225 a + 32 mu-lu ka-nag-da ba-anda-gur-ra líl-lá-da//*ša ma-a-ti is-ki-pu ana za-qí-qí*. Cf. CAD S (1983: 70) sakâpu A: *ša mati is-ki-pu ana zaqiqi <utirru>* him who rejected the country they turned to naught. gašan.mu na.an.gur.re.en: *beltu la ta-sa-kip-[in-ni]* my lady, reject me not BA 5 640:21f.; *awilum u itti ili* sà-*ki-ip itti awil*[*ut*]*i* sà-*ki-ip* that man is rejected by his god, rejected by his fellow men AfO 16 66 ii 44f; 71: *ilu mata i-zak-ki-pu* the gods will reject that country CT 40 38 K. 29992 + :27.

37. Krecher 1966: 109: '90 Honoured one, what can your city say to you? Why do you turn away? 91 Enlil, what can your city say to you? Why do you turn away? 92 What can your city Nippur say to you? Why do you turn away? 93 What can the brickwork of the Ekur say to you? Why do you turn away? 94 What can the Kiur, the great place say to you? Why do you turn away? 95 What can the brickwork of Sippar say to you? Why do you turn away? 96 What can the shrine Ebbabar say to you? Why do you turn away? 97 What can the brickwork of Tintir say to you? Why do you turn away? 98 What can the brickwork of Esagil say to you? Why do you turn away?' The preceding footnote shows that the Sumerian concept of the god's turning away is the equivalent of the god's pushing away or rejection in Akkadian. Both concepts express the same experience of alienation of divine presence from two different points of view. The Sumerian one sees the god moving away from a communion with the supplicant, the Akkadian and Hebrew one sees the supplicant being moved away from the communion with god. The passage quoted here also shows, that the city is conceived as a speaking voice, which is indeed a communal voice like the We-voice in communal lament psalms.

38. Krecher 1966: 171: b + 247 Sir, you have turned away from your city. When will you return? ... b + 257 You have turned away from the Edaranna. When will you return?

מאס 'refuse,		78.59,67;				*ta + ru* D		563, 152 (116)[39]
reject'			89.39
							šub[40]				*nadû* cf. CAD	607 a + 20[41]; 229 a + 139; 446,
											NI (1980) 68–	111[42]
											101.			100, 108–127 refrain na-an-
															šub-bé dè-ra-ab-bé[43] cf.
															157,84–92; 162 b + 179–188;
															472 a + 75–77; 529f, 85–101.

39. Krecher 1966: 590: In my field the farmer returns the basket (empty) to me = 563, 152 (116) a-šà-ga mu-un-gàr-ke₄ gi-gur ma-ra-an-gur//*[ina eq]-li-ia ik-ka-ru* giš:*pa-an ut-tir* cf. Commentary ibid. 602, 116.

40. The verbs *šub*//nadû may also mean 'to cast' as in Cohen 1988: 55, 92 e-ga-mu e-ga bi-šu-ub (var. ba- šub) me-na mu-da-zu//*šá e-ki ina i-ki it-ta-an-di* (var. *na-dì*) '(The one of) my ditches has been cast into the ditches' (60).

41. Cohen 1988: 625 a + 20: 'A storm which hurls the little child (from) the lap!' = 607 a + 20 [u4] du₅-mu-tur-re du₁₀-ub-ba ba-šub//*u₄-mu ša še-er-ra ina bir-ki na-du-ú*. The divine rejection is expressed in the power that throws down. It is indeed a refusal of any care for the human as is made explicit in the lines preceding the one quoted above: a + 13–19 'Storm which has no regard for a good spouse! Storm which has no regard for a good child! Storm which has no regard for a mother! Storm which has no regard for a father! Storm which has no regard for a spouse! Storm which has no regard for a child! Storm which has no regard for a sister! Storm which has no regard for a brother! Storm which has no regard for a friend! Storm which has no regard for a companion.' (625). This storm is the angry heart of great An (see a + 9). Cf. this complaint about the refusal of regard for people who should be esteemed (spouse, child, mother, father, sister, brother, friend and companion) with Psalm 89.39 'But now you have spurned and rejected and been angry with your anointed.' The anointed is one Yhwh should have regard for. The same idea is related to the praying community in Psalm 44.10: 'Yet you have rejected us and abased us, and have not gone out with our armies.' Psalm 74.1: 'O God, why do you cast us off forever? Why does your anger smoke against the sheep of your pasture?' Note the different renderings of the verb מאס in the NRSV (spurned, rejected, cast us off) which hints at the difficulty of a semantic comparison with Akkadian and Sumerian vocabulary.

42. Cohen 1988: 246 and 452: "Princess, genie... fallen house...!' is the cry which the city utters. Alas!' = 229 a + 139 and 446, 111 egí ᵈLamma x à-ba?-è: é-šub-xx gù-//*ru-ba-tu₄ lam-ma šá [É na?]-du-ú*. Probably here again the Sumerian šub is rendered by the Akkadian *nadû*. The house, i.e. the temple, is fallen, because it has been cast down by the rejecting god. The *balag* does not stress the action but the result of rejection.

43. Cohen 1988: 110: 108 'May 'You should not desert!' be said to you. May 'You should not desert your city!' be said to you... 127 May 'You are its lord!' be said to you. May 'You should not desert!' be said to you. May 'You are its shepherd!' be said to you. May 'You should not desert!' be said to you. May '(You are) a storm locked in a house!' be said to you. May 'You should not desert!' be said to you.' See 476: 'Indeed, you are its lord! You should not abandon it' may each utter to you. May each utter a prayer to you! 'Indeed, you are its shepherd! You should not abandon it' may each utter to you. May each utter a prayer to you! 'A storm locked in a house! You should not abandon it' may each utter to you. May each utter a prayer to you!' = 472 a + 75 za-e umun-bi bí-mèn na-an-šub-bé dè-ra-ab-bé a-a + 76 za-e sipa-bi bí-mèn na-an-šub-bé dè-ra-ab-bé a- a + 77 u₄ é-ba gi₄-gi₄ na-an-šub-bé dè-ra-ab-bé a-r[a-zu dè). Again the rejection consists of the abandonment, not in the repulsion of the supplicant(s). The praying community wishes that the interceding gods utter prayers on its behalf.

אנף 'be angry' 60.3; 79.5; šúr, huš *agâgu, ezēzu* 461,66[44]; 607 a + 11[45]
85.6

עבר Dt 'show 78.21, 59, 62; à-dib-ba *kamâlu, šabâ-* 711 b + 120[46]
anger, become 89.39 *su*
angry'

משך אף 85.6 íb-ba *uggâtu* 147, 152[47]; 213f c + 137–147
'prolong refrain íb-bé ù-na-nam[48]; 487
anger' d + 137–143; 488 d + 153; cf.
680, 7.

šà-íb-ba *nuggâtu, aggu* 322 a + 30[49], 384 a + 2[50]; 606
a + 9; 405, 37[51]; 639 a + 33[52];
cf. 652 b + 41.

šà-me-er 653 d + 78[53]

עשן אף 'smoke' 74.1; 85.b;
80.5

בער 'burn, 79.5; (83.15); *hamāṭu*
blaze up, burn 89.46
up, singe'

44. Cohen 1988: 464 Your battle..., your warring is furious = mè-zu in-[...] en-en-zu ùr-ra.

45. Cohen 1988: 625: 'Furious storm, killing people' = 607 a + 11 u_4-huš-e s[ag-gi_6 til-la]//u_4-mu èz-zu.

46. Cohen 1988: 721 At which Nudimmud is enraged = en ^{d}Nu-dím-mud-da à-dib-ba-bi. The semantic field of divine anger in Hebrew includes also the idea of God's burning and smoking nose. In the *balag* the statement of divine anger is preceded by destruction through fire: Ibid., b + 113–119: 'That city levelled by fire! That city whose fate has not been decided (favourably)! That city whose lord does not care for it! That city against which Enlil rushes! That city with which Enlil has started a quarrel! At which An frowns!'

47. Cohen 1988: 149: The storm, the angry heart of An = 147, 152 u_4-dè šà-íb-ba-an-gu-la-re.

48. Cohen 1988: 218: 'Indeed, wild with anger! The word of the lord, indeed wild with anger! The lord, the great hero, indeed wild with anger! c + 140 Muzebbasa, indeed wild with anger! Shedukishara, indeed wild with anger! Nabû, the princely, son, indeed wild with anger! Heir to the Esagil, indeed wild with anger!' = 213 c + 137 FM [íb-bè ù-na-nam]//[ug-ga]t-su kàd-ru-[...] or [... ug-ga]-t-u piri ma šaš ka-ad-ru-ti-šu c + 138 FM [umun e-ne-èm-mà-ni] íb-bé [ù-na-nam] etc.

49. Cohen 1988: 332 a + 30: 'The storm, the angry heart of An' = 322 a + 30 u_4-dè šà íb-ba-an-gu-la-ri//u_4-mu nu-ug-gá-<at> lìb-bi ša d_A-nim GA[L-ú].

50. Cohen 1988: 393: 'Oh lord! How long will your raging, your angry heart not be calmed?' = 384 a + 2 [umun]-e hu-luh-ha-zu šà-íb-ba-zu èn-šè nu-$šed_7$-dè//ezenu ni-si-idu iš-še-en-ni umun^ú hu-luh-ha-zu^ú.

51. Cohen 1988: 410: 'Who can calm your angry heart?' = 405, 37 šà-íb-ba-zu a-ba íb-$šed_7$-dè = ag-ga ŠA$_3$-*ka man-nu ú-na-ah-šu*.

52. Cohen 1988: 641: '"Oh, your angry heart!" they utter to him' = 639 b + 33 a šà-m[u-un-n]a-ab-bé-e-ne//*a-hu-lap lìb-bi-ka ag-gi i-qa-bu-šu*.

53. Cohen 1988: 664: 'All day long with an angry heart': = 653 d + 78 u_4-dù-a-ra ša-me-er-a-ta = *ka-la u_4-me ina lìb-bi ag-gi: ina nu-ug-ga-[at] lìb-bi*.

ישן 'go to sleep, sleep'	44.24	ku(-ku)	ṣalâlu	194 a + 39[54]
	cf. 78.65	nú	ṣalâlu niâlu	82 e + 143[55]; cf. 96,9, 96,14; 178 a + 50; 191,73f[56] cf. 196 b + 77–82; 203, 12[57]; 324 c + 71–73[58] cf. 378 a + 60–62; 391 a + 170–172 and more often.
		ku-ku		96,8[59] and more often.
שבח 'forget'	44.25; 74.19, 23;	ge$_{16}$-le-èm		543, 76.[60]
סתד 'hide, be hidden'	44.25; 89.47; (102.3)	ha-lam dul, šú	mašû katâmu	cf. CAD MI (1977) 397–401. 155,26.28[61] cf. 278 c + 110.112; 388 a + 87.89.

54.   Cohen 1988: 199: 'His word is a wail, a wail. He is asleep! A wail!' = 194 a + 39 e-ne-èm-mà-ni i-lu i-lu ù am-ku i-lu.

55.   Cohen 1988: 88: ['The sleeping bull!] Tell it to him = 82 e + 143 [am nú-dè d]u$_{11}$-ga-na-ab].

56.   Cohen 1988: 193: 'How long will the sleeping one sleep?' 'How long will the great mountain Enlil sleep?'' = 191, 73 [mu-lu-nú-a-e] èn-šè ba-nú-a//[. . .] a-di ma-ti sal-la-at 74 [kur-gal a-a ^{d}Mu-ul-líl èn-šè ba]-nú. Cf. ibid., 200: 'How long will the sleeping one sleep?' 'How long will the great mountain father Enlil sleep?' 'How long will the shepherd of the black-headed sleep?' 'How long will he who witnesses everything first-hand sleep?' 'How long will the bull who causes the troops to wander sleep?' 'How long will he who sleeps sleep a false sleep?'

57.   'By Enlil, who is sleeping, I shall sit (by his) forehead' = ^{d}Mu-ul-líl nú-a-ra sag-ki tuš mu-na-mar.

58.   Cohen 1988: 333: 'The bull is at rest. Why does he not rise up? Enlil is at rest. When (sic!) does he not rise up? The bison, the bull is at rest. Why does he not rise up?' = c + 71 [am al-n]ú te nu-un-zi-zi//be-lu$_4$ ša ṣal-lu mi-nam la i-te-e[b-bi] c + 72 ^{d}Mu-ul-líl am al-nú [te]//^{d}Ninnu be-lu$_4$ ša ṣal-lu mi-nam la i-te-eb-[bi] c + 73 alim-ma-am al-nú te//kab-tu be-lu$_4$ ša ṣal-lu mi-nam [la i-te-eb-bi].

59.   Cohen 1988: 108: 'Father Enlil, who sleeps a false sleep' = 96,8 [a-a ^{d}Mu-ul-líl ù-lul-la ku]-ku. Cf. CAD S (1962) 67 šalâlu: (Enlil) who is awake even when he seems to be asleep (lit. who sleeps a false sleep).

60.   Cohen 1988: 589: 'Those Anunna-gods who sit (in counsel) have forgotten me.' = 543, 76: ^{d}An-nun-na dúr-dúr-ru-na-bi me-e ba-ge$_{16}$-le-èm-mà-ne. Inanna laments over her destroyed temple and city, her captured spouse Dumuzi and her deported child (i.e. probably the city's population) and complains that her human protégés' misery came to pass because the other gods of heaven did forget her.

61.   Cohen 1988: 166: 'How long will you keep your head covered with a cloth? How long will you keep your neck in (your) lap? How long will you keep your mind covered like a reed box?' = 155,26 mu-lu sag-zu-a túg bi-dul-la èn-è//ša qaq-qa-ad-ka su-bat tu-kat-ti-ma. . . 28 šà-zu ^{gi}pisan-gin$_7$ ám-mà-ba-šu-a èn-še//li-ba-ka GIM pi-sa-an-nu tak-tu-mu. Cf. Cohen 1988: 598: 'The hierodule no longer manifests herself. How can anyone speak with her? The princess (Inanna), woe, she no longer comes out. How can anyone speak with the princess Inanna?'

נתן 'surrender, deliver, give away'	44.12; 74.19	zé-èm	nadânu	76 a + 37[62]; 80 d + 116–126 refrain du$_5$-mu-mu nu-u-ba-an-zé-èm-mà[63]; 84 f + 195. 198[64]; and more often.
כלם (H) 'disgrace, hurt; abuse; put to shame'	44.10		nâṣum ṭapā- lum ṭuppulûm	cf. CAD N II (1980) 53; AHw 1379, 1396 and Kraus (1970:145–147).
העטה בושה 'cover with shame'	89.46		pištu bâšum	cf. CAD B (1965) page?
חרף D 'taunt, reproach'	44.17; 74.10, 18; 79.12; 89.51, 52; 102.9			596f When I stand at a place of argument, indeed I am a woman who knows (all) the insults.

A comparison of the Hebrew, Akkadian and Sumerian (Emesal) vocabulary encounters the difficulty that the semantic range of the words concerned does not fit exactly and is even sometimes uncertain. We deal with dead languages, the dead language Sumerian is even only accessible through the other dead language Akkadian and the word-lists and interlinear translations of old times. A scholar nowadays cannot avoid the necessity of relating the ancient terms to renderings in modern languages as given in the dictionaries. For the inquiry presented here, the Akkadian equivalents to the Hebrew word were found through their German renderings in the dictionaries of Georg Fohrer (1971), Thomas Kämmerer and Dirk Schwiderski (1998), and Wolfram von Soden (AHw). The AHw

62. Cohen 1988: 85: 'Because of the house of Arue, which has been handed over' = 76 a + 37 é-^{d}A-du-ru-e ba-zé-èm-mà-šè.

63. Cohen 1988: 87: 'As the mountain stream goes, it destroys. 'Had he not handed over my son!' As it goes, summoned forth by the lord, it destroys. 'Had he not handed over my son!' The mother..., 'Had he not handed over my son!' Mother Damgalnunna..., 'Had he not handed over my son!' d + 120 'Had he not handed him over!' 'Had he not handed over my son!' 'Had he not handed over my son!' She enters her cella. She walks about aimlessly. 'Had he not handed over my son!' 'My son, who was washed in the holy basin! Had he not handed over my son!' 'My son, who ate from the bowl! Had he not handed over my son!' 'My one who would feed himself, rearing himself! Had he not handed over my son!' 'He who would anoint himself, growing tall! Had he not handed over my son!' 'My one at whom I would look with a measuring reed! Had he not handed over my son!'" It is not clear who this son is, for whom the goddess laments, another god, the temple or city or even a king. But the motives of destruction, anointing and handing over are similar to those in Psalm 89.39-42 given the difference that the lamenting voice is the human one of Ethan the Ezrahite according to the psalm's identification in 89.1 and he laments not for his own but for God's son (cf. 89.27).

64. Cohen 1988: 89: 'When the lord acts like An, the bull gives forth like An; he gives forth in his *bariga*-container. When Enki acts like An, when Asarluhi acts like An, the bull gives forth like An; he gives forth in his *bariga*-container.' = 84 f + 194... f + 195 am an-gin$_7$ ì -ib-zé-èm ba-rí-ga-na ì -ib-zé-èm... f + 198 [am an-g]in$_7$ ì -ib-zé-èm ba-rí-ga-na ì-ib-zé-èm.

and the wordlist provided by Maul (1988) with German translations for the Sumerian and Akkadian words lead to a list of Sumerian terms that were looked up in Mark E. Cohen's index of Sumerian terms (1988: 740–785). Thus the inquiry switched to Sumerian and English and was equipped with the English renderings of the Hebrew words in William Holladay's ([13]1993) dictionary. Almost every word has a wider semantic range than that focused on in the comparison attempted here. Hence there are twilight zones of meaning so that overlapping semantic ranges may exist even when the most common meaning of a word does not fit in the semantic field given by the Hebrew term concerned.

An example from the first semantic field of the list above, 'rejection' may illustrate the procedure and its difficulties and incertitudes. The Hebrew verb זנח is rendered in Fohrer's dictionary (1971) as 'verwerfen, verstoßen' and in Holladay's ([13]1993) as 'reject, exclude' and מָאַס as 'verschmähen, verabscheuen, ablehnen, verwerfen, widerrufen' and 'refuse, reject, disavowal (thus rejection) of earlier words'. Hence the common rendering for both verbs is 'verwerfen' and 'reject'. If one looks up the verb 'verwerfen' in a German-English dictionary one gets 'to reject, to repudiate, spurn, condemn'. Thus 'verwerfen' transports connotations which exceed the verb 'to reject', but remain still in the wider semantic field of the change from a positive to a negative relationship creating distance. Looking for an Akkadian equivalent starting from 'verwerfen' one gets e.g. the verb *nadû*. CAD N I (1980: 68) gives for *nadû*, lot of meanings, e.g. 1. to throw into... cast down... spit out... to abandon... to disregard... to repudiate an obligation... 7 to turn a city, a temple into uninhabited ruins... abandon... 8 šuddu + to repudiate, to reject, to repel (an attack), to pardon negligence, to deprive. Hence there are overlapping semantic ranges especially for the Akkadian word in the Š-stem, namely 'to repudiate, to reject'. However which meaning a translator of the verb *nadû* in an Akkadian text actually chooses depends partly on the context and partly on his subjective estimation. Is it legitimate to combine the two semantic ranges of *nadû* Š-stem, namely 'to turn into ruins, abandon' and 'to reject' as more or less visible and aggressive forms of rejection or must meaning 7 and 8 of *nadû* Š-stem be separated seriously? One Sumerian equivalent of *nadû*, šub is quite prominent in *balags* but rather in the meaning 'to cast down, to turn into ruins, to abandon' than in the meaning 'to reject'. Is it therefore legitimate to take the former meanings as a more concrete form of the latter one? Seeing that the Hebrew verbs זנח and מאס appear in Psalms 44.23 and 78.59-64,67 in the context of being killed, in Psalm 60.3 together with shaking and breaking the earth, in Psalm 74.1,4-8 with destruction, and in Psalm 89.39,41 with bringing to ruin, it seems acceptable to count those passages where šub/*nadû* in *balags* describes the fate of the lamenting city as belonging to the semantic range of divine rejection.

The semantic field of 'rejection' given by the Hebrew verbs זנח and מאס leads to a further interesting aspect of the *balags*. The Akkadian translation of the Sumerian verb *gur* 'to turn away' through *sakâpu* gives just the opposite meaning, namely 'to reject'. CAD S (1984: 70) lists the following meanings for *sakâpu* A: 1. to thrust, push away, to overturn, to reject, to set aside (kingship), depose (a king); 2. to drive back, repulse, defeat, drive out, evict; 3. to dispatch a boat, to send by boat, to drive cattle. Thus the semantic field of the verb includes 'to reject', extant in the semantic field of זנח and מאס too. But the Sumerian word *gur* does not include this semantic field. It denotes just the opposite movement of the god. The supplicant is not pushed away by the god, but the god himself turns away and leaves the supplicant alienated. Thus the Akkadian and the Hebrew verbs are closer from a semantic point of view, than the Akkadian and Sumerian verbs. If Hebrew poets had some knowledge of Mesopotamian hymnology at all, it is most likely that they understood the Sumerian expressions of the god's 'turning away, abandoning and desertion' as a divine act of rejection as does the Akkadian *sakâpu*.

Though the idea that anger and fury are combined with burning, heat and smoke as is common in psalms was existent in Akkadian[65] it does not appear in *balags*.

The Hebrew verbs ישן, שכח and סתר contain the concept of negligence and refusal to care. God sleeps, forgets and hides himself. Thus he is not experienced as approachable and helping. While the sleeping god is very common in *balags*, the idea of a forgetting god is rare and his hiding comes to the fore as covering his head, expressed with the Sumerian and Akkadian verbs dul//*katâmu*. When the god has covered his head, he is hidden and not approachable and attentive to the supplications of the praying community. This equation is corroborated through an episode, where Dumuzi covers his head with a garment in order to hide himself from his demonic pursuers (Cohen 1988: 673 c + 86 = 679f c + 81-92). Akkadian personal names express the wish that the divinity may not forget a place (AHw 631 *mašûm II* 1b GN-ON-*e-ta-am-ši*) and it may be extant in wisdom literature (BWL 38, 21; 241 iii 60), the *balags* use 'to forget' only seldom, be it for human beings (Cohen 1988: 432 c + 66 *it-tam-šu*), be it for gods as subject (Cohen 1988:589 = 534,76). The Sumerian verb 'ha-lam', which may mean 'to forget', is translated as *halâqu* 'to destroy' when it has a divine subject (Cohen 1988: 233 b + 233; 430 a + 20).

It is quite remarkable that the idea of a sleeping god, so prominent in *balags*, does only appear in one Korah (44.24) and one Asaph (78.65) psalm, both bearing the Hebrew genre indication משכיל. The third mention of ישן with divine subject in Psalm 121.4 does precisely exclude that God

---

65. CAD H 1956: 64f hamâṭu B 1c 'to be inflamed with fury'.

sleeps. This idea exists in the *balags* too, and is expressed by using the oft-repeated formulas 'sleeps a false sleep' and 'you have placed on watch a shepherd that never sleeps'. The verbs סתר (Pss. 13.2; 22.25; 27.9; 30.8; 44.25; 51.11; 69.18; 88.15; 89.47; 102.4; 104.29; 143.7) and שכח (10.11,12; 13.2; 42.10; 44.25; 74.19, 23; 77.10) with the divine subject on the other hand also appear in other psalm groups and genres and can thus by no means be regarded as typical for Korah and Asaph psalms or communal laments. It is noteworthy that the clearest resemblance between psalms and *balags* in this semantic field consists just in the concept of the 'sleeping god' in the Korah and Asaph collections. It may be added that the concept of the forgetting god, also existent in *balags*, is combined in the Asaph psalm and משכיל 74.19 with the motif of the dove (תור) so prominent in *balags* (Cohen 1988: 778 v.s. tu^{mušen} = *simmatu*). Hence there is more common vocabulary with *balags* in the משכיל genre of the Korah and Asaph collections than in the rest of the Psalter.

The idea that humans may come to shame is extant in Akkadian personal names (CAD B 1965: 6 ba-ašu 1.e and 2.b), and in šuillas, but not in *balags*.

2.2.2 *God's return (zuwending)*.

Hebrew	Pss.	Emesal	Akkadian	Cohen 1988 page, line
עור 'stir oneself up, be awake, astir, lively'	44.24	zi-zi è	*tebû* *waṣû*	324 c + 111–119[66] 95,1 ^{d}Utu-gin$_7$ è-ta … = Come out like the sun!
קיץ H 'awake'	44.24	zi-zi		324 c + 71–73[67]

---

66.   Cohen 1988: 333: 'Why does the goring bull not rise up? Why does Enlil, the goring bull, not rise up? Why does the bison, the goring bull, not rise up? Why does father Enlil, the lord of the lands not rise up? Why does the bison, the lord of Nippur, not rise up? From among the fattened sheep… why does not rise up? 324 c + 111 am du$_7$-du$_7$ te nu-um-zi-zi//*be-lu$_4$ mut-tak-pu mi-na la i-te-eb-ba*… c + 119 gukkal-IB$_2$-lá-a-ta te nu-um-zi-zi//*gu-uk-kal-ku$_4$ ina zib$^{1(UG)}$-ba-ti-ú a-lí-šu a-lí-lu$_4$ mi-nam la i-te-eb-ba*.

67.   Cohen 1988: 333: 'The bull is at rest. Why does he not rise up? Enlil is at rest. When(sic!) does he not rise up? The bison, the bull, is at rest. Why does he not rise up?' = 324 c + 71 [am al-n]ú te nu-un-zi-zi//*[be-l]u$_4$ ša ṣal-lu mi-nam la i-te-e[b-bi]* c + 72 [^{d}Mu]-ul-líl-lá am al-nú [te]//*^{d}NINNU be-lu$_4$ ša ṣal-lu mi-nam la i-te-eb-[bi]* c + 73 alim-ma am al-nú te//*kab-tu [be-l]u$_4$ ša ṣal-lu mi-nam [la i-te-eb-bi]*. Here the Sumerian verb *zi-zi* rendered in Akkadian as *tebû* stands in opposition to Akkadian *ṣalalu* 'lay down, sleep'. In this opposition to 'sleeping' it is the exact counterpart of Hebrew קיץ H 'awake'. Note also the rendering of Sumerian *am* 'bull' with *belu* 'lord' in Akkadian. Hence the Akkadian drops the Sumerian animal image for the god and instead employs a noun whose Hebrew counterpart אדוני is prominent in the Psalter.

קום 'stand up, get up; stand upright, arise, rise up; come about'	44.27; 74.22	zi-bu-um		342, 1-a + 15 zi-bi-um min ^{d}[Mu-ul-lila un]-kur-kur-ra//[t-i]-ba-a MIN ^{d}E[n-líl be-el] ma-ta-a-ti = Arise, arise, Enlil, lord of the lands!; 348,1; 352,88. 147,157f.[68]
זכר 'mention; remember'	74.2, 18, 22; 89.49, 51	mu-uš tuk	šemû רכ hasâsu	69 b + 62[69]
נבט 'look; look out, gaze; see, look at, catch sight of'	74.20; 80.15	u$_6$ di	amâru natâlu palâsu N	325 c + 119–123[70] cf. 339, 1f.
ראה 'see; percieve, become aware of; look at, consider; gaze at; get to know, become aquainted with'	80.15	i-bí dub	ṣubbum	129,108f; 159,121; 330 f + 240f[71]; 340,11; 354,165–167[72]

68. Cohen 1988: 150: 'It (i.e. the house) had risen towards the heavens; it will never again be founded. It had *stretched into* the earth; it will never again arise.' = 147,157 an-še: ì-zi mu-mu-un-da-ma[ma] 158 ki-še: ì-zi nu-mu-un-da-zi-[zi].

69. Cohen 1988: 72: 'The woman cried out in the holy house. He heard her cry in the holy house.' = 69 b + 61... b + 62 gù-né é-kù-ga mu-uš im-ma-an-tuk-a//ri-gi-im-á el-lu iš-me-e-ma. Though the Akkadian verb means 'to hear' and not 'to remember', it is used here to express the attention given to the supplication by the (angry) male god.

70. Cohen 1988: 333: 'Rising bull, gaze about! Enlil, rising bull, gaze about! Bison, rising bull, gaze about! Father Enlil, lord of the lands, rising bull, gaze about!' = c + 119 [am-z]i-g[a-à]m u$_6$-ki-ga-a-an-zé-e[n]//[...]-x lí-mur-ka... c + 122 [a-a ^{d}Mu-ul-líl-lá umun-kur-kur-ra am-zi-ga-àm u$_6$-di].

71. Cohen 1988: 139: 'Gaze at... your city which has been destroyed!' = 129,108 [...-a mu-un-hul-a u$_6$-du$_{11}$-ga-ab DU (...)] 109 [... urú-zu mu-un-hul-a u$_6$)-. Ibid., 336: 'After he of the dirges had looked about in the steppe, looked about in the steppe, after he looked about ...' = 330 f + 240 šir-re eden-na ut-du$_{11}$-ga-ta eden-na u$_6$-[d]i?//ina ṣir-hi É ina ba-re É mi-i-[t]i.

72. Cohen 1988: 341: 'Important one, go about! Gaze at your city!' = 340,11 x [...] x nígin-ù urú-zu u$_6$-ga-e-du$_{11}$. Ibid., 370: 'Look about! Look about! Let me gaze about the house! Let me gaze about the house! In the Eanna, let me gaze about the house! Caringly, let me gaze about the house!' = 354,165 i-bí du-ub-bé i-bí du-ub-bé 166 é-e u$_6$ ga-e-du$_{11}$ é-e ga-e-du$_{11}$ 167 é-an-na-ka é-e u$_6$ ga-e-du$_{11}$ é-e mí-zi ga-e-du$_{11}$.

שׁוב 'return, go back, come back; revert; turn into; turn back; change one's mind; withdraw'	80.15; 85.5 (G); 60.3 (D); 80.4,8,20 (H)	gi_4, gi_4-gi_4	*tuaru*	164f c + 247–257[73]; 178f a + 55– b + 58[74]; cf. 107 d + 273; 136 and more often; 378 a + 48–52[75]
רום H 'raise, lift up; pick up; put up, errect; take up, exalt, raise up; elevate; present offer'	89.43	zi-zi íl	*našû šaqû*	100,168[76]; cf.147, 161[77]; 179 b 86f[78] 214 c + 144[79]; 503,28[80]; 508f a + 128–132[81]

73. Cohen 1998: 171: 'Sir, you have turned away from your city. When will you return? Enlil, you have turned away from your city. When will you return? You have turned away from Uruk, from the Eanna. When will you return? b + 250 You have turned away from your city Nippur. When will you return? You have turned away from the Kiur, the Enamtila. When will you return? You have turned away from Sippar, from the Ebabbar. When will you return? You have turned away from your city Tintir. When will you return? You have turned away from the Esagil, from Borsippa. When will you return? You have turned away from the Ezida, the Emahtila. When will you return? You have turned away from the Etemenanki. When will you return? You have turned away from the Edaranna. When will you return?' = 146 c + 247 mu-lu urú-zu ba-da-gur-ra-en-na me-na-še: ì-g[i_4?]... 165 c + 257 é-dára-an-na ba-da-gur-ra-en-na me-.

74. Cohen 1988: 182f: 'Its brickwork! Restore the brickwork!' Tell it to him! ... Its (fill)-dirt! Restore the (fill)-dirt! Alas! = 178 a + 55 [e-eb-è] še-eb gi_4-gi_4 du$_{11}$-ga-an-na-ab... 178 b + 85 sahar-è sahar gi_4-gi_4 ù-(li-li). Cf. the subscripts of the *balags* as 107 d + 273 šùd-bi e-eb-[é- ...] ki! na-an-gi_4-gi_4-dè! = 114: A supplication that the brickwork of the...-temple should be restored.

75. Cohen 1988: 382f: Change (your) mind! Change (your) mind! Enlil, change (your) mind! a + 50 Enlil in the land, change (your) mind! Shepherd of the black-headed, change (your) mind! Change (your) mind! Change it! Speak to him! = 378 a + 48 à-ab gi_4-ù gi_4-ù... a + 52 à-ab gi_4-ù gi_4-ù e-ne-ra du$_{11}$-àm.

76. Cohen 1988: 111: 'My house, which had been raised up for the feast of eating emmer, rises up in sighs' = 101,168 [é imgaga-gu₇?-e ba-zi-ga-mu ér-re ba-zi-zi] cf. Krecher 1966: 57 IV 11, 187.

77. Cohen 1988: 150: 'It had risen towards the heavens; it will never again be founded. ... raise my foot.' = 147,157... 161 [x x (x)]-x-x-EL-le me-ri an-da-ab-í[l-e]

78. Cohen 1988: 183: 'When you are surpassing (as) the shining horn of heaven, inherently majestic, when you are surpassing, when you are surpassing (as) father Nanna, the shining horn of heaven, inherently majestic, when you are surpassing...' = 179 b + 86 si-mú-kù-an-na še-er-ma-al-la ní-te-na diri-ga-zu-dè za-e diri-ga-zu-dè//*na-an-na-ru el-lu ša ša-me-e e-til ra-ma-ni-ú ina šu-tu-ru-ti ka-at-tú* MIN b + 87 a-a ^{d}Nanna si-mú-kù-an-na še-er-ma-al-la ní-te-na.

79. Cohen 1988: 218 His (word) which carried the battle up to the heavens! = 214 c + 144 FM [an-na mè]-e ba-an-n[a?-íl-la-ni]//*[ana] AN-e ta-ha-zi iš-[šu-u]*

80. Cohen 1988: 512: 'raised upon the silver throne of Sumer' = 503,28 bára-kù-babbar-ra ki-en-gi-ra íl-la//*[par-rak] eb-bi ša ina KUR á-gu-ú.*

81. Cohen 1988: 514: 'Raise up! Raise up your arm to the heavens! My lord, rise up your arm to the heavens! a + 130 Nergal, raise up your arm to the heavens! Your city which you have destroyed with your massive arm! Your city which you have destroyed with your raised arm' = 508 a + 128 íl-la-ab íl-la-ab á-zu an-na//*á-qu-ú á-qu-ú id-ka ana AN-e*... 508f a + 132

מהר 'hurry; quickly; in a hurry'	79.8	ul-le-eš	*arhiš*	234 c + 244–248; 303 c + 118–123
פדה 'ransom, redeem, deliver'	44.27			197 e + 128 = 201: Guilt, dispel the guilt seven times seven! 408 f + 104 = 411; Its wall is firm. You can dispel sin!
נצל H 'snatch away; take away; pull out, extricate, rescue'	79.9			496 d + 150 His (word) which (enabled) the ruler to pile high the enemy in battle!
כפר D 'appease; make amends; provide reconciliation, atonement'	78.38; 79.9 (cf 65.4)	à-ga-ni ga-an-hun bar-ra-a-ni ga-šed₇-dè	*libbašu lunuh, kabattašu lupašših*	134 f + 225f = 141: May heaven and earth calm you! May both heaven and earth calm you! cf. 166,43f; 190,61-63 = 193: 'May I calm his heart! May I pacify his liver!' 'May I direct words to his heart and liver!' 'May I direct words to that tired heart!'
עזר 'help, support; come to the aid of'				452,80 Your throne is secure. You are the one who rules over the enemy. May you kill on my behalf.
עזרה 'support, help'	60.13			630 c + 246: Her mother, well-versed in lamentations, stands up among my people on her behalf.

urú-zu á-íl-la im-me-(hul-a-zu)//[ša URU]-ka e-mu-qan á-qa-at(var. -ti) MIN. These lines contain almost exactly the idea of Psalm 89.43 'You have exalted the right hand of his foes; you have made all his enemies rejoice.' God whose own hand is raised (89.14) and who destroys his anointed and his anointed's fortified cities (89.40) raises the hand of the anointed's enemies, who are God's means of destruction.

חסד 'obligation to the community, loyalty; faithfulness; kindness, grace'	85.5; 89.2, 3, 15, 25, 29, 34, 50	495 d + 114 The lord, the protection of the Ezida, the hero perfect in strength. 512,33 When you care for the shepherd and herdsman, who can compare (favorably) to you?
עבד 'servant; slave'	89.40	590 I shall heatedly utter 'My slave girl!' I shall grievously utter 'Oh my young maidservant!' ... 'Its servant girl who is (usually) stationed there, its servant girl is no longer stationed there. Its manservant who is (usually) stationed there, its manservant is no longer stationed there.'

Again the vocabulary is grouped into semantic fields. The first group expresses God's rising in order to change the misery. This motif is very prominent in *balags*. The second group expresses God's new bestowing of attention, by remembering, looking at and returning to the supplicants. There is also widespread evidence of this theme in *balags*. The last Hebrew verb of this group מהר, expects divine help to come quickly. This idea cannot be found in the *balags*, instead of this there exists a litany which contains the Sumerian expression *ul-le-è*, equated with arhiš 'quickly, hurrying' in *eršahungas* (Maul 1988: 454), but translated 'joyfully' by Cohen. The expression serves to qualify the attitude of humans hurrying to the sanctuary in order to implore the angry god to bestow the positive change of their fate. Since a we-group is speaking in the passages concerned (Cohen 1988: 248 cf. 202 c + 118–123), I quote them further below when the we-group prominent in biblical communal laments is treated. Here follows instead a passage, where an unidentified voice summons the people to 'hurry' to worship:

> Oh people, hurry hither to the place where An dwells! (To) the princely house, oh people hurry hither to the place where An dwells! It is at the house. The lofty first-offerings are at the house. Ablutions..., ablutions... So that at the house the heart (of) the storm will be calm, the liver (of) the storm will be calm, so that during the day the

first-offerings will be performed correctly, a + 60 so that during the day
the supplications will be performed correctly, so that during the day the
heavens, the god(s) of man will... so that Enki, the bull of Eridu will...
Enlil, come! Enlil, (...)! Oh people hurry hither! ... washed. At
evening... washed. It calms the heart (Cohen 1988: 292f ll. a + 54–64).

Liturgical summoning as in Psalm 81.2-4 is therefore not an element
exclusively restricted to Asaph psalms but belongs to the features of
communal prayers both in Emesal and Hebrew. The same is true for the
divine speech or oracle as already pointed out above (cf. Seybold 1994:
148, 150).

The following two semantic fields do not have exact vocabulary parallels
in the *balags* though their ideas are present nevertheless. In order to show
the difference in resemblance in comparison to the preceding semantic
fields, no Sumerian and Akkadian words are given. Instead quotations
from *balags* appear in Cohen's English translation. The only exceptions are
the heart pacification formulas, which serve as counterpart to the Hebrew
כפר D. This formula is more common in *eršemmas* and typical for
eršahungas and a very characteristic feature of Mesopotamian prayer
language without counterpart in biblical psalms.

Remarkable are the two quoted petitions to forgive sin, a motif more
common in *šuillas* and *eršahungas* than in *balags* and *eršemmas*. This
corresponds to the biblical evidence where the plea to forgive sin is likewise
much more extant in individual than in communal laments. However this
motif in Psalm 79.8 does fit into the genre of the latter as corroborated by
Mesopotamian evidence and its existence must not necessarily be understood as a later development in *Volksklageliedern* (against Weber 2000:
530).

Due to the fact that a female, the imploring goddess, plays an important
role in *balags*, the divine concern is less directed to a male servant as in
psalms (e.g. Psalm 89.4, 40, 51) than to a maidservant. But the concept is
identical. The male or female servant is afflicted by divine wrath and the
praying voice desires the positive relationship between the servant and his
god(s) to be restored.

2.2.3 *Construction*. The motifs of construction and destruction in *balags*
are so overwhelmingly present that the following two tables refer to
comparable expressions in the English translation of the prayers and only
indicate the Sumerian and Akkadian counterparts of the Hebrew
vocabulary when Cohen's translation is to be doubted. Whoever takes
Cohen's edition into his hands will immediately find many more. All the
examples cited below are taken from the *balag* Uru amirabi 'That city
which has been pillaged'.

The most prevalent feature in *balags* referring to construction is the oft-repeated subscript 'A supplication that the brickwork of NN (= the temple's name) should be restored'. Hence the very purpose of singing these poetical prayers is to invoke a constructive attitude of the divinity not only as regards a certain temple but also with regard to the pious community mentioning it.

Hebrew	Psalms	Cohen, Uru Amirabi
נטע 'plant; drive a nail'	44.3; 80.9	580 c + 422 mu-gi-bi alma-ma-an al-mama-[an]//se-*eh-ra u ra-ba a a-na-as-sa-ah a-á-ak-kan* = 4 <Ich,?> die Göttliche, ich reisse aus, setze (wieder) ein. Akk.: Klein und Groß entwurzle ich, setze ich (wieder) ein Volk (1989: 203) 597 I smash the mighty ones like plants. 598 I stand an the earth. Vegetation sprouts.
שלח 'give free, let go; stretch out; send'	44.3; 80.12	597 As for me, my word is a huge net stretched over the haunted swamp ... When it stretches over the seq, the sea quakes. When it stretches over the marsh, the marsh moans. 596 I cause the weak to enter the house. I expel the mighty from the house.
קנה I 'acquire, buy; redeem' II 'create'	74.2; 78.54	595 Am I not the lady of the house, the lady of the gods? ... The Eanna, (my) house on earth, has been given to me. ... That maidservant whom I touch is purified.
גאל 'redeem; deliver; avenge; lay claim; ransom'	74.2	591 Will not someone replace the holy corpse, the clean corpse. I am the young woman. Will not someone replace the one whose donkeys have been set loose?
שכן 'submit oneself; settle; stay, stop; inhabit; sojourn, be found; dwell'	74.2	589 'Oh, I want to sit down! My sitting place!' she says. ... The house ... on whose reed mat I used to lie down! ... So it is when she is in the holy house.
זרוע 'arm, forearm'	44.4; 77.16; 79.11; 89	596 I am the valour in the heart of the battle, indeed I am the arm of valour.
ימין 'right side; right hand; south'	44.4; 60.7 (// 108.7), 74.11; 89.16,18,43	595 As for me, the lady, no hand can equal my hand. 596 I make right into left. I make left into right.

The Hebrew vocabulary can be distributed into three psalm verses that serve as a paradigm for the use and meaning of the words. Psalm 44.3 reads: 'You with your own hand drove out the nations, but them you planted; you afflicted the peoples, but them you set free'. Hence planting stands in opposition to expel and liberation in opposition to affliction. The phrases quoted from the *balag* express a similar opposition between rooting out (ausreißen) and planting (einsetzen) in Volk's translation.[82] An opposition between malignity and benevolence comes to the fore in Inanna's smashing the mighty but bestowing vegetation. Both this *balag* and Psalm 80 compare the afflicted of divine wrath with a plant.

The next set of three Hebrew verbs are used together in Psalm 74.2: 'Remember your congregation, which you acquired long ago, which you redeemed to be the tribe of your heritage. Remember Mount Zion, where you came to dwell'. The idea is that a divinity takes possession of a people and a realm and dwells there. The phrases of the *balag* describe Inanna as inhabitant of her temple, which she acquired as a gift of her father Enlil. While Yhwh is able to redeem his people, Inanna asks that her spouse Dumuzi be given back to her. Other *balags* ask in a direct way: 'Why won't you hand over to the mother her child who was taken away? Why won't you hand over to the mother, to Ninurubare, her child who was taken away? ... Why won't you hand over to her who says "Oh city! Oh people!" her child who was taken away?' (Cohen 1988: 292). This passage makes clear that the goddess regards the city and its people as her child and it begs redemption from the angry male god that caused the deportation.

2.2.4 *Destruction*. Destruction is so overwhelmingly present in the *balags* that the following table simply quotes phrases of the *balag Uru amirabi* comparable to the vocabulary collected by Hieke and Veijola. Some *balag* titles even contain this vocabulary and are also cited. The *balag Uru amirabi* reveals both the compassionately lamenting and aggressively destructive aspect of goddess Inanna/Ishtar. The communal laments of the Psalter express a similar ambiguity of Yhwh's. He destroys aggressively (80.13; 89.41f) on the one hand and is begged to be compassionate and help on the other hand (74.21; 79.11).

Hebrew	Psalms	Cohen, Uru amirabi
הרג 'kill'	44.23	587 That (city), the killing (of whose people) has been ordered.

82. Cohen (1988: 596) translates 'I *have been installed as* the hierodule. *I have been installed*,' though he gives the same transcription as Volk does. His italics show that it is an uncertain, not literal translation.

פרץ 'make a breach, burst out; tear down; break through; spread out, increase'

60.3; 80.13; 89.41

590 On my road hostile bandits commit murder. In my street during the night thieves break into the homes. My houses, having been made into houses... have been torn asunder.

רעע (H) 'hurt, injure; treat badly, harm; bring calamity; cause damage; act wickedly'

74.3

Cf. 253 *Uruhulake*: She of the ruined city. 595 My utterance destroys the rebellious. 596 Indeed, I am the one who extinguishes... Cf.457ff: *Ušumgin ni si*: Instilling terror like a serpent. 500 *Agalgal buru susu*: Flood which drowns the harvest.

שרף 'burn, cauterize'

74.8; 80.17

588 That city, *levelled* by fire.
595 The fire I kindle cannot be extinguished. ... I am a blazing, rising fire. ... I am a flame raining down ash upon the rebellious.

נאר D 'dishonour, disgrace'

89.40

590 As for me, I feel strange. As for me, I feel alienated.
Cf. 47ff *Abzu pelam*: The defiled Apsu.

שבת H 'put to an end, bring to a stop; remove; let be lacking; make disappear'

89.45

593 At the command of the 'lady of heaven,' the girl, the 'mother-of-sin', is set on a dust heap. (Inanna) looks at her with death (in her) eye.
598 My name causes the scribes to stop writing. My choice name prevents the *gala*-priests from calling out (in song).

קצר ימים H 'shorten the days'

89.46 (cf. 102.24)

588 That city whose young men are sick; whose young women are sick, so that the young girls of the city are no longer happy, so that the young men of the city no longer rejoice.

חלל לארץ 'pillage to the ground'

74.7; 89.40

587 That city which has been pillaged! Oh its children!'
590 Before my very eyes my city has been strewn about. What has been taken from it? Who is aware of the property has expropriated it from me.

שסה / שסס 'plunder'

44.11; 89.42

589 Those men have plundered your dwelling places like (all the other) settlements.
595 The city, which I plunder, can never again raise its head.

אויבים / צרים 'adversaries//enemies'

89.43

588 That city which has been destroyed by war, war in which the *slave* is the antagonist!
589 The dogs, which knew me, have made me known to the enemy. The dogs, which now do not follow me, follow the enemy.

> 590 As for me, when I enter the house like a swallow, the hostile and deceitful rush at me, coming suddenly and swiftly at me.

In addition to the typical vocabulary Hieke (1997: 241f) points to the prevalence of vocatives and a we-voice ('wir'-Gruppe). Both features exist in *balags*. Examples for the vocative are to be found in many of the quotations from *balags* given in this paper. The we-voice comes to the fore as a group consisting of gods and humans proceeding to the angry god. In the following quotation I change Cohen's rendering 'joyfully' to 'hurrying' which fits better to the depiction of the procession as accompanied with lamentations:

> To the house in prayer, we go in prayer. c + 240 Lamentation... to the house, we go in prayer. Going about the house (with) lamentations... we go in prayer. (With) lamentations, we, god and man, go in prayer. We, god and man, go in prayer. Hurrying we go the (one) of the house in prayer. Hurrying we go to the place (of) the one of the house in prayer. Hurrying we go to the house to calm the heart of the storm. Hurrying we go to calm the heart, pacify the liver. Hurrying we calm the heart of the lord. Hurrying we calm the heart of An, the heart of...
> (Cohen 1988: 248 cf. 202 c + 118–123).

This section shows very clearly that the we-group in *balags* consists of human and divine beings praying together on behalf of city and temple. Hence the praying congregation sees itself in company with a heavenly congregation (cf. Ps. 89.7) and the liturgy terrestrial procedes synchronically with the liturgy celestial. A further example of the we-voice will be quoted from the *balag Abzu pelam* in the next paragraph. Gunkel's opinion that the ANE does not know a praying 'we' – quoted time and again in exegetical literature – results from a lack of knowledge due to the insufficient accessibility of *balags* at his time and must be corrected.[83]

More prevalent than the we-voice is an I-voice, which can often be identified as the one of the 'weeping goddess' (e.g. Cohen 1988: 182 ll. 28–31; cf. Dopps-Allsopp 1993: 75–90), but sometimes a *balag* explicitly

---

83. Gunkel formulated his opinion with caution adding: 'soweit ich zu sehen vermag... wenn sie sich bestätigen würde' (Gunkel/Begrich 1933: 123). Stummer (1922: 137) quoted indeed the 'Selbstaufforderung einer Gruppe von Betern... zum Besuch von Tempeln' that corresponds to the summoning quoted above. But Gunkel may have been deceived by the fact that Stummer did not identify this passage as part of a lament but calls the genre of the prayer a litany. Such a misunderstanding of cuneiform texts in the first half of the twentieth century is more than forgivable. But it throws a shadow on Hieke's accomplished analysis of the *Gattung der Volksklagelieder*, when he quotes Gunkel's opinion more than 60 years later intending to depict a difference between Hebrew and Mesopotamian prayer language (1997: 253).

makes it clear that the voice of the city is speaking: '"Princess! Princess!" is the cry which the city utters.' (Cohen 1988: 183 l. 73, 245f ll. a + 126–142). A god can even decree that the *balag* be sung by the population of the city:

> 'Let (this) lament be sung for me in its fury! I am the ruler! I am the king! Let the populace sing (this) to me! I am the son of Asarluhi!' (Cohen 1988: 218 l. c + 154f).

Hence, the I-voice may represent the congregation. This may also be the case in the Asaph psalms (Seybold 1994: 144f). However, a difference exists in the roles that the persons or voices play. This leads to the concept of actors and actants used in structuralist syntax and semantics (Greimas [2]1986: 172–186). Mesopotamian prayers differ from Hebrew ones through their actors. In Mesopotamia we have the angry and destroying male god, sometimes identified with Enlil. We have the lamenting female goddess or a group of supplicant gods and humans even referring to them as 'we'. We have the temples and the city, the people and animals, the enemies and their homeland, the mountains. In the psalms we have Yhwh as creating and angrily destroying deity. We have the city or the praying community as female lamenting voice and we-group. We have people, animals, enemies, mocking neighbours, etc. From a structuralist point of view the actors can be reduced to six actants: addressing and addressee, subject and object, opponent and adjuvant. The easiest way to fill these actants with actors is to fill the object. What do the prayers want? They want divine care and presence. He who must give the object is the addressing one, thus Enlil and Yhwh. Who shall get the object is the addressee, thus the praying group. Subject, opponent and adjuvant are filled with different actors. The following table shows this:

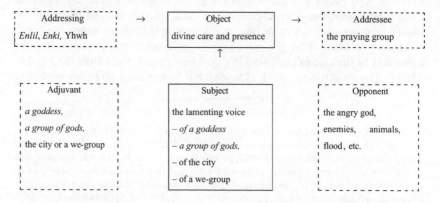

Addressing		Object		Addressee
Enlil, Enki, Yhwh	→	divine care and presence	→	the praying group
		↑		
Adjuvant		Subject		Opponent
a goddess,		the lamenting voice		the angry god,
a group of gods,		– *of a goddess*		enemies, animals,
the city or a we-group		– *a group of gods,*		flood, etc.
		– of the city		
		– of a we-group		

The subject is the one who succeeds in getting the object or providing the object for someone else. The subject is the lamenting voice, the goddess or city or divine group, which sometimes becomes a we-group in the *balag* and *eršemma*, the community or we group in the communal lament psalms. The opponents are the angry destroying god, the enemies or demonic powers. But the enemies have their power because god gives it and does not fight on the people's side. So he refrains from being the adjuvant. Adjuvants are goddesses and gods in Mesopotamia and the praying voice in the psalms. It becomes evident that the difference between Mesopotamian and Biblical laments lies primarily in the religious concept of divine powers that can help, that can be adjuvants. The Mesopotamian pantheon allows goddesses and gods to interfere. The biblical heaven is inhabited by Yhwh and lesser powers, who do not act in favour of humans unless god charges them to do so. Thus something that psalms depict as interaction between God and men, the Mesopotamian laments can depict as interaction between god and divine actors acting in favour of men. On a structural level this is nothing more than a different casting of the roles of subject and adjuvant. The italics in the table identify the actors not 'playing' in Hebrew psalms.

From the point of view of *Gattungskritik* communal laments in the third book of the Psalter share a lot of elements with *balags* from Mesopotamia. It may be legitimate to speak of a family of genres whose members all show common and specific features. This family embraces *balags* and *eršemmas*, their older predecessors, the city laments,[84] the communal lament psalms and the book of Lamentations, but even to a certain extent the individual complaints in the Psalter and in Mesopotamian worship (*eršahungas* and *šuillas*).

The common elements between *balags* and biblical laments are so prevalent that they cannot be the result of similar subject matter and similar situations that lead to poetical similarities or can be explained by 'polygenesis, wherein a genre of literature may originate independently in two different literatures' (Dopps-Allsopp 1993:5 cf. 4). On the contrary, some of the features belong to an imaginative language that seems to be restricted to the Fertile Crescent. The most prominent example is the motif of the divine shepherd and the human flock. This motif appears frequently in *balags* and biblical psalms. It is also attested in Egypt (Hieke 1997: 335–336). Thus there seems to be a clearly discernible realm in which this metaphorical language was acceptable as positive characterization of the relationship between god or human leaders and the people.

Greece, for example, does not belong to this realm. It is true that the gods Apollo and Hermes are depicted as shepherds and sometimes this

---

84. Cf. Green (1978; 1948); Michalowski (1976); Tinney (1996). For a continual tradition connecting the city laments from the third and second millennium to the *balags* and *eršemmas* form the second and first millennium cf. Dopp-Allsopp (1993: 13f); Edelman (forthcoming).

metaphor is used for political rulers too (Hieke, 1997: 338f). But originally Apollo was a foreigner and Hermes a minor god.[85] The shepherd has by no means a thoroughly positive reputation. Homer depicts Hermes as a thief that steals animals, and a teacher of robbery (Nilsson 1941: 477). When the metaphor of the shepherd is applied to the political ruler or the philosopher it takes the connotation of degrading the persons depicted as sheep to a lower worth or intelligence and unable to care for themselves (Turner 1999: 35–38). Features of the shepherd in Greek mythology and poetry, which do not apply to gods in Mesopotamian or to Yhwh in Hebrew prayers, are the link with music (Duchemin 1961) and the function of leading the souls of the departed to the netherworld.

African religions – apart from Ancient Egypt – do not embody the metaphor of shepherd and flock in order to express a relationship of care between gods and human beings (Mbiti 1970; 1974). Sheep and goats are not animals with which humans like to be compared.

Another outstanding similarity between Mesopotamian and biblical laments are the bird images. Dove and swallow, pelican and owl, sparrow and even bat describe mortals and gods afflicted by disaster. The epithet צבאות calling Yhwh a god of hosts or troops (Hieke 1997: 352–355) has a counterpart in Enlil's epithet 'who lets his troops wander' (Kutscher 1975: 49). The fact that the Hebrew epithet is almost completely restricted to the second and third book of the Psalter, i.e. the passage encircled by Asaph and Korah psalms, underlines the distinctness of that portion of the Psalter which contains features of *balags* (Pss. 24.10 + 46.8, 12; 49.9; 59.6; 69.7; 80.5, 8, 15, 20; 84.2, 4, 9, 13; 89.9). Is it mere coincidence that the Hebrew genre indication משכיל is limited to almost the same segment (Pss. 32.1 + 42.1; 44.1; 45.1; 47.8; 52.1; 53.1; 54.1; 55.1; 74.1; 78.1; 88.1; 89.1 + 142.1)?[86] Hence the superscript forms clusters from Psalm 42/43

---

85.   Nilsson (1941: 527): 'Daß Apollon aus Kleinasien nach Griechenland eingewandert ist, war schon längst vermutet worden.' See 531: 'Die Griechen sind schon früh... dem mächtigen Gott begegnet, der ihnen zwar fremd und unheimlich war, andererseits aber tiefen religiösen Bedürfnissen entsprach, so daß sie ihn anerkannten und übernahmen.' See 471: 'Hermes wird unter die großen olympischen Götter gerechnet, in Wirklichkeit ist er nicht gleichen Ranges mit ihnen, sondern nimmt eine dienende, niedere Stellung ein. Bei Homer ist er der Wegweiser und der Bote der Götter, der nicht aus eigenem Antrieb handelt.'

86.   The superscripts of Psalm 32, a psalm which is lacking in two Qumran manuscripts (Flint 1997) and of Psalm 142 may be imitations (Bayer 1982). The superscript of Psalm 88 is a redactional product mixing elements of the preceding Korah superscripts with the superscript of Psalm 89, which declares the latter to be a משכיל of Ethan the Ezrahite. While Psalm 89.1 corresponds to 1 Kings 5.11, Psalm 88 contradicts this verse by changing the affiliation of Heman in contradiction to 1 Kings 5.11 from a son of Mahol to an Ezrahite. The simplest explanation for this is, that Psalm 88.1 was created in imitation of Psalm 89.1 and unaware of this verse's link to 1 Kings 5.11. Thus 88.1 receives the terms משכיל and Ezrahite. 1 Chronicles 2.6 interprets 'Ezrahite' in 88.1 and 89.1 later on as 'son of Zerah' and ascribes Heman and

(one psalm) – 45 and 52–55 or designs extraordinary long compositions such as Psalms 78 and 89, the former one epic in style, the latter one falling into three distinctive subunits (hymn v. 2-19, divine speech v. 20-38, lament v. 39-52) and resembling to Psalm 74 in vocabulary and themes (74.13-17// 89.11-15). Psalm 74 contains a lot of elements that are extant in *balags* (divine anger v.1b; human flock v.1b; ruins v.3; divine will unfathomable v.9a; 'how long' v. 9b.10a; divine king v. 12a; supplicant a dove v. 19a). Bearing in mind that *balags* and *eršemmas* are divided into *kirugus*, which may be understood as independent poetical units and that *balags* and *eršemmas* are combined in fixed sequence both in literary catalogues and liturgical ceremonies, one may ask whether or not the clusters in Psalms 42–45 and 52–55 should be seen as coherent compositions. This question exceeds the scope of my investigation. It leads, however, to the following paragraph which treats the combination of prayers in rituals.

3. Cult Functional Approach: The Sequence of Prayers in Liturgy

Stefan Maul republished the so-called role-book of the lamentation priest (gala/*kalû*) in the New Year Feast in Asshur. The extant texts witness celebrations for three months, the year's two final ones Šabaṭu and Addaru, and the first month of the New Year, Nisanu. A previously unpublished cuneiform tablet (K 11617 Maul 2000: 402f, 408) lists the duties of the *kalû* starting on an unknown day of Šabaṭu. The first readable date is the 10th Šabaṭu in line 7'. Line 5' also starts the duties for a day. So the first day, whose duties are listed must be one day between the 1st and 8th Šabaṭu. It seems likely that the day concerned was the 5th of Šabaṭu.[87] The role-book prescribes:

Ethan the Ezrahites/sons of Zerah to the offspring of Judah. Neither Ethan nor Heman of Psalm 88 and 89 are Levites! The levitical genealogies of 1/2 Chronicles contain several Ethans and Hemans, but they never bear a patronym that identifies them either to be an Ezrahite or a son of Mahol (Rösel 1999: 214f). In sum, Psalm 32.1; 88.1 and 142.1 stem from later stages of Psalter redaction and do not procure reliable information about the significance of the term משכיל used as genre indication. What is a משכיל should be investigated in examination of the other psalms bearing this superscript. A comparability between משכיל and *balag* alluded to in this paper may well fit Koenen's characterization of משכיל as antiphony (*Wechselgesang* 1991:119). The change of speaking voices is an outstanding feature in both genres.

87. The first day preserved in the role book tablet differs from most other days, because after the recitation of a *balag* with its *eršemma* an *eršahunga* follows and then an additional *balag* with its *eršemma*. The second tablet published by Maul (2000: 409 l. 33') shows that an *eršahunga* (*Herzberuhigungsklage*) was to be said by the king himself on the 5th of Addaru. On the 5th day of several months sacrifices were offered for the benefit of the king (Cole / Machinist 1998 nos 8–11). During the New Year Feast, the 5th day of a month might have been marked by the recitation of an *eršahunga*, a genre of prayer generally said for the benefit of the king (Parpola 1993 nos 338:15, 339 r. 3; 381:2).

At the $5^{?\text{th}}$ day (of Šabaṭu you sing the balag/ÉR): Umun še-er-ma-al-la-an-ki-a (Lord, respected one of heaven and earth) (and the ér-šem-ma) Dilmun^{ki} nigin-na (Important one, go about!) ... in/into the palace. (Than you sing:) Me-e ^{d}Utu-ra a-ra-zu ga-an-na-ab-dug$_4$ ér-ša-hun-ga (I will pray to Utu/the sun god). Then Mullissu enters the akitu-house(?). (You sing the balag:) Nir-gál lú è-dè(NE) (Respected one, manifest one) (and the ér-šem -ma) Ur-sag ut-u$_{18}$-lu (Warrior, southstorm) for DN in TN (cf. Maul 2000: 408).

All five prayers indicated exist at least partly. Thus it is possible to reconstruct the liturgy, i.e. the rites performed and the prayers sung and recited, at a certain day of the Asshur New Year festival. Though it is not as if being invited to participate at the ceremonies, which must have been very impressive, *balags* and *eršemmas* being sung probably as a litany in antiphonal style between cantor and choir to the rhythm of drum beats, we are almost allowed to have a glimpse into the temple and to overhear the prayers.

But a word of caution must be given at this moment too. Neither the prayers edited by Cohen, Maul and Ebeling, nor the psalms can really represent the very texts liturgically used in Asshur or Jerusalem. The editions of Mesopotamian prayers give reconstructions put together from various copies of various times and origin. The prayers actually pronounced in Asshur may have differed in some ways from those accessible to us in the editions. The psalms likewise underwent changes that make the text in the Psalter, a book formed by several redactions and redactors, different from earlier versions of a psalm used in liturgy. The psalms treated here show traces of literary growth due to Psalter redactions.[88] Nevertheless they are quoted in this paper in their final canonical form and not in hypothetical forms they might have had previously.

There are two other days preserved, where the role book not only prescribes that a *balag* with its *eršemma* must be sung but also prayers of the individual *eršahunga* or *šuilla* type:

On the 26th day (of Šabaṭu you sing) the *balag*: Nir-gál lú e-NE and the *eršemma* Ur-sag ^{d}Utu-u$_{18}$-lu for Asshur in the house of sunrise. Then Asshur rises. He takes his seat in Esara. You place a brick. You sing É sà-ab hun-e-ta; the *šuilla* Alim-ma umun an ki-a for Asshur; the *šuilla* Nin$^?$ kur-kur-a for Mullissu. On the 5th day (of Addaru you sing) the *balag*: ^{d}Utu-gin$_7$ è-ta-na (Come out like the Sun!) and the *eršemma* šà-ba-ni ga-an-hun (I will pacify his heart) for Asshur. Then offerings. You make the king recite the *eršahunga* E-ri-zu i-bí zi bar-mu-un-ši-ib (Lord,

---

88. For literary critics on Psalms 79–83 cf. Hossfeld/Zenger (2000: 456–458, 471–473, 496).

look mercifully on your servant) to the beats of the *Liliz* drum (cf. Maul 2000: 409).

Two *šuillas* must be sung likewise at the 18th *Addaru* and the 11th *Nisanu* each time after a procession with the divine image of god Asshur, but the *balag – eršemma* composition is missing. Only one prayer probably linked to the procession proper precedes the *šuillas* which does not bear a genre indication.

Hence we get a pattern of arrangement of prayers and ceremonies exceeding the normal one of all the other days preserved. This extraordinary pattern consists of singing a *balag* with its *eršemma* followed by a procession finished always with its unfortunately not preserved introit É sà-ab hun-e-ta, and then two further prayers either again a *balag* with its *eršemma* or two *šuilas*.

5$^{?th}$ *Šabaṭu*
balag:　　　　Umun še-er-ma-al-la-an-ki-a
eršemma:　　Dilmun^{ki} nigin-na
eršahunga:　Me-e ^{d}Utu-ra a-ra-zu ga-an-na-ab-dug$_4$

Then Mullissu enters the akitu-house(?)...

balag:　　　　Nir-gál lú è-dè(NE)
eršemma:　　Ur-sag ut-u$_{18}$-lu (Warrior, southstorm)

26th *Šabaṭu*
balag:　　　　Nir-gál lú e-NE
eršemma:　　Ur-sag ^{d}Utu-u$_{18}$-lu for Asshur in the house of sunrise

Asshur's procession into the Esara temple. Offerings on a brick. (Introitus when the God's statue is deposed in the cella) é sà-ab hun-e-ta

šuilla:　　　Alim-ma umun an ki-a for Assur
šuilla:　　　Nin$^?$ kur-kur-a for Mullissu

5th *Addaru*
balag:　　　　^{d}Utu-gin$_7$ è-ta-na
eršemma:　　à-ba-ni ga-an-hun for Asshur

Then offerings

eršahunga:　E-ri-zu i-bí zi bar-mu-un-ši-ib (recited by the king).

In comparison with the sequence of psalms in the Psalter we get a pattern of communal lament (*balag* with its *eršemma* and an *eršahunga*), a ceremony (procession or offering), and an individual complaint (*šuilla* or *eršahunga*). If one combines this evidence with the two *šuillas* sung after Asshur's procession on the 18th of *Addaru* and his return from the *akitu*-house to Ešara on the 11th of *Nisanu*, then a system becomes visible. An offering is followed by one prayer (5th *Addaru*), processions are followed by two prayers (5 Šab., 26 Šab., 18 Ad. and 11 Nis.). The sequence of Psalms 79–83 fits very well into the latter pattern. Two communal laments, Psalms 78 and 80, would correspond to a Mesopotamian *balag* with its *eršemma*. Then comes Psalm 81, a psalm of procession and divine oracle, which fits the ceremonial part. Then follow Psalm 82 and 83, shorter psalms in comparison to Psalm 79 and the latter one showing both sings of an individual complaint (I-voice 83.14) corresponding to a *šuilla* and of a communal lament corresponding to a *balag*.

Do these similarities in the sequence of prayer genres reveal a liturgical pattern common in Asshur and Israel, how to celebrate a New Year Feast? This question develops into a thesis, when one takes into account that Mowinckel and Goulder could argue from inner biblical evidence alone that Asaph psalms were used during the New Year Feast. The Asshur New Year Feast seems to corroborate this. By comparing the laments used during the New Year Feast in Asshur with Psalms 79–83 one does not only find a similar sequence of prayer genres but also a similar sequence of motifs in the prayers. This points to the common pattern of festal celebration, for which I argue in this paper. In order to show this the Psalms 79 and 80 will be paralleled with a *balag*, *eršemma* and *eršahunga* from the role book of the *kalû*. Psalm 81 will be related to the ceremonies prescribed on the 26th of *Šabatu*, and the motifs of Psalm 82 and 83 will be compared with motifs prevalent in *šuillas* and *balags*. Unfortunately no *šuilla* from the role book is known. Thus we must refer in our comparison to other *šuillas*.

To make it clear right from the beginning, I do not think that Psalms 79–83 are a copy or adaptation of Mesopotamian prayers or that their arrangement results from a mere imitation of the Assyrian celebrations. I do argue that Israel and Asshur shared a linguistic (Semitic), cultural (Phoenician influence on art[89]), economic (tribute and trade), and religious (Tammuz – Ezek. 8.14, Queen of Heaven – Jer. 7.17; 44.15-24[90]) realm that comprised traditional patterns of poetical imagery and probably also

---

89. Cf. 1 Kings 5.23; 7.13 and the mention of bronze work and craftsmen from Tyre or parts of the palace in Hittite = Syrian style in Sennacherib's building inscriptions (Matthiae 1999: 88–92).

90. Cf. Frevel (1995: 353, 423–471); Nissinen (2001: 101f, 116–123; 624–626); De Villiers (2002: 624f).

patterns of liturgical celebrations. Both Israelites and Neo-Assyrians are partly heirs of the same cultural ancestors in the second millennium BCE, the Hittites and the Neo-Hittite Aramean states in Syria being among them. During the funeral ceremonies of the Hittite king a *balag* instrument was burned and from the famous *šuilla to Ishtar* published in ANET[3] (1963: 384f) two versions were found in *Hattuša* (KUB 37.36 + 37).[91]

The fact that two religions share common liturgical patterns stemming from a common religious heritage is by no means impossible. An example is the ritual of the Jewish synagogal prayer and the Christian Eucharist. In both rituals the peak of the celebration – the recitation of the *šema' Yiśra'el* and the Eucharistic Canon – is surrounded by the Trishagion (Isa. 6.3) and a prayer with the characteristic that the congregation stands during its recitation – the Amida (= the prayer said standing) consisting of 18 demands and the Our Father consisting of 7 demands (cf. Elbogen 1967: 61–67). With these similar patterns of liturgy church and synagogue do not imitate each other but follow their common legacy from Early Judaism. This example shows what we can expect to find in comparing Hebrew and Mesopotamian prayers and their arrangement in Neo-Assyrian liturgy and the biblical Psalter. We will find common features at a common position in the celebrations and the sequence of psalms, not texts that resemble each other in every detail.

Psalm 83, the last psalm of the Asaph collection contains elements that resemble those of the first *balag* prescribed on 5[th?] of *Šabatu:* Umun še-er-ma-al-la-an-ki-a. Unfortunately only the first part from this *balag* is preserved. The comparison with the relatively short Psalm 83 will be given later.

The *balag* must be completed on the 5[th?] and 22nd of *Šabatu,* and 3rd of *Addaru* with the *eršemma* Dilmun[ki] nigin-na. But only on the 5[th?] of *Šabatu* it is followed by the *eršahunga* Me-e [d]Utu-ra a-ra-zu ga-an-na-ab-dug[4]. While the *eršemma* is addressed to Enlil, obviously identified with Asshur, the supreme god of the pantheon, the *eršahunga* is addressed to the sun god Utu/Shamash. Thus the ritual prescribes a series of different prayers belonging to different genres and addressing different gods.

Psalm 79 does not resemble the *balag* Umun še-er-ma-al-la-an-ki-a, but in some degree another *balag*, to which the same *eršemma* must be attached on an unidentifiable day in *Šabatu,* the 1st and the 17th *Addaru.* This *balag* is called *Abzu pelam* 'The defiled *apsu*'.

Psalm 79 speaks of the defiled temple in Jerusalem. The *balag* speaks of the defiled *apsu*, and *apsu* is both the subterranean waters and Ea's temple.

---

91. Cf. Kassian/Korolëv/Sidel'tsev 2002: 457 (KUB 39.14 + Z. 10'): 'They burn [down] ([GIŠ]BALAG[ii]-ma) B-instrument...'; Reiner/Güterbock 1967; Groenewald 1996.

Thus we have the temple lament *Abzu pelam* followed by an *eršemma* and the temple lament Psalm 79 followed by Psalm 80.

balag: Abzu pelam

The **defiled** Apsu! Pillaged Eridu! Faithful house! The defiled Apsu! Pillaged Eridu! Faithful house! House of Enki! Faithful house! House of Damgalnunna! Faithful house! House of Asarluhi! Faithful house! House of Panunanki! Faithful house! House of Sukkalmah! Faithful house! House of Muzebbasa! Faithful house! House of Nammu! (10) Faithful house! House of Nanshe! Faithful house! House of Ara!

When the Apsu had been built upon a pure place, when Eridu had been built upon a good place (so too were) my still Eengur, my standard, which was purified, my main courtyard, the Apsu... my main courtyard, the Apsu... my [...] a perfect thing, (20) my holy throne, set up where the sun rises, Tintir, my city where there are sighs, my open house, into which gifts were brought, my chamber of cedar by the edge of the sea, my inner sanctum of the Apsu which no man has ever seen.

Tears at its front, tears at its interior, in tears one enters at its front, in sighing one exits from its interior.

Why does the Apsu turn against me at every shore? Faithful house, why does the Apsu turn against me at every shore? (30) House of Enki, **why** does it turn against me at every shore? House of Damalunna, **why** does it turn against me at every shore? House of Asarluhi **why** does it turn against me at every shore? House of Panunanki, **why** does it turn against me at every shore? House of Sukkalmaham, **why** does it turn against me at every shore? House of Muzebasa, **why** does it turn against me at every shore? House of Nammu, **why** does it turn against me at every shore? House of Nanshe, why does it turn against me at every shore? House of Ara, **why** does it turn against me at every shore?

Psalm 79

1 O God, the nations have come into your inheritance; they have **defiled** your holy temple; they have laid Jerusalem in ruins. 2 They have given the bodies of your servants to the birds of the air for food, the flesh of your faithful to the wild animals of the earth. 3 They have poured out their blood like water all around Jerusalem, and there was no one to bury them.

4 **We** have become a taunt to our neighbours, mocked and derided by those around us.

5 **How long**, Yhwh? Will you be angry forever? Will your jealous wrath burn like fire?

Because of the defiled Apsu, **we** are hurrying to him. (40) **As for us**, because of the defiled Apsu, **we** are hurrying to him. Because of the desecration, **we** are hurrying to the lord Enki. Because of the defiled Apsu, the lord no longer dwells in the Apsu. Because of the desecration, the lord Enki no longer dwells in Eridu. The lord no longer dwells in the Apsu. The lord is silent for me. The lady Danmalnunna no longer dwells in Eridu. The lady is silent for me.

Its lady... goes to him because of her defiled house. She goes to him [... and] because of her pillaged assembly hall. She goes to him because of **her destroyed cattle pen**. She goes to him because of **her destroyed treasure house** and **her slain people**. (50) She goes to him because of her defiled funerary offerings. She goes to him because of her corridor through which men (now) traipse. She goes to him because of her holy places which have become estranged. She goes to him because of her defiled great banquet hall.

Day and night she cries out. She goes to him. She cries out over her destroyed cattle pen. She goes to him. She moans over **her uprooted sheepfold**. She goes to him.

She walks about stooped over in her house. She cries bitterly. She walks about (aimlessly) in her defiled cella. She cries bitterly. She walks about (aimlessly) in **her levelled treasure house**. She cries bitterly.

(60) '(My) possessions are in (the eye of) a storm!' she says **feverishly**. Oh, my lady! 'What will become of me?' she says **feverishly**. The lady of the house! 'Enlil, **how long** will it continue?' she says **prostrating**. She goes to him because of her defiled house and pillaged city.

As for me... Where can I go?

Treasure house! Treasure house! Faithful house! Treasure house! Treasure house! **To where have your people been carried off?** Faithful house! House of Enki! Faithful house! House of Damgalnunna! Faithful house! House of Asarluhi! (70) Faithful house! House of Panunanki! Faithful house! House of Sukkalmaham! Faithful house! House of Muzebbasa! Faithful house! House of Nammu! Faithful house! House of Nanshe! Faithful house! House of Ara!

6 Pour out your anger on the nations that do not know you, and on the kingdoms that do not call on your name. 7 For they have devoured Jacob and **laid waste his habitation**.

8 Do not remember against us the iniquities of our ancestors; let your **compassion** come speedily to meet us, for we are brought very low. 9 **Help us**, O God of our salvation, for the glory of your name; deliver us, and forgive our sins, for your name's sake.

10 **Why** should the nations say, 'Where is their God?' Let the avenging of **the outpoured blood of your servants** be known among the nations before our eyes.

Your youngsters and adults, your youngsters for whom you cared, the adults who traversed the highways, **your sheep** with bent legs, (80) your kids with trailing beards, your female kids covered with wool, our artfully crafted ornaments of shuba-stone, your wealth of shuba-stones and lapis-lazuli, **(to where have they been carried off?)**
He who was familiar to the house is no longer in attendance. Who is left to care for you? The gala-priest who knew the chants is no longer in attendance. Who is left to care for you? The harp, your advisor, is no longer in attendance. Who is left to care for you? ... Who is left to care for you? House, to where has your maidservant been carried off? She is no longer in attendance. Who is left to care for you? To where have your people been carried off? To where have they been led away? They are not in attendance. Who is left to care for you?

11 Let the groans of the **prisoners** come before you; according to your great power preserve those doomed to die. 12 Return sevenfold into the bosom of our neighbours the taunts with which they taunted you, O Lord! 13 Then we your people, **the flock of your pasture**, will give thanks to you forever; from generation to generation we will recount your praise.

(90) I wander about the place that has been pillaged. I wander about. I wander about. I wander about the place that has been pillaged. (The one of) my ditches has been cast into the ditches. (The one of) my canals has been thrown into the canals. He who goes for wood has been carried off. He who goes for water has been carried off. He who carried wood no longer carries wood for anyone. He has been carried off. He who carried water no longer carries water for anyone. He has been carried off. The dogs, which knew me, **have made me known (to) the enemy**. The dogs, which (now) do not know me, follow the enemy. (100) The flocks of birds do not acknowledge my fledglings, who must pick at the ground. My bird does not acknowledge (its) marsh. It flies away. ... killed.

(Break of the composition to the end of the kirugu)

I wander about the place that has been pillaged. ...

[...] you [...] *(Break in the composition.)*

... return... to Nippur ... Your house, your seat, ...

(b + 110) Your clay returns to its Apsu. ... Your reeds return to their canebrake. ... Your beams return to their forests. ... rising waters... standing waters... By the edge of the sea... at her wails tears are held back. The smell of the offerings has been destroyed. The aroma has been destroyed (for) the gods.

The lord has been installed as a lord... The lady has been installed as a lady... Ninlil has been installed in the Kiur. ... (b + 120) Ninmah has been installed in Kesh... installed...

May he cause him who approaches me to submit. May the word of great (An) cause him who approaches me to submit. May the word of Enlil cause him who approaches me to submit.

(The remainder of the composition is not preserved).

The beginning of both poems is marked by the description of the defiled sanctuary. The enemies do not appear in *balags* as acting forces as in the psalms. Hence, the *balag* does not list the enemies' deeds as in Psalm 79.2-4. The Sumerian restricts itself to state the result of the deed: temple and city are defiled and pillaged. The *balag* continues with the story of the building of Apsu. A voice is speaking in the first person singular. Divine word is expressed. It is the voice of the lamenting goddess, the lady of the temple, the wife of king Enki. This section remembers a constructive period in the past and reminds to the description of the vine being planted by God in the following psalm, Psalm 80.9-14. It ends with the motif of tears similar to Psalm 80.6.

The emotional imploring for compassion, forgiveness and help in Psalm 79.8f has a counterpart in the emotional depiction of the feverishly perplexed and agitated goddess who decides to go to the angry male god and prostrate herself imploringly before him.

The question 'why' is pronounced by the speaking I-voice and similar to the question in Psalm 79.10a. There are the questions 'where can I go' and 'where is their god', both carrying the idea that goddess or god abandon their city and people (cf. ll. 45ff the lord. . . no longer dwells in. . .). There are the questions 'how long', typical for the Hebrew and Mesopotamian lament, and in both cases combined with the very name of the angry god, Enlil and Yhwh. Just here Enki is called Enlil in the *balag*, just here the Tetragram appears in Psalm 79, which in the Elohistic Psalter stresses the importance of the address.

In the following section the I-voice becomes a we-voice as in the biblical laments and can thus be compared to Psalm 79.13. The psalm motivates God by a vow pronounced by the we-group. The *balag* motivates the god by a group of gods hurrying to him and praying for the Apsu and the city Eridu. The scene changes again. Now the goddess implores Enki because of the defiled temple and her slain people. These motives are roughly equivalent to Psalm 79.1-4, 10b allowing for the difference that the imploring role in the psalm is played by the community and not by the goddess. The people have not only been slain but also carried away (l.65ff). Deportation follows the defeat as imprisoning in Psalm 79.11. Both poems hope for a turn of fate. Psalm 79 asks God to turn his anger from his people to other nations and avenge their misdeeds. The *balag* hopes for the return of Lord and Lady to temple and city, a new installation and the submission of those who approach (ll. b + 109ff).

Probably it is again the female voice of the goddess who wants everyone (him) who approaches her to submit. But given the identity of praying community in the psalm and imploring goddess in the *balag* as fulfilling the role of subject who succeeds in getting the object wanted, it is the same on a structural level. It is the same indeed, because if everyone approaching the goddess as Lady of the temple is doing this in a submissive way, this must be true for foreign people too. But if the foreigners are approaching the goddess in a submissive way, they are pilgrims bringing gifts and not enemies hostile to temple and city. Thus if Enki's word becomes true the same peaceful result is given as asked in the psalm.

The *balag* is much longer than the psalm and both prayers have elements that are not extant in the other, but some elements that they share come in a roughly parallel sequence: 'defiled – we – why, where, how long – your sheep/flock of your pasture – carried off/prisoners'. This common sequence is continued in Psalm 80 and the *eršemma* Dilmun^ki nigin-na in combination with the *eršahunga* Me-e ^dUtu-ra a-ra-zu ga-an-na-ab-dug4.

Psalm 80 is printed in the right column and in the left one the *eršemma* plus the *eršahunga*. Psalm 80 bears traits of both prayers prescribed as appendix to the balag. One could almost say, Psalm 80 is a mixture of an *eršemma* and an *eršahunga*. Cohen gives an English translation for the *eršemma*, Maul a German one for the *eršahunga*. Thus the English text in the left column belongs to the *eršemma*, the German text to the *eršahunga*. Both prayers are given completely and in their order.

eršemma: dilmun^ki nigin-na
eršahunga: me-e ^dUtu-ra a-ra-zu ga-an-na-ab-dug4

(1) Important one, **go about!** ... **watch over**... your city. Honoured one, important one, **go about!** ... **watch over**... your city. Lord of the lands go about! Lord whose pronouncement is true, go about!
(5) Enlil, **father of the nation**, go about!

Shepherd of the black-headed, go about! He who witnesses (everything) first-hand, go about! Bull who causes the troops to wander, go about! He who sleeps a false sleep, go about! (10) Lord Enki, go about! **Warrior**, Asarluhi, go about! Lord Enbilulu, go about! **Warrior** Mudugas, go about! Lord Dikumaha, go about! (15) Warrior Utulu, go about! Lord of heaven and earth, go about!

1 [Ich] will zu **Utu/Schamasch** ein Gebet sprechen!
2 [Zu dem **He]lden**, dem Mannhaf[ten, Schamasch, (will ich ein Gebet sprechen)]
3 Zu dem Herrn des Ebabbar, etc. 4 Zu dem Bärtigen, dem Sohne des Ninggal, etc. 5 Zu dem des [reinen] Heilig[tums, etc.] 6 Zu dem Ri[chter der Götter, etc.
7. Zu dem, der die Entscheidung der Anunna-Götter fällt, (will) ich [ein Gebet sprechen!)]
8 'Es genügt! **Wie lange noch?**' will ich zu ih[m sagen!] 9 'Er ist groß. Nicht [ ]' [will] ich [(zu ihm sagen!)] 10 'Dein Herz möge sich mir gegenüber beruhigen!' will ich [(zu ihm sagen!)] 11 'Dein Gemüt möge sich mir gegenüber besänftigen!' will ich [(zu ihm sagen!)]

Psalm 80:1 To the leader: on Lilies, a Covenant. Of Asaph. A Psalm.

2 **Give ear,**

O **Shepherd of Israel**, you who lead **Joseph** like a flock!

You who are enthroned upon the cherubim, **shine forth** 3 before Ephraim and Benjamin and Manasseh. **Stir up your might**, and come to save us!

4 Restore us, O God; let your face shine, that we may be saved.

5 O Yhwh **God of hosts,**

how long will you be angry with your people's prayers? 6 You have fed them with the bread of tears, and given them tears to drink in full measure. 7 You make us the scorn of our neighbours; our enemies laugh among themselves.

x + 3 Deinen Nacken bzw. **dein Haupt wende her zu mir**, mein Flehen nimm an! x + 4 Mein Haus, das gebaut wurde, mein **Ziegelwerk** baust du? (wieder?) auf.

Go about in your **city**, Nippur! In the brickwork of Ekur, (in) the kiur and the Enamtila (and) in the brickwork of Sippar go about! (20) In the shrine Ebabbar, the Edikukalama (and) the brickwork of Tintir go about! In the brickwork of the Esagil, the shrine Eturkalama (and) in the brickwork of Borsippa go about! In the brickwork of the Ezida, the shrine Emahtila, (25) in the brickwork of the Etemenanki, the shrine Edaranna, (and) the brickwork of Isin go about! (In) the [shrine] Egalmah and the shrine Erabiri (go about)! **In your city which has been flooded, washed away, in your Nippur which has been flooded, which has been submerged beneath the waters**, (30) in your city which has been flooded, washed away, in your Sippar which has been flooded, which has been submerged beneath the waters, in your city which has been flooded, washed away, in your Tintir which has been flooded, which has been submerged beneath the waters, in your city which has been flooded, washed away, (35) in your Isin which has been flooded, which has been submerged beneath the waters, your city which must (carefully) check the weight of the grain (whose supply) has been cut off, (where) the glutton spends the day without eating, (go about)!

She who has a new spouse says, 'My spouse!' She who has a little child says, 'My child!' (40) My young girl says, 'My brother!' (In) the city my mother says, 'My child!' The young child says, 'My father' They make those standing in the street restless. These youngsters go mad; these adults go mad. (45) (In) Nippur these youngsters go mad; these adults go mad. (In) Tintir these youngsters go mad; these adults go mad. In Isin these youngsters go mad; these adults go mad. **The dogs carry off those spread far and wide. The wolves carry off** those who are scattered. (50) The dancing places are filled with ghosts. The street is not sated with its joy.

x + 5 sum.: Was **mein Geschenk** anbelangt, das ich? machte, so sättigt sich das Land an seiner Fülle.

x + 6 [ ] ... möge er setzten, ich möge nicht umgebracht werden!

8 Restore us, O God of hosts; **let your face shine**, that we may be saved.

9 You brought a **vine** out of Egypt; you drove out the nations and planted it. 10 You cleared the ground for it; it took deep root and filled the land. 11 The mountains were covered with its shade, the mighty cedars with its branches; 12 it sent out its branches to the sea, and its shoots to the River.

13 Why then have you **broken down its walls**, so that all who pass along the way pluck its fruit? 14 **The boar** from the forest **ravages it**, and all that move in the field feed on it. 15 **Turn again**, O God of hosts; **look down from heaven**, and **see**; **have regard** for this vine, 16 the stock that your right hand planted.

17 They have burned it with fire, they have cut it down; may they perish at the rebuke of your countenance.

18 But let your hand be upon the one at your right hand, the one whom you made strong for yourself. 19 Then we will never turn back from you; give us life, and **we will call on your name**.

x + 7 Dein Herz möge wie das Herz einer
leiblichen Mutter für mich an seinen Platz
zurückkehren!
x + 8 Wie eine leibliche Mutter, ein leiblicher
Vater, (möge es für mich) an seinen Platz
(zurückkehren!)
[It is] an *eršemma* of Enlil.
Ein [E]*ršahunga* an Utu.

20 **Restore us**, Yhwh God of hosts; let your face
shine, that we may be saved.

The *eršemma* begins with the address 'important one' and the imperative
'go about... watch over'. So the praying community asks for the god's
presence and watching. Psalm 80 starts with an imperative asking for
God's listening. Both are begging for divine attention. Psalm 80 continues
with the address 'Shepherd of Israel', thus combining the motive of the
divine shepherd and the human flock with the nation's name. The *eršemma*
calls Enlil 'father of the nation' and 'Shepherd of the black-headed', i.e. all
mankind. Then the *eršemma* continues with martial aspects of Enlil which
may be equated with the psalm's imperative 'stir up your might'. The
psalm's enthronement motive recalls Enlil's enthronement over Sumer in
balags. The psalm's imperative 'shine forth' underlines the solar aspect of
Israel's god. His presence is comparable to the shining sun. This element is
repeated in a refrain in verses 2, 4, 8 and 20. This solar element gives a link
to the *eršahunga* to the sun god Utu/Shamash, whose first portion is cited
in the left column. Utu is a warrior (*Held, Mannhafter*) as Enlil and Yhwh,
addressed 'God of hosts'. L. 6 calls Utu judge of the gods. This is
important for Psalm 82, where Yhwh is visualized in a scene depicting
judgments of other gods. So Psalm 82 also contains motives of the sun god.
Psalm 80.5 and l.8 of the *eršahunga* share the question 'how long'. L. 10
contains the heart pacification formula. If the god's heart must be pacified,
he is angry as states Psalm 80.5. The tear motive of Psalm 80.5 is also
extant in *balags* and *eršemmas*, but it has no counterpart in the *eršahunga*
cited. The motive of mocking neighbours in Psalm 80.7 lacks in
Mesopotamian laments. This may be regarded as typical Hebrew or
perhaps West Semitic. The refrain in 80.8 combines the demand to let the
face shine upon the praying community with the imperative 'restore'. So
care and restoration come together. The *eršahunga* does the same with
other words. Care is expressed as turning the god's head to the prayer, and
restoration is expressed as the rebuilding of brickwork (l.x + 3f). When the
praying voice speaks of my brickwork (*Ziegelwerk*), this shows also that
the praying person is someone, who may count the brickwork of temples
and cities as his own. The praying voice is the king's voice. One will find no
clearer hint of the king in these prayers, but external evidence from letters
and rituals shows that just *eršahungas* were prayed by and for the king and
his family.

Psalm 80.9-16 draws us back to the *eršemma*. These verses tell the story of a vine planted by Yhwh now afflicted by Yhwh and spoiled by animals. A story of construction in the past – not in the image of a plant but in that of a building – we met in the *balag* Abzu pelam. The image of devastating animals comes later in the *eršemma*: Dogs and wolves carry corpses of slain men spread far and wide and not buried. Though the images differ, the ideas are similar. God is connected with the people. It is 'his' city Nippur as it is the vine planted by Yhwh. But suddenly the divinity destroyed its property by breaking down the walls, by flooding the city.

The next portion of the *eršemma* shows a characteristic element of *balags* and *eršemmas*. A change of the speaking voice. It is not quite clear, who she is that has a new spouse, a little child, speaking in the first person 'my young girl'. It must be a female. It is a goddess or the city.

While curses as in Psalm 80.17b are missing in most Mesopotamian laments the prayer for the king and the vow in 80.18-19 exists. The *eršahunga* prescribed in the role book contains the vow in form of the gift (*Geschenk*) mentioned and the prayer for the king can be compared to the demand not to be killed. The last passage of the *eršahunga* shows a typical element of this genre. The pacified heart of the divinity may return to care for the suppliant like a father or mother. So the prayer can vision himself as son of a god or goddess.

Having equated a *balag* with Psalm 79, an *eršemma* plus an *eršahunga* with Psalm 80, we encounter three further songs. The introit É sà-ab hune-ta is always ordered when a divine statue is set down after a procession. According to the pattern shown above, either a second *balag* plus *eršemma* or two *šuillas* follow. Thus three additional songs must be sung. Three psalms follow after Psalms 79 and 80 in the Asaph collection. So we can try to compare Psalm 81 to the song related with the procession, Psalms 82 and 83 to *balag* plus *eršemma* or two *šuillas*. As a matter of fact ancient tradition appoints Psalm 81 to the New Year Feast be it the one in Tishri or the one from earlier times in Nisan (Delitzsch 1883: 578). The psalm begins with festive sound and music probably accompanying a procession (81.2f). It mentions ordinances to celebrate festal days and both the New Moon and the Full Moon (81.4f). The dates of processions with the divine statue mentioned in the role book coincide with the New Moon (expected on 29th–1st in a month according to the moon calendar, a period enclosed by processions on the 26th/5th) and the Full Moon (13th–15th, followed or preceded by processions on the 18th or 11th).[92] Hence, Psalm 81 would fit perfectly to be sung at several processions during a longer period of feasting which covered New and Full Moon of a month as is true for the

92. To watch out for New Moon and Full Moon was the task of Assyrian scholars (Parpola 1993: nos 63, 80, 94, 105, 110, 116, 121, 123–126, 135, 142, 145, 146).

New Year Feast in Asshur. The sermon or oracle (81.6-17) may be a later addition or contain later added elements (Loretz 1999: 140). Its character and function will be treated in the next paragraph.

Psalm 82 is a composition too short to be compared with a *balag*, but neither does it show resemblance with *šuillas* or *eršahungas*. A frequent element in the latter prayers is nevertheless the motive of the divine judge which is prominent in Psalm 82 too. But Simon B. Parker (1995: 535–538) argues convincingly that in the epic scene narrated by the psalm Yhwh is not judging but accusing the gods, the supreme god of the divine assembly 'tactfully' not being exposed by name. Yhwh accuses the other gods of not being just judges, i.e. not to be good shepherds. The psalm contains a lot of mythological motifs that are extant in Mesopotamian mythology, the accusations of one god in divine assembly and his condemnation to die, i.e. the descent into the netherworld (Nergal and Ereškigal), the rise to supreme power of a member of the divine assembly through killing another deity (*Enuma Elish* cf. the Baal cycle in Ugarit). Yhwh does not kill another deity, he simply declares them to be mortal. 'But their fall and death have only been announced, not realized. The myth gives assurance that their (mis) rule is doomed, but present reality insists that their practice and tolerance of injustice continues. Where the myth stops short of explaining how God's announcement is realized in its narrative world, the liturgical response calls upon God to assume authority and power, and to initiate his just governance of the universe in the real world' (Parker 1995: 558). Hence, Psalm 82 may be seen as a short prayer which tells a myth that narrates, or better, invokes the rise of the national deity to supreme power, as does *Enuma Elish*, the New Year Feast myth at Babylon (Levenson 1988: 6f).

Psalm 83 astonishes with its martial content as finale of the Asaph collection.[93] The climax of the appeal to God to manifest himself, culminating in the demand of military help against hostile peoples in Israel's vicinity (including Asshur) as the goal of all the Asaph psalms, can rather be described than explained (Weber 2000a: 81 n. 73). An explanation could be that the final sequence of the Asaph collection simply follows a liturgical arrangement, extant in Asshur's New Year Feast, that invokes Mullissu, a manifestation of belligerent Ishtar, in the final prayer of days with procession. Perhaps it is due to the procession of Mullissu's statue on the 5th? of *Šabaṭu* that no prayer is directed to her on this day. Instead, the ceremonies end with a *balag* and *eršemma* to the warrior gods Nergal and Ninurta. Hence the belligerent motifs do appear

---

93. Millard (1994: 103) states, 'daß mit der Asaphpsalmkomposition das einzige klare Beispiel einer Komposition mit Klageschluß im Psalter vorliegt'.

also in the final prayers of this procession day. Psalm 83 contains elements of *balags*[94] and of *šuillas* to Ištar.[95]

4. *Do Psalms 79–83 reflect a Liturgy for the New Year Feast?*

In order to understand the internal logic of the arrangement of Psalms 79–83 we must first of all discuss Psalm 81. Since the text of the introit É sà-ab-hun-e-ta is still unknown, the song book of the *kalû* does not yield information. But the description of ceremonies for the New Year celebration preserved in other documents and collected by Maul (2000: 393–401) sheds light on the meaning of processions with Asshur's statue. As in many cultures, the New Year Feast in Asshur was also a period when it was desirable to obtain some knowledge about the fate during the beginning year. In Babylon the fixing of the New Year's fate was linked to the procession with Marduk's statue, more precisely the statue's appearance on that day. In combining ritual knowledge from Babylon with the ceremonies in Asshur one might understand Psalm 81 as a combination of both a New Year procession and New Year fate fixing turned into the literary form of a poem.

The 26th *Šabatu* during the New Year celebration is the day when the king makes the face of Asshur shine. Asshur's statue is carried in solemn procession from the temple of Dagan to his own temple Ešara. On its way the procession stopped on the sunrise gate. Here the king made Asshur's face shine. The statue is lifted again and carried in procession to Asshur's temple, set down with offering and singing of É sà-ab-hun-e-ta (Maul 2000: 396). What does it mean, when the king makes the god's face shine? Most probably this ritual act had the character of an ordeal or the decision of the country's fate for the next year. There is a series of omens called *umma âlu* and concerned with the look of Marduk's statue on the New Year festival in Babylon. Having the Neo-Assyrian esteem for every form

---

94. Cf. *balag* Umun çe-er-ma-al-la-an-ki-a Cohen (1988: 413–417): Enlil's epithet 'sheltering roof' with the idea of divine protection in Psalm 83.3; Enlil's martial qualities attacking the disobedient land, i.e. those in opposition to the god, with 83.2; Enlil's and God's silence; the description of Enlil in l. 25 of the balag that combines flame and storm with 83.15. While Psalm 83 uses several imperatives, in order to indicate how Israel's god shall destroy the enemies, the *balag* describes Enlil's skill as warrior in rhetorical questions and mythological images of the divine net and a fight with sea, swamp and river. Cf. in the Ninurta eršemma Ur-sag ut-u18-lu l. 11 'When you are the warrior goring the rebellious land, (verily a flood)'.

95. The one in ANET3 (1963: 384f); Ebeling (1953: 130–137), addresses the goddess as able in handling weapons, causing fight, star of martial cries, causing brethren to fight each other, lady of the battlefield (6–12). Ištar is judge and benevolent to the poor (l. 13, 25f; cf. Ps. 82.2-4). The praying voice asks 'how long' the enemies may look angrily unto the supplicant, plan falsehood, lie, and mock the supplicant (l. 56–59).

of mantic in mind, it is most probable that this series was applied to the statue of Asshur too.

The series *umma âlu* contains quite a lot of possibilities of how the statue of the god can shine or look like. If the god's face is blackish there will be darkness and plague in the land. If his face is white, there will be famine and the king will die. If his face is green, Enlil will defeat the enemy countries. If his face is red, Enlil will bestow wealth to the land. If his face shines, Enlil will enlighten the land and bestow wealth. If the face freezes, the gods will hand the land over to the enemy (Sallaberger 2000: 239). It is amazing how these omens resemble God's scolding words in Psalm 81.9-17.

Israel's fate is at stake. But unlike Babylon and Asshur it is not dependent on the look of the divine face but on submission under the divine will. At least this is so according to the final text Psalm 81 has now in the canonical Psalter. But according to Loretz (1999: 140), Psalm 81.5-11a, 12-16 may be an addition from later times. Hence the divine speech – an element so common in *balags* – may have consisted of 81.11b,17 only.

> 11b: Open your mouth wide and I will fill it.
> 17: I'll feed you with the finest of the wheat,
> and with honey from the rock I satisfy you.

If this reconstruction is reliable, the divine gifts consist, as in Babylon, of wealth. A later redaction enlarged this New Year's oracle with patterns of post-exilic Jewish theology. Perhaps unintentionally it made the resemblance to the *omina* even closer by adding the defeat of the enemies. But according to biblical theology calamity threatens in case of disobedience. Mowinckel thought that the psalm witnesses cultic prophecy. But this is not the case. The psalm is prophecy turned to literature, frozen prophecy being repeated time and again because it is always true. As Loretz (ibid.) states, the post-exilic 'modernizing' of the psalm made it fit for the Feast of New Year and may indicate that Psalms 79–83, our alleged chain of psalms for the liturgy of the New Year Feast, was used in pre- and post-exilic times.

The sequence of Psalms 79–83 shows such a great similarity with the prayers used in Asshur that one hardly can avoid the conclusion, that the five last psalms of the Asaph collection represent a liturgical sequence of prayers for one single day of the New Year Festival in Jerusalem. Are these similarities in form and arrangement due to direct borrowing? If we understand direct borrowing as translating a Mesopotamian prayer into Hebrew, then the answer must certainly be no. But if we understand borrowing as influence by forms, elements and even liturgical arrangements that were common in the ANE, then there was borrowing. The ANE provided a pool for motives, phrases and vocabulary, from which poets could draw in Mesopotamia as in Israel. Probably the ANE also provided liturgical customs about how to arrange a New Year celebration.

It was the purpose of this paper to show how many elements of the communal laments stem from an ANE pool and not from an immediate religious reaction to a historical event. Hence those elements cannot be used for dating. Nevertheless there is a lot of evidence in the psalms of the Asaph collection that they may originate in circles of the Northern kingdom that fled to Jerusalem after 722 BCE (Weber 2000b: 530–532). If it were poets belonging to this group of Israelites who composed psalms in forms similar to those extant in Mesopotamia, this would coincide with the close geographical, cultural and political relationship the kingdom of Israel had with the Neo-Hittite states in Syria.[96]

Bibliography

Ahlström, G.W. 1959 *Psalm 89: Eine Liturgie aus dem Ritual des leidenden Königs* (Lund: CWK Gleerup Vörlage).

Auwers, J-M. 1994 *Le psautier hébraï que et ses éditeurs: Recheres sur une forme canonique du livre des psaumes: Dissertation présentée pour l'obtention du grade de docteur en philolgoe biblique* (3 vols.; Université Catholique de Louvain, Faculté de théologie et de droit canonique).

—2000 *La composition littéraire du Psautier: Un état de la question* (Cahiers de la Revue biblique, 46; Paris: Gabalda).

96.   I do not see enough evidence to follow Goulder's (1982) thesis that the Korah psalms stem from liturgical celebrations in the sanctuaries of Dan and Bethel. In comparison to his thesis that all the Asaph psalms form a liturgical setting for the New Year Feast in Jerusalem going on for *several* days (1996), I confine myself to Psalms 79–83 only and should like to stress that according to Neo-Assyrian evidence these psalms were most probably used in the liturgy of *one* day of the New Year Feast. During the Neo-Assyrian period people from Israel and Judah might have been present at *akitu*-festivals in Kalhu, where Samaritans and delegations from Judah are mentioned in wine lists (Postgate 1973; Dalley / Postgate 1984; Oded 2000), Nineveh, where king Manasseh of Judah had to build the arsenal, or Haran, an important stop on the way from the Mediterranean Sea to Mesopotamia (Pallis 1926: 21f; Parpola 1993: 274, no. 338:9f). One copy of War Rituals, which embodied *balags, eršemmas* and *eršahungas* belonged to the chief *kalû* of Sin in Harran according to its colophon (Elat 1982: 18 l. 10'). It cannot be excluded that king Manasse and his soldiers fighting alongside Assurbanipal at his campaign in Egypt became witness of such a War Ritual. Though the prayers were sung and said in Emesal, their Akkadian translation and their various repetitions of similar formulas probably meant that the knowledge of the prayers' content and imagery was not restricted to the clergy. For cult in Neo-Assyrian military camps cf. Pongratz-Leisten/ Deller/Bleibtreu 1992. On the other hand the Babylonian exile led a Judean elite to Mesopotamia, and forced cultural exchange (Ps. 137.3). Many Emesal prayers exist in copies form the Seleuchid period, which makes these manuscripts roughly contemporary to the oldest psalm scrolls found in Qumran.

Bayer, B. 1982 *The Titles of the Psalms: A Renewed Investigation of an Old Problem* (Yuval: Studies of the Jewish Music Research Centre, 4; Jerusalem: Magnes Press, The Hebrew University).

Begrich, J. 1928 'Vertrauensäußerungen im israelitischen Klagelied des Einzelnen und in seinem babylonischen Gegenstück', *Zeitschrift für die alttestamentliche Wissenschaft* 46 (NF 5): 221–260.

Berges, U. 2002 *Klagelieder* (Herders theologischer Kommentar zum Alten Testament; Freiburg im Breisgau [u.a.]: Herder).

Black, J. 1998 *Reading Sumerian Poetry* (Ithaca, NY: Cornell University Press).

Bouzard, W.C. Jr. 1997 *We Have Heard with Our Ears, O God: Sources of the Communal Laments in the Psalms* (Society of Biblical Literature. Dissertation Series, 159; Atlanta: Scholars Press).

Cavigneaux, A. 1998 'Sur le balag Uruamma'irabi et le rituel de Mari', *NABU* 46 Nr. 43.

Cohen, M.E. 1974 *Balag-compositions: Sumerian lamentation liturgies of the second and first millennium B.C.* (Sources from the ancient Near East, 1,2; Los Angeles, Calif.: Undena Publ.).

—1981 *Sumerian hymnology: the Eršemma* (Hebrew Union College Annual Supplements, 2; Cincinnati: Hebrew Union College).

—1988 *The canonical lamentations of ancient Mesopotamia* (2 vols; Potomac, Md.: Capital Decision Ltd.).

—1993 *The cultic calendars of the ancient Near East* (Bethesda, Md.: CDL Press).

Cole, R.L. 2000 *The shape and message of Book III: (Psalms 73–89)* (Journal for the study of the Old Testament. Supplement series, 307; Sheffield: Sheffield University Press).

Cole, S.W./Machinist, P. 1998 *Letters from Priests to the Kings Esarhaddon and Assurbanipal* (State Archives of Assyria, 13; Helsinki: Helsinki University Press).

Dahood, M.J. 1968 *Psalms II: 51–100: Introduction, Translation and Notes* (AB, 17; New York: Doubleday).

Dalglish, E.R. 1962 *Psalm fifty-one in the light of ancient Near Eastern patternism* (Leiden: Brill).

Dalley, S./Postgate, N. 1984 *The tablets from Fort Shalmaneser* (Cuneiform texts from Nimrud 3 Brit. School of Archaeology in Iraq. [Bagdad]).

—1998 'Yabâ, Atalyâ and the foreign policy of late Assyrian kings', *State Archives of Assyria Bulletin* 12: 83 – 98.

De Villiers, G. 2002 'Where did she come from, and where did she go to? (The Queen of Heaven in Jeremiah 7 and 44)', in *Old Testament Essays* 15: 620–627.

Delitzsch, F. 1859 [⁴1883] *Biblischer Commentar über die Psalmen* (Biblischer Kommentar über das Alte Testament; 4,1; Leipzig: Dörfling und Franke).

Dobbs-Allsopp, F.W. 1993 *Weep, O Daughter of Zion: A Study of the City-Lament Genre in the Hebrew Bible* (Biblica et Orientalia, 44; Rome: Pontificial Biblical Institute).

Doeker, A. 2002 *Die Funktion der Gottesrede in den Psalmen: eine poetologische Untersuchung* (Bonner Biblische Beiträge, 135; Berlin: Philo-Verl.-Ges.).

Duchemin, J. 1961 'Dieux pasteurs et musiciens: Hermès et Apollon', in *Académie des inscriptions & belles-lettres: Comptes rendus des séances 1960* (Paris: Klinchsieck): 16–37.

Durand, J-M./Guichard, M. 1997 'Les rituels de Mari', in D. Charpin and J.-M. Durand (ed.), *Florilegium marianum III: Receuil d'études à la mémoire de Marie-Thérèse Barrelet* (Paris): 19–78.

Ebeling, E. 1953 *Die akkadische Gebetsserie 'Handerhebung'* (Institut für Orientforschung <Berlin, Ost>: Veröffentlichung 20; Berlin: Akad.-Verl.).

Edelman, D. forthcoming 'The "Empty Land" as a Motiv in City Laments,' manuscript forthcoming in: G. Brooke (ed.) *Issues in Historiography* (Journal for the study of the Old Testament. Supplement series; Sheffield: Sheffield University Press).

Elat, M. 1982 'Mesopotamische Kriegsrituale', *Bibliotheca Orientalis* 39: 5–25.

Elbogen, I. 1967[³1931] *Der jüdische Gottesdienst in seiner geschichtlichen Entwicklung* (Olms Paperbacks, 30; Hildesheim: Olms Reprogr. Nachdr. der 3., verb. Aufl. Frankfurt a. Main).

Emmendörffer, M. 1998 *Der ferne Gott: eine Untersuchung der alttestamentlichen Volks-klagelieder vor dem Hintergrund der mesopotamischen Literatur* (Forschungen zum Alten Testament, 21; Tübingen: Mohr Siebeck).

Engnell, I. 1969 *A rigid scrutiny: Critical essays on the Old Testament* (Nashville, Tenn.: Vanderbilt Univ. Pr.).

Falkenstein, A. 1931 *Haupttypen der sumerischen Beschwörung literarisch untersucht* (Leipzig: Hinrichs'sche Buchhandlung).

—1953 'Zur Chronologie der sumerischen Literatur', *Mitteilungen der Deutschen Orient-Gesellschaf*, 85: 1–13.

Ferris, P.W. 1993 *The genre of communal lament in the Bible and the Ancient Near East* (Society of Biblical Literature. Dissertation series, 127; Atlanta, Ga.: Scholars Press).

Flint, P.W. 1997 *The Dead Sea psalms scrolls and the book of Psalms* (Studies on the texts of the Desert of Judah, 17; Leiden: Brill).

Fohrer, G. ⁵1989 *Exegese des Alten Testaments: Einführung in die Methodik* (UTB für Wissenschaft: Uni-Taschenbücher, 267; Heidelberg, Wiesbaden: Quelle & Meyer).

—1971 *Hebräisches und aramäisches Wörterbuch zum Alten Testament* (Berlin: de Gruyter).

Frevel, C. 1995 *Aschera und der Ausschließlichkeitsanspruch YHWHs: Beiträge zu literarischen, religionsgeschichtlichen und ikonigraphischen Aspekten der Ascheradiskussion* (2 vols. Bonner Biblische Beiträge, 94/1/2; Weinheim Beltz Athenäum).

Gerstenberger, E.S. 1980 *Der bittende Mensch: Bittritual und Klagelied des Einzelnen im Alten Testament* (Wissenschaftliche Monographien zum Alten und Neuen Testament, 51; Neukirchen-Vluyn: Neukirchener Verl.).

—1988, 2001 *Psalms: Part I & II and Lamentations* (2 vols.; The Forms of the Old Testament Literature 14, 15; Grand Rapids, Mi.: Eerdmans).

Goulder, M.D. 1981 *Studies in the Psalter. Vol. 1: The Psalms of the Sons of Korah* (Journal for the Study of the Old Testament. Supplement series, 20; Sheffield: JSOT Press).

—1996 *Studies in the Psalter. Vol. 3: The Psalms of Asaph and the Pentateuch* (Journal for the Study of the Old Testament. Supplement series, 233; Sheffield: JSOT Press).

Green, M. 1978 'The Eridu Lament', *Journal of Cuneiform Studies* 30: 127–167.

—1984 'The Uruk Lament', *Journal of the American Oriental Society* 104: 253–279.

Greimas, A.J. [2]1986 *Sémantique structurale* (Paris: Presses Universitaires de France).

Groenewald, A. 1996 *Poëtiese konvensies in 'n jong-babiloniese handopheffingsgebed aan die godin Ištar* (MA thesis, University of Pretoria).

Gunkel, H./Begrich, J. 1933[[4]1985] *Einleitung in die Psalmen: die Gattungen der religiösen Lyrik Israels* (Göttingen: Vandenhoeck & Ruprecht).

Gunkel, H. 1911 [[4]1926] *Die Psalmen* (Göttinger Handkommentar zum Alten Testament, 2,2; Göttingen: Vandenhoeck & Ruprecht).

Hallo, W.W. (ed.) 1989 *The Bible in the light of cuneiform literature: Scripture in context, III* (Ancient Near Eastern texts and studies, 8; Lewiston: Mellen).

—1990 *The Context of Scripture, Vol. 1: Canonical Compositions From the Biblical World* (Leiden; Boston; Köln: Brill).

—2000 *The Context of Scripture, Vol. 2: Monumental Inscriptions From the Biblical World* (Leiden; Boston; Köln: Brill).

Hieke, T. 1997 *Psalm 80: Praxis eines Methodenprogramms: Eine literaturwissen-schaftliche Untersuchung mit einem gattungskritischen Beitrag zum Klagelied des Volkes* (Arbeiten zu Text und Sprache im Alten Testament, 55; St. Ottilien: EOS-Verl.).

Holladay, W.L. [13]1993 *A Concise Hebrew and Aramaic Lexicon of the Old Testament* (Grand Rapids MI: Eerdmans; Leiden: Brill).

Hooke, S.H. (ed.), 1933 *Myth and Ritual: Essays on the Myth and Ritual of the Hebrews in Relation to the Cultic Pattern of the Ancient East* (Oxford).

Hossfeld, F.-L./Zenger, E. 2000 *Psalmen 51–100* (Herders theologischer Kommentar zum Alten Testament; Freiburg im Breisgau: Herder).

Hossfeld, F.-L. 1997 'Das Prophetische in den Psalmen: Zur Gottesrede der Asafpsalmen im Vergleich mit der des ersten und zweiten Davidpsalters,' in F. Dietrich and B. Wilmes (ed.), *Ich bewirke das Heil und erschaffe das Unheil (Jesaja 45,7): Studien zur Botschaft der Profeten: Festschrift für Lothar Ruppert zum 65. Geburtstag* (Forschung zur Bibel, 88; Würzburg: Echter): 223–243.

Kämmerer, T.R./Schwiderski, D. 1998 *Deutsch-Akkadisches Wörterbuch* (Alter Orient und Altes Testament, 255; Münster: Ugarit-Verlag).

Kassian, A./Korolëv, A./Sidel'tsev, A. 2002 *Hittite Funerary Riual šalliš waštaiš* (Alter Orient und Altes Testament, 288; Münster: Ugarit-Verlag).

Koch, K. 1964 [[5]1989] *Was ist Formgeschichte? Neue Wege der Bibelexegese* (Neukir-chen-Vluyn: Neukirchener).

—2002 'Der König als Sohn Gottes in Ägypten und Israel,' in E. Otto und E. Zenger (Hg.), *'Mein Sohn bist du' (Ps. 2, 7): Studien zu den Königspsalmen* (Stuttgarter Bibelstudien, 192; Stuttgart: Verl. Kath. Bibelwerk): 1–32.

Koenen, K. 1991 'Maškil – 'Wechselgesang'. Eine neue Deutung zu einem Begriff der Psalmenüberschriften,' *Zeitschrift für die alttestamentliche Wissenschaft* 103: 109–112.

—1996 *Gottesworte in den Psalmen: eine formgeschichtliche Untersuchung* (Biblisch-theologische Studien, 30; Neukirchen-Vluyn: Neukirchener).

Krecher, J. 1966 *Sumerische Kultlyrik* (Wiesbaden: Harrassowitz).

Kunstmann, W.G. 1932 [1968] *Die babylonische Gebetsbeschwörung* (Leipziger Semitistische Studien NF, 2; Leipzig: Hinrichs; repr.: Leipzig: Zentralantiquariat der DDR).

Kutscher, R. 1975 *Oh Angry Sea (a-ab-ba hu-luh-ha): The History of a Sumerian Congregational Lament* (New Haven, London: Yale University Press).

Lambert, W.G. 1975 *Babylonian Wisdom Literature* (Oxford: Clarendon Press).

—1997 'Processions to the akîtu House,' *Revue Assyriologique* 91: 49–80.

Landsberger, B. 1926 'Die Eigenbegrifflichkeit der babylonischen Welt,' *Islamica* 2: 355- 372.

Levenson, J.D. 1988 *Creation and the Persistence of Evil: The Jewish Drama of Divine Omnipotence* (San Francisco: Harper).

Levin, C. 1982 *Der Sturz der Königin Atalja: Ein Kapitel zur Geschichte Judas im 9. Jahrhundert v. Chr.* (Stuttgarter Bibelstudien, 105; Stuttgart: Verlag Katholisches. Bibelwerk).

Livingstone, A. 1989 *Court Poetry and Literary Miscellanea* (State Archives of Assyria, 3; Helsinki: Helsinki University Press).

Loretz, O. 1999 Konflikt zwischen Neujahrsfest und Exodus in Psalm 81 in: A. Lange, H. Lichtenberger and K.F.D. Römheld (ed.) *Mythos im Alten Testament und seiner Umwelt: Festschrift für Hans Peter Muller zum 65. Geburtstag –* (BZAW, 278; Berlin: Walter de Gruyter) 127–143.

Matthiae, P. 1999 *Ninive: glanzvolle Hauptstadt Assyriens* (München: Hirmer).

Maul, S.M. 1988 *'Herzberuhigungsklagen': die sumerisch-akkadischen Ershahunga-Gebete* (Wiesbaden: Harrassowitz).

—1994 *Zukunftsbewältigung: eine Untersuchung altorientalischen Denkens anhand der babylonisch-assyrischen Löserituale (Namburbi)* (Baghdader Forschungen, 18; Mainz am Rhein: Von Zabern).

—1999 'Gottesdienst im Sonnenheiligtum zu Sippar,' in B. Böck, E. Cancik-Kirschbaum and T. Richter (ed.), *Munuscula Mesopotamia: Festschrift für Johannes Renger* (Alter Orient und Altes Testament, 267; Münster: Ugarit-Verlag): 285–316.

—2000 'Die Frühjahrsfeierlichkeiten in Aššur,' in A.R. George and I.L. Finkel (ed.), *Wisdom, Gods and Literature: Studies in Assyriology in Honour of W.G. Lambert* (Winona Lake, In.: Eisenbrauns): 389–420.

—2001 'Eine neubabylonische Kultordnung für den "Klagesänger" (kalû)', in T. Richter, D. Prechel and J. Klinger (ed.), *Kulturgeschichten: Altorientalische Studien für Volker Haas zum 65. Geburtstag* (Saarbrücken: SDV): 255–265.

Mayer, W. 1976 *Untersuchungen zur Formensprache der babylonischen 'Gebetsbeschwörung'* (Studia Pohl: Series Maior, 5; Rome: Biblical Institute Press).

Mbiti, J.S. 1970 *Concepts of God in Africa* (London: S.P.C.K.).

—1974 *Afrikanische Religion und Weltanschauung* (De-Gruyter-Studienbuch; Berlin [u.a.]: de Gruyter).

Michalowski, P. 1989 *The lamentation over the destruction of Sumer and Ur* (Mesopotamian civilizations, 1; Winona Lake: Eisenbrauns).

Millard, M. 1994 *Die Komposition des Psalters: Ein formgeschichtlicher Ansatz* (Forschungen zum Alten Testament, 9; Tübingen: Mohr).

Mowinckel, S. 1921–1924 [reprint 1966] *Psalmenstudien* (6 vols. Skriftur utgitt av Det Norske Videnskaps-Akademi i Oslo; Kristiana: J. Dybwad; reprint: Amsterdam: P. Schippers).

—1962 *The Psalms in Israel's worship* (2 vols; Oxford: Oxford University Press).

Nasuti, H.P. 1988 *Tradition history and the psalms of Asaph* (Society of Biblical Literature. Dissertation series, 88; Atlanta, Georgia: Scholars Press).

Nilsson, M.P. 1941 *Geschichte der griechischen Religion.* Vol. 1. *Bis zur griechischen Weltherrschaft* (Handbuch der klassischen Altertumswissenschaft, 5,2,1; München: Beck).

Nissinen, M. 1998 *References to Prophecy in Neo-Assyrian Sources* (State Archives of Assyria Studies, 7; Helsinki: The Neo-Assyrian Text Corpus Project).

—2001 'Akkadian Rituals and Poetry of Divine Love', in R.M. Whiting (ed.), *Mythology and mythologies: methodological approaches to intercultural influences; proceedings of the second annual symposium of the Assyrian and Babylonian Intellectual Heritage Project held in Paris, France, October 4–7, 1999* (Melammu symposia, 2; Helsinki: Neo-Assyrian Text Corpus Project) 93–136.

Obiego, C.O. 1984 *African image of the ultimate reality: an analysis of Igbo ideas of life and death in relation to Chukwu-God* (Europäische Hochschulschriften, 23; 237; Frankfurt am Main u.a.: Lang).

Oded, B. 2000 'The Settlements of the Israelite and the Judean Exiles in Mesopotamia in the 8th–6th Centuries BCE', in: G. Galil and M. Weinfeld (eds.), *Studies in Historical Geography and Biblical Historiography: Presented to Zecharia Kallai* (Supplements to Vetus Testamentum, 81; Leiden: Brill): 91–103.

Pallis, S.A. 1926 *The Babylonian Akîtu Festival* (Det Kgl. Danske Videnskaberne Selskab. Historisk-filologiske Meddelelser 12,1; Ko/benhavn: Host).

Parker, S.B. 1995 'The Beginning of the Reign of God – Psalm 82 as Myth and Liturgy', *Revue biblique* 102: 532–559.

Parpola, S. 1992 *Letters from Assyrian and Babylonian Scholars* (State Archives of Assyria, 10; Helsinki: Helsinki University Press).

—1997 *Assyrian Prophecies* (State Archives of Assyria, 9; Helsinki: Helsinki University Press).

Pongratz-Leisten, B. 2002 'The Other and the Enemy in the Mesopotamian Conception of the World,' in R.M. Whiting (ed.), *Mythology and mythologies: methodological approaches to intercultural influences; proceedings of the second annual symposium of the Assyrian and Babylonian Intellectual Heritage Project held in Paris, France, October 4–7, 1999* (Melammu symposia, 2; Helsinki: Neo-Assyrian Text Corpus Project) 195–231.

Pongratz-Leisten, B./Deller, K./Bleibtreu, E. 1993 'Götterstreitwagen und Götterstandarten: Götter auf dem Feldzug und ihr Kult im Feldlager,' *Baghdader Mitteilungen* 23: 291–356.

Postgate, J.N. 1973 *The Governor's palace archive* (Cuneiform texts from Nimrud, 2; Baghdad: British School of Archaeology in Iraq).

Reiner, E./Güterbock, H.G. 1967 'The Great Prayer to Ishtar and its two Versions from Bogazköy', *Journal of Cuneiform Studies* 21: 255–266.

Rösel, C. 1999 *Die messianische Redaktion des Psalters: Studien zu Entstehung und Theologie der Sammlung Psalm 2–89** (Calwer theologische Mono-graphien, A 19; Stuttgart: Calwer Verl.).

Sallaberger, W. 2000 'Das Erscheinen Marduks als Vorzeichen: Kultstatue und Neujahrsfest in der Omenserie Schumma alu,' *Zeitschrift für Assyriologie* 90: 227–262.

Seybold, K. 1994 'Das "Wir" in den Asaph-Psalmen: Spezifische Probleme einer Psalmgruppe,' in K. Seybold and E. Zenger (eds.), *Neue Wege der Psalmenforschung: FS Walter Beyerlin* (Herders biblische Studien, 1; Freiburg u.a.: Herder): 143–155.

—1996 *Die Psalmen* (Handbuch zum Alten Testament, 1/15; Tübingen: Mohr).

Soden, W. von 1965–1981 *Akkadisches Handwörterbuch* (3 vols.; Wiesbaden: Harrassowitz).

Steymans, H.U. 1998 'Der (un-)glaubwürdige Bund von Psalm 89', *Zeitschrift für Altorientalische und Biblische Rechtsgeschichte* 4: 126–144.

—2002 '"Deinen Thron habe ich unter den großen Himmeln festgemacht": Die formgeschichtliche Nähe von Ps 89,4–5.20–38 zu Texten vom neuassyrischen Hof,' in E. Otto und E. Zenger (eds.), *'Mein Sohn bist du' (Ps. 2,7): Studien zu den Königspsalmen* (Stuttgarter Bibelstudien, 192; Stuttgart: Verl. Kath. Bibelwerk): 184–251.

Stummer, F. 1922 *Sumerisch-akkadische Parallelen zum Aufbau altestamentlicher Psalmen* (Studien zur Geschichte und Kultur des Altertums, 11; Paderborn: Schöningh).

Tate, M.E. 1990 *Psalms 51–100* (Word Biblical Commentary, 20; Waco, Tex.: Word Book Publishers).

Tinney, S. 1996 *The Nippur Lament* (Occasional Publications of the Samual Noah Kramer Fund, 16; Philadelphia: University of Pennsylvania Museum).

Turner, J.D. 1991 'The history of religions background of John 10', in J. Beutler and R.T. Fortna (ed.), *The Shepherd Discourse of John 10 and its Context. Studies by members of the Johannine Writings Seminar* (Monograph series. Society for New Testament Studies, 67; Cambridge: Cambridge University Press): 33–52, 147–150.

Veijola, T. 1982 *Verheißung in der Krise: Studien zur Literatur und Theologie der Exilszeit anhand des 89. Psalms* (Annales Academiæ Scientiarum Fennicæ. Ser. B, 220; Helsinki: Suomalinen Tiedeakatemia).

—2000 'Das Klagegebet in Literatur und Leben der Exilsgeneration am Beispiel einiger Prosatexte', in T. Veijola, *Moses Erben: Studien zum Dekalog, zum Deuteronomismus und zum Schriftgelehrtentum* (Beiträge zur Wissenschaft vom Alten und Neuen Testament, 8, 9; 149; Stuttgart: Kohlhammer): 176–191.

Volgger, D. 1994 *Notizen zur Textanalyse von Ps. 89* (Arbeiten zu Text und Sprache im Alten Testament, 45; St. Ottilien: EOS-Verl.).

Volk, K. 1989 *Die Balag-Komposition Úru Àm-ma-ir-ra-bi: Rekonstruktion und Bearbeitung der Tafeln 18 (19'ff.), 19, 20 und 21 der späten, kanonischen Version* (Freiburger altorientalische Studien, 18; Stuttgart: Steiner-Verl. Wiesbaden).

Weber, B. 2000a 'Psalm 83 als Einzelpsalm und als Abschluss der Asaph-Psalmen', *Biblische Notizen* 103: 64–84.

—2000b 'Zur Datierung der Asaph-Psalmen 74 und 79', *Biblica* 81: 521–532.

—2001 'Der Asaph-Psalter – eine Skizze', in B. Huwyler, H-P Mathys, and B. Weber (eds.), *Prophetie und Psalmen. Festschrift für Klaus Seybold zum 65. Geburtstag* (Alter Orient und Altes Testament, 280; Münster: Ugarit-Verl.): 117–141.

—2002 Weber, Beat: 'Akrostichische Muster in den Asaph-Psalmen', *Biblische Notizen*, 113: 79–93.

Widengren, G. 1937 *The Accadian and Hebrew Psalms of Lamentation* (Stockholm: Atkiebolaget Thule).

Zenger, E. 1999 'Psalm 82 im Kontext der Asaf-Sammlung: Religionsgeschichtliche Implikationen', in B. Janowski und M. Köckert (eds.), *Religionsgeschichte Israels: formale und materiale Aspekte* (Wissenschaftliche Gesellschaft für Theologie: Veröffentlichungen der Wissenschaftlichen Gesellschaft für Theologie, 15; Gütersloh: Kaiser, Gütersloher Verl.-Haus): 272–292.

—2000 'Psalmenforschung nach Hermann Gunkel und Sigmund Mowinckel', in: A. Lemaire und M. Sæbo/ (eds.), *International Organization for the Study of the Old Testament, Congress volume, Oslo 1998* (Vetus Testamentum Supplements, 80; Leiden: Brill): 399–435.

—2001 'Von der Psalmenexegese zur Psalterexegese,' *Bibel und Kirche* 56: 8–15.

SPATIALITY IN PSALM 29

Pieter M. Venter
Pretoria, RSA

1. *Introduction*

The discipline of *Critical Spatiality* seeks 'to reintroduce spatiality in an ontological trialectic that includes historicality, sociality, and spatiality' (Flanagan 1999: 26). Critical spatiality studies the spatial aspect of the biblical text and relates it to the socio-historic context in which it originated. It understands space in the framework of the social experience and conceptualization of the physical space in which people live. Space is not only perceived as concrete geophysical reality ('first space' cf. Matthews 2003:12) but also the way in which this space is conceived (so called 'second space') and the way in which it is related to the ideology of the author and of the society ('third space').

Critical spatiality theory, therefore, provides a tool for social-historical reconstruction (cf. Camp 2002). Spatial analysis of biblical literature can provide a window into the ancient world of the Bible. By including critical spatiality in the exegetical process the toponyms used in a passage can be related not only to the perceptions related to them, but also to the specific idea world of the text's author.

In Psalm 29 explicit toponyms occur. Lebanon, Sirion and the desert of Kadesh are indicated as areas where God exerted his power. Throughout the psalm God's sovereignty is conceptualized in spatial terms. A critical spatial analysis of these spaces not only leads to information about how they were perceived in Israel, but also to the ideological context from which this psalm originated.

2. *First space in Psalm 29*

Three places are explicitly named in Psalm 29: Lebanon, Sirion and Kadesh.

Lebanon occurs in verses 5 and 6. Lebanon is the name for the mountain ridge in Syria. It is almost 160 kilometres long, running from Southwest to North East. It is marked by white limestone on its ridge and occasionally snow. It is from this feature it got its name as the 'white mountain'.

The Lebanon range is a direct continuation of the hills of northern Galilee. The range is marked by several peaks varying from 1,630 to 2,600 metres high. To the west the range sweeps down to the Mediterranean Sea.

To the east it is flanked by the parallel Anti-Lebanon mountain range, with the Biqa valley between them (cf. Josh. 11.17).

Lebanon is identified with cedar trees in Psalm 29.5. The rulers of Egypt, Mesopotamia and Syria-Palestine used Lebanon's cedars and conifers as building material. These cedars were often symbols of majesty and strength in biblical imagery (cf. Judg. 9.15; 1 Kgs. 4.33; 2 Kgs. 14.9, Pss. 92.12; 104.16; Cant. 5.15; Isa. 35.2; 60.13). They were also symbols of earthly pride which was subjected to divine wrath (cf. Isa. 2.13; 10.34; Jer. 22.6; Ezek. 31.3-14; Zech. 11.1-2).

Mount Hermon is found in the southern half of the Anti-Lebanon range mentioned above. Psalm 29.6b names it שְׂרִין. The Sidonians called Hermon 'Sirion'. The name the Amorites used was 'Senir' (cf. Deut. 3.9). These names were already used during the fourteenth century BCE. In the Ugaritic texts of the fourteenth/thirteenth centuries BCE Lebanon and Sirion are described as the origin for the timber used for Baal's temple (cf. Pritchard 1950:134a). The use of the word pair Lebanon and Sirion can be seen as standard expression in Phoenician literature ('stehende Redeweise – Kraus 1966: 237). Zaphon, Amanus, Tabor and Hermon are mentioned together in Psalm 98.13. In Isaiah 2.12 the cedars of Lebanon and the large trees of Bashan are grouped together.

The desert of Kadesh mentioned in Psalm 29.8b is often identified as Kadesh-Barnea, an oasis in the Wilderness of Zin. Both the names Kadesh and Kedesh are used for cities that were ancient sanctuaries in Canaan. Kadesh is used for cities of Judah and Kedesh for cities in the north (cf. Cohen 1962:1). The name 'Barnea' is appended to Kadesh to distinguish it from other sites with the same name. Seybold (1998: 99, n. 59) puts the Kadesh of Psalm 29.8 in the same area as Lebanon and Sirion. He links it to the Orontes area rather than the wilderness at Negeb. Kraus (1966: 237) understands Lebanon and Kadesh as geographical opposites which strangely belong together as traditional border markers for the north and southern extremes of old Israel. With Lebanon and Kadesh a description is provided of the *Herrschaftsbereich* of the king which probably was a traditional old Canaanite geographical identification (cf. Kraus 1966: 238). It came from the royal high god tradition.

The desert of Kadesh is sometimes conceived in terms of the southern boundary of Israel. Ezekiel makes Meribath-Kadesh part of the southern border of his idealized land of Israel (Ezek. 47.19; 48.28). In Deut 33.2 the advance of God from his holy mountain is described. The words in this verse usually translated as 'from the ten thousand of holy ones' should be amended to read 'from Meribath-Kadesh' (cf. Cohen 1962: 2). As Kadesh is linked to the desert it can be included in the boundary formula 'from the wilderness and Lebanon and from the River Euphrates to the western sea' (Deut. 11.24; Josh. 1.4), i.e. within these South-North and East-West limits.

3. *Second space in Psalm 29*

The names Lebanon, Sirion and Kadesh and other spatial references are used as represented or imagined space in Psalm 29. Specific ideas or meaning is attached to the spaces in the psalm. These attached ideas should be studied by firstly investigating the way in which these spaces are used in the structure of the poem and secondly how these spaces became part of the poem during its literary growth.

3.1 *The structure of the poem*
The poem is structured as a symmetrical unit. It consists of four symmetrically arranged *inclusios*. Indication of place is found in three of the four *inclusios* of the poem. Spatiality plays an all important role in the poem. To understand the meaning of this spatiality the use of spatial references has to be studied in each separate *inclusio*.

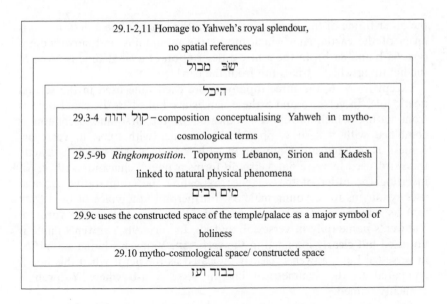

3.2 *Space in the central inclusio (29.5-9b).*
The three specific toponyms Lebanon, Sirion and Kadesh are found in vss. 5b, 6 and 8b. All of these verses belong to the central inclusio of vss. 5-9b. Jeremias (1987: 33) identified these verses as a 'Ringkomposition'. Five poetic lines describing the disastrous effects of God's thundering voice on objects in nature are structured here in an A-B-C-B¹-A¹ scheme. A poetical description of the storm which unearths trees (vss. 5a-b and 9a-b) forms

5 קוֹל יְהוָה שֹׁבֵר אֲרָזִים			**The voice of Jahwe** breaks the cedars
וַיְשַׁבֵּר יְהוָה אֶת־אַרְזֵי הַלְּבָנוֹן		The Storm	Breaks **Jahwe** the cedars of **Lebanon**
6 וַיַּרְקִידֵם כְּמוֹ־עֵגֶל לְבָנוֹן			He makes skip like a calf **Lebanon**
וְשִׂרְיֹן כְּמוֹ בֶן־רְאֵמִים	Earthquake		**Sirion** like a young ox
7 קוֹל־יְהוָה חֹצֵב לַהֲבוֹת אֵשׁ	Lightning		**The voice of Jahwe** strikes with flashes of lightning
8 קוֹל יְהוָה יָחִיל מִדְבָּר			**The voice of Jahwe** strikes the desert
יָחִיל יְהוָה מִדְבַּר קָדֵשׁ			Shakes **Jahwe** the desert of **Kades**
9 קוֹל יְהוָה יְחוֹלֵל אַיָּלוֹת			**The voice of Jahwe** twists the oaks
וַיֶּחֱשֹׂף יְעָרוֹת			**He** strips the forest bare

the outer frame of this central inclusio. In the inner frame a description is given of the earthquake which moves the mountains and surroundings (vss. 6a-b and 8a-b). In the centre a description of a single line is given of the lightning which strikes fire from the earth (v. 7).

Except for v. 6, the three toponyms are each time used in the second poetic line. In verses 5 and 8 these names are linked to the exact objects from nature which have been indicated in the first line. Lebanon is combined with אֲרָזֵי in v. 5b, which coincides with אֲרָזִים in verse 5a. Kadesh is in linguistic combination with מִדְבַּר in v. 8b, which is exactly the word used in verse 8a. Verse 6b forms a poetic chiasmus with v. 6a, inverting the order of the sentence, repeating the comparative כְּמוֹ and uses synonyms for a young male ox. Furthermore the voice of God (יְהוָה קוֹל) as acting agent in verses 5a and 8a is repeated in the form of Yahweh's name only in verses 5b and 8b. In verse 9b Yahweh's name is not used but clearly intended in the verb חָשַׂף. Yahweh's name is omitted in verse 6a, but Yahweh is clearly indicated as the actor when this line is compared to the symmetrical line in verse 8 a-b where Yahweh is explicitly named.

The northern geophysical names Lebanon, Sirion and Kadesh of the Syrian desert (cf. Jeremias 1987: 42), which Israel usually understood as outer boundary of its settlement area (cf. Jeremias 1987: 42 n. 39), are linked in the different poetic lines to the forest, mountain and desert areas of Upper Galilee. These names, however, function here not in terms of boundary markers but as concrete indications of nature sites. Through poetic parallelism the explicit northern names of Lebanon, Hermon and Kadesh are described in terms of the forests, mountains and deserts in the most northern areas of Israel.

What is more, in the poetic lines these names are simultaneously used as conceptualization of Yahweh's acts and deeds. By relating them to Yahweh they now express what Yahweh and his voice does and who Yahweh really is. Metaphorically the natural force of lightning is used to indicate how Yahweh subjects these areas to his power. He breaks, twists and strips the trees in this area. He makes Lebanon and Hermon jump. He shakes the desert of Kadesh. He strikes the earth with fire. All of these expressions relate the area to Yahweh's acts and indicate his manipulation of this space to conceptualize his personal identity (cf. Matthews 2003: 16). They are zones of Yahweh's influence and indicate by the way they are interpreted in the poem the identity Yahweh enjoys in the community of Israel.

In the second *inclusio* (29.3–10a) a different kind of space is used. The phrase 'voice of God' (קול יהוה) was used in a prominent position at the start of the first lines of verses 5, 7, 8, and 9 in the central '*Ring-komposition*'. The same phrase is used in the same position in verses 3a and 4a-b.

```
3 קול יהוה על־המים אל־הכבוד
   הרעים יהוה על־מים רבים:
4 קול־יהוה בכח
   קול יהוה בהדר:
```

The first line of verse 3 and both lines of verse 4 are also started with the phrase קול יהוה. The pattern found in verses 5 and 8 that the voice of God as acting agent in the first line is repeated in the form of only Yahweh's name in the next line, is also found in verse 3b. What is more, Yahweh is also related to space in nature to conceptualize his identity in verse 3. These features link verses 3-4 to the central *inclusio* in verses 5-9b.

The space indicated in verses 3-4, however, is not in the same category as that of verses 5-9. It does not indicate the geophysical area of the sea adjoining the dry land, but through the use of attributes like רבים is a traditional mythical concept which indicates the primeval sea as a cosmic power.

This move towards the use of mythological concepts for cosmic phenomena is also found in verse 10a, right after the central '*Ring-komposition*'. Yahweh's identity is conceptualized there in terms of his manipulation of the space called the 'flood' or 'heavenly sea' (מבול), a synonym for the cosmic sea in verse 3. This links verse 10a to verses 3-4 and completes the second *inclusio*.

Two phenomena, however, disturb this neatly concentric structure. Firstly, v.10a is closely linked to verse 10b by repetition of Yahweh's name, the verb ישב and the inverted order or chiasmus by which the two lines are linked.

יהוה למבול ישב **10**   Yahweh is over the flood enthroned

ישב יהוה מלך לעלם: Enthroned is Yahweh as king forever

This causes overlapping between the second and the third *inclusio*.

3.3 *Third inclusio (29.9c-10b)*.

In verse 10b a third category of spatial terms is intended. When Yahweh 'sits' (ישב), a royal throne is intended. This can be indicated as a constructed or manufactured space. The same kind of space is used in verse 9c. Here Yahweh is in his temple/palace where all cry 'Glory!'. In virtue of overlapping contents and the same kind of space used, 29.9c and 29.10b forms an *inclusio* around 29.10a. This makes the third *inclusio* (29.9c-29.10b) to be different from the 'neat' *inclusio* formed by 29.3-4–29.10a. It is still an *inclusio*, but not of the same order as the second *inclusio* which included 29.5-9b.

9c ובהיכלו כלו אמר כבוד:
10a יהוה למבול ישב
10b ישב יהוה מלך לעלם:

The same kind of overlapping between two *inclusios* is also found between verse 9c and the next *inclusio*.

Holiness (כבוד) used in v.9c was the central concept in Israel's life. 'It was the major concept by which the nation-culture structured and classified everything in its world – people, places, objects and times' (Rhoads 1992: 147). According to Israel's cultural maps of people, time and places the temple was the 'primary religious symbol of Judaism' (Freyne 1980: 260). In verse 9c the created space of the temple is linked to the ceremony in which Yahweh is hailed as Kabod! The same term is used twice in verses 1 and 2. This links the third *inclusio* to the fourth *inclusio* found in 29.1-2 and 29.11.

3.4 Fourth inclusio (29.1-2 and 29.11)
The fourth *inclusio* uses no spatial terms at all. This *inclusio* only refers to person categories (עם and בני אלים and יהוה). The term כבוד (honour) in verses 1c and 2a, the combination כבוד with עז (power) in verse 1c and the use of עז in verse 11a are the main indicators of the contents of the fourth *inclusio*.

This analysis of the concentric structures found in Psalm 29 indicates that three types of space are used in the different *inclusios* of the psalm. In the central *Ringkomposition* (29.5-9b) specific toponyms from the northern area are linked to geophysical space and used as conceptualizations of God's power over nature. In the second surrounding *inclusio* (29.3-4, 29.10a) mythological concepts of the cosmos (the sea and the flood) are used to express Yahweh's royal rule of the cosmos. In the irregular third *inclusio* (29.9c-10b), partly overlapping with the second 'mythological *inclusio*' artificial or constructed space (palace/temple) is used to depict Yahweh as the God who rules the whole world. In the outer frame (29.1–2, 29.11) or fourth *inclusio*, no spatial reference is used. Yahweh is simply stated as the God of כבוד ועז (honour and strength) who should be praised by his people and all living beings.

3.5 Socio-literary background
The different inclusios in the poem indicate that the poem is compiled from different literary units. These units are probably of different provenance. They can either be from the same time in history or even from different times. In tradition history research they are evaluated as 'Wachstumspuren' (Jeremias 1987: 32) representing different 'Wachstum-phasen' (Seybold 1996: 122). The different *inclusios* of the poem are then related to different phases in its literary growth and to different origins. As a different type of space is found in each inclusio it is logical to presume that the different types of space also represent different stages in the history and a different socio-historical context. Each type of space has to be studied against the background of its probable time and socio-historical context. This leads us to an investigation of the psalm's literary growth and its background.

In tradition criticism either informal Canaanite influence is accepted or the use of a formal ancient Baal hymn. Some would suspect influence of Ugaritic texts but limit it to certain poetical figures of speech. Others would be of the opinion that the Baal religion has influenced Yahwism at essential points. Still some others would identify a concrete hymn as the basis for the psalm. However, whether a specific *Textvorlage* in the form of a Baal or El Psalm which developed into the present text is supposed, or it is interpreted as what Zenger (2003: 164) calls an artful combination of El and Baal 'Theologumena', both sides agree that

Canaanite elements are reflected in the psalm. Like Psalms 46–48, 76 and 93 which deal with God as King by including Canaanite, Egyptian or Assyrian ideas, Yahweh is conceptualized in Psalm 29 by inter alia using traditional Baal and El elements. The main question for an investigation of *Critical Spatiality* in the psalm, however, is what contribution form-critical and traditio-historical analysis of this Canaanite background can make to a better understanding of the represented or imagined space in Psalm 29.

A major issue in the study of the psalm is the question why this original Canaanite material was used and why the material was rewritten several times. Kloos's (1986: 124) theory is 'that Yhwh possessed his Baal traits from the beginning'. His study of Exodus 15 and Psalm 29 shows that Baal traits were attributed to Yahweh by the Israelites right from the beginning and that the Baal traits were an essential element of Yahweh's character. At the time when the psalm was composed Yahweh was credited with the same properties as Baal in the Ugaritic Baal-Yam myth (cf. Kloos 1986: 123). The conception of God in terms of Baal traits was not polemical against the Baal religion *per se*, but was done in a time and a region where these available notions were merely used to conceptualize Yahweh's identity.

On the other hand Jeremias (1987: 30) sees an obvious polemical trend in the often repeated use of the Yahweh name in the psalm. Spieckermann (1989: 175) understands the explicit combination of cedar trees-Lebanon-Sirion as indication of a polemic against Baal. In the Ugaritic Baal Cycle the cedar wood from the Lebanon area is used to build the temple for Baal. When Yahweh's lightning strikes the cedars on Lebanon and makes the mountains of Lebanon and Sirion shudder, it is a way of expressing Yahweh's superiority to Baal. He destroys the material used for Baal's temple. According to Spieckermann (1989: 177) we have here the theological dexterity of a poet who undertook the challenge to adapt Canaanite mythology. He succeeded to formulate Yahweh's 'alleinigen Herrschatsanspruch in nicht für ihn erbauten Tempeln und in nicht für ihn konzipierten Theologien (=Mythologie)[1]' (Spieckermann 1989: 177).

Whether the Baal concepts were merely taken over from Baal religion or indeed used to polemize against Baal in favour of Yahweh, it is still clear that Baal terminology was used to conceptualize Yahweh's identity.

This supposed Baal material is mainly found in the central parts of Psalm 29. Since W. H. Schmidt (1966) the trend was to discern at least two sections in the psalm. The one section in the middle of the poem reflects

---

1. Translated: Yahweh's claim to be recognized as the only Lord in terms of temples which were not built for him and theological concepts not designed for him = mythology.

traditions of the storm god Baal Hadad. The other section forms a frame for the first. In this section mainly El traditions are found.

There are different types of theories on the way these two sections came together. One type of theory is found with Jeremias (1987). According to his theory there was an original hymn on Baal's reign from the mountain of Saphon. From there he ruled with weapons of thunder and lightning (cf. Jeremias 1987: 41). This formed the 'Grundbestand' of verses 5-9a. This *Baalhymnus* was probably from northern provenance as can be seen in the geographical terms Lebanon, Sirion and Kadesh of the Syrian desert (cf. Jeremias 1987: 42, note 39). In this hymn Baal's thundering voice and his irresistible military power were praised.

In Jeremias' second phase of the psalm the frame of verses 3-4 and 10 was added to this *Baalhymnus*. It included the key word מבול (heavenly sea/ flood) in verse 10. In a third step taken in Jerusalem an El tradition was linked to the *Baalhymnus*. By this time it was transferred to Yahweh. By adding verses 1, 3 and 9 the dynamic elements of the Baal tradition were put into a framework of static elements from the El tradition (cf. Jeremias 1987: 42). By enriching the psalm with an El tradition the new theme of Yahweh's honour (vss. 1, 2, 3, and 9) was developed.

In terms of the different types of space used we can deduct from Jeremias' theory that the toponyms Lebanon, Sirion and Kadesh were already present in the first phase of the *Baalhymnus*. As the hymn was originally used in the northern area, it used references to northern sites to conceptualize Baal's identity as god of thunder and of war. Lebanon, Sirion and Kades were not mere names of northern places, but indications of the god Baal and his power revealed in the thunder storm. In the second phase mythological terms like מבול were added to indicate cosmic phenomena rather than regional phenomena. According to the view represented in this second addition there was also a great sea or primeval flood in the world. This sea presents a cosmic power with which the gods wage war. In the third phase the scene shifted to Jerusalem where terms from the better known El tradition were used. These terms give preference to static notions like throne, honour and temple. The old Baal terms were reconceptualized in terms of the concepts of the El tradition. Yahweh's power is now conceptualized not only in terms of his combat with nature and primeval forces, but also in terms of the Royal God who sits upon his throne in his temple and reigns the world.

Another type of theory is represented by Seybold (1996 & 1998). He interprets Psalm 29 as an original 'mythisch geprägter Hymnus' (Seybold 1996: 121) which deals with Yahweh's triumph over chaotic powers. This poem was changed into a theophany liturgy with a cultic background (cf. Seybold 1996: 121). In the 'poetischer Grundtext' (Seybold 1998: 94) or 'Primärtexte' (Seybold 1998: 95) a sevenfold קול יהוה was used, based on an old Canaanite mythical confession of Baal who uses seven lightnings and thunders to exert his power (cf. Seybold 1998: 95, note 43). In the same way as in Psalm 93 and the Sumerian-Akkadian *amatu* hymns, Yahweh is depicted as the Cosmic King who has the power (עז) to rule the thunder, the primeval ocean, the land, the desert and all creatures. Typical late bronze Hadad-Baal expressions are used to describe Yahweh's acts in terms of a Syrian-Canaanite god. The impression is created that Yahweh took over the features of a god of thunder here (cf. Seybold 1998: 96). These traditional Baal elements are put in the frame of a divine council. Yahweh bears all the royal insignia of the warrior who rules over heaven and earth and is honoured by all living beings including his own people.

According to Seybold's theory a shift towards a theophany liturgy already took place during the first phase of the development of the text. In the basic seven *Theologumenon* the deity rules as divine warrior over the flood, the trees and the desert. His identity is conceptualized in terms of his ability to combat with nature forces and break their power. He operates in terms of the complex of myths in the late bronze Ras Shamra Texts which Gray (1962: 328) calls 'Baal and the Waters'. In these myths Baal champions the gods against the insult and tyranny of the unruly waters, called Sea and River. He overcomes its forces in a grim struggle. He then disperses the water to become a good servant. Baal then acclaims himself as king. In these texts space is conceptualized in typical mythological language as threatening forces from nature which are subdued by the deity.

In Seybold's next phase a 'redaktionelle Überarbeitung' (Seybold 1998: 94) took place by using 'Narrativsätze' (Seybold 1998: 97) to form 'Doppelkola'. Parallellism with the existing lines was created by adding explanations, amplifications and corrections in narrative form to form double poetic lines. By using these narrative sentences the original psalm was changed into a theophany which could be used in the liturgy at the temple (cf. Seybold 1998: 100). Yahweh now becomes the אל הכבוד who formerly became visible in the thunder but is now honoured at his temple. The content of the psalm is related to the every day living reality ('erlebten Realität' – Seybold 1996: 123). The purpose of this concretization of the psalm was to advance the cultic worship of God's people. It was done *inter alia* by the inclusion of the specific place names Lebanon, Sirion-Hermon and the desert Kadesh. These geographical references probably indicate the 'Entstehungsbereich im alten Mittelsyrien' (place of origin in old central Syria) (Seybold 1998: 99). Seybold (1998: 99) speculates that these names can even be linked to the 'altisraelitische Heiligtum am Füsse des Hermon' (old Israel sanctuary at the foot of Hermon) near Dan. The explicit mentioning of the temple-palace and the obvious correspondence with the Korah and enthronization psalms lead Seybold (1998: 101) to the conclusion that in the reworking of the psalm 'das nördliche Tempelheiligtum in Dan vor allem in Frage kommt' (especially the northern sanctuary at Dan comes into mind). As far as circumstances are concerned this remodelling of the older 'Gewittergott-Ikonographie' (Seybold 1998: 100) into a theophany liturgy took place in a time when the nature based agriculture oriented Canaanite pantheon was replaced by the Phoenician Baal-Shamen ideology in which Baal and El tradition were united (cf. Seybold 1998: 101). In its conflict with this religion Yahwism used the same conceptualizations to propagate Yahweh as the only Cosmic King.

Before interpreting Seybold's theory in terms of the type of space used in the psalm, I would like to refer to a third type of theory found in Zenger. Zenger (2003: 164) acknowledges that Psalm 29 is an artful combination of older El and Baal *theologumena*. He declines, however, to reconstruct any Canaanite *Textvorlage* for the psalm. Zenger is rather interested in studying the psalm as a Yahweh royal hymn that was probably used in the liturgy at the Yahweh royal festival during the autumn. What is of concern to us in his study is the spatial orientation Zenger finds in the psalm. The three different parts (1–2, 3–9, 10–12) he identified in the psalm, are linked together by the scene of Yahweh the king on his throne (cf. Zenger 2003: 167). Between God's throne and the מבול there exists a spatial relevance (cf. Zenger 2003: 167). In the Jerusalem cult tradition the flood is on a vertical axis, the cosmic opposite of the throne of God. From his throne God reigns with military might over the primeval flood. A distinction is not made here between God's throne in heaven and his presence in the temple in Jerusalem. The throne of Yahweh is rather 'mythische Chiffre seiner universalen Königsmacht' (mythical cipher for his universal power as king) (Zenger 2003: 167–168). The relation between God's throne and the mighty waters/flood is intended rather qualitatively than physical.

The geographical references in verses 5-9 do not refer to the thunder storm between Lebanon and anti-Lebanon, but rather present a horizontal world scene with the temple in Jerusalem in its centre (cf. Zenger 2003: 168). He reads the geographical reference to Kadesh in verse 8 as a reference to the southern desert at Kadesh Barnea. Between the extreme sites of Lebanon-Sirion in the north and Kadesh Barnea in the south lies Jerusalem in the centre with Yahweh's throne in the temple. God's throne is thus put in the centre of both vertical and horizontal axes. In spatial terms we have in Psalm 29 'die hymnische Konstituierung eines "Weltbilds", das JHWH als den königlichen Triumphator über alle Formen des Chaos feiert und so JHWHs die Welt erfüllende und dominierende Herrlichkeit kultisch vergegenwärtig'[2] (Zenger 2003: 168).

In terms of space Zenger works with a centralised world view. Qualitatively as well as quantitavely Yahweh's throne stands at the centre

---

2. The hymnic constitution of a view of life in which Yahweh is praised as the King who triumphed over all forms of chaos and therefore a cultic presentation of God's glory which fills the world and prevails everything.

of the physical as well as the mythical world. Zenger's synchronic analysis unfortunately dismisses the Baal-El tradition and the northern locations in the *Ringkomposition* in verses 5-9b too easily as integral constituents of the meaning of this throne of God. The contribution found in the two previous studies to understanding what determined the representation of the second space in the poem gets lost in the process.

It is also obvious that the meaning of the three toponyms Lebanon, Sirion and Kadesh is totally different in each of the three types of theories referred to. The names are either ascribed to different phases of the poem or to a geographical function which supports the centrality of Jerusalem in the spatial orientation.

At this stage we can return to Seybold's theory. In terms of space, mythological spatiality was already used in the primary text of his theory. Hadad-Baal terminology was used from the beginning to describe Yahweh in terms of the divine warrior who fought the primeval flood and who ruled as God of thunder over the elements of nature. In Jeremias' theory the mythical element of the flood was only added during the second phase of the psalm. In Zengers' theory the mythical element of the מבול is inherent to a qualitative-quantitative throne centred cosmic spatiality.

In terms of Seybold's theory of a second redactional reworking into a fully fledged theophany liturgy, another type of space was also introduced into the psalm. Two features from everyday life were included in the psalm to advance the cultic worship. The first is the physical temple in Jerusalem. The אל הכבוד is honoured at his temple building. Compared to the mythological concepts of thunder and flood, this is an artificial or created space. This temple is, however, not the mere physical space which Seybold suggests. In the *Narrativsätze* added to form the *Doppelkola* a narrative strategy is followed which transforms the physical space of the temple into a technical social space. It functions as the most holy place where his people honour their Holy God. Its meaning is determined by the identity of the God whom they honour at the temple. His identity is conceptualized in terms of the accumulated Baal-El traditions reflected in the poem. The Yahweh of the temple is also the God who reigns from his throne in the temple over the primeval flood and powers of nature. The received space of the temple is in relation to Yahweh also the conceived space in the poem conceptualized in terms of all the previous Baal *theologumena*.

The second feature from every day life included in the psalm according to Seybold's theory was the names Lebanon, Sirion and Kadesh. Seybold hinted at the possibility that the inclusion of these names can be related to a reworking of the older material at the temple of Dan at the foot of Hermon. Jeremias understands these geographical terms as indications of a northern provenance of the *Baalhymnus*. The names were already included at the first phase of the psalm. In Seybold's theory these names were only included in a second phase to advance the cultic worship. Seybold's idea that the concretization of the psalm can be linked to the old sanctuary at Dan near Hermon is not totally improbable. Some possibilities for a northern provenance of the linking of mythological spatiality to artificial spatiality already at the temple at Dan should be explored.

Jeremias (1987: 29) remarked that Psalm 29 can be linked to a Canaanite background much more than any of the other psalms. In his studies of a northern Hebrew dialect, which he calls 'Israelian Hebrew (IH)', Rendsburg (1990: 4) found ample evidence in Psalm 29 that it is of northern origin. He studied not only the list of toponyms mentioned in the poem, but also several items of linguistic evidence supporting a northern provenance for this poem (cf. Rendsburg 1990: 35–37).

Goulder (1982) proposed the theory that the Korahite Levites originating from Dan later joined the Jerusalem priesthood and maintained an independent position and even opposed the Zadokites. In terms of this theory they could also be the bearers of a psalm like Psalm 29 originating from the sanctury at Dan. At Dan they had immediate contact with Baalism and could have used Baal notions to either express their ideas on Yahweh (cf. Kloos 1986 above) or to polemize against the religion of their neighbours. This conceptualization using nature as well as mythological spatiality was probably developed at the sanctuary at Dan and related to revelatory sites in the surroundings like Lebanon, Sirion and Kadesh. These formulations already in existence at the sanctuary of Dan explicitly formulated for cultic purposes were later taken over in Jerusalem and applied to the temple there. Exactly the same happened with Deuteronomy 32 and Psalm 78 where the northern ark narrative and material originating at Shiloh was applied to the temple in Jerusalem when the northern shrine came to an end.

The tradition of northern cultic sites is also found in literature of the third century BCE. In the Book of the Watchers (*1 Enoch* 1–36) Hermon, Dan and Abel-Main are explicitly named as areas of religious activity. These references 'constitute a tradition of northern Galilean provenance which, in turn, reflects visionary activity in the area of Dan and Hermon' (Nickelsburg 1981: 585). Levi's commissioning in the *Testament of Levi* (2–7) runs parallel to the events in *1 Enoch* 13–14. In both books the events take place in exactly the same geographical setting of Abel-Main and Mount Hermon.

This brings us to the conclusion that those central sections in Psalm 29 where spatiality is used to characterize Yahweh are from northern provenance, probably from Dan. The three types of space used – toponyms of places in nature, mythological cosmic space and created space at the temple – originated at the northern sanctuaries and were used there in conceptualizing Yahwism within a context of co-existing Baalism. As conceived space these spatial references are to be interpreted in their northern context where they were heavily influenced by Baal ideology in its development form Hadad-Baalism to El conceptualization. In turn these spatial references determined the characterization of Yahweh presented in the psalm. With the increasing centralization of the temple in Jerusalem and phasing out of other cultic centres like those in Dan and eventually in Samaria this psalm with its 'strange' formulations was included in the liturgy of the temple in Jerusalem. The fourth *inclusio* (29:1–2, 11) was added to the older northern form of the psalm. No spatial references were used this time. Conceptualization of Yahwism now became person-orientated. Yahweh's כבוד ועז depicted in terms of the old Baal-El spatial contents is now related to the בני אלים[3] and the עם. They honour Yahweh at his temple in Jerusalem.

4. *Third space in Psalm 29*

Third space is primarily social space. It is not mere physical space or the way in which this space is conceived from a certain perspective, but the way perceived spaces are integrated into the ideology of society. Within the power relations in society it is a set of relations are produced through every day practice (cf. Flanagan 1999: 29).

The 'Lived Space' in Psalm 29 is the set of relations between Yahweh and the 'mighty ones'/his people. These relations are determined by the character of Yahweh. His character is pictured in terms of four concentric areas in which his כבוד ועז is experienced on different but congruent levels. For the three areas at the centre of this picture conceived space is used. Yahweh is firstly experienced in terms of the old Baal-Hadad concepts as the Divine Warrior and God of Thunder as it was already formulated at the temple at Dan. The spaces of Lebanon, Sirion and Kadesh with its cedars and nature forces witness to Yahweh's power and might. Building on this geographically based witness a second larger area is presented where Yahweh's power and his honour is experienced. In terms of the mythical concept of the mighty primeval flood and Baal's triumph and subjecting of these waters, Yahweh is depicted as a king who reigns over this cosmic force. Interlinked with this circle a third area is presented where Yahweh is sketched in terms of a king who sits on a throne. Building upon the concepts of the inner circles of Yahweh who overpowers forces of nature and who rules over the cosmic powers, Yahweh's reign formulated in the third concentric circle in terms of the created space of thrones and temples, is a reign which includes the space of the whole cosmos. All of these are included in the fourth concentric circle. Although no spatial

---

3. The בני אלים could be a mythological cosmic concept intending the population of heaven. Then a spatial aspect forms part of the concept. Here it is merely interpreted as persons related to Yahweh who acknowledge his honour and power and pay homage to Him.

references are used here Yahweh's כבוד ועז formulated in terms of his relation to the mighty ones and his people include the cosmic space used in the inner circles to proclaim his relation of power to everything in the cosmos.

In this way a lived space is presented in Psalm 29 in poetical language where every one and everything is related to Yahweh's honour and his power. The call upon the mighty ones and the people of Yahweh to acknowledge his glory and splendour and worship Him is substantiated by enouncements in language which relates the different spaces of the cosmos to Yahweh's characteristic power and glory. It can be depicted with a diagram:

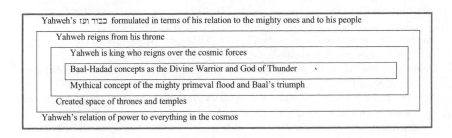

Bibliography

Camp, C.V. 2002 *Storied Space, or Ben Sira 'Tells' a Temple*. At http://www.cwru.edu/affil/GAIR/Constructions.html.

Cohen, S. 1962 sv Kadesh, Kades-Barnea, in G.A. Buttrick (ed.), *The Interpreter's Dictionary of the Bible* (New York: Abingdon).

Flanagan, J.W. 1999 'Ancient perceptions of space/perceptions of ancient space', S*emeia* 87: 15–43.

Freyne, S. 1980 *Galilee from Alexander the Great to Hadrian 323 BCE to 135 CE. A STUDY OF SECOND TEMPLE JUDAISM* (NOTRE DAME, INDIANA: GLAZIER & UNIVERSITY OF NOTRE DAME PRESS).

Goulder, M.D. 1982 *The Psalms of the Sons of Korah* (JSOT SS, 20; Sheffield: JSOT Press): 51–84.

Gray, J. 1962 sv Baal (Deity) in G.A. Buttrick (ed.), *The Interpreter's Dictionary of the Bible* (New York: Abingdon): 328–329.

Jeremias, J. 1987 *Das Königtum Gottes in den Psalmen. Israels Begegnung mit dem kanaanäischen Mythos in den Jahwe-König-Psalmen* (Göttingen: Vandenhoeck & Ruprecht): 29–45.

Kloos, C. 1986 *Yhwh's Combat with the Sea. A Canaanite Tradition in the Religion of Ancient Israel* (Leiden: EJ Brill).

Kraus, H-J. 1966 *Psalmen I* (BKAT; Neukirchen-Vluyn: Neukircher Verlag).

Matthews, V.H. 2003 'Physical space, imagined space, and 'lived space' in ancient Israel', *Biblical Theology Bulletin* 33(1): 12–20.

Nickelsburg, G.W.E. 1981 'Enoch, Levi, and Peter: Recipients of Revelation in Upper Galilea', *Journal for Biblical Literature* 100/4: 575–600.

Prichard, J.B. 1950 *Ancient Near Eastern texts relating to the Old Testament* (Princeton: Princeton University Press).

Rendsburg, G.A. 1990 *Linguistic Evidence for the Northern Origin of Selected Psalms* (The Society of Biblical Literature. Monograph Series, 43. Atlanta, Georgia: Scholars Press).

Rhoads, D. 1992 *Social Criticism: Crossing Boundaries*, in J.C Anderson & S.D. Moore (eds.), *Mark and Method. New Approaches in Biblical Studies* (Minneapolis: Fortress Press):135–161.

Schmidt, W.H. 1966 *Königtum Gottes in Ugarit und Israel: zur Herkunft des Königsprädikation Yahwehs*. Berlin: Walter de Gruyter.

Seybold, K. 1996 *Die Psalmen* (HAT, I/15; Tübingen: Mohr [Siebeck]).

—1998 *Studien zur Psalmenauslegung* (Stuttgart: Kohlhammer): 85–111.

Spieckermann, H. 1989 *Heilsgegenwart. Eine Theologie der Psalmen* (Göttingen: Vandenhoeck & Ruprecht): 165–179.

Zenger, E. 2003 *Theophanien des Königsgottes JHWH. Transformationen von Psalm 29 im Psalter*, in E. Zenger (Hg.), *Ritual und Poesie* (Formen und Orte religiöser Dichtung im Alten Orient, im Judentum und im Christentum. Freiburg: Herder): 163–190.

THEOPOETICAL AND LITURGICAL PATTERNS OF THE PSALMS WITH REFERENCE TO PSALM 19

Cas J. A. Vos
Pretoria, RSA

1. *Introduction*

The rays of the sun strike the brown earth, resonant with the hum of insects, at different angles in different places. Similarly, readers and listeners have different perspectives on the Psalter, a collection of poems written to be sung. In this article, I explore some of these perspectives.

2. *Theopoetry*

Amos Niven Wilder (1976) is the author of *Theopoetic: theology and religious imagination*. Wilder explored the role of the artistic element in biblical interpretations. Through his use of the concept *theopoetry* Erich Zenger (2000) expresses both the poetical and the prayer-like tone of the psalms in their individual text form. I would like to use this term to reflect the particular nature of the psalms as poetry. The psalmists, via the vehicle of their poetry, frequently call upon God. Sound gives a poem a voice. The primal source is the imagery (Krog 2002: 12). Thus the poetry of the psalms lends a distinct sound and colour to the way the psalmists spoke about, and to God. God is not the sole subject in the psalms; another central theme is God in relation to mankind and the universe.

It is clear in the psalms, that the Israelites saw themselves as God's people. God chose Israel to be a communicative partner, not a passive object of his historical will. The psalms are the outcome of this relationship and communication. In this dialogue, Israel stands before God as 'we' and 'I' (Zenger 1997: 23). The psalms are also Israel's answer to the search for God and the mystery of God. A study of these lyrical poems tells us how Israel regarded itself in relation to Yahweh (Von Rad 1966: 366–367).

The essence of the psalms, although it sounds contradictory, is to understand God, to enter into a living communion with him, to reach out for the unattainable and to cling to God (Zenger 1997: 23). The psalms reveal that God holds tightly onto those who extend their arms to him. The struggle with the incomprehensible is part of mankind's existence even now, but the psalms can be helpful and encouraging.

Gerhard von Rad (1966: 366) and Erich Zenger's (1997: 22–23) indication that the psalms are 'answers' is acceptable, however the psalms are also many other things. In the psalms we can find reflections of pleading, struggles (Ps. 22), reproaches (Pss. 42, 43), complaints (Ps. 13), longings (Ps. 84) and other prayer-like emotions. Therefore, regarding the psalms as answers only is taking too narrow a view.

In the psalms, which are 'answers', and in those, which reflect encounters with God, the 'I' and 'we' emerge conspicuously as speakers. 'I' and 'thee' frequently fuse into each other (e.g.: in Ps. 40). It has often been debated whether the 'I' is individual or collective, but this is a modern distinction. Even when a single Israelite says 'I', he is conscious of the fact that in the sight of God to whom he prays, he is bound into the 'we' of God's people. Conversely, the 'you' of God's people, is a community that knows that their lives are as indivisible and vulnerable as that of the 'I' (Zenger 1997: 23). All this comes to the fore in the poetic expression of the psalms.

Any student of the psalms needs to take cognisance of the unique character of poetry. It should also be borne in mind that poetry acquires a different voice and bears a different stamp in each language. When reading the psalms, the specific character of Hebrew poetry must always be kept in mind (cf. Van der Lugt 1980; Watson 1986; Hossfeld & Zenger 1993, 2000; Prinsloo 2000; Martin and McEvenue 2001: 131–136).

In a literary approach, the emphasis is on the poetic nature of the psalms. Some of the most moving poetry is to be found in the psalms. While not all the psalms are of the same literary standard, their language, imagery, architecture and sounds are nevertheless intense and moving (Zenger 1997: 35). In the words of Herman de Coninck (1995: 11), a poem affords linguistic, visual and possibly even meditative pleasure to the reader. We experience the same when reading a psalm.

3. Conversation and related groups

It is a characteristic of a volume of poetry that it does not consist of loose texts. An anthology is meticulously planned and each poem has its own voice and temperament. Poems are also grouped in sections and are finely in tune with one another. One should be able to hear the poems breathe.

In the psalms there is also a distinct discourse and relationship between the poems, but, eventually, there is a sense of totality. This framework also applies to the Book of Psalms (cf. Westermann 1984: 12). The juxtaposition (*iuxtapositio*) and the concatenation (*concatenatio*) of the Psalter are compositionally, editorially and theologically meaningful (Braulik 1995: 59; Zenger 1998: 12; Schuman 2002: 35). Modern biblical research has proved that the Psalter is to be understood as a text meant for meditation. Its preamble, Ps. 1, welcomes the user of the Psalter as someone who continuously 'murmurs the Torah' and the 'directives of Yahweh':

> His joy is the Torah of the Lord;
> he murmurs his Torah by day and by night (verse 2).

The Hebrew verb הגה, which is translated here as 'to murmur,' does not denote an intellectual reflection, but it means 'to recite, to repeatedly utter words in an undertone' (Braulik 2003: 5).

Adjacent psalms are often unified by themes, or by the events that they describe. When analysing Ps. 19, its positioning and function have to be considered.

Niek Schuman (2002: 38–39) made a significant contribution to our understanding of the interrelation of Pss. 15–24. He points out that the king is the subject of many of the psalms in this group. This focus begins in Ps. 18, where the 'I' cannot be anyone but the king. In the last line his identity is revealed. The 'I' represents the anointed of Yahweh. Yahweh promises his everlasting devotion to the anointed ones and their descendants (Ps. 18:51). Pss. 20 and 21 subsequently contain a prayer of victory for the king, as well as an expression of thanksgiving for the victory that has been attained.

Ps. 16 is a song of confidence. The singer has come to know beautiful abodes and he has even been saved from death. In stark contrast to this, there is the supplication of a person who is suffering, due to false accusations. In the group formed by Pss. 18–21, we find a different pattern. Ps. 22.1-22 is a lament by someone surrounded by enemies. The second part of Ps. 22.22-32 has a difference in tone. In liturgical language: after a nearly bottomless *kyrie*, follows a celestial *gloria*, ending with divine justice. Then follows Ps. 23, another song of confidence.

Schuman (2002: 39) has identified the following links between psalms in this group: related terms and themes link Ps. 15 to Ps. 24 (cf. Prinsloo 2000: 53, 62), Ps. 16 to Ps. 23, Ps. 17 to Ps. 22 and Ps. 18 to Pss. 20 and 21. Ps. 18, a confidential prayer of the king who was saved by God, is bound editorially to the 'twin psalms,' Pss. 20 and 21, due to its positioning and formulation. These twin psalms are prayers for the king going to war, or returning victorious (Braulik 1995: 66). According to Millard (1994: 166), twin psalms are always situated at the editorial beginning, middle and end positions of compositions. Ps. 18, together with Pss. 20 and 21, belongs at the centre of the group formed by Pss. 15-24. These psalms frame the Torah hymn, Ps. 19 (Braulik 1995: 66).

Ps. 19 shows various thematic similarities with the psalm group 15–24. The praise of the Torah forms a link between the various themes in the psalm group, one of which is the way of the righteous and of a righteous king. The cosmic order represented by the course of the sun (Ps. 19.2-7) is reflected in the ethical order which the Torah teaches (Ps. 19.8-12) (Schuman 2002: 39). The thematic relationship between Pss. 18 and 19 can be described as follows: the servant of Yahweh (Pss. 18.1; 19.12, 14), perfection (Pss. 18.24, 26; 19.14); protection from debt (Pss. 18.24; 19.14). Keywords such as 'orders' (9b) and 'legal verdicts' (10c) are also found in Ps. 18.21, 25.

Ps. 19.12-15 forms a concise parallel with Ps. 18.26-32 (Arneth 2000: 101–102, note 56). An analogy of the law of reprisal in Ps. 18.26 *et seq.* can be found in Ps. 19.12. Wisdom terminology is also present in Ps. 19.8-11. The consecration 'my Rock' takes up the verdict of trust of Ps. 18.3, 47 (Hossfeld 1993: 130).

Arneth (2000: 101–103) has argued that Ps. 19 was not included as an expansion of Ps. 18.26-32 in the psalm collection 15–24, as concluded by Hossfeld (Hossfeld & Zenger 1993: 130). Arneth says that Ps. 18, which is already linked in 2 Sam. 22 to 2 Sam. 23.1-7, was available to the psalmist. The correlation between Ps. 19 and 2 Sam. 23 is as follows:

2 Sam. 23.1b and Ps. 19.5b-7.
2 Sam. 23.2a, 3a and Ps. 19.2-5a.
2 Sam. 23.3b, 4 and Ps. 19.9b-10.
2 Sam. 23.5-7 and Ps. 19.12-14.

Ps. 19's dependence on 2 Sam. 23.1-7 is another argument for the literary unity of the psalm. The direction of reception between Ps. 19 and 2 Sam. 23.1-7 is clear: Ps. 19 is the receiver and 2 Sam. 23 is the donor (Arneth 2000: 109). Therefore Ps. 19's dependence on 2 Sam. 23.1-7 should not be seen to suppress the individual voice and theopoetry of Ps. 19.

Arneth's argument for the dependence of Ps. 19 on 2 Sam. 23.1-7 does not discount its numerous thematic links with the psalms in the group 15–24.

Ps. 19 ends with a prayer (Ps. 19.13-15). The concept of the king representing the ethical order is not unfamiliar in the Oriental worldview. He personifies divine right and divine justice in society (cf. Ps. 72) (Schuman 2002: 39). The law-abiding intercessor for the poor in Israel in Ps. 18 is also the supplicant of Ps. 19, who acknowledges God's ordinances in Creation and in the Torah.

The word 'servant' is mentioned 38 times in the psalms, with 14 mentions in the Torah Ps. 119. An excellent servant of God is the supplicant who does not stray from the Torah (Berges 1999: 22). According to Ps. 18, the anointed of Ps. 20.6b, 7, whose prayer will be heard, are also the Torah-devout servants of Yahweh in Ps. 19 (Hossfeld & Zenger 1993: 130).

4. *Interpretation*

Ps. 19 is an exceptional poem; on the one hand, its poetic beauty entrances the reader, but on the other hand, the reader is concerned about its interpretation (Potgieter 1991: 106). The interpretation is made difficult due to the seemingly irreconcilable differences presented by the nature psalm (lines 2–7) and the Torah psalm (lines 8–15) (Potgieter 1991: 106; Zenger 1997: 191). Hence, the unity of this poem must be questioned. Is it a unit, or is it made up of two separate poems, which were later combined? Both these views can be found in the literature of the exegesis of the Psalter.

Exegetes like Morgenstern (1945: 506–507), Weiser (1962: 197), Van der Ploeg (1971: 134), Steck (1980) Petersen (1982: 85) and Knierim (1991: 439–458) postulate that Ps. 19 originally consisted of two independent poems. According to this view, the first part (verses 2-7) was an original sun-hymn, which in time grew with the addition of part B (verses 8-11) and part C (verses 12-15). Zenger (1997: 191) also supports the view that there was a shorter psalm, which celebrated the Torah as the 'sun of life' (verses 2-11). Other contributions made the psalm a prayer, i.e.: an offering to Yahweh. Many other exegetes regard the poem as a single composition (Clines 1974: 12–13; Gese 1982: 7; Deissler 1966; Dohmen 1983; Meinhold 1983: 12; Glass 1987: 147–159; Spieckermann 1989: 67–68; Potgieter 1991: 106; Hossfeld 1993: 128–129; Mays 1994: 97; Wagner 1999; Arneth 2000: 108–109).

Apart from the question of whether a poem consists of two parts, or one, there is the question of intertextuality. Intertextuality can be distinguished on numerous levels: there is intertextuality in the psalm group 15–24 and it is also claimed that inter-textuality exists in the Old Testament canon (cf. 2 Sam. 23.1–7). A third distinction is concerned with the degree to which a poem corresponds with the ancient Eastern texts and cultic patterns. These points are all considered in a liturgical, theopoetical analysis.

When interpreting Ps. 19, we do not consider the literary aspects separately and only then examine the theopoetical result. We look at the text as at a living body – the bone structure forms the literary part, while life-giving blood is the theopoetical part.

In general, it is accepted that the poem can be divided into two main parts, namely verses 2-7 and 8-15 (Kraus 1978: 298–299; cf. Spieckermann 1989: 61). Zenger (1997: 189, 191); Hossfeld (1993: 128); Seybold (1996: 85) and Arneth (2000: 92) distinguish a tripartite. Lines 2–7 and 8–11 have unity, but in terms of the third stanza, academics differ slightly. According to Hossfeld (1993: 128) and Zenger (1997: 189), the last stanza, (verses 12-14), forms a whole, while verse 15 serves as a concluding directive. However, Potgieter (1991: 108); Seybold (1996: 85); Arneth (2000: 92) and Kruger (2002: 113–115) are of the opinion that verses 12-15 form a whole.

Ps. 19 can be divided into three stanzas. Each of these has three subdivisions. The coherence between the various stanzas can be schematized as follows (Potgieter 1991: 108):

Stanza		Subdivision
I The nature and God.	A(2-3)	The heavens declare.
	B (4-5)	The earth resounds.
	C (6-7)	The place of the sun.
II The law of the Lord.	D (8-9b)	The law is perfect.
	E (9c-10)	The statutes of the Lord are right.
	F (11)	The law is precious.
III Man and God.	G (12-13)	Hidden trespasses.
	H (14)	Presumptuous sins.
	I (15)	Man's songs of praise.

This structural analysis is based on considerations of formality and content. Formal criteria are chiefly based on the morphological and syntactical combinations. What makes the above structure especially remarkable is the consistent pattern of the units, which are repeated in all three stanzas. While the first two units of each stanza show a parallel build-up, the pattern of the third unit differs in many respects from that of the preceding units (Potgieter 1991: 108. Cf. also Kruger's (2002: 113–117) colometrical division).

In the first stanza, the first two units consist of two distichal lines. In contrast, the third unit starts with a monostich. This is followed by a distich, which ends in a tristich. The first two units of the central stanzas build up to a climax in the same way; they both consist of three distichal lines with a parallel, syntactical pattern. This similarity is strengthened by a consequent 3–2 metrical pattern. The first two patterns of the last stanza both begin with the particle *gam* and both consist of two distichal lines.

In his analysis of a song by Assurbanipal (669–630 BCE) for the sun god, Arneth (2000: 84, 90) came to certain conclusions. According to him, a comparison between Ps. 19 and KAR III,105 is not aimed at demonstrating a literary dependence between the two texts, but rather at finding literary technical patterns in KAR III,105 that could clarify Ps. 19 and also shed light on the composition of Ps. 19. The Šamaš song (KAR III,105) is composed in three parts. The Šamaš and Assurbanipal parts have a parallel construction. In spite of the parallel ordering of the benedictory and maledictory sayings, the chiastic composition of the conclusion is the focal point. The parallel arrangement of the passage KAR III,105, the Šamaš and Assurbanipal parts, is repeated in reverse in the concluding benedictory and maledictory series. A similar structure is found in Ps. 19.2-7, 8-11 and 12-15 (Arneth 2000: 108, note 72).

The following chiastic construction of lines 2-7a can be observed (Arneth 2000: 95–96):

A verse 2   2 nominal sentences (chiasmus).
B verse 3   2 reversed syntactical sentences. Predicate Imperfect.
C verse 5a   2 reversed syntactical sentences. Predicate Perfect.
C' verse 5b   1 reversed syntactical sentence. Predicate Perfect.
B' verse 6   1 reversed syntactical sentence. Predicate Imperfect.
A' verse 7a   2 nominal sentences (chiasmus).

Certain textual links occur in the structure of verses 2-7. There is a link between verse 2 and verse 5b, as well as between verse 5a and verse 7a. This is the basis for the parallel that develops between the text blocks formed by verses 2-5a and 5-7a. Verse 3 and verse 6 were included in the context, but it is significant that verse 4 was not (Arneth 2000: 94–95).

A further pattern that can be found in the structure of the poem is the similarity between the third units of the various stanzas. In verses 6-7 of stanza 1, a double comparison is used to describe the activity of the sun. Verse 6 compares the rising of the sun to a bridegroom's arrival and also to the arrival of a hero. Similarly a double comparison is also made in verse 11 of stanza II to describe the quality of God's instructions. To stress their value, they are likened to gold and honey.

This construction is used, where the preposition *min* has also been used in conjunction with the subsequent noun to form the comparative. This is unlike verses 6-7, where only the preposition k^e is used to make the comparison possible. Verse 15, as the third unit of stanza III, conforms to this pattern, when a metaphor concludes the poem (Potgieter 1991: 108). The third units of the various stanzas show a similarity in the use of the comparison. The comparisons are applied in an ascending line, culminating in the metaphor in the last stanza (Potgieter 1991: 108).

Verses 2-7, as well as verses 12-14 exhibit an astoundingly identical, climactic pattern by means of the compositional parallelism. The words 'and there is nothing hidden from its heat' (verse 7c) is thematically bound to the expression 'and may the meditation of my heart be acceptable in your sight'. The threads of the text also weave verse 7c and 13b together with the word 'hidden' (Arneth 2000: 107) and herewith the image of the sun radiates through the poem. In verse 7c nothing is hidden from the glow of the sun and in verse 13b, Yahweh is implored to free the supplicant from that which is hidden from him. Therefore, Yahweh's exoneration brings that which is hidden in the dark, out into the light.

Stanza 1 (verses 2-7) and stanza 2 (verses 8-11) have a parallel structure in the sense in that the second part (verses 5b-7; verses 9b-10) is illuminated by the image of the sun. This is not the case in the first subdivisions (verses 2-5a, verses 8-9a) (Arneth 2000: 107). In the third stanza (verses 12-14), verse 12a refers to the image of the sun (Arneth 2000: 107). The arrangement, however, is exactly reversed: verse 12a refers to verses 5b-7 and verses 9b-10, while verse 14 correlates with verse 8 (Arneth 2000: 107–108). This poetic interweaving unifies the poem on both a compositional and a literary level.

In verses 2-7, concepts of communication like 'message', 'knowledge', 'words' and 'voice' appeal to human insight and acoustic perceptions. In verses 8-11, however, varying concepts are used for the divine Torah and the appeal is directed chiefly at the human will. Legal concepts like *dābār* (word) and *'imrā* (pronouncement), which overlap with the first group are avoided (Hossfeld 1993: 129).

The three stanzas (verses 2-7, 8-11, 12-15) are introduced by a theme word: verse 2 – glory = the prevalent works of God in his Creation; verse 8 – Torah = teachings of the God of Israel; verse 12 – 'your servant' = living under the rule of the reigning Yahweh (Zenger 1997: 191).

In this psalm, as in the other psalms, the primary subject is the relationship between God and mankind. However, unlike in other psalms, it is only in the last line that God is addressed in person or the relationship between God and mankind is mentioned. In some of the other psalms, either God is praised for his salvation, or the misery of the human condition is lamented. Ps. 19, however, is distinguishable from the other psalms, in that human need and human praise are very subtly expressed and then only at the end of the poem (Potgieter 1991: 109). Although God is praised throughout the psalm, this praise is derived from other sources, namely nature and the Torah, by which mankind comes to know God and self.

It is usually surmised that heaven and the sun sing God's praises in the first stanza (verses 2-7) (cf. Ps. 148.1-5). However, according to Zenger (1997: 192), these lines really reflect a sense of 'knowing' on the part of heaven and the sun, as well as their perpetual testimony. This testimony is chiefly directed at mankind 'living under the sun'. The content of this message could be formulated from Ps. 148.6: 'He (God) has established for them (the firmament and the sun) a decree (law) that will never pass away.' It is this dispensation and these life-rhythms that are decisive for creation. This is summarised in Gen. 8:22:

> As long as the earth endures,
> seedtime and harvest,
> cold and heat,
> summer and winter,

day and night
will never cease.

It is into this basic order that the existence of Israel is interposed (cf. Jer. 31.35 *et seq.*). The same creations of God, namely heaven/sky, day/night and earth/ground, made in the first three days according to Gen. 1, are also described in the first two stanzas of Ps. 19. However, they are not arranged in the same order (Potgieter 1991: 109). The Creation itself is not the main focus of the poem; instead its function and its witnesses are described. According to Dohmen (1983: 505), the first two lines of the stanza function as the introduction and the heading. This parallelism, which has a chiastic arrangement, describes how the heavens declare God's glory (Van der Ploeg 1971: 136; Kraus 1978: 300; Spieckermann 1989: 62–63). To quote Spieckermann (1989: 63): the Creation is God's glory, his doxology. Through the use of the literary strategy of chiasmus, one of the main themes of the poem, namely the praising of God, is brought to the fore:

The heavens declare the glory of God,
the skies proclaim the work of his hands.

The subjects are placed at the sides, the verbs directly next to them, with the topic of praising God in the centre (Kruger 2002: 117). The question is, whether the *nomen rectum 'ēl* in the genitive construction *'glory of El'* should be seen as a common noun or a proper noun. As a proper noun it would refer to the Canaanite god *El*, being honoured, as God is honoured in Ps. 29.1-9. As a common noun, it would refer to the Creator, God, which implies monotheism as it appears in Isa. 40.18; 43.12 and 45.22 (Hossfeld 1993: 132). Due to the psalm being placed within the context of the Creation, makes me inclined to choose the argument for the common noun.

The introductory *Stichwort* 'heaven' is repeated in verse 7. This creates an *inclusio*, which frames verses 2-7 to form a whole (Arneth 2000: 93). Verse 7a is arranged chiastically, exactly as verse 2. Heaven is the highest expanse over the globe and the place of the enthroned presence of God (Hossfeld 1993: 132). The hymn in praise of heaven is directed at God who is represented in Zion and whose radiance reaches all lands (Isa. 6.3). Just as the royal court and the royal garments represent the glory of a king, so the whole of Creation represents the glory of God (Van der Ploeg 1971: 136).

Heaven is defined by the parallel concept, firmament. The firmament is the place that separates the ocean from the sky and thereby creates a space in between, for living creatures to exist. The application of this concept relates to exilic and post-exilic literature (Ezek. 1.22 *et seq.;* 10.1; Gen. 1; Ps. 150.1; Dan. 12.3 and *Sir.* 43.8) (Hossfeld 1993: 132). The proclamation of the heaven and the firmament is vaguely paralleled in Pss. 50.6; 97.6, which proclaims divine justice, as well as in Job 12.7-9, where the whole animal world announces its creation (Hossfeld 1993: 132). The firmament (Gen. 1.7 *et seq.*) proclaims the 'works of his hands' (Ps. 8.4) (Van der Ploeg 1971: 135; Kraus 1978: 300; Seybold 1996: 86).

Verses 3-5 repeatedly describe an aspect of this glory, this power. The spatial dimension of the world is mentioned (verse 2), followed by the temporal dimension. At first it is declared that this proclamation of God's glory takes place unceasingly, by day and by night. The New Afrikaans Bible translation of the Hebrew word *nb'* to mean 'to report a message', is neutral, while the root word has a nuance of bubbling and frothing (cf. Prov. 8.4, where it is used in connection with water) (Kruger 2002: 114). According to Kraus (1978: 300), the meaning of the Hebrew verb is to bubble, sparkle, or tingle and implies animated and excited speech. Verse 3 (Eng. 19.2) may be translated as follows:

> In mounting excitement one day passes the message on to the next. One
> night imparts knowledge to the next (Kruger 2002: 114).

The verb 'to impart knowledge' can mean to make known (Ezek. 15.17; 32.6, 10, 17; 36.2) and this is also a reference to trust i.e.: of a priest (Hos. 4.1; 6.6) (Kraus 1978: 300). The message that passes from one day to the next, the knowledge communicated from one night to the next can be likened to two choirs singing alternately (Nötscher). Verse 4 of the first stanza continues as follows:

> They have no speech, there are no words;
> no sound is heard from them (Eng. 19.3).

Verse 4 is exceptional. It does not merge smoothly into the whole (Spieckermann 1989: 64, note 10). Furthermore, it does not fit the chiastic pattern of verses 2-7. Its construction also differs from the context in which it is placed (verses 2, 3, 5a). Verse 4 deviates from binary parallelisms and consists of either three nominal sentences, or two nominal sentences and a relative sentence (without *'šr*) (Arneth 2000: 95). The verse also poses problems in terms of content. In verse 2 *et seq.*, the 'glorious message' (Spieckermann 1989: 62) of the heavens, the firmament, day and night, is introduced. Verse 4 interrupts this chain of thought, in that the execution of the announcement becomes thematic, i.e.: the presence of speech and language, as well as the audibility of the heavenly voices is opposed.

Verse 5a links up with verse 3, without verse 4 being of any significance (Arneth 2000: 95), making it possible that verse 4 was a later interpolation (Arneth 2000: 95). In poetry, it is customary for logical and linguistic patterns to be penetrated to open up new, surprising insights. The function of verse 4 may be to serve as a counterbalance and a preparation for verse 8 *et seq.*, where the Torah takes centre stage (Arneth 2000: 95).

The tidings and the knowledge disclosed by the heavenly bodies cannot be heard (Westermann 1984: 179). This inaudibility (Ps. 19.4) points to the autogenous analogy and mysterious witness of heaven and the firmament, which rises far above man (Van Uchelen 1971: 131, 135; Kraus 1978: 302; Hossfeld 1993: 132; Mays 1994: 97; Seybold 1996: 86). There is also another way to explain verse 4: the inaudibility of the heavenly bodies could indicate that mankind is deaf to the polyphony of their voices. Verse 5a-5b explains the spatial magnitude of the announcement of glory.

On a text-critical level the reading of *qawwām* in line 5a is a problem, because the normal lexical meaning of *qāw*, namely measuring-rod or measuring-line, does not make sense within the parallelism. Either the word must have another lexical meaning, like speech or manner of speech, which fits in with the context, or a textual emendation should be made (Potgieter 1991: 107; Seybold 1996: 85). Most commentators prefer to change the text to *qôlām*, 'their voice or their sound', so that it corresponds to the Septuagint text, which fits well into the context (Dohmen 1983: 502 *et seq.*; Westermann 1984: 178; Spieckermann 1989: 60; Gese 1991: 142, note 142; Hossfeld 1993: 131; Seybold 1996: 85; Arneth 2000: 91; Kruger 2002: 115). The parallel in verse 4b requires the reading 'their voices' (Arneth 2000: 91). Van Zyl (1996: 142–144) concludes that *qāw* can also have the lexical meaning of speech and command. This possibility fits well into the context of the parallelism and therefore, verse 5a could be translated as follows:

Their voice goes out into all the earth,

and verse 5b follows:

their words to the ends of the world (Eng. 19.5ab).

There is an apparent contradiction between verses 4ab and 5ab. In verse 4ab the 'non-acoustic' character of the praise of Creation is mentioned, while verse 5ab stresses its audibility. Gese (1982: 3) declares this poetic contradiction to be typical of the wisdom genre (Kruger 2002: 115). Everything does not always add up in poetry; there is always space for the irreconcilable and the contradictory.

It has often been pointed out that Ps. 19.5b-7 and also Ps. 19.8-15 fall within the traditional, historical, Mesopotamian context (Spieckermann 1989: 66–67; Arneth 2000: 82–83). In the late pre-exilic times a parallel was already being drawn between Yahweh and the heavenly bodies (Arneth 2000: 82). After discussing the aspects of time and space in relation to the proclamation, the poet focuses on the sun as a creation of God, in verses 5-6 of stanza 1. Verse 5c reads:

> In the heavens he has pitched a tent for the sun (Eng. 19.4c).

The sun as a 'tent in the heavens' is also found in Assyrian-Babylonian texts (Arneth 2000: 83).

The firmament is made of light from which, God weaves a tent for the sun (Hossfeld 1993: 183) (cf. Isa. 40.21 *et seq.;* 42.5; 44.24; 45.12; 51.13; Jer. 10.12; Zech. 12.1; Job 9.8; Ps. 104.2). In verse 6a, the tent metaphor becomes a bedchamber metaphor, as this is the place from which the sun rises at daybreak. 'Therein' refers to the heaven/firmament (verse 2) (Spieckermann 1989: 63–64). In this manner, a logical bond is created between stanza 1 (verses 2-5b) and stanza 2 (verses 5c-9), in which the sun is the theme (Kruger 2002: 113). The sun has been given a fixed abode and a specific function in the heavens that proclaim God's glory. It rises on the side of the heavens and sets on the other side (verse 7ab). The sun illuminates the entire world; it comes forth like a bridegroom from his bedchamber. The description of the sun as a bridegroom possibly refers back to the description of *Šamaš's* wife *Aja* as 'his beloved bride' (Arneth 2000: 83; Spieckermann 1989: 60, 66–67, footnote 19). Like a hero (Van der Ploeg 1971: 138), hastening to his destination, the sun hastens to its task (Zenger 1997: 193; Arneth 2000: 95). In the Assyrian-Babylonian world, the sun was regarded as a hero/warrior (Arneth 2000: 82–83).

Hence, the sun becomes imagery for God, as it too, is life-giving and life-supporting. There are conspicuous similarities to the sun god in Mesopotamia and Egypt, who was the protector of justice, a lawgiver, judge, rescuer and avenger (Spieckermann 1989: 66–67; Hossfeld 1993: 133; Koch 1993; Hutter 1996: 43–44; Zenger 1997: 193; Seidel and Schultz 2001). The judicial function of the sun god is strikingly described in the *Šamaš* hymn (cf. Hutter 1996: 62). The characteristics of a judge are ascribed to *Šamaš* by the morality element of Babylonian theology. No sin can be concealed from him and he is the champion of those who determine right and righteousness (Hutter 1996: 62). The epiphany of the sun is not only evident in its physical changes, but also in the victorious transition from chaos (darkness, calamity, death and the underworld) to the cosmos (clarity, bliss, life and the world of the living) (Hossfeld 1993: 133). The sun drives the darkness away; the time of anxiety and chaos comes to an end. The sun's rays penetrate everything and illuminate both the good and the bad (Zenger 1997: 193–194). Nothing is hidden from its light (verse 7c; cf. *Sir.* 43.1-5) (Seybold 1996: 87).

As in Gen. 1, the sun is described as one of the great lights created by God. It is placed on a fixed course and has a task to perform. God is glorified by the deeds that he performs, which set an example and allow mankind to know God and themselves better (Spieckermann 1989: 66; Potgieter 1991: 110).

In terms of the internal structure of verses 8-11, Arneth (2000: 96–97) has commented as follows: in verse 9a (commands), as in verse 10b (judgments), the nouns, which represent Yahweh's ordination, are in the plural. In verse 8, verse 9b and verse 10a the singular is used. The structure of verses 8-11 can therefore be represented as follows:

Verse 8a	Singular: the law of Yahweh.
Verse 8c	Singular: the testimony of Yahweh.
Verse 9a	Plural: the statutes of Yahweh.
Verse 9c	Singular: the commandment of Yahweh.
Verse 10a	Singular: the fear of Yahweh.
Verse 10c	Plural: the judgments of Yahweh.
Verse 11	Conclusion.

Verses 8-11 cover the parts, which consist of three stiches each, in which sayings of Yahweh are discussed. This pattern can also be seen in the composition of verses 2-7a. This unit may be divided into two sections: verses 2-3; verse 5a, verses 5b-7a. Both sections contain three stichoi. The second subsection, verses 9b-10, which forms a parallel to verses 5b-7a, begins in verse 9c with lexemes, which also reflect the image of the sun (Arneth 2000: 97):

> The commands of the Lord are radiant,
> giving light to the eyes (Eng. 19.8c).

The king's function of dispensing justice appears in KAR III,105, as well as in Ps. 19. Just as the sun god was the guardian of the cosmic order, the Assyrian king as a representative of that order had the same function. He was responsible for dispensing justice on his subjects, e.g.: '... he protected his subjects that you entrusted to him, in justice' (line 14 – reverse line 3). Also, '... in abundance and in justice he protects the subjects of Enlil' (line 14 – reverse line 7). In Ps. 19 the king's function of meting out justice is transferred to the Torah (Arneth 2000: 109).

Arneth (2000: 83) points out that the relationship between Yahweh and the sun is not central to the psalm – the king's function to dispense judgment and justice is more prominent (2 Sam. 8.15). The king's right of admission to the Godhead stems from this.

In the 19th century, Hengstenberg (1842: 435) pointed out that the focus on the sun in verses 5c-7, immediately before verses 8-11, infers that the Torah also functions like the sun (cf. the predicates sublime, pure, exalting, illuminating). Everything said about the sun in verses 2-7 also pertains to

the Torah (Van Uchelen 1971: 132). The Torah is the beloved bridegroom
of Israel, the warrior victorious over evil and the judge who reveals all
(Zenger 1997: 194).

Arneth (2000: 97 *et seq.*) points out that the sun symbol, which
elucidates verse 9c and d is also mentioned in 2 Sam. 23.3. There it relates
to the rule of the king (cf. KAR III,105 and the prologue to the so-called
Codex of Hammurabi). We find related expressions, parallels and certain
identical words in Ps. 19 and 2 Sam. 23 (Arneth 2000: 98–102).
Considering that Ps. 19 relies heavily on 2 Sam. 23, we find that the
classic royal function, namely the dispensing of judgment and justice in Ps.
19 is ascribed to the Torah of Yahweh (Arneth 2000: 102; Otto 2000: 208).

Verse 8 of strophe II begins with a construct construction, with Yahweh
as *nomen rectum*. This pattern is then repeated six times, where the *nomen
regens* varies, but the *nomen rectum* is stressed (Arneth 2000: 96). This
variation serves to focus on an attribute, which varies repeatedly (cf. the
relationship to Ps. 119). It is not by chance that the theme is placed in the
centre of the poem, i.e.: between verses 2-7 and 12-15. Verses 8-9b and 9c-
10 give a series of three parallel views, which describe the character and
essential features of God's ordinances and their effects on mankind.

The third ordinance of the two units deviates repeatedly from the
grammatical pattern of the two preceding ordinances, by replacing the
feminine singular with the masculine plurals. Furthermore, the previous
two specific statements are consolidated into a more general statement
(Potgieter 1991: 110; cf. also Kruger 2002: 118). When, for example, we are
told in the first two statements, that the law of Yahweh is perfect and
trustworthy, the third statement provides confirmation: the precepts of
Yahweh are right. Similarly, the first two statements of the following
series, namely that the commands of Yahweh are pure and virtuous, are
confirmed as the truth.

If one accepts the unified composition of the psalm, the hermeneutic key
is a theology of wisdom, with which the Torah is also regarded and which
is in keeping with the order of Creation. If we accept this frame of
reference, it becomes clear why the poet prays for order in his own life
(verses 12-15), at the end of the poem (Kruger 2002: 119).

The ordinance of God is perfect. Kraus (1978: 304–305) rightly contends
that the traditional translation of Torah as law implies rigidity. However,
Torah also implies 'indicator for life' (Kruger 2002: 113), or 'prescription'
(Hossfeld 1993: 133) and functions as a mediator in specific instances
between God's Word and his teaching of the priests (cf. Hag. 2.11 *et seq.*;
Hab. 1.4; Isa. 2.3) (Seybold 1996: 87). This concept is found especially in
Deuteronomy (cf. Otto 2000). The word 'perfect' comes from sacrificial
terminology. The faultless and pure animal is called 'perfect' and describes
the *sufficientia* of the Torah (Kraus 1978: 305). In verses 8 *et seq.* the
supplicant is the beneficiary of the blissful workings of the Torah

(Spieckermann 1989: 71). The result of the Torah is that it revitalises life, restores strength and makes a new life possible (Seybold 1996: 87). The Torah is bound to wisdom in a twofold manner: like wisdom, it appeals to one's total being and all of one's understanding, will and vitality. This effect also pertains to the entity: wisdom and Torah become identical (Hossfeld 1993: 134).

Different words are used to describe and explain the wealth of the Torah. The word '*ēdût* (witness), i.e.: law, is a central concept in the priestly literature, which describes the similarity between Yahweh and his people (Hossfeld 1993: 133). It also suggests an ordinance, which has the force of a statute (cf. the so-called royal protocol, Ps. 2; 81.6; 122.4; 132.12; Exod. 25.16 *et seq.*) (Seybold 1996: 87). The testimony of the Lord is trustworthy. It gives wisdom to the inexperienced person who is easily led astray (Prov. 1.22; 7.7; 9.6; 19.25; 21.11; Ps. 119.130). Orders, *piqqûdîm*, suggest the authority of the lawgiver (Hossfeld 1993: 133). In this instance, the subject appears to take the form of concrete directions and stipulations (cf. Pss. 103.18; 111.17; 119) (Seybold 1996: 87).

The commandments of the Lord are righteous; they gladden the heart. Commandment, *miswā*, describes the separate commandments, but also the entirety of the law (cf. Deut. 6. 25; Exod. 24. 12; Ps. 119. 96) (Hossfeld 1993: 133). The commandments of the Lord are radiant and they illuminate the eyes. The word 'radiant' is a further link between the first and second parts of the poem. This is because 'radiant,' which is used elsewhere in connection with the sun (cf. Song 6.10: 'radiant as the sun') is a reference here, to the Torah (Fisch 1990: 122). The expression '(t)he commandments of the Lord are radiant, giving light to the eyes', means that they grant new vigour to ones sight (Kraus 1978: 306). When a person is ill, his eyes are dull; when he is healthy his eyes are clear (cf. 1 Sam. 14.27).

Verse 8 starts, as was pointed out previously, with a *constructus* nexus, in which Yahweh forms the *nomen rectum*. This pattern is repeated in the following sections, where the *nomen regens* varies, but the *nomen rectum*, in contrast, is stressed. In verse 10a there is a deviation from this scheme (Arneth 2000: 96). The relationships are turned around in the first half stich. The accent is now on the fear of the Lord (the worship of Yahweh and his glory) which the Lord expects (Kruger 2002: 116). The fear of Yahweh is pure (evident), it holds steadfast, for ever. It is wisdom (cf. Prov. 1.7; 9.10) (Hossfeld 1993: 133). The fear of the Lord which holds 'steadfast for ever' alludes to the performance of the heavenly bodies and the light of Creation (cf. Ps. 33.9 where the same root, '*āmad*, is used in this connection) (Fisch 1990: 122). The *mišpātîm* (the law of judgments, the legal adages and the verdicts) point to the authority of the judgments (Hossfeld 1993: 133; Seybold 1996: 87). The judgments of the Lord are true; all of them are righteous. They rectify, direct, i.e.: they establish order (Seybold 1996: 88).

These decrees are from God, they derive characteristics from him. It is also true, that God is perfect, trustworthy and pure (Potgieter 1991: 110). Furthermore, all these characteristics belong to the semantic category of morality and affirm that God expects mankind to be morally correct (Potgieter 1991: 110). The third unit, (verse 11), ends this second strophe with a double comparison, in which a value judgment is pronounced on God's commandments. The final conclusion is that these commandments are valuable to mankind (Potgieter 1991: 110). The Torah is more precious than anything yearned for, by the ancient civilisations of the Orient. (Gold was the wealth of kings, honey was the food of the gods and the dessert at a banquet) (Zenger 1997: 194).

The concluding third unit, like verses 2-7 and verses 8-11, is divided into two parts, which are introduced by *gam* (verses 12, 14). Both units, verses 12-13 and verse 14, correspond to an identical lexeme, followed up in series: first a servant is mentioned (verses 12, 14a) and in the following stich, the root *nqh* (exoneration) is used – verse 13, verse 14d. Verse 15 forms the conclusion (Arneth 2000: 104).

The following pattern can be distinguished in verses 12-15 (Arneth 2000: 104):

Verse 12a	Further
Verse 12a	Servant
Verse 13a	Exonerate
Verse 14a	Even more
Verse 14a	Servant
Verse 14d	Be free
Verse 15	Conclusion

The following chiastic pattern can be distinguished in verses 12-14 (Arneth 2000: 105):

A	12ab
B	13ab
B'	14ab
A'	14cd

According to Seybold (1996: 85–86), the third strophe (verses 12-15) offers the key to the comprehension of the finely composed text. This is as far as the components A (verses 2-7) and B (verses 8-11) occur as citations from the lips of the supplicant of verse 12 *et seq.* (cf. verse 15a). In his exegesis, Seybold says, that the creation hymn (verses 2-7) and the Torah of Yahweh (verses 8-11) have been prepared with a view to a prayer of petition (cf. verse 7b and verse 12 *et seq.*, verse 10ab and verse 14 *et seq.*). This becomes especially clear in verse 11, with the focus on the *mišpāṭîm*. In verse 12 *et seq.*, the poet pins his hopes on the promise (Seybold 1996: 86).

The third strophe formally distinguishes itself from the previous sections in terms of its subject matter. For the first time, Yahweh is addressed in prayer (verses 12, 14, 15) and the supplicant is introduced as the 'servant of Yahweh' (verses 12, 14). The focus of the Torah piety also changes: the Torah promises a rich reward, but warns that the pious should not be dominated by 'intentional sins', as the Torah is not their sole protector anymore – Yahweh will forgive all their hidden sins (Hossfeld 1993: 130; cf. also Seybold 1996: 86).

In contrast to the consistent use of the singular, which occurs from Ps. 18.1 to Ps. 144.10, the servants are nearly always mentioned in the plural, in the concluding part of the fifth Book of Psalms (Pss. 107-150) (Berges 1999: 22). The singular 'your servant' in strophe III (verses 12-15), expresses the fact that the poet is personally involved in the events. The personal tone of the poem is apparent from the fact that the poet twice refers to himself as 'your servant' (verses 12a and 14a).

In two closely structured units (verses 12-13 and 14), the elements of which are arranged chiastically, mankind's conduct is tested in the light of God's commands. This is done in two ways. Firstly, a statement is made, confirming that the burden of human life becomes lighter when the commands are followed. The verb *zhr* in verse 12 can be translated as 'warn' or 'lighten'. The root *zhr* occurs in Ezek. 8.2 and Dan. 12.3, meaning 'lustre' (Kruger 2002: 116).The announcement that following the commands lightens mankind's path on earth, establishes a relationship between the light of the sun and the illuminating commands of the Torah (Fisch 1990: 122). Secondly, it is petitioned that God pardons hidden transgressions (Potgieter 1991: 110).

Obeying the commands of the Torah will be richly rewarded. According to Prov. 22.4 this means wealth, honour and life (Hossfeld 1993: 134). Those who have been pardoned find that life brings 'great rewards', i.e.: happiness for others, as well as themselves (Zenger 1997: 192). In verse 13, there is a reference to 'unwitting wrongdoing,' i.e.: sins that the supplicant is not aware of having committed. Behind verse 13, we can discern the priestly theology of sin, which differentiates between conscious and unconscious transgressions (Lev. 4.13; Num. 15.22; cf. Pss. 119.21, 118) (Hossfeld 1993: 134).

In the Babylonian text collection *Surpu*, reference is made to the Babylonians' consciousness of sin. The *Surpu* deals with the unconscious transgressions, which place mankind under the 'curse' of the gods. This leads to mankind's forfeiting communion with the gods, with the result that his life is threatened (Hutter 1996: 62–63). After the question, 'who can discern his errors?' follows a prayer asking for forgiveness of unconscious transgressions. The sun metaphor also illuminates the double use of the root *str* ('hidden') in verse 7c ('nothing is hidden from its heat'), verse 13b ('(f)orgive my hidden faults', literally meaning, exonerate me from that which is hidden). Also illuminated is the Torah, from which nothing is hidden and which brings everything to light (Fisch 1990: 123). As nothing can be concealed from the heat of the sun, likewise no transgression can be hidden from God's Torah.

In the next unit (verse 14), the elements are interchanged and the request that mankind be restrained from committing arrogant deeds is put first. Then follows the statement that he will be free from sin and immaculate (Potgieter 1991: 110). In the light of the co-text, this verse does not mean that the poet is praying that arrogant people be kept away from him (Kruger 2002: 116). Unlike other psalms, the poet's need is not physical, i.e.: threat from illness, or the enemy. His need comes from a moral level and is concerned with his transgressions against God (Potgieter 1991: 110; Seybold 1996: 88). The poet's transgressions might have been committed unknowingly, or unintentionally and for these reasons, were concealed. Alternatively, if they were intentional, they would have sprung from human pride when in direct confrontation with God (Potgieter 1991: 110). The lexeme, *rāb,* occurs in verse 12b and also in verse 14d. This forms a frame for verses 12-14 (Arneth 2000: 104–105). The lexeme also has another function. It creates tension between the 'great reward' and the 'great sin'. The Torah resolves the tension. It offers the 'great reward', while the Giver of the Torah accomplishes liberation from 'great sin'.

After the poet has made his distress known to God and begged for forgiveness, his hymn of praise is rendered in the form of a consecration, in the last unit of strophe III (verse 15) (Zenger 1997: 194). The poet uses statements from sacrificial language ('acceptable' and 'in your sight') and ends the psalm giving thanks and immolation to God (Hossfeld 1993: 134; Zenger 1997: 195). 'To be acceptable' is a technical term for suitable offerings to God in his sanctuary. Sacrifices in the temple service were aimed at exoneration and correction (Lev. 4–5; Num. 15.22-31) (Mays 1994: 100).

A nexus is formed between verse 11, which ends the previous main section, and verse 15a, which forms part of the last section. In verse 11c and 11d, the judgments of Yahweh are said to be sweeter than honey and tasty on the tongue. In verse 15a, the poet asks that his words, refreshed by the Torah, be acceptable to God and this also pertains to his thoughts (literally: the thoughts of my heart) (cf. Prov. 15.28; 24.2; Pss. 1:2; 49:4). The sounds of the poet's words are like a colourful fountain from his mouth. In addition, the heart as the core of thought and life, is also the womb of words.

The offering of the life of Yahweh's servant is potentially a perfect sacrifice under the sun of the Torah. At the same time, the servant trusts in

God's gracious forgiveness, should he transgress against the Torah, as a result of human weakness or limitation (Zenger 1997: 194).

Even the metaphoric titles, 'My Rock and my Redeemer', with which the poet addresses God at the end of his poem, are respectively derived from nature and the judicial world (cf. the combination 'rock and redeemer' in Ps. 78.35). 'Rock' is at the centre of the chaos threatening Creation, and the 'redeemer' is at the centre of the enslaving forces of history. In Ps. 18.3, Yahweh is called a 'Rock'. 'Redeemer' is a word that comes from judicial language. The avenger of blood is named in Deut. 19.6 and the same word is used for the man who 'redeems' the family land in Ruth 2.20. In Deutero-Isaiah there is the suggestion that Yahweh has 'redeemed' Israel from exile (Isa. 41.14; 43.14). In Job 19.25 Job calls God his 'Redeemer', because he will deliver him from his misery. The poem is therefore linked with the last unit, both formally and in substance and has a climatic conclusion.

A literary theopoetical analysis reveals that the poem is a unit. The text, which is woven into a unit, is made up of many different threads. The poet's mastery is to be seen in the way in which he has used rhythm and imagery to create segments and then larger blocks of text. The result is a melodic and apparently effortless poem that fills us with delight. The psalm is woven like a many-coloured tapestry. This interweaving of various textual traditions lends colour and uniqueness to the poem. All these elements combine to serve the purpose of theopoetry.

5. *Bridging function of psalms*

In many ways the psalms fulfil a bridging function between divergent denominations, which previously avoided each other (Schuman 1995: 1). The psalms are songs, which have been given key positions in the Jewish and Christian traditions, in the Greek Orthodox and Western churches, in the Roman Catholic tradition and also in many of the reformed churches (Schuman 1998a: 374–375; Kaspar 1999: 96). The psalms bring together people from different worlds, traditions and periods (Vos 2001: 358).

6. *Influence of psalms on liturgy*

The psalms are more than liturgy and liturgy is comprised of more than merely psalms. Therefore, the psalms cannot simply be clothed in liturgical vestments. To distinguish the liturgical character of the psalms, different liturgical aspects should be considered.

The psalms have been spared from criticism, more than other parts of the Old Testament. A reason for this is that the psalms started to bear the stamp of the piety of the Church very early on and also belonged to the official liturgy of the Church (Zenger 1997: 15). Yet, there were objections to certain psalms, especially the 'vindictive psalms', a prime example of which is Ps. 137.

The Book of Psalms is the book in the Bible, which exerted the greatest influence on the liturgy, not only in Old Testament times, but also in the Jewish and Christian churches.

The early Church arose out of the psalms and hence, celebrated their liturgy (Schuman 1998: 172). This is illustrated by the place and function accorded to the psalms by one of the fathers of the Church, St. Augustine. It is significant, that the Scripture readings virtually always consist of three parts. Firstly, there is the recitation of a part of the Old Testament, or a part of the New Testament, which does not belong to the Gospel. A psalm and a Gospel reading then follows. The aforementioned format was, in earlier times, also upheld in the Synagogue – a psalm frequently followed a reading from the Torah. This was later abolished in the synagogues, because the psalms had been taken over by the Christians and given a messianic interpretation. However, the practice of reading psalms as a part of lectures remained with the Christian church (Van Oort 1991: 62).

The new interest in the liturgy prompted questions regarding the meaning and function of the psalms in the liturgy (Schuman 1998: 165; 1998a: 377–378; 2001: 250–252). In the *Ecumenical Protestant Churches* reference is made in the liturgy to 'the psalm for this Sunday', which usually determines the pattern of the service in terms of the liturgical theme for the year. This is then given out as the *proprium,* together with a specific text as a refrain and the 'prayer for the Sunday' (Schuman 1998: 166–167; Monshouwer 1998: 423–449).

The singing of the psalms in the church service always reminds us of the vigorous origins of Israel, Judaism, the Temple and the Synagogue (Barnard 1985: 66–102; Schuman 1998a: 375).

In 2001, a versification of all 150 psalms in Afrikaans was introduced (Liedboek van die Kerk 2001). This strengthened the influence of the psalms on the liturgy.

6.1 *Psalms as a prayer book and a reader*

Zenger (2003: VIII) is of the opinion that the 'ritual space' and the 'ritual time' of the psalms could constitute the cult, but that the psalms could also have come into being from outside the cult, by recitation and meditation. In the psalms, the cultic events take place on a three-dimensional level: the familiar/personal faith, the spatial and group religion, the state and national religion (i.e. religion in the home, the local sacred institutions and the empirical temple). We are dealing, then, with everyday cultic semiotics Zenger 2003: VIII).

The Psalms, as a book of religious poems and instruction, can be understood as a 'reader' and a book of meditation (Braulik 1995: 60; Zenger 1997: 34). The psalms are not a collection of individual or once-off prayers, but a collection of formulary texts, which serve as ritual prayers. The vitality of the psalms is seen in the fact that the poems are prayers (Westermann 1984: 11, 13, 19–21; Kaspar 1999: 96; Oeming 2002: 381–382). A multiple prayer collection, which is dependent on the presence of a good and merciful God, can be found in the psalms (Spieckermann 2003: 152). Different types of prayers appear in the psalms, e.g. laments, songs of praise and psalms of confidence, which are again moulded into various forms (Westermann 1984: 12). Laments and psalms of praise may be merged in the same psalms (compare Ps. 13). The psalms are increasingly seen as the book of prayer and meditation of the lesser people standing at a critical distance from the post-exilic temple aristocracy and their social eminence (Zenger 1998a: 323; Berges 1999: 15).

I would endorse the view that the scribes, priests and Levites played a decisive role in the composition of the Psalter (cf. Spieckermann 2003: 158). The tradition summarised the secrecy of the psalms as follows: 'Do not trust in miracles, but say the psalms' (Zenger 1997: 11). Those who say the psalms are in conversation with God, and those who pray the psalms and listen to their dictates are not only confronted by the realities of life, but are also 'sent' to life; the psalms are prophetic and apostolic prayers. Psalms transport those who pray into intrigue and politics, as well as into meditation and strife (Zenger 1997: 13; also compare Braulik 1995: 60–61).

Some are of the opinion that the psalms as so-called set prayer formularies standing in the way of creativity, spontaneity and imagination, but this is untrue. It is an illusion that humans are capable of always expressing their experiences, needs, troubles and longings, spontaneously and creatively. There are moments of desperation, dejection, fear and suffering when they are bereft of speech. In such circumstances the psalms can provide the words to express these feelings (Westermann 1984: 13–16; Zenger 1997: 14).

The psalms protect us from becoming boring and stereotypical in our needs. The psalms are a gift from God, teaching us to pray. Prayer means to search for words that would make sense in a specific situation. The psalms provide these words and make us a part of the event of prayer.

Psalms are like bread; one can argue about bread. It could be said that whole-wheat bread is healthier, but people have their own preferences. One can analyse bread, break it down into its chemical components, but only those who eat it, gain life and strength from it (Zenger 1997: 15).

Those who find joy in the psalms (Ps. 1.2), those who call from the depths (Ps. 130.1) and those who sigh thankfully to him 'who dwells on high' (Ps. 113.5-6) will experience that 'man lives by every word that proceeds from the mouth of the Lord' (Deut. 8.3). This means that he lives off the Bread and the Word given to him by God (Zenger 1997: 15).

In contrast to the prayer literature from the ancient Orient, it is characteristic of the psalms of Israel that not only the 'I', is heard, but also the 'we' of the congregation and the nation (Braulik 1995: 74). The subjects in a psalm can change in an instant; hence with a few additions, individual psalms are often extended to involve the whole of Israel.

Braulik (1995: 74–75) is of the opinion that there was a historical progression from the 'I–prayers' to the 'we–prayers' in the psalms. It had something to do with the communal experience of the catastrophes during the Babylonian exile, the social conflicts of the Persian period and the confrontations with the unfamiliar Hellenistic powers. Hence, it is possible that there is a 'people's congregation', without state and cultic institutionalisation, behind ten of the twelve Asaph psalms from the exile period. The 'we' that occurs in some psalms is a reflection of a communal religion. The typical Old Testament concept of regarding a collective entity as individual makes it possible to simultaneously interpret individual laments and songs of praise, collectively. This is most apparent in the Davidic collection (Braulik 1995: 75).

When all of Israel prayed together, the enemy constituted those nations who threatened Israel. A large part of Israel praying together, was representative of the whole of 'real Israel' 'speaking'. In such an event, the rest of Israel would be regarded as part of the enemy. This group was usually comprised of those who were suppressing the poor (Braulik 1995: 77. Compare Berges 1999: 14–21).

The psalms as prayers are an exercise of the Torah. Those who repeat the psalms and live according to the psalms, maintain the world and life-order of God (Zenger 1998: 47). The prayer of the psalms does not become a private and self-centred religious act, but reaches out to others near and far, liturgically, pleadingly, with praise, or in a confessional or celebratory way. The focus of the final concept of the psalms is not so much on the temple cult, but on individual and collective situations in life. There is nothing strange about this – the prayers had to sustain the Jews in the worldwide Diaspora, far from the temple and its officials (Spieckermann 2003: 157).

Christians pray the psalms because they express the plenitude of life. The wealth of the words is superior to any attempt made by an individual to create his own prayer. When we pray, we experience not only our own needs in the psalms, but also a sense of being bound to the communion of the faithful. Those who pray the psalms do not do so as isolated individuals, but as representatives of all believers, and surely of all mankind (Reemts 200: 29). Athanasius wrote in a letter to Marcellinus that man not only experiences something of God and the history of salvation in the psalms, but also comes to know himself as though in a mirror. 'In any case, I am convinced that man's whole life is embraced by the words of the psalms.'

The *iuxtapositio* of the psalms indicates the skilful use of existing material and lexical correspondence. The texts come into dialogue with each other and mutually act as contexts for one another. The *concatenatio* or concatenation of keywords forms verbal networks, including the mutual incorporation of motifs between adjoining psalms. However, these were also extended further into their surroundings and even across whole groupings of psalms. To create such connections, additions were inserted, words were exchanged and whole bridging psalms were probably even created. Often, the composition was strengthened by a play between isolated announcements and their fulfilment in subsequent psalms (Braulik 2003: 318).

The psalms teach us to meditate. They teach us to visualise the depths, heights, wide expanses and narrow straits of our existence. The psalms teach us to lift up our eyes and to see letters written in the sky. If we look closely, we will even see God's Name shining in the heavens.

7. *Psalms as a book of songs*

In the previous section, we discussed the psalms as a prayer book, but it must be remembered that prayer and song cannot be separated (Oeming 2002: 376). *Qui cantat bis orat* (St. Augustine). From a historical, theological and literary perspective, I regard the psalms as a book of songs. The psalms contain some hymnals of the Levitical Musical Guild of the Temple of Jerusalem (Strydom 1994: 11–12; Zenger 1997: 33). According to 1 Chron., independent groups were formed for the singing of psalms. They all belonged to the Levitical priesthood (Spieckermann 2003: 150). The following can be traced back to the sons of Levi, Kehat and Merari: Heman, Asaph and Etan (cf. 1 Chron. 6.16-28, 33, 39, 44; 16.41 *et seq.*, 25; 2 Chron. 5.12; 35.15). Heman's lineage goes back to Korah (1 Chron. 6.37), amongst others. These are the names that are also found in the psalm titles: Heman, Asaph, Etan, Korah and Jeduthun. These facts, as well as how the songs were used in the temple cult can be traced back to 1 Chron. 16.8-36 and especially back to Jesus, *Sir.* 50.15-21.

According to these sources, a Levitical choir, accompanied by music, recited the psalm text. The (two) priests, from the sacrificial altar, announced the beginning, the caesura and the end of the psalm recital, by means of trumpet blasts. The Levitical choir stood on the wide steps, which led to the 'priest's court' where the sacrificial altar was situated. From there, the people could hear and see the choir quite well. The artistic text collage was compiled from Pss. 105.1-15; 96.1-13 and 106.1, 47–48

(Spieckermann 2003: 151), which reveals the foundation of the theology of the Book of Chronicles.

In terms of the composition, the focus was on the past (a retrospective on the history of Ps. 105), the present (praise singing of Yahweh from Ps. 96) and the future of the people of God (prayer in Ps. 106 for liberation from the enemies) (Braulik 1995: 69–70). The people, as a rule, only sang the chorus, or the antiphony. The sentence '(y)our kindness, O Lord, endures for ever' (compare Ps. 136), or the exclamation 'hallelu-Jah' (= praise Yah[weh]), or the confirmation '(a)men, amen' (so it is, so it shall be!) were all used as antiphonies (Strydom 1994: 12, 16; Zenger 1997: 34).

In the fourth book of psalms (Pss. 90–106), we find the golden thread used to call on other nations to consent to Israel's praise of their God and King – that God led and protected his chosen people. His being and his work are praised in the climactic end to the hymn, as are his grace and his mercy (Spieckermann 2003: 151–152).

Not one of the titles of the psalms belongs to the actual time of inception; hence directions are given regarding the compilation of the single psalms into a collection. The compilation shows signs of the association between the Old Testament and various psalms, while the spirituality is revealed of the group that prayed and meditated on these psalms (Zenger 1997: 28).

Many of the titles suggest the musical form a psalm should take. Indications are also given of the melody in which a psalm should be sung. The melodies of known folk songs were used as a basis (Zenger 1997: 28–29). The melody, (D)eath of a Son can be linked to Ps. 9 and Ps. 56 was sung to the melody of (D)o not Destroy It! Directions are also given for the instrumental accompaniment, e.g.: 'with stringed instruments' (Ps. 4), 'with flute' (Ps. 5) and 'on an eight-stringed harp, with bass voice' (Ps. 6). It is supposed that the compiler did not mean these indications to be technical directions. The directions for Ps. 6 indicate that the psalm was prayed/sung by those who were longing for the messianic times and according to the rabbinical tradition, the eight-stringed harp was the instrument of these times (Zenger 1997: 29).

Other titles suggest either the real, or the merely fictional cultic use of a psalm. Ps. 30 is recommended 'for the dedication of the temple', Ps. 92 'for the Sabbath day' and Ps. 100 'for thanksgiving'. Such would be the directions for the real use of the psalms in the cult of the Second Temple, especially because it is more likely that the psalms originated from other situations in life (Zenger 1997: 30. See also Lohfink 2003: 76; Groenewald 2003: 148, 270). These headings therefore indicate a change in '*Sitz im Leben*'.

In most cases, the titles of the psalms refer to the names of the groups, or individuals to whom the psalms were connected. A psalm is linked to David 73 times, twelve times to Asaph (a prominent Levite of the post-exilic period, for whom a guild of temple musicians is named), twice to

Solomon; four times to the Jeduthun, and once to Moses, Heman and Etan (Zenger 1997: 30). 'The sons of Korah' and 'for the sons of Korah' could be understood as referring to a psalm from the collection of the sons of Korah. However, the mention of Moses or David was intended as an editorial indication and explanation only; it was not intended as historical information. The supplicant should be able to imagine how and why this psalm (Ps. 90) was prayed by Moses or David, because of the allusion in line 3 to Gen. 3.19. The supplicant should then also be able to pray the psalm with Moses or David in communal prayer (Zenger 1997: 30).

In Chronicles David is neither a supplicant nor a singer of psalms. He is the founder and organiser of the temple music, probably even the inventor of instruments, as well as the commissioner for the writing of psalms and their setting to music (Braulik 1995: 69; Zenger 1998: 41). The David of the psalms (with the exception of Ps. 30) does not stand in any liturgical context. On the contrary, his feet are firmly on the ground, as he is both a victim of persecution and a sinner. He is also someone who is threatened by enemies and is then saved from them. In the psalms, he clings to God. The psalms are not concerned with his official duty as king; instead David is depicted as a figure with which to identify. 'As David, so every man' (Millard 1994: 230–234; Kleer 1996; Zenger 1998: 41).

The psalms linked to David's name make up a collection. These psalms have 'biographical' titles and especially in the Books of Samuel, they are so intertwined with narratives, that they are cast in a narrative mould (Mays 1986: 148; Zenger 1998: 41).

Pss. 50 and 73–83 are associated with Asaph. In these psalms, the accent is on divine judgment, the divine oracles and an appeal regarding God's actions in the past. This all points to a prophetic background and reference can be made to 2 Chron. 29.30; 1 Chron. 25.1-6 and to the sons of Korah (Pss. 42–49; 84–88). These psalms originated in the Jerusalem cult and the many references to Zion are clear proof.

There is no doubt that the titles of the psalms were added to the texts later, as they reflect the historical conscience of some of the psalms, rather than the historical foundation. The titles also serve to bind groups of psalms together, where communal theological concepts can be distinguished (Zenger 1998: 27).

I would now like to discuss the psalms as a book of songs from a literary perspective. The accent is on the hymns and the psalms represent the sanctum where God had to be sought and praised and from whence his benediction and salvation came. Psalms are not about a substitute for the temple or the temple cult. Instead, they are about a meeting with Yahweh in his temple in Zion, from where he reigns as the King of Israel and of the whole world (Zenger 1998: 47; Berges 1999: 15).

There are three theopoetical ways to speak to God in the psalms: via the lament, the prayer or in praise (Spieckermann 2003: 137; Gerstenberger

2003: 76). In the Hebrew, praise is distinguished contextually, but not semantically (Westermann 1977: 20–28). We can find idioms in direct and indirect speech in the psalms. There are also the actions of speech such as accusation, trust, self-reflection, the giving of praise to the king and to other people, etc. The three actions of speech, however, form the core of the psalms (Spieckermann 2003: 137).

The praise in the hymns follows different patterns (Spieckermann 2003: 137). There are hymns which call for praise by naming the supplicant and giving reasons for the praise (Pss. 100; 148). There are also hymns, which make use of *participia* to describe God's nature (Pss. 104; 147).

An entire anthropology is embedded in some of the hymns and is directed towards the praising of God (cf. Pss. 8 and 103) (cf. Irsigler 1997: 1–44 on Ps. 8). Ps. 23 is a psalm of trust and is woven with a delicate hymnal thread. Even the prayer of lament ends in praise (Ps. 13). The hymnal function in the psalms of lament can be clarified with two examples. In Ps. 22 – an individual psalm of lament – verses 4-6 have the function of creating an antipode to the lament. In this manner, the individual history of suffering is inserted into the history of trust and the salvation of Israel. In Ps. 74 – a people's lament – the hymnal core, verses 12-17, creates hope after the catastrophe of 587–586 BCE by uniting with the temple theology of Jerusalem (Spieckermann 2003: 138).

In the fourth and fifth Book of Psalms (Pss. 90–106; 107–150) the hymnal formulas and hymnal-woven text compositions increase (Zenger 1997a; Kratz 1996; Spieckermann 2003: 142). The psalm-group 90–100 is a hymnal group, which celebrates the universal kingship of God. Ps. 96 deals with the question of how nations are expected to attain salvic knowledge. In Ps. 96, it becomes clear that it is expected that Israel's worship will have a particular effect on the nations (Ps. 96.1-4). Again, we notice the basic form of the hymn: imperative, addressee, vocative and *kî* (verses 1-4). However, the imperatives are liturgical only in part (three repetitions of 'sing'). They are followed by verbs, which characterize the form of speech usually directed at people outside the community of worship.

The poem refers to a messenger of victory, who informs people that do not know about the positive outcome of a battle, about Yahweh. More importantly, *sphr* stands for the narrative of an individual who has been saved. It also stands for the worshipping service, to which he/she invites relatives and friends. It is fitting to express gratitude towards Yahweh, even at such a casual gathering. This involves thanking him, (addressing him in the second person) and the telling of the salvation to the 'brothers' who need to learn this for themselves. The term 'new song' belongs to the category of a song of thanksgiving (cf. Pss. 40.10; 144.9 *et seq.*). This song is 'new', because it tells of Yahweh's new act of salvation.

It is possible that Ps. 1 was created as a precursor to Pss. 90–100 and together with Ps. 2, it forms the hinge for the hymnal conclusion in

Pss. 90–100 (Spieckermann 2003: 143). Pss. 1 and 2 also function as a portal to the 'house' of the psalms. The title of Ps. 90 as '(a) prayer of Moses the man of God', introduces Moses as the man who became one with the Torah. This unity fixes the Torah instruction as a way of life for Israel under the banner of a song of praise (Ps. 1). This brings us to the point where praise of God as King is a universal injunction to all the earthly kings and nations (Spieckermann 2003: 143).

The self–summons to praise God, '(p)raise the lord, O my soul,' (Pss. 103.1; 22; 104.1, 35), gives an individual–universal (Ps. 103) and royal, cosmic (Ps. 104) perspective on God's praise. Pss. 104–106 are editorially linked by the jubilant invocation '(h)allelujah' (Pss. 104.35; 105.45; 106.1, 48). Pss. 106 and 107 are linked by the introductory hymnal invocation, '(p)raise the Lord. Give thanks to the Lord, for he is good; his love endures for ever' (Pss. 106.1; 107.1).

Pss. 105–107 are compositions, which revolve around the history of salvation and the nation's catastrophes. The chorus of Ps. 107 is an incentive to praise God for his mercy and miracles (Ps. 107.8, 15, 21, 31, 43). The twin psalms 111 and 112 have hymnal features. The composition of the two psalms, as well as the twofold '(h)allelujah,' indicates that both should be read as texts of praise (Spieckermann 2003: 144). The Egyptian hallel, Pss. 113–118, has an introductory '(h)allelujah'. The '(h)allelujah' also reverberates in Pss. 115.18; 116.19 and 117.2. In Ps. 116, the hymn of thanksgiving and the votive offering are bound to the local sanctuary or the temple of Jerusalem, to where the sacrifice was brought (Janowski 2003: 98).

Ps. 118 is well known, because it is part of the Easter liturgy. This psalm starts and ends with '(g)ive thanks to the Lord, for he is good. For his love endures for ever.' This forms an *inclusio*. Ps. 134 concludes the collection of pilgrimage psalms, (Pss. 120–134), with a hymnal call: 'Behold, bless the Lord...' (Ps. 134.1-2). Ps. 135 corresponds to Ps. 134 (cf. Ps. 135.1 *et seq.*, 19–21) while the antiphonal hymn, Ps. 136, corresponds to Ps. 135 (cf. Pss. 135.3 to 136.1). The hymnal echo '(g)ive thanks to the Lord, for he is good. His love endures for ever' (Ps. 136.1) also reverberates in Pss. 106 and 118.

A series of prayers principally attributed to David, (Pss. 137–144), in which the lament dominates, culminate in the acrostic Ps. 145. In this psalm, praise for the Lord, who commands royal power, is declared. His kingship is for all times and encompasses all generations (Ps. 145.11-13). In Pss. 146–150, hymnal sounds vibrate. These psalms begin and end with '(p)raise the Lord'. Each hemistich in Ps. 150 breaks out in a '(h)allelujah' (Loader 1991: 165; Spieckermann 2003: 144). Due to the precise regularity with which the exclamation '(h)allelujah' appears, the page layout or visual appearance of the printed poem emphasizes the laudatory character of the song (Loader 1991: 165). The entire Ps. 150 is a hymn.

The praise has a theopoetical function, because giving praise is part of life. Praise and the lack of praise face each other as life and death (Von Rad 1966: 381).

Contrary to Zenger's (2000: 434) view that the Psalter is a popular book of eschatological wisdom. Spieckermann (2003: 158) regards it as a book, a roll, that was in the hands of the priests and scribes. There it became an authoritative agent, a source of insight and an inspiration for theological practise (theopoetry – CJAV) when praising God. These two viewpoints need not exclude each other totally. The Psalter, as a vital book encompassing all experience, managed to reach the ordinary people, even though it was in the possession of the priests and the scribes.

In the time of Jesus, although the psalms were not the official liturgical songs and prayer books of the Jewish congregation in the temple and synagogue services (Barnard 1985: 146; Füglister 1998: 329–352), they were sung by a guild of vocalists, accompanied by musicians. The hallel was sung, (Pss. 113–118), during Passover (also the Feast of the Tabernacles). Here, we could also refer to the song of praise in Mt. 26.30, which was sung after the Holy Communion. On the way to the temple for Pentecost or the Feast of the Tabernacles, pilgrims' songs were sung (Pss. 120–134). The joy of the Torah was a further reason for jubilation (Pss. 1; 19; 119), and before the Sabbath morning, Ps. 72 was sung (Barnard 1985: 583; Albrecht 1987: 9; Strydom 1994: 20–21).

The Christian church has assimilated the psalms. In the rich tradition of Christendom, the Psalter is one of the sources from which we live and sing.

8. *Psalms as hymns*

In this section I begin by discussing the different approaches to the versification of the psalms. This is followed by a consideration of the musical aspects. A versification of the psalms involves theological, hymnological and hermeneutic choices. There are two possible ways of versifying the psalms in lyrical form. The first option is to follow the rhythmic movements and metaphorical structure of the Hebrew psalm and to versify the psalm as a strophic hymn. A versification of this kind is essentially a faithful versification of the Hebrew psalm. This does not mean, however, that every line has to be versificated literally – or indeed at all. A versification of Ps. 119 would require, for instance, that the versifier should do justice to the theopoetic underpinnings of the psalm. Where this approach is followed the psalms can be creatively turned into verse without losing their essential character. The aim of this approach is to allow the voice of the original psalm to be heard as clearly as possible. The second possibility is a free versification of the Hebrew psalm. The result may be that the psalm is coloured by the New Testament perspective to such an extent that the basic patterns of the Hebrew psalm may even be changed. My study and understanding of the psalms suggests that the first approach to a versification is preferable.

The musical aspects are discussed in the following paragraphs. In the Jewish and Christian tradition, the psalms form the core of the repertoire of the hymns. If one opens a *Liber Usualis,* (the Gregorian monk's book), the texts are mostly from the psalms (Winter 2000: 139).

One of the pre-reformatory musical forms was a plain recitative. The text was recited in a specific, melodic pattern. The subordination of the melody gave power of expression to the text. The caesuras between the lines emphasised the meditative character of the recitative (Winter 2000: 141).

Since the fifth century, the liturgical movements have been accompanied by the singing of psalms. Since that time, the entrance, the sacrifice and the communion have been encompassed with antiphonies, which have become more artistic. Eventually, a point was reached where the congregation could no longer sing along. Only one or more chanters sang the antiphon. In the eleventh century, only the psalm verse of the antiphon remained (Winter 2000: 142–143).

The fundamental structure of the pre-reformatory accompanying psalms – psalm strophes with a chorus – can be used meaningfully in public worship at certain liturgical moments. The musical structure of Pss. 111 and 112, with the antiphonies, can be used for various liturgical acts. In Ps. 111 the refrain verse reads:

> Let us exult in awe of the Lord,
> in our song his glory praise.

The refrain verse in Ps. 112 is:

> God from plenitude provides;
> protection for his servant loyal.

This praise song is only one example.

9. *Liturgy as a creative process*

Neither the Old nor the New Testament presents a rigid, prescribed form into which the liturgy should be moulded. During the ages, however, a living Christian tradition came into being from, among others, the primal sources of the Old and New Testament and the later traditions of the Church (Barnard 1985: 66–383; Strydom 1994: 9–144; Schuman 1998: 26–36). These traditions have a definitive character. Certain patterns, colours and sounds are noticed. However, each generation of believers must interpret the ancient sources and traditions of the Church anew, within the demands of their time, without being unfaithful to the traditions in which a definitive liturgy exists.

The process of glassblowing creates a useful metaphor for reflection on creative liturgy. My poem, 'The Glass-blower', leads us into a study of the liturgical process:

Glass-blower
La Rochère, 1475
His spirit looms over dark
voids, chaos broods.
Let there be light!
In his fire-ripe oven he stokes
molten glass, incandescent and fragile.
Through his pipe he blows her heart to beating,
suckles bubbles from her lungs.
His eyes approve the glowing curves of hips,
her flaming form he baptises in Holy Water,
revives her, then
clinks her without a crack.

It is clear upon a first reading, that the subject of this poem is a glass-blower who is skilfully making a vase. The reference to the creation of the earth in Genesis, in the first two lines, engenders a contextual framework within which the creative process of the glass-blower finds a parallel. This enables us to think anew and on various levels about the liturgy as a creative process.

The liturgist creates a liturgy, which has to be handled with care, because it is extremely delicate and fragile. Even if the liturgy has been carefully shaped in advance, it can shatter in the heat of the moment, when the congregation comes together in the flesh. The hallmark of the liturgy is that, regardless of how carefully it has been created, there is no guarantee of an inspirational service.

It is the task of the liturgist to breathe life into the liturgy, so that the congregation can experience the liturgy as a living event. The liturgist needs to remove every possible flaw and meticulously remove the 'bubbles' that could mar the beauty of the liturgy. The liturgist must scrutinize the radiant sequence of liturgical events and ensure that the liturgy is beautiful in the eyes of the congregation and of God. The liturgy, should be something of a work of art in terms of its design. The design differs from that of the making of a vase, as the liturgy provides the vehicle, which allows the liturgist and the congregation to raise a toast to God. In the liturgy we celebrate the glory of God.

The metaphor of the glass-blower's pipe serves to bring the liturgical miracle into being. The metaphor also makes the psalms into the glass-blower's pipe, which creates the wonder of the liturgy. The liturgist as a glass-blower can use the psalms to perform an act of creation in miniature. All the liturgical acts and movements can be created through the psalms. It may be said that a liturgy is 'blown' from the psalms.

10. *Psalms tuned in to liturgy*

The choice of psalms is determined not only by the liturgical tradition, but also by various exegetic points of view (Braulik & Lohfink 2003a: 236). This means that in the case of the psalms, the texts must be woven into the liturgy. In this manner, they acquire their own, unique pattern in the liturgy. In terms of the choice of psalms for the liturgy, their liturgical place and function must be carefully selected. The psalms should not be forced into the liturgy. The psalms acquire a liturgical voice, which is determined by the liturgical context and the event.

A certain rhythm and way of celebrating the glory of God comes to the fore in the liturgy, while, at the same time, the church year unfolds. This must be taken into account when choosing the psalms.

The psalms create a liturgical meaning. In this regard, inter-textuality between texts is of great importance. Braulik (2003: 325–326) presents an example where he demonstrates inter-textuality between Ps. 103 and 'The Lord's Prayer' in Mt. 6. The following surprising links can be found:

Ps. 103	The Lord's Prayer (Mt. 6)
As a father… (verse 13).	Our Father
throne in heaven… (verse 19).	which art in heaven
his holy name… (verse 1).	hallowed be thy name.
his kingdom rules… (verse 19).	Thy kingdom come.
… who do his will… (verse 21).	Thy will be done
everywhere in his dominion (verse 22).	on earth as it is in heaven.
satisfies… with good things … (verse 5).	Give us this day our daily bread
who forgives all your sins (verse 3).	and forgive us our trespasses as we forgive those…
he remembers that we are dust (verse 14).	And lead us not into temptation
who redeems your life from the pit (verse 4).	but deliver us from evil.

Inter-textuality and links with other passages should be deliberately sought in the liturgy. This results in the creation of a meaningful liturgy.

11. *Psalms as liturgical acts*

11.1 *Introit psalm*

This is usually referred to as the psalm of entry, or introit psalm. The ritual of the 'introit' has its origin in the Middle Ages. In one of the Roman churches, the pontifical High Mass was celebrated and solemn psalm singing commenced when the pope and his retinue made their way into the church. This eventually grew into a complete procession (Schuman 1998: 167).

In the inaugural psalm, the congregation can express its joy at coming into the presence of the Living God. The strophes, which are sung, can also be alternated with readings of parts of the psalm. Ps. 84 can be used in this way.

11.2 *Votum*

The *votum* can be done as a prayer, but also as a declaration. It is also possible to present the *votum* as a song (Vos 1997: 202). The liturgist can use Ps. 19.2 and 15 for this purpose:

> The heavens declare the glory of God;
> the skies proclaim the work of his hands (Eng. 19.1).

Ps. 19.2 is a declaration of God's power, and then follows the declaration of independence in Ps. 19.15:

> May the words of my mouth
> and the meditation of my heart be acceptable in your sight.
> To this the congregation can respond:
> O Lord, my Rock, my Redeemer (Eng. 19.14).

11.3 *Benediction*

The liturgist's salutation forms the pronouncement of the benediction. The congregation that receives the benediction is a blessed congregation, to whom God comes with mercy and peace. By the salvation brought by Christ and dispensed by the Holy Spirit, the congregation is in a holy relationship with God. It is this congregation which receives God's benediction (Vos 1997: 212).

The following benediction can be compiled from the psalms:

Liturgist: May God bless you from Zion,
                  he who created heaven and earth.
Congregation: Amen.

11.4 *Glory to God*

Some of the psalms are excellent songs for praising the Lord. Where the whole psalm has been taken from the original text, it is possible that the objection of liturgical limitation could be raised, i.e. that because of the psalm's length and range, the whole psalm cannot be utilised liturgically. This objection could be obviated by using different strophes for different liturgical acts, as in the case of Ps. 19.

The first strophe of Ps. 19 may be used as a praise song. The psalms offer a creative challenge to the liturgist to use them in a liturgically meaningful way.

11.5 *Prayers*

The elements of prayer, which encompass praise, worship and the admission/expression of faith (Vos 1997: 62) could fruitfully draw material from the psalms. Pss. 8 and 19 present material for praise, while an expression of worship could be created from Ps. 84. An admission/expression of faith could be taken from Ps. 103.

11.6 *Law*

In the liturgy, the law has various functions (Barnard 1985; Vos & Pieterse 1997). Ps. 19.8-11 (Eng. 19.7-10) tells us that the law is a source of direction, joy and instruction.

Liturgist: The law of the Lord is perfect –
reviving the soul.
The testimony of the Lord is trustworthy –
making wise the simple.
The statutes of the Lord are right –
rejoicing the heart.
The commands of the Lord are radiant –
giving light to the eyes.
The fear of the Lord is clean –
enduring for ever.
The judgments of the Lord are true –
and righteous altogether.
More to be desired are they than gold,
more than much fine gold;
sweeter also than honey
from the honeycomb.

11.7 *Confession of guilt*

The confession of guilt can be taken from Ps. 19.13-14ab (Eng. 19.12-13ab).

Liturgist: Who can discern his errors?
                    Forgive my hidden faults.
Congregation: Keep your servant from presumptuous sins;
                    let them not rule over me.

11.8 *Exoneration*

Ps. 19.14cd (Eng. 19.13cd) presents a theme for exoneration:

Congregation: Then I will be blameless,
                    innocent of great transgressions.

11.9 *Scripture reading and sermon*

The psalms present a challenge to the liturgist to uplift the congregation
with the sermon and transport them into a poetic world. In the sermon, the
theopoetry can take on a homiletic structure, texture and posture (Vos
1999). Each sermon is cast in a certain mould. Looking at it from another
perspective, we could say that the sermon is given wings. This is the
structure. The texture is the language, which holds the poem together.
Language lends itself to various stylistic devices in order to express
thoughts. Language is the homilist's indispensable and unique instrument.

Posture is the body of a sermon. A sermon needs to have a body, which
must reach out and touch, or move the reader/listener. It can be said of the
psalms that they have posture. They are fleshed out every time someone
reads them or listens to them. The homilist has to mould the psalms in his
sermon in such a way, that they have posture for the listener and lead to
greater understanding.

11.10 *Prayer*

The elements of prayer, i.e. the confession of guilt, exoneration and
intercession, abound in the psalms. For confession of guilt, we refer to Pss.
51 and 103. Exoneration can be found in Pss. 51 and 103. Pss. 17 and 116
are examples of psalms containing the element of intercession.

11.11 *Votive offering*

The following votive offering can be compiled from Ps. 136:

Liturgist: Give thanks to the Lord, for he is good,
                    give thanks to the God of gods,
                    give thanks to the Lord of lords, (verses 1-3).
Congregation: for his love endures for ever.

	for his love endures for ever.
	for his love endures for ever.
Liturgist:	Give thanks to the Lord, for he is good,
	give thanks to the God of gods,
	give thanks to the Lord of lords (verses 1-3).
Congregation:	to the One who remembered us in our low estate,
	and freed us from our adversaries,
	who gives food to every creature (verses 23-25).
Liturgist:	Give thanks to the God of heaven (verse 26):
Congregation:	for his love endures for ever.

11.12 *A song of reply*

This song must relate to the sermon.

11.13 *A benediction*

Ps. 134.3 may be used as a benediction.

Liturgist:	May the LORD,
	the Maker of heaven and earth,
	bless you...
Congregation:	Amen.

12. *A last note*

To reiterate, the psalms offer a mechanism for the liturgical glass-blower to produce a creation in miniature. All the liturgical acts and movements can be created from the psalms. With the aid of the psalms, the liturgist can make a glass creation that is without a crack or a flaw.

Bibliography

Albrecht, C. 1987 *Einführung in die Hymnologie* (3. Auflage. Göttingen: Vandenhoeck & Ruprecht).

Arneth, M. 2000 Psalm 19: Tora oder Messias? *Zeitschrift für Altorientalische und Biblische Rechtsgeschichte* 6: 82–112.

Barnard, A.C. 1985 *Die erediens* (2de druk. Pretoria: N.G. Kerkboekhandel).

Berges, U. 1999 *De armen van het boek Jesaja. Een bijdrage tot de literatuur-geschiedenis van het Oude Testament* (Katolieke Universiteit, Nijmegen: Nijmegen).

Braulik, G. 1995 *Christologie der Liturgie. Der Gottesdienst ser Kirche – Christusbekenntnis und Sinaibund, Questiones Disputatae* (Band 159; Freiburg-Basel-Wien).

—2003 Psalms and Liturgy: Their reception and contextualization, *Verbum et Ecclesia* 24/2: 309–330.

Braulik, G. &; Lohfink, N. 2003a *Osternacht und Altes Testament* (Berlin, Bern, New York, Oxford, Vienna: Herder Verlag).

Clines, D.J.A. 1974 'The Tree of Knowledge and the Law of Yahweh (Psalm XIX)', *Vetus Testamentum* 24: 8–14.

De Coninck, H. 1995 *Intimiteit onder de melkweg Over poëzie* (De Arbeiderspers Amsterdam – Antwerpen).

Deissler, A. 1966 *Die Psalmen* (Düsseldorf: Patmos).

Dohmen, C. 1983 Ps. 19 und sein altorientalisher Hintergrund, *Biblica* 64:501–517.

Fisch, H. 1990 *Poetry with a Purpose. Biblical Poetics and Interpretation* (Bloomington: Indiana Univerity Press).

Foster, B.R. 1997 'The Shamash hymn', in W.W. Hallo & K.L. Younger (eds.), *The Context of Scripture. Volume I* (Leiden: Brill): 418–419.

Füglister, N. 1988 Die Verwendung und das Verständnis der Psalmen und des Psalters um die Zeitenwende, in J. Schreiner (Hrsg.), *Beiträge zur Psalmenforschung. Psalm 2 und 22* (FzB, 60; Würzburg: Echter Verlag): 310–348.

Gerstenberger, E.S. 2003 'Psalmen und Ritualpraxis', in E. Zenger (Hg.), *Ritual and Poesie* (Freiburg, Basel, Wien: Herder Verlag): 73–90.

Gese, H. 1982 'Die Einheit von Psalm 19', in E. Jüngel, et al (Hrsg.), *Verifikationen. Festchrift für Gerhard Ebeling zum 70. Geburtstag* (Tübingen: J.C.B. Mohr [Siebeck]):1–10.

—1991 *Alttestamentliche Studien* (Tübingen: JCB Mohr [Siebeck]).

Glass, J.T. 1987 'Some observations on Psalm 19', in K.G. Hoglund, et al (eds.), *The Listening Heart. Essays in Wisdom and the Psalms in Honor of Roland E. Murphy* (JSOT SS, 58; Sheffield: Sheffield Academic Press): 147–159.

Groenewald, A. 2003 *Psalm 69: Its structure, redaction and composition* (Münster: LIT VERLAG).

Hengstenberg, G.W. 1842 *Kommentar über die Psalmen. Erster Band* (Berlin: Oehmigke).

Hossfeld, F.-L. & Zenger, E. 1993 *Die Psalmen I. Psalm 1–50* (Neue Echter Bibel. Würzburg: Echter Verlag).

Hossfeld, F.-L. & Zenger, E. 2000 *Psalmen 51–100* (HThKAT; Freiburg, Basel, Wien: Herder Verlag).

Hutter, M. 1996 *Religionen in der Umwelt des Alten Testaments, I* (Stuttgart, Berlin, Köln: Verlag W. Kohlhammer).

Janowksi, B. 2003 'Dankbarkeit – Ein anthropologischer Grundbegriff im Spiegel der Toda-Psalmen', in E. Zenger (Hg.), *Ritual und Poesie* (Freiburg, Basel, Wien: Herder Verlag): 90–136.

Kaspar, P.P. 1999 *Musica sacra: Das grosse Buch der Kirchenmusik* (Graz, Wien, Köln: Styria).

Kleer, M. 1996 *Der liebliche Sänger der Psalmen Israels cc Untersuchungen zu David als Dichter und Beter der Psalmen* (Bodenheim: Philo Verlagsgesellschaft).

Knierim, R.P. 1991 'On the Theology of Psalm 19', in D.R. Dans et al (Hg.), *Ernten was man sät* (FS. Klaus Koch, Neukirchen: Neukirchen-Vluyn): 439–458.

Koch, K. 1993 *Geschichte der Ägiptiche Religion. Von den Pyramiden bis zu den Mysterien der Isis* (Stuttgart, Berlin, Köln: Verlag W. Kohlhammer).

Kratz, R.G. 1996 'Die Tora Davids. Psalm 1 und die doxologische Fünfteilung des Psalters', *ZThK* 93: 1–34.

Kraus, H.-J. 1978 *Psalmen. 1. Teilband Psalmen 1–59* (5. grundlegend überarbeitete und veränderte Auflage. Neukirchener: Neukirchener-Vluyn).

Krog, A. 2002 *Met woorde soos met kerse* (Kaapstad: Kwela Boeke).

Kruger, P. 2002 'Die Hemel vertel die eer van God': Natuur, Skriftuur en die bidder in Psalm 19', *Verbum et Ecclesia* 23(1): 111–124.

Liedboek van die NG Kerk 2001 (Kaapstad: NG-Kerk Uitgewers).

Loader, J.A. 1991 'God se hemelgewelf', in C.J.A. Vos & J.C. Müller (reds.), *Mens en Omgewing* (Halfway House: Orion).

Lohfink, N: 1993 'Was Wird anders bei kanonischer schriftauslegung ? Beobachtungen am Beispiel von Psalm 6', *Studien zur biblisher Theologie* (Stuttgart: Katholisches Bibelwerk 263–293).

Martin, F. and McEvenue, S. 2001 'De Bijbel als literatuur: poëtische en narratieve teksten', in E. Eynikel, E. Woort, T. Baarda, A. Denaux, (eds.), *Internationaal Commentaar op die Bijbel. Band I* (2de uitgawe. Kok: Kampen).

Mays, J.H. 1986 'The David of the Psalms', *Interpretation* 40: 143–155.

Mays, J.L. 1994 *Psalms* (Interpretation; Louisville: John Knox).

Meinhold, A. 1983 'Überlegungen zur Theologie des 19 Psalms', *ZThK* 80: 119–136.

Millard, M. 1994 *Die Komposition des Psalters Ein Formgeschichtlicher Anzatz* (Tübingen: J.C.B. Mohr [Siebeck]).

Monshouwer, D. 1998 'Informatie en documentatie', in P. Oskamp & N. Schuman (reds.), *De weg van de liturgie: Tradities, achtergronden, praktijk* (Zoetermeer: Meinema).

Morgenstern, J. 1945 'Psalms 8 and 19A', *HUCA* 19: 491–523.

Oeming, M. 2002 'An der Quelle des Gebets. Neuere Unterschungen zu den Psalmen,' *Theologische Literaturzeitung* 127 (4): 368–384.

Otto, E. 2000 *Das Deuteronomium im Pentateuch und Hexateuch* (Tübingen: J.C.B. Mohr [Siebeck]).

Peterson, C. 1982 Mythos im Alten Testament. Bestimmung des Mythosbegriffs und Untersuchung der mythischen Elemente in den Psalmen (BZAW, 157; Berlin: Walter de Gruyter).

Potgieter, J.H. 1991 'Natuur, Skriftuur en die mens is getuienis van God,' in C.J.A. Vos & J.C. Müller (reds.), *Mens en Omgewing* (Johannesburg: Orion).

Prinsloo, W.S. 2000 *Die lof van my God solank ek lewe* (Irene: Medpharm Publikasies).

Reemts, C. & Bielefeld, P. 2000 *Schriftauslegung. Die Psalmen bei den Kirchenvätern* (Stuttgart: Verlag Katholisches Bibelwerk).

Ridderbos, J. 1955 *De Psalmen I (Psalm 1-41)* (Kampen: Kok).

Schuman, N.A. 1995 '*en wat zij zong hoorde Ik dat psalmen waren.' Over psalmen en liturgie* (Kampen: Intreerede, 22 September 1995).

—1998 'De Psalmen', in P. Oskamp & N.A. Schuman (reds.), *De weg van de liturgie: Tradities, achtergronden, praktijk* (Zoetermeer: Meinema).

—1998a '... Die weet gehad heeft en geen weet gehad,' *Skrif en Kerk* 19(2): 373–380.

—2001 'Psalm 91: tekst, context, en een diversiteit aan herlezingen', in P. Post, G. Rouwhorst, T. Sheer, R. Steensma en L. Tongeren (reds.), *Jaarboek voor liturgieonderzoek, deel 17* (Groningen, Tilburg): 237–256.

—2002 *Pastorale. Psalm 23 in Bijbel en Liturgie verwoord uitgebeeld* (Zoetermeer: Meinema).

Seidel, M. & Schultz, R. 2001 *Kunst & Architektur. Ägypten* (Köln: Könemann Verlagsgesellschaft).

Seybold, K. 1996 *Die Psalmen* (HAT 1/15; Tübingen: J.C.B. Mohr [Siebeck]).

Spieckermann, H. 1989 *Heilsgegenwart. Eine Theologie der Psalmen* (Göttingen:- Vandenhoeck & Ruprecht).

—2003 'Hymnen im Psalter – Ihre Funktion und ihre Verfasser,' in E. Zenger (Hg.), *Ritual und Poesie* (Freiburg, Basel, Wien: Herder Verlag): 90–136.

Strydom, W.M.L. 1994 *'Sing nuwe sange, nuutgebore'. Liturgie en Lied* (Bloemfontein: NG Sendingpers).

Van der Lugt, P. 1980 *Strofische structuren in de Bijbels-hebreeuwse poëzie* (Kampen: Kok).

Van der Ploeg, J.P.M. 1971 *Psalmen* (Roermond: J.J. Romen).

Van Oort, H. 1991 *Augustinus' facetten van leven en werk* (Kampen: Kok).

Van Uchelen, N. A. 1971 *Psalmen I* (POT; Nijkerk: Callenbach).

Van Zyl, A.H. 1966 Psalm 19, in *Proceedings of the Ninth Meeting of 'Die Ou-Testamentiese Werkgemeenskap in Suid-Afrika' and Proceedings of the Second Meeting of 'Die Nuwe-Testamentiese werkgemeenskap van Suid-Afrika'*, held at the University of Stellenbosch [Biblical Essays]: 142–158.

Von Rad, G. 1966 *Theologie des Alten Testament* (Band 1; München: Chr. Kaiser Verlag).

Vos, C.J.A & Pieterse, H.J.C. 1997 *Hoe lieflik is u woning* (Pretoria: Raad vir Geesteswetenskaplike Navorsing).

Vos, C.J.A. 1999 'n Raaisel in die spieël. Kantaantekeninge van Letterkunde en Homiletiek', in C. Lombaard (red.). '... *In die wêreld...*'. (Johannesburg: RAU): 93–106.

—2001 'n Perspektief op die nuwe Psalmomdigting', *Hervormde Teologiese Studies*, 56 (2 & 3): 357–376.

Wagner, J.R. 1999 'From the heavens to the heart: the dynamics of Psalm 19 as prayer', *CBQ* 61(2): 245–261.

Watson, W.G.E. 1986 *Classical Hebrew poetry. A guide to its techniques* (2nd edn, JSOT SS, 26; Sheffield: University of Sheffield).

Weiser, A. 1962 *The Psalms: A Commentary* (London: SCM).

Westermann, C. 1977 *Lob und Klage in den Psalmen 5, erweiterte Auflage* (Göttingen: Vandenhoeck & Ruprecht).

—1984 *Ausgewählte Psalmen* (Göttingen: Vandenhoeck & Ruprecht).

Wilder, A.N. 1976 *Theopoetic: Theology and the Religious Imagination* (Philadelphia: Fortress).

Winter, C. 2000 'Zet de zang' (Psalm 98: 4): De Psalmen in de liturgie, in J.W. Dyk, P.J. van Midden, K. Spronk & G.J. Venema (reds.), *Psalmen*. (Maastricht: Uitgeverij Shaker Publishing): 139–149.

Zenger, E. 1997 *Die Nacht wird leuchten wie der Tag* (Freiburg, Basel, Wien: Herder Verlag).

—1998 *Der Psalter in Judentum und Christentum* (FS. N. Lofhink; Freiburg: Herder Verlag).

—1998a *Einleitung in das Altes Testament* (KST, Band 1,1; Freiburg, Basel, Wien: Herder Verlag).

—2000 'Psalmen', in F-L. Hossfeld, & E. Zenger (Hrsg.), *Psalmen 51–100* (HThKAT; Freiburg, Basel, Wien: Herder Verlag).

—2003 'Vorwort', in E. Zenger (Hg.), *Ritual und Poesie* (Freiburg, Basel, Wien: Herder Verlag): 7–9.

INDEX OF BIBLICAL TEXTS

INDEX OF NAMES

GENERAL INDEX